AT HOME IN RENAISSANCE BRUGES

Julie De Groot

AT HOME IN RENAISSANCE BRUGES

Connecting Objects, People
and Domestic Spaces
in a Sixteenth-Century City

Leuven University Press

Published with financial support of the KU Leuven Fund for Fair Open Access, the Universitaire Stichting van België, and The Centre of Urban History at the University of Antwerp.

Published in 2022 by Leuven University Press / Presses Universitaires de Louvain / Universitaire Pers Leuven. Minderbroedersstraat 4, B-3000 Leuven (Belgium).

ISBN 978 94 6270 317 9 (Paperback)
ISBN 978 94 6166 438 9 (ePDF)
ISBN 978 94 6166 439 6 (ePUB)
https://doi.org/10.11116/9789461664389
D/2022/1869/14
NUR: 694
Layout: Crius Group
Cover design: Anton Lecock
Cover illustration: Sixteenth-century kitchen interior in The Miracle of the Broken Sieve, left panel of retable, © Royal Museums of Fine Arts of Belgium (Brussels), inv 334, photo: J. Geleyns.

TABLE OF CONTENTS

PART 1
CROSSING THE THRESHOLD: THE ORGANISATION OF DOMESTIC SPACE

PART 2
DOMESTIC OBJECTS IN CONTEXT

GENERAL INTRODUCTION

Early fifteenth-century travellers such as Spanish writer Pero Tafur praised the city of Bruges because of its liveliness and economic activity: 'Bruges was a large and wealthy city, and one of the greatest markets of the world [...] anyone who has money, and wished to spend it, will find in this town alone everything which the world produces'.[1] Bruges had played an important role in the European network of trade already since the mid-twelfth century.[2] In this capacity, it offered a remarkable quantity and variety of consumer and luxury goods. Not only the ducal court could happily thrive there, but local and international merchants found their way to Bruges as well, lured as by favourable business opportunities in this important northern European trade centre.[3] Artisans were attracted by this environment of creativity as well, among them several of the most renowned painters of the age.[4] Wealthy craftspeople and the higher middling groups in Bruges society provided an important local demand and increasingly proved to be keen consumers of luxury goods themselves.

In the middle of the fifteenth century, however, the Bruges economy became increasingly affected by unfavourable conditions.[5] Due to shifts in international trade networks, whereby land trade regained importance, Antwerp's location on the Scheldt river allowed it to develop into a new trade hub for both maritime and continental trade.[6] Strong competition in the production of cheaper cloth in neighbouring centres caused the Bruges traditional wool industries to decline. Consequently, the city had to look for alternatives to keep its economy running and reconverted its industries from producing heavy woollens towards a more differentiated economy with the production of luxury goods, luxury textiles and accessories.[7] However, some economic and political problems left a deeper impression on the city's commercial activities. The Flemish Revolt against Archduke Maximilian of Austria caused an occupation of the Bruges outer port of Damme, which not only seriously disrupted trade but also prevented the import of raw materials and the export of finished products by local craftspeople.[8] The economic warfare of the Habsburg duke clearly undermined the city's attractiveness. To make things worse (and to further weaken Bruges's trade position), the archduke ordered foreign and local merchants to leave the city and to settle in the more loyal Brabantian city of Antwerp.[9] Large groups of local and foreign merchants and craftspeople left the city – some only temporarily, but others were not planning to return soon and started to build a new life in the Scheldt city. Although the Bruges government made several concessions to foreign nations in terms of trade and tax privileges, it did not succeed in keeping all nations in the city permanently. So, at the dawn of the sixteenth century, international trade found a new focal point in the new metropolis of Antwerp.[10] Vigorous attempts were made to reverse the downwards spiral and to attract (and keep) foreign trade, such as new channels and government initiatives regarding infrastructure, the construction of better roads in and to the city and up-to-date streets. In 1562 the city government asked painter and engraver Marcus Gerards to make a large city map to highlight the renewed accessibility of the city from the sea. The map was intended as a deliberate promotional stunt to promote Bruges as a reliable and easy accessible trade city. Gerards's city map was a clear attempt by the city government to bring the infrastructure the city had to offer for trade and commerce to the attention of foreign nations. The map therefore presented an idealised image of an economically thriving city, highlighting its most important public places: the large squares and stately public buildings such as commercial halls, the city crane, churches and the city hall. However, notwithstanding these efforts, it was clear that international trade could only be revived for a short period of time.[11]

Despite the sharp decline in international trade from the fifteenth century onwards, the Bruges economy as a whole turned out to be relatively resilient. Although Bruges gradually lost its position in international trade to Antwerp, the city continued to play a strong role in regional trade.[12] But, of course, this transition came at a price. The negative effects were greater for people working in the supporting trades than for the large merchant families in Bruges.[13] The latter were able to keep increasing their wealth thanks to monopolies on certain products and the spreading of their trade activities both over Bruges and Antwerp.[14] Also textile traders, entrepreneurs and already wealthier master craftsmen could benefit from the increased production in the fustian and say industry and from an increase in scale within their companies. Other craftspeople, textile workers and shopkeepers, on the other hand, were more sensitive to declines in purchasing power and had a particularly hard time, especially in the second half of the sixteenth century, due to sky-high inflation. Nevertheless, the decline of the Bruges economy must be put into perspective: it mainly affected international trade, not regional trade, which grew in strength even beyond 1600. And the city could still thrive on its former wealth and glory during much of the sixteenth century.[15] This is probably also the reason why travellers such as Ludovico Guicciardini praised Bruges even in the sixteenth century as a 'seer

schooner heerlijcke machtighe ende groote stadt. [...]', specifically mentioning that
'der menschen wooninge zijn hier meestendeels veel heerlijcker ende kostelicker dan
in eenige andere stadt'.[16] Others noticed the many stone facades of the houses and
the size of these domestic dwellings as well. Even the Bruges city map made by Marcus Gerards, originally meant to promote the commercial opportunities of Bruges,
meticulously described various types of houses and other dwellings. So even though
the city map was intended to promote Bruges as an interesting place to work, it also
recommended the city as an interesting place to live – with its wide, tidy streets,
well-maintained houses and beautiful squares and markets.

All this suggests that the gradual transition of the Bruges economy (and society?) from an international metropolis to a sizeable provincial centre during the
long sixteenth century,[17] with clear economic ups and downs and many social consequences – especially for the lower social groups in the city – were not immediately
visible on the streets, especially not in the first part of the sixteenth century when
there were even signs of continuing prosperity.[18] But did that also apply to the situation within the walls of citizens' houses? Even if this process was neither sudden nor
total, it must have had an effect on the daily lives of all of its citizens; on consumption practices and possibilities, on tastes and lifestyles, on the ways people organised
their lives and living spaces. In most studies on the early modern Bruges economy,
however, this aspect seems to be forgotten. Therefore, this book is about the material
culture of these dwellings and the domestic life of its residents. It will focus predominantly on the houses of the 'middling sort', a group of citizens described as neither
very rich nor very poor.[19] In her new book on artisans, material culture and everyday
life in Renaissance Italy, Paula Hohti describes this social group as 'those who occupied an economic and social position between merchants, lawyers, and notaries, on
the one hand, and workmen and day labourers, on the other',[20] though we tend also
to include the merchants in our analysis. This middling section of the population is
interesting to consider, because it has often been associated with the profound social
and economic changes of the period.[21] Little attention has been paid, however, to the
central importance of the home and its specificities at this social level or to its role
in negotiating the heterogenous nature of middling status.[22] Scholars such as Paula
Hohti have already convincingly shown that despite, or even because of, economic
fluctuations, it is necessary to undertake a study of the spaces and possessions of the
middling groups in urban society to allow for reasons other than social recognition
that would motivate families from the artisan classes to acquire various types of material artefacts.[23] Indeed, even for the people of the middling to lower social strata of

society, home meant more than just a building or a place. And because this population probably had to adapt the most to a new way of consumption throughout the
sixteenth century, the middling groups of urban society are the subject of this book.

Sixteenth-century homes have received less systematic scholarly attention in the
Low Countries than public spaces mostly because of trends in the research field of
urban space: the study of the public sphere of the city or the (social) production
of urban public spaces remain highly ranked, even when it is generally agreed that
more research is needed on what urban people said and thought about urban spaces.[24] Surely, these studies have provided – and will continue to provide – a valuable
basis for understanding some of the ways in which individuals formed and communicated their identities in or to the public, but relatively little attention has thus far
been paid to domestic space as a context for creating and shaping urban identities.[25]
The problem is that historians and social theorists that have accorded all the pre-
miums to public spheres have approached city dwellers merely as members of the
public urban community, thereby remaining ignorant of 'private' living conditions.
Domestic space has received attention only in its guise as the antithesis or binary of
public, commercial space and the outside world, especially for the Low Countries.[26]
But, as Lynne Walker has argued, 'these binary categories often serve to diminish
the significance of specifically domestic interiors, privileging instead the facade over
the inside, the public building over the private home'.[27] Nonetheless, homes were
places of prayer and private devotion, of comfort, sociability and conviviality, work
and household labour, family memories, love and marriage, children and household
servants, cooking and eating, joy and mourning; contexts where particular aspects
of the identity of urban citizens took shape. Therefore, we need to go back to the *basic* questions of how people lived, the reality they experienced and the way they interpreted what surrounded them, as well as their values and attitudes towards home
and public life. The organisation of rooms and domestic spaces, the decoration of
the interior of these spaces and the use of furniture or a study of the material translation of this home life offer the best ways to answer these questions.

This book, therefore, will follow Alexa Griffith Winton's argument that aspects
of the spatial theory of Henri Lefebvre and his followers, which considers space as a
social construct, are also relevant to the study of the interior.[28] In this view, the interior, too, 'is never the sum of its architectural components, or the objects within it,
but is rather produced by the people who inhabit it'.[29] In other words, this book will
argue that there are strong connections between the individual and the interior; the
domestic (space) did not exist apart from the households that are productive of it.[30]

The Spatial Turn

In recent decades, the concept of space has managed to reach the status of a category of analysis and even of an 'almost accepted dogma' in many disciplines of the humanities.[31] Historian Leif Jerram started his polemic article on the viability of this 'spatial turn' with the thought-provoking observation that, in historiography, 'much fuss has been made of the "spatial turn" in recent years, across a range of disciplines. It is hard to know if the attention has been warranted'.[32] He argues 'that space is a primary category through which the human experience needs to be analyzed and explained', but that the 'spatial turn' itself is actually only an extension of the cultural turn, theorising about concepts and their cultural meanings, and only of little help in engaging with what he called 'the matter and substance of human experience'.[33] His most important critique on the 'spatial turn' in historiography is formulated through a citation of historian Ralph Kingston. Kingston observed, in a recent review essay on the spatial turn in history, that 'much of the use that historians have made of space has been, essentially, a replay of the cultural turn, where space has been viewed as a repository of cultural meaning, rather than as a physical "thing" that structures human action'.[34] Jerram therefore strongly advocates to study space as material – the only problem he foresees is that, as Thomas Gieryn proposes, 'there is a tipping point when infinite malleability takes on a solid form that is not immutable, but very hard to change'.[35] It follows to some extent what Daniel Roche had suggested as well; according to him, a house was like 'petrified time, [...] built in the past and modified by successive generations which have unified the ways things are arranged in it'.[36] But although houses indeed tend to suggest stability and invariability, interiors were personal creations, a translation of the way people lived, whereby material goods defined the meaning of a certain room; therefore, interiors were likely to be more dynamic and fluid over time.[37]

Key to the interpretation of spaces, therefore, is revaluing the agency of the people that constructed these spaces (and their interiors) as well as reconsidering the agency of the objects that constituted these spaces. The limits of domestic space did not restrain people, but they had to create strategies to circumvent or adapt to boundaries and spatial constraints. People were also proficient in adapting available space to their own taste, needs and desires, and they actively used the existing advantages and deficiencies of spaces to create their own environment. Just as we cannot reduce space to a barrel full of cultural significance, perceptions and representations, we must not reduce its users and creators to passive entities either, handed over to the steering capacity of the space itself. Edward Soja understood 'spatiality' already in 1989 as 'simultaneously a social product (or outcome) and a shaping force (or medium) in social life'.[38]

Reclaiming Domesticity

The study of the late medieval and early modern domestic interior is certainly a rapidly growing field of inquiry, although there is an increasing imbalance towards one specific geographical area: Renaissance Italy. Once scholars were convinced of the fact that the interior of the pre-modern house itself was worth studying, and not just a tool to map the house's stylistic developments and decorative idiom like many late nineteenth-century and early twentieth-century scholars did,[39] attention quickly concentrated on the interiors of the large Renaissance palazzi built in the chief locations of Italian Renaissance culture such as Venice, Siena, Florence and Rome.[40]

It was Richard Goldthwaite who was the first to assert firmly that it was essentially the consumer mentality of Renaissance Italian urban consumers that was both the 'creative force' behind their identity construction and used as a means to express this identity in public (or rather *to* the public).[41] First the facade of the house and later also its interior were considered to be crucial outward expressions of family status, wealth and cultural values.[42] These houses were constructed and designed to proclaim the status and identity of their inhabitants to the wider community, as an outward expression of the moral economy that was governed by the *padre di famiglia* indoors.[43] It was as if the house became a precious and well-preserved worldly good as well, to be treasured and safeguarded from hostility and assaults on the family honour.[44] It is therefore not surprising that the *casa* itself was the subject of intense contemporary debates, as 'people became acutely aware of how their status could be reflected by the rank of the dwelling they lived in'.[45] In treatises on architecture (Leon Battista Alberti,[46] Antonio Filarete,[47] Giacomo Lanteri[48]) and on the vices and virtues of wealth creation and luxury consumption (Giovanni Pontano and his concept of *splendour*), the building and furnishing of these magnificent houses was not only discussed but also stimulated, because architectural patronage and expenditure on furnishings were seen as outright virtues rather than vices.[49] Indeed, in Giovanni Pontano's theory, 'the splendid man was expected to surround himself with objects that reflected his aesthetic discernment, civility and cultural standing'.[50] Treatises on household management, on the other hand, provided readers with instructions to achieve a solid structure and good organisation of the *casa* (and so the household).[51] Because the *casa* as representing both house and household proclaimed the status and virtue of the family, a strict and good organisation was a matter of the utmost importance.

For the southern Low Countries, however, the study of domestic culture and interiors remains confined to later periods[52] or to some fragmented studies that each have examined only one facet of the interior or of domestic life, inspired by archaeology and building history[53] or art history and material culture studies,[54] without integrating all these facets of space, people and objects into one study. But perhaps this lack of research on 'early forms' of domestic culture in the southern Low Countries is to some extent also due to the contested validity of the use of the concept of domesticity or *huiselijkheid* in studies on societies that were not situated in seventeenth-century Holland nor in the nineteenth century.

On the one hand, a strand of scholars, including Witold Rybczynski and Philippe Ariès, believe that the concept of domesticity, which they see as devotion to internal family values and to the home itself, originated only in the seventeenth-century northern Low Countries or in the Dutch Golden Age.[55] This assumption was based on seventeenth-century genre paintings of idyllic domestic interiors, like the many everyday scenes of the paintings of Pieter de Hooch.[56] In Rybczynski's words, 'it was the atmosphere of domesticity that permeated de Witte's and Vermeer's paintings'.[57] Other scholars, however, believe that our present-day notions of 'home' and 'domesticity' have to be understood as the inheritance of the nineteenth century's cult of the home.[58] According to them, the true meaning of 'home', 'domesticity', 'home culture' and notions associated with the home such as 'privacy' and 'comfort' originated in nineteenth-century debates and thus is specific to this bourgeois ideal. Following this theory, scholars working on earlier periods could not study the creation of homes in societies prior the Industrial Revolution without being accused of thinking anachronistically.

However, rooted as they were in the long-standing tradition of studies on vernacular architecture and the archaeology of everyday life, it was mostly British scholars who stepped into this debate to attest to the assumption that domesticity would have been a concept known of only in the modern world.[59] In the introduction to their volume on medieval domesticity, Goldberg and Kowaleski assert that, even for people living in the medieval period, 'home' was 'an evocative word that meant rather more than just a building or a place'.[60] According to them, the concept of domesticity, as well as the concept of, for example, comfort, is indeed flexible in meaning, and its content depends heavily on the geographical and historical context.[61] In fact, it is historically contingent.[62] Moreover, Felicity Riddy has convincingly shown that this 'set of values associated with a particular mode of living' was already apparent in fourteenth- and fifteenth-century England.[63] Indeed, even in medieval times, people 'occupied physical structures that constituted homes, which were built, organized and furnished in ways that are consciously or unconsciously reflective of their particular cultural values'.[64] And in their most recent book, Catherine Richardson and Tara Hamling have proven that these values were not confined to the homes of the elite either, but were also present in the houses of the urban middling classes.[65] Jeanne Nuechterlein, in turn, provides further evidence in a visual iconography that rapidly gained popularity in the fifteenth-century Netherlands – that of the Virgin in a fully developed domestic interior. This type of iconography was especially attuned to the lives of the (more well-off) urban citizens, using a recognisable domestic interior as its setting.[66] So the idea of having or creating a *home* was, therefore, not new in the sixteenth century.

So the problem does not necessarily lie in the actual use of the concept of domesticity for pre-modern societies; the real issue at stake here is that historians studying the pre-modern period have to be careful not to use the nineteenth-century interpretation of domesticity to study other past realities, because this ideology of home is specific to the era of industrialisation, of factories and factory workers, of male breadwinners and of growing population and urbanisation.[67] But the experience of being at home and the need to create a home is not historically and culturally specific: it is as old as humankind itself. In every era, 'homes promise security, retreat, rest, warmth, food and the basis for both a family life and for full participation in social life'.[68] Every society (and even each social layer in society) has its own interpretation and translation of what home entails. And domesticity was translated differently in every period and in every culture.

At Home in Renaissance Bruges

The material culture in sixteenth-century Antwerp is well represented in historiography,[69] but, as far as Bruges is concerned, it seems that historians have followed a similar shift from Bruges to Antwerp as many contemporary artisans and merchants did.

Perhaps scholars have found it counter-intuitive to study the consumption of (luxury) goods in a city that had an unstable economy throughout the sixteenth century? A minimum of resources is indeed indispensable for the consumption of everyday goods, let alone of luxuries,[70] such as objects to furnish the domestic interior.

The growing presence of wealthy local and international merchants in Antwerp has long been seen as one of the explanatory factors for the success of, among others, the booming art market in the Scheldt city.[71] But the question arises whether we have to see the Antwerp art market as a benchmark for other urban centres. Robert Lopez claimed in the 1950s that the 'crust of preconceived impressions' on the interconnection between economic wealth and cultural investment is still not easily pierced.[72] Even 'the [Italian] Renaissance was neither an economic golden age nor a smooth transition from moderate medieval well-being to modern prosperity', because it was also grounded in a period of economic stagnation.[73] 'Culture', according to Lopez, 'was a new way for the Italians to gain prestige when economic wealth, which had given them status before, was declining'.[74] What mattered most for Raymond Van Uytven, who discussed whether economic prosperity was the essential condition for the consumption and production of luxuries, is that, even during a depression, 'the rich may grow in number and in wealth while the poor get poorer and more numerous'.[75] Looking at the social and demographic data Heidi Deneweth provides for Bruges, this social-gap scenario fitted sixteenth-century Bruges well.[76]

In 1544, it was estimated that no less than 25 per cent or a quarter of the Bruges population lived below the poverty line, caused by high levels of unemployment and inflation.[77] The city government hoped to recover from economic stagnation and to improve Bruges's competitive position by freezing wages at the 1500 level. However, due to a sharp rise in prices during the sixteenth century, the purchasing power of especially the middling groups was severely affected. In the 1580s, the purchasing power was only one-fourth of the level of around 1500, again causing people to look for better opportunities elsewhere.[78] Moreover, religious and political troubles during most of the second part of the sixteenth century triggered major migration as well. From the late 1560s onwards, the city acted as a safe haven for poor Anabaptists who had fled the Bruges hinterland and Artesia out of fear of prosecution, for Calvinists and for people from the impoverished surrounding countryside. At the end of the sixteenth century, however, groups of Calvinists were forced to migrate out of the city to better places because of the intolerance of the Spanish Catholic regime in Bruges. And because Calvinism was popular mainly among the higher income groups like merchant-entrepreneurs and wealthy craftspeople,

it was especially the more wealthy Bruges residents who migrated out of the city
once again.[79] However, because the population dropped by as much as 34 per cent
at the end of the sixteenth century, and because the total number of Calvinists in
the city was relatively low especially when compared to Antwerp, both Deneweth
and Vandamme have argued that not only Calvinists but also other citizens, like
skilled craftspeople, left the city to search for happiness elsewhere.[80] So due to these
religious and political troubles and also because of economic shifts (e.g. towards the
manufacture of cheaper textiles), the majority of Bruges's population in the 1590s
was comprised mainly of unskilled and proletarianised wage labourers with a smaller group of middle-class shopkeepers and artisans and international and local merchants.[81] So the social composition of the city was clearly subject to change, and it
seems that the gap between the lower social groups of society and the more wealthy
skilled craftspeople, entrepreneurs and merchants grew increasingly larger. In short,
while Bruges merchants and entrepreneurs and some of the middle groups still enjoyed the relative economic growth that characterised especially the first half of the
sixteenth century in Bruges (mainly because of a strong position in the regional
market and a relatively good position in parts of the international trade), this was by
no means the case for the lower social groups. This variety of income groups was undoubtedly also visible in the city's housing stock. The city plan by Marcus Gerards
makes it clear that the city of Bruges was an amalgam of various types of houses.
Whereas poorer people were obliged to rent a room or cellar, the more prosperous
households were able to own a house with several rooms and outbuildings.

Sources and Challenges

In this book, we have chosen for a broader view and not for a method focused on case
studies dealing in specific detail with the individual houses, households and categories of things. This choice was made possible thanks to the series of sources preserved
in the archives of Bruges. There is a lot to be said for studying case studies using clusters of source materials, but this will be further explored in separate publications. At
first sight, it seems difficult to recover (let alone to reconstruct) late medieval and
early modern interiors from two-dimensional historical documents. But, in the absence of descriptions of how spaces were used and experienced in the past, we needed
to adopt a pragmatic approach; in other words, we situated ourselves imaginatively

and phenomenologically in the spaces we wish to understand.[82] Floor plans are rarely available for the fifteenth and sixteenth centuries,[83] and even those floor plans that have been reconstructed from archaeological research do not fully allow to assess the whole three-dimensional picture.[84] The various techniques used to analyse the use and meaning of the (formerly) built environment, including planning analysis and access analysis,[85] could be instrumental in showing potential interactions between the users of the different compartments of a dwelling, but they do not do justice to the actual *experienced* reality, because they were mostly based on ground plans and archaeological evidence only.[86] Architectural history, in turn, had already turned away from churches and large public buildings starting in the 1970s. Architectural historian Luc Devliegher was a pioneer in 'architecture mineure', with a focus on the ordinary house. He delivered groundbreaking and internationally followed research on the facades of ordinary houses, but his book *The Houses of Bruges* also contains a few floor plans with interior layouts and photos and drawings of decorative elements.[87] The Bruges examples in *Building through the Ages* also have several photos of interiors, and on a local level, Bruges's interiors have been widely discussed in the brochures for Open Monuments Day in Bruges.[88] But in general, this discipline has been mostly concerned with the exteriors of buildings and with architects, rather than with the interior of houses and their actual users.[89] The most promising way to enter the domestic sphere of fifteenth- and sixteenth-century houses and to grasp the lived reality of domestic spaces, therefore, is a close study of the (materiality of the) domestic interior using post-mortem and confiscation inventories.[90]

Inventories

Giorgio Riello commented that 'put in a very simplistic way, the drawback of inventories has never been deemed to be their particular nature, but their complex and demanding processing'.[91] Indeed, 'the archival work of transcription, compilation, standardisation, and – with the beginning of the information age – database design has been central to the use of inventories'.[92] My colleagues Inneke Baatsen and Isis Sturtewagen, with whom I created the database, and me were lucky to be able to construct a relational database based on an impressive corpus of inventories for one city, allowing for both a longitudinal research and an in-depth analysis. For this study, no less than 502 Bruges inventories were analysed, from five different archival series divided over six sample periods. To achieve more or less representative

Table 1. Inventory Types and Sample Periods

| | POST-MORTEM INVENTORIES | | CONFISCATION INVENTORIES | | | |
| | BASTARD INVENTORIES | INVENTORIES OF CITIZENS | ARREST COURT | ARREST WP | COUNCIL OF TROUBLES | |
SAMPLE PERIOD	GENERAL STATE AR-CHIVE (GSA)	CITY ARCHIVE BRUGES (CAB)	CITY ARCHIVE BRUGES (CAB)	STATE ARCHIVE BRUGES (SAB)	GENERAL STATE AR-CHIVE (GSA)	TOTAL
1438–1444	69	-	-	-	-	69
1450–1500	-	-	-	33	-	33
1500–1510	-	-	-	10	-	10
1528–1549	-	5	52	-	-	57
1559–1574	-	58	156	-	7	221
1584–1600	-	63	49	-	-	112
TOTAL	69	126	257	43	7	502
	195		307			

Source: Database of inventories © IB, JDG & IS

samples for both the late fifteenth and sixteenth centuries, we had to draw sources from several series of different types of both post-mortem and confiscation inventories. Well-chosen samples of inventories were closely studied, balancing between thick-description and quantitative analysis. Table 1 illustrates the different types of inventories I used for this study and the numbers of sources per sample period that were recovered.

Inventories are lists of all the household movables and/or stock goods people owned; these inventories were drawn up for a variety of legal and administrative procedures.[93] The most common event in which an inventory was produced was the death of a citizen and property owner.[94] But inventories were also necessary in other situations. Indeed, another important occasion on which the household chattels were inventoried was in the case of debt collection.[95] When the creditor was not immediately compensated by the debtor, the debtor's assets were to be taxed and, if necessary, confiscated and publicly sold by representatives of the city government to reimburse the creditor. This means that such an *arrest* or confiscation inventory could be drafted at any moment in a person's life, whereas post-mortem inventories were only drafted when a person (who was a *poorter* or burgher of the city) had died. Both types of inventories were therefore constructed in a particular legal and administrative context whereby different concerns, intentions and actions, as well as several different stakeholders, were involved.[96] A confiscation inventory was ordered by the city government to meet the interests of the creditor, whereas a post-mortem inventory first and foremost concerned a legal distribution of the estate among the heirs.[97] It follows that the main aim of any kind of inventory was not to literally represent the material or domestic culture of a household; the only task of the appraiser was 'to assess goods and chattels and value them'.[98] The fact that inventories 'are [...] forms of representation that are influenced by social and legal conventions [...]'[99] and that 'the taking of an inventory was not simply an act of accounting. It was something more akin to an act of translation'[100] has urged scholars to warn against a straightforward use of these sources.[101] Lena Orlin even labels them 'works of fiction', simply because they do not exactly mirror the daily lives of people, because some goods were often missing (especially objects of low value) and sometimes entire rooms were not included either.[102] Nevertheless, although we must indeed be aware of the fact that inventories are not exhaustive records of the contents of domestic space, we are still inclined to follow Riello in revaluing the document as a source by reminding scholars that inventories were somehow still linked with the lives of the people involved, so 'appraisers connected inventories to social and cultural attitudes and values'.[103] As Adrian Evans has formulated it, these sources 'contain information about past domestic objects and spaces, which also bear the traces of embodied existence'.[104] Especially when they are taken together in large numbers and simultaneously scrutinised for the micro details that they contain (e.g. object descriptions, object classifications, object groupings, object locations, room descriptions), 'they can help us to paint a reasonably detailed picture of domestic spaces and domestic objects'.[105] Inventories are mostly considered the best foundation for a quantitative understanding of interiors with a focus on the relative levels of expenditure on goods in each part of the house. The reason for this is that 'many things found in late medieval registers – an item of dress, a bed set, a dozen trenchers, an old boot found in a rented room – are nearly mute, no more than a word or two [...]'.[106] But we have (re)valued inventories especially for their qualitative values considering, for example, the practical and aesthetic relationships between goods in the same room. Like the French historian and archaeologist Françoise Piponnier insisted, every object, regardless of its value, has something to say.[107]

Despite the great value of inventories in this regard, historiography constantly reveals that inventories are not without flaws. First, they do not record perishable items (or not all perishable items – some did include large pieces of cheese, meat and wine) and sometimes lump together items of low(er) value (such as crockery, household textiles, prints and cheap books). Second, they tend to neglect fixed furnishings such as nailed benches and bedsteads.[108] But some items such as bed curtains and sheets could hint at the presence of a fixed bedstead, already partially solving this issue. Third, they present values that the goods would obtain if sold and not original purchase prices. Furthermore, post-mortem inventories tend to show the resale value of the listed goods rather frequently and consistently, but confiscation inventories, on the other hand, only rarely provide this information, notwithstanding the fact that the document was drafted to repay a debt. Fourth, inventories provide only a 'snapshot' of ownership, neglecting the dynamics of purchasing patterns.[109] Indeed, we have to be aware that household chattels of all kinds were not only bought on the commodity market, but that they could also enter the house in other ways – as a gift from family members or friends, by inheritance, bought on the second-hand market or brought into marriage by one of the two partners.[110] Some items were therefore very personal, such as jewellery or a family picture, whereas other items bought on the second-hand market were mostly practical in nature. Fifth, both post-mortem and confiscation inventories cannot shed light on the relationship between consumptive practices and the life stage of consumers.

Both types of sources were compiled at a particular moment in time. This means that both sources are rather static in nature, presenting only one situation or household configuration. However, this does not have to mean that we know nothing about the social background of the person in question, especially not in the case of post-mortem inventories, because we are often informed about the owner's social and family background at the time the post-mortem inventory was drafted. The preamble of such a document clearly states the marital status of the deceased person, the name of the spouse (and potential former spouses), sometimes also the names of family members (mother, father, brothers and sisters), the names of any children and whether these children were still minors and needed legal guardians. Sometimes, we also know the circumstances of death (e.g. plague or disease) and the place where the person died. The text also mentions the occupation of the deceased citizen and if not, this information could often easily be inferred from other data in the inventory (e.g. in the part on debts). The post-mortem inventory was, in a sense, also a realistic document, especially because it also recorded the outstanding debts of the household. So during life, people could keep up appearances of well-being by wearing expensive and high-quality robes, but when they died, it became clear how deep in debt they were.[111] Therefore, although the inventory still presents the situation at one particular moment in time, it does not necessarily mean that the people who left such a document were nameless, abstract figures. In the case of *arresten*, there is often a lot less information about the individuals involved, though we often know the name of the debtor, the debtor's marital state, the name of the spouse and the debtor's occupation. Finally, inventories tend to be socially discriminating, because they systematically under-represent the lowest status groups, such as poor people and unskilled labourers. The poor did not leave inventories behind, because household goods had to be valuable enough to be listed, and one had to pay the scribe or appraiser who listed the goods as well.[112] That means that the more wealthy middle groups of society are particularly well represented in these written sources.

In short, inventories as historical sources pose some interpretational problems and each type of inventory has its own set of possibilities and difficulties. As we have already discussed, we will use two different types of inventory: post-mortem inventories, which are, in general, more complete; and records of debt collection. The latter are usually detailed in their description of objects, but they do not always mention each and every room in the house, making it difficult to map the entire domestic geography of these dwellings.[113] Moreover, these sources do not mention any form of real estate or immovable property, nor do they enlist other debts and credits. The majority of the guildsmen in the sample and whose inventory was detailed enough to discuss the particularities and distinguishing features of retail and/or production space(s), for example, left behind a more confined confiscation inventory. This means that we cannot be a hundred per cent sure of the fact that all the objects in that room were included in the inventory by the appraiser (because his task was only to inventory and value goods to pay off a certain debt) *and* that all the other rooms of the house were added to the list as well. But even though the details in these confiscation records could be compromised by their very nature and genesis, these sources are useful to analyse; for example, the location of retail and/or production at home and these spaces' (most important) contents should be analysed especially because they were compiled more 'spontaneously' and often more unexpectedly then their post-mortem counterparts. People often had less time to change or hide things than the surviving relatives of deceased citizens. Moreover, to contextualise the contents of shop interiors, we tend to supplement the data from confiscation inventories with regulations concerning retail space and display of goods found in guild statutes and court records. And because transactions outside the normal market circuit (i.e. in artisan's shops) were looked at with greater suspicion and were therefore strictly regulated (with risk of a penalty if the rules were not followed),[114] we assume that these regulations were, in general, complied with. These confiscation records are supplemented with a couple of inventories of confiscated goods that were made in the context of the religious persecutions under the rule of the Duke of Alva around the year 1567 (infra).

The layout of inventories also differed depending on the origin of the document. The most common layout of confiscation inventories or *arresten* presented a room-by-room division, whereas post-mortem inventories usually presented the house's content in groups of goods (e.g. all the metal goods, linen, household textiles, woodwork, clothing), often, but not always, because goods were clustered into one room, decontextualising the objects and disarranging the spatial layout of the entire dwelling. Consequently, it complicated the study of domestic space enormously. The part on domestic space is therefore predominantly based on confiscation inventories.

In what follows, we will discuss each archival series of inventories separately to fully grasp the original context wherein the documents originated.

Inventories of Burghers of Illegitimate Birth

A remarkable collection of sixty-nine inventories of Bruges burghers of illegitimate birth or *bastaardgoederen* could be identified from the bailiff's accounts from the period between 1438 and 1444.[115] As determined by customary law, the so-called bastard's privilege, or *bastaardijrecht*, enabled the count to confiscate the estates of the *bastaarden* who died childless and left no direct legitimate heirs.[116] If there was a spouse and no children, the count had to be satisfied with only half the estate.[117] In other cases, the entire estate was confiscated, valued and publicly sold. In 1289, Count Guy de Dampierre gave his right to the estates of *bastaarden* to the city, but after the city revolted against Duke Philip the Good in 1436, the duke took the privilege away from the city and he put the city bailiff, his main local representative, in charge of receiving this taxation.[118] During 1438–1444, the level of detail and the amount of information on rooms, material culture and social status are exceptional, especially for this early period in time. Before this period (in the city's accounts) and afterwards (in the accounts of the special receiver of Flanders), the entries in the accounts were summary, and they only gave the name of the deceased, the buyer of the estate and its total value. Most inventories were concentrated in the period when the bastard's privilege had just returned to the duke. And these inventories were also most detailed. Undoubtedly, the phenomenon can be linked to an operation of catching up with the arrears in the previous period of political turmoil.[119] The higher numbers of inventories in both 1438 and 1439 can also likely be ascribed to the general mortality crisis in these plague years. For the interpretation of the inventories, this is a lucky coincidence, because people were probably less prone to have anticipated confiscation after death and had little opportunity to refashion their estates and hide the best parts from confiscation by the bailiff.[120]

Post-Mortem and Confiscation Inventories from the Deanery of Saint Donatian (Proosdij van Sint-Donaas)

Some enclaves enclosed within the city walls still fell under the authority of the provost and canons of the ecclesial seigniory of Saint Donatian. The seigniory was a fully-fledged domain with its own statutes and laws, jurisprudence and administrators.[121] It therefore operated outside the urban jurisdiction. Within the city, the deanery consisted of two separate quarters: the Proosse and the Kanunnikse. Information and documents about the houses and their inhabitants who fell under the Proosse and the Kanunnikse was therefore generated and preserved by a separate administration.[122] Today, these documents, including the post-mortem and confiscation inventories, can be found in the series of *Wettelijke Passeringen*, or Legal Proceedings, kept in the State Archives of Bruges. Forty-three confiscation inventories have been recovered from the ledgers of the Legal Proceedings. Most of these inventories are situated in the fifteenth century as well, enlarging the source base for this part of the research period. The earliest *arrest* dates from 1457, and the latest in our sample from 1511.

Confiscation Inventories in the Protocollen of the Vierschaar in Bruges

The twelve aldermen of the city of Bruges that resided in the local court of justice, the Vierschaar, were assisted by city officials or clerks who were authorised to draft and ratify acts between citizens of Bruges, such as agreements on property taxation and rents, donations, estate divisions and bailouts.[123] Of these acts, the *minuten* (or the original draft texts) were written in special registers or *protocollen*. The clerks were obliged to keep these registers and submit them to the city council when they wanted to end their duties. Most of these registers (for the period between

1520–1786) are now preserved in the City Archives of Bruges. In practice, the protocols of the clerks are completely similar to, for example, the Antwerp aldermen's
registers. Schouteet mentions that several clerks were also notaries. The difference
lies in the fact that, from a legal point of view, all transactions relating to real estate
(e.g. sales, name and plot changes of real estate, mortgages, judgements) had to be
passed by the aldermen.[124] Even if someone had executed an initial contract before
a notary, the deed still had to be entered in the protocols of the clerks and executed
before notaries. People quickly saved themselves the trouble and time of registering
and paying a deed twice. Matters that were still done before civil law notaries for
privacy reasons were marriage contracts, business contracts, inheritances and inventories. However, hardly any of those old notaries have been preserved in Bruges.

Some of the *protocollen* contained *arresten*. When someone could not or would
not repay a debt, the creditor could appeal to the city magistrate, after which the
bailiff and two aldermen, accompanied by one clerk, could confiscate the debtor's
goods.[125] When, after a public reading of the confiscation, no rejections or opposi-
tions against the arrest were expressed, the bailiff could confiscate the goods within
a period of twenty-one days. After the period had passed, the creditor could demand that the confiscated goods be publicly sold by one of the four *ghesworen stock-
houders* of the city.[126] For small debts, the procedure was less complicated and the
goods could be confiscated impromptu, at only a day's notice to the debtor and with
permission of the aldermen. Consequently, when nothing changed, the goods were
publicly sold by the *stockhouder* in the town hall within a mere eight days.[127]

For our research, we consulted all the ledgers or *protocollen* of the clerks that
were active during the period under study. The ledgers of fifteen clerks were examined, and we managed to recover no less than 257 of such confiscations or arrests.[128]

Staten van Goed and Post-Mortem Inventories

Post-mortem inventories are the most well-known and most comprehensive group
of documents arising from the orphans chamber or *wezenkamer*, of Bruges. One of
the duties of the guardians was to accurately record the orphan's share in the legacy.
To determine this share, full inventory of all movable and immovable property of
the mortgaged house, including debts and funds or credits, needed to be made. An
important element in this was drafting an inventory of goods. The orphans' registers were already in use from 1398 to 1410, and continued to be used until the

beginning of the eighteenth century. Estates were also listed here, but according to medievalists, this only contains that part of the inheritance that actually belongs to the minor orphans. Some of those estates in the orphans' registers are also extensive. But for this research, we chose to use the so-called *Staten van Goed*, which are more coherent. These post-mortem inventories have been preserved for Bruges only from the first half of the sixteenth century onwards.[129] The earliest post-mortem inventory is from 1528, but a more systematic registration took off from the 1540s. After a citizen of Bruges died, an inventory of the estate was required to be composed within six weeks.[130] Two guardians were appointed to assist the surviving spouse (or other relative) during registration. In the end, the inventory had to be agreed on by all beneficiaries and settled the actual partitioning of the estate.

In general, some sort of sequence seems to have been followed in the compilation of inventories. After the aforementioned preamble – introducing the deceased person(s), the legal heirs and their guardians – sometimes a short reference is made to parts of a premarital contract. As customary law decreed that upon marriage all the goods accompanying the spouses became shared and joint possession, it entailed that all the household goods were to be appraised and divided among the heirs upon the death of one of the spouses. But as some goods were deemed either personal or necessary for living or working, some goods that were often specified in the contract were exempt from appraisal. On most occasions, these goods entailed clothing, a bed, bedding, jewellery, money and professional tools. For our research, this means that these goods were not part of the inventory itself, so caution is due when considering the 'completeness' of the inventory. The same goes for goods that were to be bequeathed in a last will or testament. Especially silverware, linen and pieces of the wardrobe of the deceased, but sometimes also beds and paintings, were promised to a particular person and therefore not included in the post-mortem inventory either.[131]

After the premarital contract, the landholdings, farmland and other immovable property that was (partially) owned, leased or burdened with rents were appraised. In some cases, the available cash in the house (*'t ghereede ghelt*) was counted as well, but this amount was mostly limited, because most households still greatly relied on credit.[132] Having counted the money and inventoried the immovable wealth of the household (when available), the appraisers moved on to the more complex and detailed part of the estate, the inventory of goods (*boedelinventaris*). Subsequently, the household's debts and credits were summarised, often together with the costs for the funeral and the administration.

The inventories are certainly not evenly distributed across the different sample periods. As can be gleaned from table 1, there are only five post-mortem inventories for the first sample period of the sixteenth century, complemented by fifty-two confiscation inventories. For the third sample period, the situation is even more worrying: only ten confiscation inventories have survived the test of time. For the majority of calculations, sample periods two and three were therefore merged.

Confiscations of the Council of Troubles

The large sample period 1559–1574 not only includes post-mortem inventories and confiscation inventories that were drafted due to economic debt but also inventories of confiscated estates because of political and religious defiance. During the religious troubles in the Low Countries, lots of estates were seized after their owners were executed or outlawed by the Spanish rulers. The Council of Troubles (*Bloedraad*) was one of the councils, issued by the ferocious Duke of Alva, who prosecuted heretics or people suspected of heresy.[133] When found guilty, all the household chattels of those involved were confiscated. If the person whose property was confiscated was married, half of the property went to the 'royal majesty' and was publicly sold, and the other half remained the property of the spouse. However, only seven of such Bruges confiscation inventories have survived the test of time in the national state archives in Brussels.[134]

Social Stratification[135]

The middling sort clearly were not a coherent social group in the late medieval and early modern period. The phrase 'middling sort' is a historiographical construct, often used as a collective term for the broad mass of the working population – from artisans and tradespeople to educated professionals.[136] So the source material is not only very diverse in its typology but also includes several different social groups. The very nature and origin of the sources determines that neither the poorest layer nor the richest segment of urban society can be studied, but it seems that even the middling groups of society were heterogeneous too. So for an in-depth analysis of the material and domestic cultures of the urban middling groups, it was imperative to devise a method to socially stratify the inventories. Only then was it possible to make comparisons over time and to say something about the representativeness of the sample for the whole of the population at a given moment in time. However, both the complexity and diversity of the surviving inventories complicate the quest for a social stratification.[137] In previous research, several types of parameters were already in use to establish a certain kind of social stratification; the number of rooms, a parameter for stratification that was formulated by Bruno Blondé and that was based on the strong statistical correlation between the number of rooms (and therefore house size) and wealth, was most commonly used, in addition to the total value of the estate (including capital, creditworthiness and total debt)[138] and occupational labels.[139] Other researchers have linked the estates with taxation records as an external classification criterion, but for Bruges, these sources are not available (or not for the whole of the city and for each sample period).[140] The estimated value of the total household can also be valuable for a stratification of the households.[141] The most useful inventory is the one that lists items separately and gives each item both a quantity and a value, but inventories following this pattern are rare,[142] especially in Bruges. Moreover, the differences between post-mortem and confiscation inventories entails that such a parameter is not useful for both types of sources. Confiscation inventories only rarely give information for the value of the entire estate (supra).

To assess source-technical and chronological differences and to account for differences between post-mortem and confiscation inventories, we have developed a method for establishing social stratification. This method was inspired by research that used 'wealth signifiers'.[143] The first step in the process was assessing occupational labels, because they present an interesting starting point for measuring the social status of households. Approximately one-third of the inventories mention the (main) occupation of the head of the household. Singling out shopkeepers and artisans enabled us to situate the so-called 'middling groups' in the sampled households.[144] Not only the inventories with occupational labels were identified as such but also the inventories with professional workspace, tools and/or shop provision were added to the list. As a result, for each sample period, at least 20 per cent of the households could be identified as belonging to the middling groups of Bruges. But to further socially differentiate this wide diversity of occupational labels categorised as middling groups, another parameter was needed.

We could have used the rental values listed in the so-called *penningkohieren* (the theoretical annual rental value of owner-occupied houses and the effective annual rental value of rented houses). To assess the social profiles of Protestant reformers in Bruges, Ludo Vandamme reconstructed the wealth of these individuals by calculating the total value of their estates.[145] When comparing their assets to the rental value of their houses, he observed a remarkable correlation between assets and rent. This underscores the representative function of the *penningkohieren*. From the early sixteenth century onwards, the central government levied this newly in-troduced taxation on 5 to 10 per cent of the annual housing value.[146] Heidi De-neweth has established an overview of all the housing values of the city from 1571 to 1583.[147] Deneweth furthermore linked the data on housing values to the registers of the *zestendelen* produced in 1569, providing the exact location of a specific house and the names of its owners and/or tenants.[148] She proposed a social stratification based on rent value categories whereby households were classified into six groups, ranging from those living in the cheapest dwellings, worth less than 240 s. a year, to the wealthiest families, living in houses worth over 1440 s. a year. As the median value of all Bruges's rent values for 1583 was calculated at only 240 s., a consider-able share of Bruges's inhabitants must have lived in cheap and presumably small houses. However, due to missing data, we could find a link with taxation for only ninety-seven inventories.

Graph 1. Classification of Households According to Yearly Rent Values (N=97)

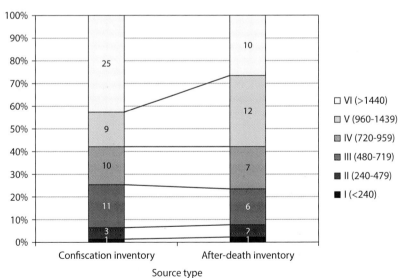

Source: Database of inventories © IB, JDG & IS – Database of rent valuations of Bruges (1571/1583) © Heidi Deneweth.

Graph 2. Stratification of Post-Mortem Inventories (N=190)

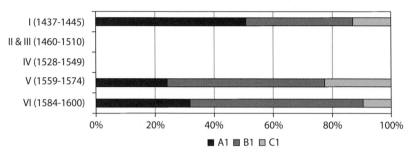

Source: Database of inventories © IB, JDG & IS

Graph 3. Stratification of Confiscations (N=307)

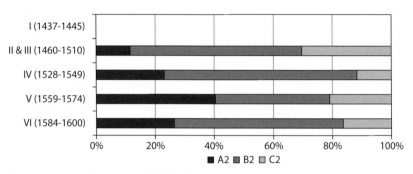

Source: Database of inventories © IB, JDG & IS

Graph 1 compares the summarised statistical results for classification according to source type. Several things can be gleaned from this graph. First, it illustrates how every social group is represented in the sources. Second, both types of inventories almost equally represent groups I, II, III and IV. Third, confiscation inventories exhibit a surprisingly more 'high-profile' character than the post-mortem inventories, because a greater share of their wealthiest group was represented by group VI. The sources therefore agree with the idea that inventories are, in general, biased towards the higher echelons of society. Relatively speaking, the studied households do not belong to the poorest groups of society, although certainly not only the very high end was represented either. However, the *kohieren* were not available for all the sample periods and are therefore not useful as a parameter for constructing a stratification for all the sample periods. But they do present an interesting picture of the heterogeneity of the middling groups in Bruges.

The only metric applicable to all the inventories seems to be the total count of the number of records of goods registered (hereafter, Record Unit Count or RUC). While the total value of household assets was not mentioned in all inventories (especially not in the confiscation inventories), we do have a total count of the number of records of goods registered. This counts every time a record was put in the database. This means that a record unit could comprise more than one object. While it hides high numbers of objects contained in one record, it gives a good account of the variety of material culture.[149]

When testing whether this parameter could serve as a valid 'wealth signifier', we had to conduct several statistical tests to measure correlation with other parameters already surveyed (i.e. rental value and room number). In the end, we chose to construct a two-tailed social stratification that takes into account the difference between the two source types. The results, a layering of our sources (A: lower middling groups in inventory population, B: middle groups and C: higher middling groups), which allows for comparing between different sample periods, are shown in graphs 2 and 3. All in all, we have tried to remedy the heterogeneity of the sources.

The social stratification of the confiscations mirrors the city's economic ups and downs fairly well. In times of scarcity, less affluent households were more vulnerable to confiscation, meaning a rise in the share of group A, which explains the differences between sample period II&III and sample period IV. When looking at the second half of the sixteenth century, the group B of middling groups further shrinks, whereas group A grows. The late sixteenth-century crisis is therefore nicely reflected in this stratification. Only at the very tail end of the century, we see small signs of recovery, with an expanding group B.

The Structure of the Book

In two separate but related parts, this book will dig into questions about how daily life and social identity were negotiated and materialised in the dwellings of a city that was making the transition from an international trade hub to a middle-sized, regional city. By doing so, this book will reassess the crucial importance of domestic space in reproducing cultural identities, forging power relations, defining social status and organising economic activities. This book is not a history of family life,[150] though its findings shed interesting new light on such a concept; rather, our concern here is with the way behaviours were located within the material environment of the household.[151] The first part of the book will focus on spatial dynamics and social and domestic practices, using the organisation of rooms, objects and different household goods as proxies to approach room use. In this part, home culture will thus be studied from a combined object- and space-based approach. Marta Ajmar-Wollheim and Flora Dennis noticed that early scholars of the domestic interior focused predominantly on domestic practices and social meanings of the house but neglected to include the artefacts.[152] These scholars considered objects merely as props and not as items fulfilling a participatory role in daily practices. Furthermore, most attention still went to the study of valuable objects rather than everyday items,[153] and in some cases, the study of artefacts even overshadowed the study of domestic practices,[154] detaching objects from the domestic spatial settings in which they performed a certain function.[155] Recent studies, however, have underscored the primacy of domestic objects in creating the social spaces of the late medieval and early modern home.[156] Indeed, the spatial organisation of a house as well as its decoration and the movable goods it housed all represented a way of life and a way of understanding the world.[157]

The first chapter in this book opens the door and considers how internal spaces were pragmatically and emotionally demarcated. For many people, the household was also the centre of work of various kinds, which reflects the crucial relationship between the house and the activities of labour. Indeed, the shop, the workshop and storage spaces can be seen as liminal spaces that both divide the interior from the exterior and allow for a connection between the internal life of the house and the outside world of the city. Because late medieval dwellings are often suspected of being predominantly 'public', harbouring little 'private' space, mainly due to the presence of labour activity within their walls, it is imperative to start with a study of these threshold spaces, questioning shifting levels of permeability and changing degrees of intrusions into the inner realm of the home.[158] But the shop or the retail space on the ground level of a house was only one way (or one site) in which public life would link with the domestic practices and material culture of the household. Houses could contain different types of these transitional sites.

In the next part of this chapter, we move to allegedly one of the most private, most gendered and most formal spaces in the interior: the *contoor*, translated as the office or study. In historiography about Italian Renaissance interiors, the study is seen as 'the quintessential Renaissance space'.[159] Although in Bruges, we did not come across any references to the word 'study' or *studoor*, as was the case in six-teenth-century Mechelen and Antwerp,[160] we did find rooms labelled *contoor*, or 'office', especially in houses of Bruges and Hispano-Bruges merchants. Obviously, the latter was used more often than not in a formal, businesslike way, ideal as a shel-ter for preserving letters, business communications and account books, although even rooms used for business could double as places for quiet contemplation.[161] The question is then what functions these Bruges *contoren* had and to what extent these rooms were comparable to the Italian Renaissance studies many scholars have al-ready written about. The design and furnishing of this type of space and its location in the domestic geography of the house could tell a lot about its use and its func-tional capacities.

In the second thematic chapter, the concept of 'functional specialisation' is fur-ther questioned. The concept was invented when researchers began to inquire when exactly rooms became specialised in use and furnishings. In this chapter, the theme of 'running the house' is further elaborated by focusing on several particular room types that were at the heart of the home, starting with one of the first rooms to be la-belled with a functional name: the kitchen. The particularities of this room are then used to question the specificities of related spaces such as the bedroom (or sleeping room), the dining room and the 'best room', or the *salette*.

The second part of this book places the decorative object in the spotlight. The chapters in this part consider the objects that filled the rooms discussed in the first part of the book, giving the opportunity to question the material contexts in which people moved around. We suggest in this part of the book that the visual aspects and the material characteristics of decorative objects induced different kinds of be-haviour among their users. The definition of the category of 'decorative objects' is of course entirely arbitrary, and choices had to be made which objects were to be included, because households traditionally harboured all kinds of objects that were both functional and aesthetic.[162]

In (art) history and especially in the study of Early Netherlandish art, there has been a tendency to reduce this category of 'decorative objects' to the story of pan-el painting.[163] Traditionally, a division was made between the 'major', or 'fine', and 'minor', or 'decorative', arts; architecture, sculpture and painting were assigned a pri-mary nature, whereas other arts such as ivory carving, glass working, goldsmithing, furniture making and textile work were lumped together into a secondary group.[164] As early as 1568, Vasari theoretically proposed such a division, claiming that the primary arts were the result of genius and intelligence and not merely of artisanal skill.[165] Though this division was therefore initially applied only to the Italian arts, it was not long before it spread across Europe and was used even in the eighteenth and nineteenth centuries to give certain arts a pejorative association. Nonetheless, such a hierarchy of aesthetic values was foreign to the inhabitants of fifteenth- and sixteenth-century Europe, whose inhabitants 'valued a multiplicity of objects in diverse media',[166] and no separation existed between 'fine arts' and 'crafts' as we understand them today. Several objections to this traditional division have already been made by new generations of art historians.[167]

Nonetheless, in this second part of the book, we deliberately start the discussion with a focus on paintings underlining that, despite the attention this topic has received, we actually know very little about paintings as consumables, as objects that were meant to be used in a specific context and at a specific moment in time. This is what Larry Silver has labelled a 'new art history', which lies close to what was called 'art in context',[168] moving 'into a more inclusive vision of what constitutes visual culture in its historical period'.[169] One of the interesting exceptions is the work of historian Anne-Laure van Bruaene, who pays attention to this in her book on chambers of rhetoric, in which she points out that certain types of prints were popular with the middle groups of society and had the purpose to interiorise new religious and social values. Once that was done, those prints disappeared from interiors.[170] But the fact remains that the focus on paintings is far more a historiographic and art historical debate than it was a historic reality. Textiles were present in many households in greater numbers than paintings and played an important role in the organisation of domestic sociability. In the second chapter, we will therefore turn to decorative textiles such as cushions, bed curtains, table rugs and tapestries. These textiles were actively used in the structuring of the house and its inner workings precisely through their connection with furniture. Though considered more stable in style, material and finish, (seating, storage and sleeping) furniture evolved throughout the sixteenth century, both in use and finish. In this chapter, we therefore aspire to look for evolutions throughout the period in the creation of domestic comfort and to reveal related social practices of creating or sustaining privacy, sociability and self-fashioning.

Instead of studying the mere ownership of paintings, household textiles and furniture, we have put these objects in their original context, a real tour de force. Approaching objects as non-textual forms of communication allowed for them to serve as ideal proxies for questioning social and cultural practices.[171] After all, 'knowing about people's possessions is crucial to understanding their experience of daily life, the way they saw themselves in relation to their peers and their responses to and interactions with the social, cultural and economic structures and processes which made up the societies in which they lived'.[172]

PART 1

CROSSING THE THRESHOLD:
THE ORGANISATION OF DOMESTIC SPACE

INTRODUCTION

On 20 February 1595, all the movables belonging to Pieter Hendrick Winkelman, his wife Katelijne Vander Capelle and their two children were listed by reason of Pieter's death.[1] The appraiser, Sproncholf, went through all eleven rooms of the family's house and recorded all the objects found in those spaces. The inventory that resulted from this action has a room-by-room layout – only money (and some silver objects) and jewellery were listed separately. The appraiser used a mixed nomenclature for defining the rooms: some rooms were labelled with a one-purpose or specialised label such as *contoor*, 'kitchen', 'sleeping room' and 'laundry kitchen', whereas other rooms were named after their location in the house (and according to their location relative to other spaces) such as 'room above the *salette*' or 'front room'. Winkelman's post-mortem inventory therefore illustrates a possible layout of a house of a relatively wealthy family (highest social class in the sample) at the end of the sixteenth century. But even more importantly, his inventory shows that most of the rooms in the dwelling were not completely separated from each other, but were rather connected in space and function. In the Winkelman family's house, the service room (*bottelarij* or buttery), for example, was located near the kitchen so within easy reach of the kitchen staff. The nursery, on the other hand, was situated next to the bedroom (*'t kynder camerken neffens de slaepcamere*). This allowed the mistress of the house to monitor her children, because it shortened the distance between her and her infants. Service rooms such as the *vaulte*, the laundry room and the wood cellar were mentioned together as a group at the end of the inventory, illustrating their shared supporting role in the running of the household. Pieter's *contoor*, in turn, was clearly spatially connected to the hall.

Historian Chris King formulated a critique on a current in consumption research that has refocused its attention from architectural morphology of houses to home life; in his view, 'the built environment has often been treated as a passive backdrop or container for the expanding world of movable domestic objects rather than being seen as an integrated and active component of "material culture" conceived as a totality'.[2] And according to Amanda Vickery, 'the home is the setting, though perhaps not always the subject for most discussions of consumerism'.[3] King proposes, therefore, to question the changing material environment of domestic contexts in this period as well as the furnishings and material objects contained within them.[4] In this first part of the book, we will question the changing character of domestic spaces and their contents as constitutive of a broader changing domestic culture, a domestic culture that interacted with the world outside. In this context, it was the interaction between people (or users and often owners of space), objects, fixtures and fittings and the orientation of the room itself in the spatial layout of the house that constituted a room's role in the house or household. The chapters in this first part aspire to question the disposition of rooms and the arrangement of the interior. This means that some of the methodologies used in building history and archaeology (especially of access analysis) are not entirely abandoned, and some of their basic assumptions are even firmly integrated in the current study. In one of the first chapters, for example, we will show that shops were usually functionally and spatially separated from the rest of the living space and that *contoren* were often part of or an annex to a larger room. Furthermore, the spatial layout of houses did not simply provide a setting for the daily life of the household but also 'a material means of expressing cultural identities and actively negotiating changing social, economic and political relationships'.[5]

In what follows, it is the connectivity between rooms that will be of particular interest, because it plays an important role in the (changing) functionality of some spaces. It also epitomises changes or continuities in underlying cultural and social practices. In addition to the methodology of access analysis that has focused pre-dominantly on how a building works to interface the relationship between occupants, and especially between residents and visitors, we will focus on the interaction between daily functions like working, eating, sleeping, cooking, leisure, sociability and service.

In this type of research, it is important to be aware that not every citizen lived in a large multistorey house. Indeed, the practicalities of available space and pre-existing facilities dictated spatial arrangements.[6] The gradual depopulation of the city probably made rent and housing in Bruges cheaper and life more comfortable than it was in the expanding and crowded cities of Antwerp and Brussels.[7] The very poor lived in wooden cabins with straw roofs or in attics and cellars in the poorer neighbourhoods of the city,[8] but the slightly more affluent citizens or lower middle groups occupied a couple of rooms in larger houses or rented small houses. Only the much wealthier higher middle groups were able to afford houses with several rooms and multiple floors. Nevertheless, a concern with domestic space can most probably be found throughout the social pyramid, but wealth seems to have been an important determining factor in the ability to rationalise and organise the domestic environment.[9] In this respect, Lena Orlin concluded for Tudor England that the evolution towards more purpose-specific spaces 'may have developed out of desires other than privacy, including the will to impose order on possessions and activities'.[10]

Functional Specialisation: A Subject of Discussion

Within the ongoing scholarly debate on domestic spaces, it has been repeatedly stated that the sixteenth-century house was characterised by a growing number of rooms and an increasing specialisation of room use (a process of so-called 'functional specialisation' or 'spatial specialisation'), whereby spaces were divided from each other and each daily activity (e.g. eating, sleeping, cooking receiving guests) had its own locus.[11] In this vein, scholarship on the so-called great rebuilding in Tudor England in the later medieval and early modern period has been concentrated largely on early modern architectural changes in the plan and form of houses (open halls gained ceiling, fireplaces were installed and rooms were separated) in cities and in the countryside.[12] Although these architectural transformations have been identified especially in early modern England,[13] the same trends 'towards more specialised domestic spaces and more elaborate material culture and decoration within the domestic sphere' have been identified 'across different social groups and many different national contexts'.[14] For several Renaissance Italian city palaces, for example, Elizabeth Currie found that rooms other than the bedroom became more 'carefully thought over and developed their own distinctive character' over the fifteenth and sixteenth centuries.[15] Even in sixteenth-century Antwerp, Carolien De Staelen noticed an evolution towards a more differentiated room use, especially in the larger houses, which she labelled as organising living space 'according to Italian fashion'.[16] But apart from her study, the spatial developments in the late medieval and early modern middle-class houses in Flanders and Brabant have remained relatively underexplored. Perhaps this might have been a consequence of the long-defended idea that it was only in the second half of the seventeenth century that the 'functional specialisation' of rooms first made its debut in the Low Countries.[17]

   A strong current in scholarship has further elaborated on this idea of increasingly segregated spaces to formulate the hypothesis that spaces were increasingly accorded a rank within the spatial (and social) hierarchy of the house.[18] This hierarchy was based on the assumption that 'buildings and interiors were constructed to convey social meanings as well as for practical purposes'.[19] Some scholars started to use the terminology of sociologist Erving Goffman[20] to differentiate between 'frontstage' and 'backstage' spaces, meaning public versus more private rooms.[21] Goffman saw human behaviour as a stage performance. He argued that even in ordinary situations, individuals tend to present themselves and their activity to others. Through this 'impression management', individuals guide and control the impression others form of them, doing (or not doing) certain kinds of actions while sustaining their performance before them.[22] These performances have a 'front' and 'back' aspect and were staged in a certain space or a particular material context. Historians have further developed this theory and talk about 'frontstage' spaces or public display spaces where people performed a particular part of their (and their family's) identity and 'backstage' spaces or less important spaces where props are stored, 'costumes can be adjusted, and an actor can come out of character'.[23]

Using Goffman's theory, scholars have argued that some rooms, such as exotically furnished studies, sumptuous parlours and well-furnished chambers, became important social 'frontstage' spaces, while other rooms, such as kitchens, bedchambers and service rooms, became more or less private, secondary 'backstage' (work)places.[24] Unfortunately, it follows that historiography has hardly done justice to these 'secondary' and more mundane spaces as subjects of study, especially compared to the more public and often more decorated reception rooms.[25] It is only recently that this 'old' debate on the hierarchy of spaces was re-examined and that spaces such as kitchens, laundry rooms, cellars and corridors but also seemingly 'private' spaces such as bedrooms were reconsidered from a user perspective.[26] So although still very much associated with female, backstage and repetitive everyday labour, these service rooms are gradually receiving more attention from historians of home life. This growing attention is highly warranted, because it was exactly these spaces that played a vital role in the (changing) spatial dynamics in the domestic geography as a whole.[27] Lena Orlin underlines this by stating that 'for most early moderns [...], the highest degree of particularisation was associated with storage and service rooms'.[28] It remains debatable, however, whether the appearance of a separate cooking space, for example, can be linked to the 'old' modernist linear approach of the functional specialisation concept, because kitchens could have housed several functions at the same time. But the main question here concerns the cultural values or shared ways of thinking behind the (re)structuring of the domestic environment.[29]

What's in a Name? The Nomenclature of Domestic Space

Although the value of inventories to study domestic space has been widely disputed, they offer plenty of possibilities. The layouts of 53 per cent of the inventories in the sample present a room-by-room division, suggesting that the appraising was based on 'a perambulation of the house'.[30] Other inventories were of a piece-by-piece model, based on the listing of individual items or groups of items, with or without logical order.[31] Even though inventories are static, subjective and not exhaustive sources, the nomenclature that is used in the room-by-room inventories could still give a good idea of the room disposition of houses, a feature of inventories that has been insufficiently considered.

In the process of inventorying goods, it was the task of the appraiser to assess goods and chattels and value them as accurately as possible. So it was of the utmost importance that these goods were also accurately described and that the more valuable items were distinguished from the less valuable ones. When walking through the house, the appraiser therefore had to systematise a method to structure the domestic space and to link certain items to certain spaces. Hence, the appraiser (and others) used a specific nomenclature for the spatial diversity, suggesting a shared way of thinking about domestic space.

In inventories in general, and in the Bruges inventories in particular, there were different ways to distinguish each room from another; some rooms were identified by function, others by their orientation in the house (upstairs or downstairs) or location on the floor (back or front). Only in exceptional cases were rooms identified by the main colour scheme of the interior (e.g. white room or green room) or by the individual or individuals that used them (e.g. 'room of the consul of the Spanish Nation', 'sleeping room of the deceased') (table 2). In the literature, it is often suggested that most rooms in pre-modern inventories were defined according to their orientation in the house, especially because scholars were convinced that room use was not yet fixed.[32] In the Bruges case, however, the difference between the number of rooms that were defined according to function or room use and the number of rooms that were defined according to orientation is rather small (graph 4).[33] So even though defining rooms by their location was still in use, more diverse purpose-specific labels entered the nomenclature throughout the period as well.

But what does it mean when an appraiser identifies a certain room as 'shop' or 'kitchen' and another as 'back room'? What does it reveal about contemporary assumptions underlying the structuring of domestic space? What prompted the

Table 2. Variety of Functional Room Labels

SAMPLE PERIOD	VARIETY
1438–1444	8
1450–1500	9
1528–1549	6
1559–1574	21
1584–1600	14

Source: Database of inventories © IB, JDG & IS

Graph 4. Room Labels in Bruges Inventories (all sample periods, n=265)

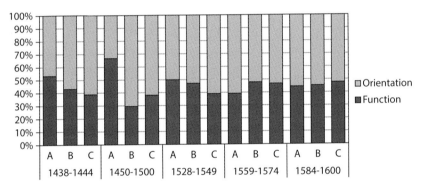

Source: Database of inventories © IB, JDG & IS

appraiser to define a particular room as, for example, 'kitchen'? And were these labels then in some way illustrative of the gradual evolution towards the debated functional specialisation of spaces?

In recent decades, historians of home life and material culture studies have approached these room labels in inventories with a certain suspicion. When scholars linked the labels with the rooms' contents, it soon turned out that these rooms were 'still' multifunctional in nature even when they were labelled with seemingly specialised names.[34] The labels were therefore quickly considered to be meaningless, and the functional subdivision of rooms reflected in the name tags was seen as an eighteenth- or nineteenth-century (elite?) phenomenon.[35] Indeed, scholars such as John Loughman and John Michael Montias concluded that for sixteenth-century cases, room labels were useless and that 'the function of a room can only be inferred from its contents.'[36]

Yet when considering the value of sixteenth-century room labels and the spatial layout of houses, we have to be careful not to throw the baby out with the bathwater. In a recent article, Giorgio Riello stated that 'the repetition of similar nomenclatures or locations of objects suggest the existence of a shared way of thinking about the domestic space that is conveyed in inventories'.[37] Indeed, there must have been a good reason why an appraiser would have named a room a 'sleeping room' even though other objects referring to other room functions were present there as well. Perhaps the appraiser was influenced by the object cluster that most attracted attention? Or the appraiser had learned that, notwithstanding these other objects in the room, this particular room layout combined with these particular objects indicated a room that was predominantly used to sleep in? In the case of the sleeping room, this could have been the bed with all its appurtenances; in the case of the kitchen, it was probably the hearth and all the cooking gear. Nevertheless, it was certainly a room that was, at least in words, separated from other rooms.

Seemingly specialised rooms such as kitchens and sleeping rooms often contained other object categories as well (like a well-made bed in a kitchen) and were therefore able to accommodate other, potentially related, household activities, perhaps during other times of the day or on particular occasions.[38] So in these cases, cooking and sleeping can be considered as the *primary* functions of these particular spaces, accompanied by other, secondary functions.[39] Hence even when a room was not entirely 'specialised' in use, there still was a certain hierarchy in the functions that were fulfilled there. Therefore, the room labels appraisers used were therefore highly suggestive of a more rationalised spatial disposition of household activities. It does not mean, however, that it was always clear to the appraiser what functions a space exactly served. The double labels such as '*camere ofte cuekene*' and the use of the undefined label 'room' or *camere* (with or without additional information about its orientation in space) could all point to the often varied character of certain spaces and the difficulty appraisers could have in defining a room.[40]

Table 3 illustrates the percentages of inventories with a room-by-room layout (per sample period) that were equipped with seemingly purpose-specific rooms. This table is revealing in several ways. First, it seems that some of the nomenclature changed over time, as new labels entered the vocabulary of the appraisers, such as *salette*, and others disappeared, such as 'dining room'.[41] It also suggests that certain rooms, such as the *contoor*, occurred only exceptionally. But the most interesting result is that the kitchen was the most commonly used label to identify a particular type

Table 3. Percentage of Inventories with Specialised Room Labels in Bruges (total number inventories with rooms per sample period; n=337)

PERIOD	SLEEPING ROOM	KITCHEN	DINING ROOM	CONTOOR	SALETTE	SERVICE ROOMS
1438–1444 (38)	3%	68%	11%	0%	0%	45%
1450–1500 (37)	3%	54%	41%	3%	0%	14%
1528–1549 (52)	4%	67%	50%	0%	0%	2%
1559–1574 (154)	5%	81%	6%	5%	2%	7%
1584–1600 (56)	16%	88%	0%	4%	16%	14%

Source: Database of inventories © IB, JDG & IS

of room throughout the whole sample period. No less than 88 per cent of the sampled households in the sixth sample period had at least one room labelled as kitchen!

However, even though the room label 'kitchen' clearly remains present throughout the period, the material constellation of and the common thinking about seemingly fixed spaces such as kitchens might still have changed. Our aim for this chapter therefore is to consider the material culture of seemingly specialised rooms as a pars pro toto to measure the evolutions in room use in Bruges houses throughout the sixteenth century. Other rooms such as dining rooms and sleeping rooms will be measured in their connectivity with the kitchen and with other spaces from the hypothesis that the more specialised a room became, the more other spaces needed to house some of its 'redundant' functions. But first, we will start our analysis at the threshold of the house, questioning the permeability of domestic spaces and the alleged dichotomy between the public life of commerce and the private life at home. We will then further enter the house, questioning the characteristics of the kitchen and its associated service rooms, moving further to other somehow, functionally connected spaces such as dining rooms, *salettes* and sleeping rooms. Reconstructing fifteenth- and sixteenth-century room uses and domestic geographies is a challenging task, because there was no such thing as a typical Bruges house type.[42]

CONNECTING THE HOUSE TO THE STREET?
THE SHOP AND WORKSHOP

Introduction

In 1551, Bruges painter Pieter Pourbus completed the portrait of Jacquemyne Buuck and her husband Jan van Eyewerve; this painting was probably commissioned by the couple on the occasion of their wedding (fig. 1).[1] The portrait consists of two separate pendant paintings, one for each spouse. The couple was staged as if they were standing in a room of a multistorey house (perhaps even their own house) on the Vlamingstraat in Bruges, right across from the Vlamingbridge, a place of great commercial activity, because many ships had to pass through the bridge to reach the Waterhalle, where they could unload.[2] Judging from their clothes and accessories – Jan's black velvet doublet fitted with fashionable long slashes and leather gloves, the gold embroidery on Jacquemyne's white linen *colette*, her golden necklace and ring, and her finely decorated leather gloves, long fur sleeves, velvet sleeves and probably velvet tippet with damask lining[3] – these people belonged to the higher social echelons of Bruges society.[4] Their citizenship and Jan's link with (the wine) trade was made clear through the vistas behind both subjects. The window or vista behind Jan offers a view of the city crane, the Kraanplaats and the Vlamingbrug, all important centres of trade in sixteenth-century Bruges. But the window behind Jacquemyne shows a fragment of the tower of Saint John's chapel and a house with a shop called 'de Haene' or 'the Rooster'.[5] So a shop – not a market square or stall – was depicted as a pendant for retail, while the city crane was used as a pendant for the wholesale business in Bruges.

The scenes behind the sitters in portraits such as these were often gendered. In this case, the city crane would then symbolise (manly) trade and business, and the shop would refer to (feminine?) retail. In the double portrait by the Leiden painter Cornelis Engelbrenchtz (1515) of brewer Dirck Ottenz and his wife Cornelia, the vista behind the brewer depicts the business of the donor as well, while a shop was painted behind the image of his wife.[6] Was this a coincidence? Why exactly a shop

Fig. 1. Portraits of Jan van Eyewerve (left) and his wife Jacquemyne Buuck (right), Pieter Pourbus, 1551, Oil on Panel, © Groeningemuseum, Bruges, www.artinflanders.be

was depicted behind the donator is not yet entirely clear. Were the wives of both tradespeople connected to the sale of derivative products? Or was the shop more a symbol for steering the household and making sure that all the necessary consumables were bought, a task linked to the lady of the house?[7] The question nonetheless arises about the position of the shop – often part of a dwelling – in a late medieval commercial urban centre, where markets were held on a regularly basis and where guilds fiercely oversaw the production in each of their members' workshops. The fact that a shop was depicted might indicate that shops were already well integrated in the retail circuit of late medieval Bruges. But because production regulations were fierce, to what extent did the shop connect to the rest of the building?

In the painting of Pieter Pourbus, barrels, tubs and trays with all kinds of merchandise were positioned right in front of the house, in the front window and in the corridor that leads up to the shop (fig. 2). Below the wooden structure of the shop, there was a hint of yet another type of retail activity that took place there: a man displaying and selling some goods from a small, simple and movable wooden counter (fig. 3). The small vista in the portrait of Jacquemyne, therefore, depicts a vivid scene of retailing both inside and outside the house; a woman is closing a deal with the

Fig. 3. Closer detail of the shop in *The Rooster* and the counter in front of the shop, detail in the portrait of Jacquemyne Buuck, Pieter Pourbus, 1551, Oil on Panel, © Groeningemuseum, Bruges, www.artinflanders.be

Fig. 2. Detail of the shop in The Rooster and the counter in front of the shop, detail in the portrait of Jacquemyne Buuck, Pieter Pourbus, 1551, Oil on Panel, © Groeningemuseum, Bruges, www.artinflanders.be

shop owner or shop assistant inside the shop, whereas another woman is entering the space of the shop. Although goods were on display outside, the transaction took place in the interior space of the shop. So the shopping occurred partly inside the house and partly outside of it.[8] Or in the words of Peter Stabel, the shop, therefore, 'offered a combination of privacy and openness'.[9]

But a shop was only rarely situated in a building that did not fulfil other functions as well. The shop in this painting was positioned on the ground floor of a multistorey building, so in all likelihood, the house also contained spaces other than the retail outlet at the front. How did shops – such as the one on the painting – relate to other sites of commerce and business and to the more domestic spaces in the same building?[10] The main research question then is to what extent this commercially furnished retail or production space situated in a dwelling interrelated with the personal living spaces of shop owners and their families.[11] Was the material culture of the home consciously brought into the shop (objects such as paintings and statuettes or textiles, chairs, tables and cushions) and actively put to use to attract customers?[12] To what extent were 'domestic values' or practices associated with do-mestic life such as devotion, social interaction, (family) honour and comfort[13] pres-ent or to be performed in the business area of a house?

'Historians and the Nation of Shopkeepers'

Research on the specificities of retail space in the late medieval and early modern period in the Low Countries is still in its infancy.[14] Several historiographic con-cerns are responsible for this lack of attention. Most research on retail practices was, until recently, predominantly focused on developments in the British commercial landscape in general and on the great evolutions (or rather *revolutions*) in the nine-teenth century in particular.[15] The retail systems before this period were seen as 'backwards' and 'traditional'; shops before the nineteenth century were presented as 'dark, unappealing places' and as 'a mere exchange point of goods for money'.[16] So areas of retail were confined to markets, stalls and the tiny, busy workshops of artisans (*werkwinkels*).[17] Not only did the pre-industrial consumer suffer from a lack of a well-developed consumer mentality, pre-modern (and especially late medieval) shops were deemed to have been too small and too full of tools and utensils to be labelled shops.[18] This presumed lack of a well-developed consumer mentality also meant that pre-modern shop owners were not expected to test commercial seduc-tion strategies, because pre-modern consumers were, according to classical theory, insensitive to marketing techniques.[19] After all, according to that same theory, mar-keting strategies and new sales techniques were only invented in the nineteenth and twentieth centuries.[20]

   According to Ilja Van Damme, who wrote a review article on the current state of affairs in the historiographical debate on retail mechanisms, a recent scholarly interest in retail developments and in the rise of the shop has arisen due to a growing fascination for middle-group people in society, a new history of guilds and crafts, and especially to a renewed interest in consumption patterns and material culture.[21] And because these interests manifested themselves for the early modern and late medieval periods, they sounded promising for the study of the late medieval and early modern shop. As a kind of counterweight to the dominance of British studies in this field, scholars started to catch up with research about retail developments in continental European (urban) contexts.[22] But also the focus shifted slightly to the period before the nineteenth century,[23] and the existence of a pre-industrial consumer was finally acknowledged. However, this focus did not go any further back then the seventeenth and early eighteenth centuries, leaving the late medieval and early modern period still underexposed.

Furthermore, in this new strand of research, the interest in retail and consumption developments was mostly focused on the experiences of the consumer or the individual shopper and not on the practices of shopkeeping. Research was driven by what John Benson and Laura Ugolini have labelled a 'demand-led model'.[24] It was a development that was probably caused by the current interest in material culture and consumption patterns that were focused on the buyer and not directly on the seller. One exception to the rule in this state of affairs is a series of articles that was published in the volume *Buyers and Sellers*, in which the focus was on both parties to the retail transaction.[25]

Whereas scholars of the late modern period have to be encouraged not to forget market selling, hawking and peddling, 'since non-fixed shop retailing continued to play a vital role in the late modern economy',[26] scholars of the medieval and early modern period have to be reminded that besides selling products on the weekly, daily or international market, fixed shop retailing was an important part of the late medieval and early modern urban economy as well. Indeed, the scholarly interest in retail systems in late medieval and early modern cities was focused mostly on the patterns of periodic retail and the urban distribution system as a whole. It was instigated primarily by a close scrutiny of market practices and retailing structures, questioning the degree of control of corporate bodies mostly organised into craft guilds.[27] Shops arguably had an odd place within this retail system controlled by the guilds, because these spaces were more difficult to control than outdoor markets. Some types of hoops for barrels, for example, were forbidden to be sold indoors in shops but had to be sold on the market by coopers.[28] Recent research has already convincingly proven that a late medieval urban market system was mainly characterised by multidimensionality; several distinct market systems and retail outlets coexisted, and it was the specificity of commodities that determined what form of exchange was preferred.[29] But artisans could have had several different retail outlets to sell their goods, depending on the time of year. Bruges turners, for example, could retail their goods from their shops as well as from a market stall.[30]

Just like markets and halls, shops were under the control of guilds and other corporate institutions.[31] Guilds decided, for example, how many retail outlets their members were allowed to operate and proclaimed whether and how members were allowed to display their products to the public. According to their *keuren* or guild regulations, turners, for example, had to choose whether they would sell their goods from their shops or from a market stall during a fair, because they were not allowed to run two *meesterijen*, or two selling outlets, at the same time.[32] The deans of the guilds also frequently visited shops and houses belonging to members of their own guild or to members of other guilds to verify whether the regulations had been complied with, whether there were foreign goods sold in the Bruges shops and to sanction product quality.[33] That these searches were often traumatic for the shop owners and their family members – especially when the deans of one guild entered the shop and house of guild members of another guild – was made clear in Harald Deceulaer's research.[34] They were experienced as infiltrations into the private realm of a guildsman, so there must have been a strong connection between the (work)shop of the guildsman, his family honour and his house. And there must have been at least psychological boundaries between workspace, domestic space and the street.[35] Were these psychological boundaries also materialised? And were these boundaries maintained by the shop owner himself during the act of shopkeeping or producing goods?

As we have seen, the act of shopping – and therefore the existence of *full-grown* shops – was for a long time considered to be something of the nineteenth century, something that did not yet exist in a late medieval urban context.[36] The groundbreaking volume by Evelyn Welch, *Shopping in the Renaissance*, was one of the first to start a new debate after providing convincing proof that the shop and the act of shopping 'already' existed in Renaissance Italy, though she warns that 'the experience of the Italian Renaissance challenges rather than reinforces a sense of linear transfer from past to present'.[37] In the chapter on markets and shops, Welch cites the words of the Italian theorist Leon Battista Alberti, who in his 1471 treatise on architecture described his ideal version of the *bottega* or shop: 'Within the city, the shop that lies beneath the house and provides the owner with his livelihood should be better fitted out than his dining room, as it should appear more in keeping with his hopes and ambitions'.[38] Translating this according to Alberti's principle of the hierarchy of spaces, the shop was then the (aspired) outwards expression of the respectability and (professional) status of the shop owner or artisan – even more so than the owner's (otherwise, according to Alberti, luxuriously furnished) dining room. So the shop as a retail space and sometimes also as a space of manufacture most likely had to serve several purposes, but above all, it had to convince outsiders of the credibility of the craftsperson playing a role in the commercial system of the city. But what were these purposes in reality? Moreover, regardless of all the guild regulations, shop owners and artisans still needed to sell their goods and had to encourage customers of substantial or modest means to buy their goods. These customers therefore needed to know the quality of the goods that were for sale in the different shops and probably wanted to have a choice of goods as well. So to what extent was the shop designed to seduce the potential customer to buy some of the shop's goods? Did a shop's interior actually matter? Or as Bruno Blondé and Ilja Van Damme have put it, 'was shop design functional' in selling sixteenth-century material culture?[39]

Shops and Shopping in Bruges

Shops were only one selling outlet or retail circuit in the commercial landscape of late medieval and early modern Bruges. But the 'rise of the shop' was one important characteristic of late medieval retailing.[40] As Felicity Riddy rightly asserts, this concept of 'shop', or *winckele*, in a late medieval context is, however, ambiguous, because 'it can imply "workshop" as well as "place of sale" because in some crafts – such as shoemaking and tailoring for example – goods for sale were made on the premises'.[41] Indeed, the typical artisan was not only a retailer or shopkeeper or a person 'who does not actually work upon, make or manufacture the goods he sells'.[42] Most artisans were what historians would call 'producer/retailers'.[43] In any case, the shop both as a place of sale and as a place of manufacturing was seen as a semi-private (or semi-public) space, protected from the outside world (in contrast to market stalls) and excluding certain people (such as thieves) when needed. It also represented an open invitation for customers (merchants and guild members) to interact with the shopkeeper and to buy some goods. And because the open market allowed visibility, comparison, price controls and guarantees of quality as well as common agreement on value, shops needed to match these requirements to be credible.[44]

The character of these spaces and the extent to which domestic life penetrated the realm of work, production and commerce (and vice versa) were, in all probability, highly dependent on the nature of the craft and the method of exchange.[45] Indeed, there were different infrastructural requirements for different types of commercial enterprises.[46] This is also the reason why it is important to consider *both* shop interior and business activity to say something about the potential interconnection

between shop design, retail space and domesticity. Mercers' shops were, in all likelihood, furnished and organised differently than bakeries and the shops of turners.
Indeed, not every craft needed to have a shop as a place of retail in the first place;
the dwellings of weavers and shearers, for example, combined manufacturing and
living accommodation, because they most likely produced their goods indoors to
sell them to a merchant or entrepreneur. So the extent to which their production activities penetrated domestic life was probably different from, for example, stocking
makers and hatters who had a room or a shop where they would sell their products
direct to their customers. Nonetheless, in each case, visitors, business associates and
customers had to cross a threshold – figuratively or literally – to close a deal or en-
gage in social and business interaction.

 Shop owners and artisans used the exteriors of their shops to make themselves
and their trade visible on the street.[47] On the one hand, they were obliged to do
so, because customers and guild officials had to know where particular shops were
to be found.[48] On the other hand, artisans and retailers were probably eager to attract potential buyers to sell their wares. Colourful and large shop signs with names
and symbols, *voorwinckels*, or outdoor displays of goods, colourful shop fronts and
counters were used to attract the attention of passers-by.[49] However, the actions
that were taken by the city authorities against infringements of the public space
undoubtedly also had consequences for the shopkeepers. The pavements and streets
in Bruges were, at one point, so cluttered with the stalls that were erected by shopkeepers in front of their shops and by the counters of street vendors that the city
had to intervene by levying a tax on all the stalls that hindered traffic.[50] Craftspeople
who did not have sufficient space to store their raw materials or finished goods in
or behind their own house and therefore simply left them on the street were also
dealt with more strictly. According to Deneweth, this led to craftspeople having less
stock on hand or looking for additional storage space or an extra workshop.[51] The
signboards, which until then, protruded above the street to attract attention from
afar, also had to be attached to the facades. That way, they would no longer hinder
passers-by and carts with loads.[52] Iconography, such as the image of 'the Rooster'
house mentioned before, signals the importance of the exterior of shops (shop signs
and the presentation of goods outside the shop, for example) in creating a retail environment in and around the physical location of the shop. But how intriguing the
exterior design of shops is, it is a subject not treated here, because there is almost no
data about the specificities of the exterior of late medieval shops in Bruges. Yet by
looking at the objects inside the shop, crucial characteristics of the interior of these

sixteenth-century commercial outlets can be deduced.[53] This chapter is therefore about the shop interior and its connection with the rest of the domestic environment, focusing on furnishing, interior decoration and the display of goods, fittings and tools.

Benson and Ugolini argue that to stress the innovative nature of early modern retailing, most researchers' attention has been concentrated on what they call the 'minority of urban, often London-based, innovative, "modern" shopkeepers at the expense of the majority of retailers, particularly "traditional" craftsmen-retailers such as shoemakers, tailors, saddlers, bakers and cabinetmakers, about whom we still know all too little.'[54] Indeed, most research was focused on the so-called 'high-class shop design' for which most material survived. In contrast to earlier research on shop design, we chose to include all types of retail in the sample in the survey.

For our sample, we first selected all the inventories (with room indication) of people who worked at home (forty-four inventories out of 502);[55] some sold their products in a room labelled *winckele* or *vloer*; others simply produced goods (or intermediary goods) and sold them to a merchant or had their *toog* or shop elsewhere.[56] The latter was, for example, allowed for members of the Bruges painters' guild from 1475; those artisans of the guild that produced their goods in a small room at the back of the house and did not have the space to have a counter (or shop) in their own houses were allowed to have a shop (or counter) elsewhere.[57] To be able to say something about the character of the retail space and/or production spaces at home, we divided the inventories (and professions) into subcategories according to product (or commodity) and profession. Most artisans produced or sold consumer durables and semi-durables, but some shop owners such as grocers and bakers, sold foodstuffs: altogether, they served a wide range of customers. So in general, we do not limit ourselves to the inventories comprising shops alone, but also include inventories of craftspeople that were only producing goods without selling them directly to the consumer. These artisans, including weavers and dyers, worked at home as well, occupying a certain amount of space in the whole of the domestic space indoors.

The inventories that meet the criteria for this chapter were spread over time. Some date back to the fifteenth century, while others date from the mid sixteenth century. We are aware that differences and evolutions must have occurred during this period of nearly a century and a half, but because the data are so limited in number and according to Bert De Munck, major changes in the structure of the craft guilds already occurred in the thirteenth and fourteenth centuries and then again from the end of the sixteenth and during the seventeenth century,[58] we are inclined to look at all the inventories from different time frames together when discussing the interiors of shops and workplaces and the character of the retail environment.

In what follows, we will discuss each category of retail separately, taking the differences between the various trades – and even among artisans from the same craft – into account. Questions considering the spatial and internal organisation of the retail or production space will be posed, focusing in short on visibility, security and accessibility, in other words, its location in the house (accessibility for costumers, links between retail space and storage space, between retail space and space of production and between commercial space and domestic space, importance of light and display windows), its content and furnishing (presence of decorative items, traces of devotion, furniture, supplies and display of goods) and the act of buying and selling while paying attention to guild regulations and the specificities of the trade.

Category 1: *Faiseurs de rien, vendeurs de tout*

The first subcategory or group of people with shops comprises retailers, people using a shop to display and sell different products that they have not made themselves (occasionally supplemented with a small quantity of products for public sale they have produced themselves). In addition to the mercers and grocers, a herring and a dairy seller also make up part of this category of retailers. These artisans and retailers lived in houses of various sizes, but the houses contained at least one room that was labelled by the appraiser as *winckele*. In some cases, however, such as in the inventories of grocer Pieter van Steenkiste, dairy seller Christoffel de Valcken and Margriete, grocer Ingel Potter's wife, the shop was not described as such. However, the presence of merchandise in boxes, bags, baskets and barrels situated at the front of the house might indicate that the room called the *vloer* in the inventories served the purpose of a shop as well. In mercer Rubrecht Hanevil's inventory, we even find the label *vloer ofte winckele*, or 'floor or shop', indicating that the floor could fulfil similar functions to a room labelled *winckele*.

Mercers and grocers were retailers of different kinds of goods, ranging from yarn to majolica plates, hollowware, soap, colophony and spices (the last applies particularly to the grocers).[59] In most cases, they did not produce the goods they sold. In some studies, these retailers were therefore labelled '*faiseurs de rien, vendeurs de tout*'.[60] The inventories of Rubrecht Hanevil (1563),[61] Pieter Van Steenkiste (1530)[62] and Luc van Slingelande (1480)[63] were the most detailed mercers' and grocers' shops of our sample. Luc Van Slingelande's shop or *'t winkelken* was situated at the front of the house, next to a little room that seems to have been some a sort of annex of *'t winkelken*. The shop contained tubs with butter, a chest with some linen and an unspecified quantity of wicker wood. The shops of Rubrecht Hanevil and Pieter van Steenkiste, on the other hand, were situated at the front of the house as well, but their goods also included spices, exotic fruits and sugar, in addition to wool and yarn. The shops of both retailers were located in the middle of the international quarter of the city – in the Vlamingstraat – with their exotic fruits and spices possibly attracting many of the international merchants that lived and worked in that neighbourhood.

All the goods the grocers and mercers sold were displayed in containers such as barrels, baskets, boxes and tubs. The shop owners used different display fittings to show different types of goods. The rarer and more expensive the goods were, the smaller the containers (and the smaller the quantity) in which the goods were shown to the customer. In the shop belonging to Rubrecht Hanevil, who sold larger quantities of wool and cotton yarn and all kinds of exotic (and imported) fruits, nuts and spices, these differences in display are very apparent. Plums, currants, almonds, capers and olives were put on display in larger tubs and barrels, whereas the more expensive spices such as cinnamon, saffron, mastic and mace (*foelie*, or the netting around the nutmeg fruit) were shown to customers in smaller boxes (*dozen*) and so in smaller quantities. Inneke Baatsen calculated the prices of these spices and the number of days a master mason in Bruges had to work to buy one ounce (or twenty-seven grams) of a particular type of spice. Her results indicated that although most of these spices were not as unaffordable as previously assumed, they were still considerably more expensive than local fruits and herbs and the dried fruits, olives and other wares the grocer had for sale.[64] One might assume that the limited quantity of spices that was for sale could be explained by the relatively high prices the grocer had to pay to the supplier. Welch asserted for the Italian mercers and apothecaries as well that 'the large capital investments in the stock contained within their shops made these spaces more like storehouses or treasure-chests than open areas for browsing'.[65] But on closer inspection, it seems that other strategies were at play as well. The remaining stock of the spices was in fact preserved in a special *cruutcamere* in Hanevil's cellar. Although we cannot tell for sure what this *cruutcamere* actually looked like, it is clear from the inventory that it contained several small bags of different qualities and types of ginger, pepper, salt, cloves and anise. So not only were certain quantities of spices stored and preserved elsewhere, some of the spices in this *cruutcamere* were not offered for sale in the shop at all. Perhaps the grocer would have wanted to limit the array of spices on sale in the shop to ensure that customers could not enter and browse the full stock? In this way, grocers could limit to some extent the access to the shop (and goods), had control over what was shown and could force contact between them and potential buyers.[66] Moreover, the enclosed nature of this storeroom could better protect the shop owners and their goods and stock from theft.[67] Especially in the case of the expensive spices, it was necessary to have larger quantities stored in enclosed spaces to better protect and preserve their integrity.

Except for the small quantity of spices Hanevil kept in his cellar, all the other goods were on display in the shop. Retailers – like any other guild member – had to guarantee the quality of the goods they had on offer.[68] Many guild statutes insisted, therefore, that manufacture would take place in public to ensure the quality of the production process and of the raw materials that were used and to facilitate control.[69] Because retailers did not produce their own goods, it might follow that they had to display the goods that were on sale as clearly as possible and all in the same space. According to Bert De Munck, retailers and artisans had to adopt strategies aimed at 'reducing information asymmetries' (i.e. 'the seller of a product having more or better information on product quality than the buyers, resulting in a lack of trust among the latter').[70] In the houses of the retailers in our sample, we could therefore find no trace of stock or commodities elsewhere in the house, except for the aforementioned cellar and *cruutcamere* of Hanevil. But even in the latter case, the spices were stored in a closed entity separate from the other objects in his cellar. So there was no risk of the spices getting compromised or mixed up with other wares not to be sold. All the other rooms in the houses of Hanevil, Van Steenkiste and Van Slingelande were furnished as living rooms with beds, chairs, tables, cooking and eating utensils, hearth equipment, clothing and accessories, but without stock, groceries or any other tools or objects that would have played a role in the retail business of their trade.

The same goes for herring seller Wouter van Gheldre (1502)[71] and dairy seller Christoffel De Valcke (1584).[72] Although other rooms in their houses were also mentioned in their inventories, and some of the rooms were also located at the front of the house, such as Van Geldre's kitchen, there were no stock or tools found elsewhere than within the boundaries of the shop.

The case of grocer Ingel Potters (1469)[73] is somewhat different, caused by the small size of his abode, though the same basic assumptions apply to his shop as

well. Ingel Potters and his wife Margriete inhabited two small rooms on the Braam-
berg, situated *onder de menhalle* (attached to the small meat hall, or Oostvleeshuis),
owned by the butchers' guild.[74] The first room was labelled *winkel* or 'shop' and
contained all kinds of exotic fruits such as oranges, figs, dates and currants, as well
as dried herring and majolica dishes. Some of the goods were displayed in a cabinet
(*schaprade*), but most were displayed in barrels, tubs and baskets, like the wares of
the other two grocers in the sample. The second room was described as 'back room'
and harboured cooking utensils, kettles, a table, three chandeliers and a bed, indicating that the room was particularly used as a cooking, eating and sleeping area. No
stock or tools were found in the latter room either, but a bed, a bench (*lijs*), two cabinets (*schaprade*) and several items of tableware were found in the shop, suggesting a
mixture of living and working in the same room. Was it because the back room was
too small to harbour all the furniture the couple needed for comfortable living? Or
were some pieces of furniture and tableware taken from the back room and put in
the shop to facilitate appraisal? We can only guess. The fact remains, however, that
although some pieces of furniture that were not intended to be used in the shop
(like the bed) were found in the shop at the time of the appraisal, the commodities
that were on sale were clearly separated from the furniture and remained visible to
the eyes of the public outside and in the shop.

The interiors of these shops showed no sign of decoration or seating furniture. The shops of the grocers, the mercer, the herring and the dairy seller simply
contained the wares that were on sale. This does not mean, however, that the retailers could not have had a strategy to entice potential customers to buy goods.
But it was mostly the quality, variety, colours and sometimes even rarity, smell and
sight of the wares themselves that had to do the trick and convince the customer
to buy goods – far more than the design of the shop. The only thing the retailer
could do to lure customers into the shop and persuade them to buy products was
organising the presentation of the goods and making this the key visual focus for
the customers. Showing smaller quantities of certain spices, for example, as in the
case of grocer Hanevil, could hint at the rarity of these goods, stimulating the potential buyer to do some business and eventually purchase them. Displaying larger
quantities of other goods, for example, of dates, currants and olives, could in turn
seduce potential buyers to indulge in the richness of taste, smell, bite and shape of
the goods displayed right in front of their eyes. Moreover, as Claire Walsh asserts for
the eighteenth-century London shops, drawers, boxes and parcels had the positive
connotation of being organised and expressing visually the good management and

organisation of the stock.[75] In other words, in the shops of the retailers of foodstuffs and spices, it was the goods themselves that were the decoration of the space and the invitation to come in and do business. The interiors emphasised quantity, choice and accessibility and the good reputation of the well-organised and well-informed retailer. The only 'decoration' we came across in Ingel Potters's shop was the *papegay metten huuscken* or the parrot in his cage. Van Damme and Deceulaer both noticed the presence of birdcages in shops of retailers of different sorts, but they interpreted it as a means to attract the attention of passers-by or as the pet animal of the seller.[76] In the context of this Bruges shop of exotic fruits, we would suggest that the parrot was either on sale as some other foreign product (as it was summarised together with the other wares) or that it was a sort of 'mascot' of the shop, underlying the exotic character of the goods on sale and filling the retail space with colour and noise.

Category 2: Cloth and Linen Sellers

Fernand De Vlime (1562),[77] Claes De Man (1464)[78] and Jacob Obbelaer (1564)[79] were also retailers – like the grocers, mercer, and herring and dairy sellers – so most likely did not produce or manufacture anything themselves but sold both fabrics and finished products made from the same type of fabric they had for sale. Nevertheless, in spite of the fact that they were selling a different kind of product, the same principles also appear to have applied to these sellers and their houses. Fernand De Vlime was a seller of especially *Friesch* cloth[80] and *Friesch* cloth products such as children's stockings, gloves and mittens, headwear and nightgowns (*nachtkeerels*). But his most important commodity was the cloth itself; eighteen rolls of Frisian cloth and fourteen *flassages* or smaller pieces of the same type of fabric were registered in his shop. The finished products in cloth, in contrast, were only available in smaller quantities; only three nightgowns, one hood and five pairs of *boxen*, a sort of trousers. Linen seller Jacob Obbelaere sold fabric and finished products as well. Apart from the rolls of linen fabric of all measurements and colours, he sold all types of collars, tablecloths and shirts. The latter were probably displayed in the three *lijnwaet schaprades*, or cabinets, mentioned in his inventory. Linen seller Claes De Man, on the other hand, mainly sold finished linen products such as tablecloths (of different sizes), shirts for men and women, and linen pillowcases. So although these three men sold different types of fabric, they all displayed the commodities they had for sale in the space that was labelled as a shop, and none of them had

stock or raw materials elsewhere in the house. All the other rooms in the houses of
De Vlime, Obbelaer and De Man were furnished with objects and furniture that
bore no reference to their trade or could be of use in the shop itself. So here as well,
all the wares that were sold by the retailer had to be on display in (or outside in
front of) the shop, making the wares visible to the public and to guild officials. The
trades that were only selling goods without producing them themselves were looked
upon with greater suspicion, because no monitoring was possible of the quality of
the raw materials used or the production process. The retailers had to rely on their
intermediaries or suppliers, and the guilds and customers, in turn, had to rely on the
expertise of the retailers in selecting and selling products of the best quality.

Another remarkable thing two of the three textile retailers had in common
was the presence of some decoration in their shops – two small pictures in Obbelaere's shop and a painted cloth in De Vlime's – as well as seating furniture such
as chairs and benches. Herein lies a major difference with the shops of the other
retailers discussed earlier. In his research on eighteenth-century Brussels, Roger De
Peuter interpreted the presence of seating, paintings, mirrors or other decorative
items in shops as part of a particular retail strategy of the shop owner.[81] According to De Peuter, these items and furniture enticed customers to come in and feel
as comfortable as in their own home. Claire Walsh made a similar remark in her
study of shop designs in eighteenth-century London.[82] Bruno Blondé and Ilja Van
Damme, in turn, used the presence of paintings as a proxy to see whether shops
were conceived as part of the larger living culture of the house or as distinct places
in eighteenth-century Antwerp.[83] Perhaps the chairs in the shops of the fabric retailers were placed there for the customers who were waiting for a fitting or to ask
for more information about sizes and dimensions and to negotiate prices once the
seller was available? But perhaps the explanation should not be too far-fetched; the
seller could have had a rather practical use in mind. Chairs were indeed perfect for
displaying textiles: the retailer simply had to unfold a piece of textile and drape it
over a chair, so it was more visible and wouldn't touch the floor and get dirty. And
perhaps the painted cloth in De Vlime's shop was a reference to his textile trade?
Curiously, the retailer did not own any more paintings than the one canvas piece he
had on display in his shop. However, we do not know the theme of the cloth painting nor of the two smaller panel paintings in the shop of linen seller Obbelaere, so
it remains difficult to interpret. Obbelaere's latter two paintings, by contrast, were
part of a larger collection of four, of which one was displayed in an undefined room
and one in his front room.

Category 3: Producer/retailers

The third category is slightly more comprehensive and includes inventories of people who not only sold their products in the shops but also manufactured the goods they sold. Hatters, bonnet makers, belt makers, wheelwrights, shaft makers, painters, turners and coopers were all part of this category. They were called producer/retailers. In most cases, the shop was therefore not only a retail outlet but also the artisan's workplace – although there were some exceptions to this rule. Consequently, differences between these crafts in shopkeeping and organising production and retail occurred, though similarities between them can be demonstrated as well. One of these similarities is that in each case and notwithstanding the production technique, the retailing of products took place at the front of the house. The more dangerous occupations used fire to produce their goods, such as belt makers and bakers, and often had a workplace that was detached from the shop and often also detached from the house itself. In general, the organisation of retail spaces of the producer/retailers was different from the shops of the retailers we have already discussed. The sale of bonnets, for example, seems to have occupied more space in the house than the retail of spices and dairy products.

Most bonnet sellers did not themselves make the bonnets they sold – the process of bonnet making involved multiple steps of production performed by specialised craftspeople, such as wool spinners, knitters, fullers and dyers.[84] This clearly differed from the hatters, who made their own hats. In the inventories of the *mutsenreeders* in our sample, we could not trace any tool of the trade, though there were some references to piles and baskets of wool. So it might seem possible that the *mutsenreeders* did not perform all the production phases in the process of making bonnets, but restricted themselves to the end process of felting and finishing.[85]

In our sample, we have two *mutsenreeders* who both sold bonnets: Stevin Sremont (1541)[86] who lived and worked in the Carmersstraet, and Jan Martin (1541)[87] who resided in a house on the east side of the river Reie, between the Snaggaard and Olie bridges. Although their houses were of different sizes – Jan Martin's house was probably much larger, because it contained more rooms (at least nine rooms), than Sremont's (at least four rooms) – the spatial organisation of their professional activities was very similar.

In Stevin Sremont's house, the *vloer*, or floor, at the front was used as a shop. According to the inventory, the space contained an unspecified quantity of unprocessed (*rauwe*) or unfelted white bonnets, some components of particular bonnets (*vizieren*), some wool and a small counter (*wynkelkin*). Furthermore, the space contained one bench, a scale or balance and one cabinet (*schaprade*), probably used as a fitting to display the bonnets. The shop furniture was completed by three barrels and eight baskets. Other items in the shop were pieces of armour such as a *busse*, or arquebus, and two *wapenstocken*, or pointed weapons, which could be peaks, halberds or spears. The shop was also equipped with a hearth (one of the few in our sample), which was also used to cook food, given the presence of a spit and grill, pots, pans and kettles. Except for the bench and the cabinet that were of use in the shop, no other pieces of furniture (chairs, smaller benches or tables, suggesting eating or dining facilities) were found. Because only his sleeping room contained another hearth, the heated floor was probably the best location in which to cook food as well as to sell the bonnets. The hearth and the kettles might also have served a double use and could have played a part in the process of felting as well, because warm water was needed to felt the yarn. Fellow bonnet seller Jan Martin's shop had only a *buffet* or a cupboard, a long bench, five barrels and two baskets of wool and several unfelted (*onghereede*) bonnets.

Intriguingly, it seems that only the unfelted or unprocessed bonnets were on display in the shops of both gentlemen, complemented with some components or accessories (*vizieren*) of specific types of bonnets and some wool. But strangely enough, no finished or felted specimens were mentioned. So it was the intrinsic qualities of the goods that added value to the shop. The felted pieces were stored in another room in the house – in both houses, a room probably situated right next to (or behind) the shop. In Sremont's case, this room was labelled the 'back room', and in Martin's inventory, the room was situated next to the shop (*neffens de vloer*). In both rooms, the appraisers found a large cabinet in which to put finished and felted bonnets (*groote schaprade omme bonetten inte leggen*). At the time of appraisal, these cabinets were not empty either, and they contained an unspecified number of red and black bonnets in Sremont's case and no fewer than sixty-seven white felted bonnets and forty-eight black felted bonnets in Martin's case. Besides this bonnet cabinet, other pieces of furniture were mentioned in these rooms in both inventories: a chair in Martin's inventory, and a cupboard, a bench, a table, a chest and a mirror in Sremont's.

In Sremont's house, the felted (and therefore finished) bonnets might have been kept elsewhere to avoid the smells and the smoke produced when using the hearth. But there were also strong similarities between the retail spaces of both *mutsenreeders* and these cannot be coincidental. It is difficult to assess the reason behind the spatial distinction between felted and unfelted bonnets. Perhaps the unfelted bonnets that were on display in the shop were used as samples or fitting models that customers could fit and try while discussing preferred sizes, measurements and colour. The bonnets that were stocked in the other room were then probably the finished goods that were awaiting a final fitting and perhaps a final retouch. The fact that there was also a mirror and a chair in the back room where the finished bonnets were stored, clearly indicates that finished or nearly finished bonnets were tried on beforehand. So the act of selling a bonnet was probably done in several stages: an initial stage of consultation with a customer, followed by a production stage that – in this case – ended in the artisan's house itself and a final fitting stage. Elizabeth Currie found a similar course of events for Florentine and Milanese tailors. She even found that some of the tailors made use of workshop books that were consulted by the clients first to select the models they preferred.[88]

It follows that, in contrast to the shops of the retailers discussed before, the retail space of the *mutsenreeders* comprises more than one room. Moreover, in the inventories of the bonnet sellers, we could find some traces of wool supplies in other rooms of the house. In Sremont's case, wool was found in the front room, and the wool in Martin's house was stored in the rooms upstairs. Interestingly, though the finished products were not on display in the shop but were stocked in other spaces near the shop, we could still see a kind of spatial limitation to the spread of retail or professional tools, goods and activities in the house. Cooking utensils and hearth equipment were found in Sremont's shop, but no tools of the trade nor samples of bonnets were found in other domestic spaces in the house except for one. The same goes for Martin's house; unfelted bonnets were on display in the shop, and finished products were kept in another room. The finished bonnets were not immediately visible to the public, but they were easily accessible when needed in case there was guild inspection or when requested by customers. Only for the raw materials, in this case wool, could we say that there was some sort of spill over from the business area to the domestic space.

Belt maker, or *riemslager*, Yserael Negheman (1541)[89] had a *werckhuus*, or detached workplace, where he produced the copper rings that were used to assemble the metal belts. The *werckhuus* included a trestle table, baskets with coals, an undefined quantity of copper rings that were probably already made there by the artisan and several pieces of hearth equipment such as bellows, shovels and tongs. In the shop (in this case labelled *vloer*), the appraiser found thirteen copper rings, tools and specialist items needed for the shop's main business, as well as some kettles and two balances or scales. The back room was used as a living area and was equipped with all the necessary furniture such as a well-made bed, cabinets, cupboards, chandeliers, eating utensils and so on. But no stock or tools were found there. Although it is difficult to deduce, because there is not much information given in the inventory, the raw production of forging brass rings near a fireplace may have been done in a separate space because of fire hazards. But the finishing of the products and the retail sales took place in the shop at the front of the dwelling. Though there were other rooms in the house, the presence of tools typical for the craft and needed for working on the goods was spatially restricted to the detached workplace and to the shop.

Hatter Silvester van Pamele (1571),[90] who lived and worked in the Korte Noordzandstraat in Bruges, had a shop where he produced hats in front of his customers. His shop contained artisan's tools, six finished hats and several moulds for hats that were – according to the inventory – hanging by the shop door. In this way, potential buyers and passers-by were immediately informed about the nature of the shop and could also immediately see what types of hats were available. Wool that was probably used by the hatter in his manufacturing process was stored in the back room and upstairs in the *camere onder tdack*. But as with the belt maker, there are no tools or finished products found in rooms other than the shop. A similar layout of the commercial environment can be found in the house of turner Rombout de Doppere (1583).[91] His floor was also his shop, and it contained all his artisan's tools, including a particular chair (*mansstoel*), a basket and a saw. The courtyard was used as a storage place for the wood: large piles of wood were found there, accompanied by bundles of firewood.

That raw materials were often stocked or stored in rooms and places in the house other than the shop or workplace becomes evident when we look at the records of the two shaft makers, Jan Duivelinck (1559)[92] and Sander Collet (1568).[93] The inventory of Jan Duivelinck, who also lived in the Korte Noordzandstraat, is most detailed. His ground-floor room *vloer* was used as a retail and manufacturing site, storing an undefined number of spikes and sticks, another eight sticks used to make torches and artisan's tools (*alaam*). His back room was used to store another quantity of the goods he produced and sold: a pile of brewers' forks and a bunch of hammer shanks. Except for a chest, there were no other pieces of furniture or other items found in that room. The back room is mentioned in the inventory immediately after the floor or shop, so it was probably seen and used as an annex to the shop. In the front room, kitchen and upper room (probably the attic), raw materials such as several pieces of wood were stored, next to some smaller quantities of produced goods such as spikes and sticks for torches. This is quite unusual though and to some extent, in sharp contrast to the regulations of most guilds. Finished goods should by all means be made visible to ensure product quality and to discourage fraud. But in the inventory of fellow shaft maker Sander Collet, the only craft-related items that were found elsewhere in the house were different types of *houd dienende ten ambochte vanden schachtmakers*, or wood used by the shaft makers. So perhaps Jan Duivelinck's house and shop were simply too small to house all the products, all the woods and all his tools at the same time. The surplus of products was then spread throughout the house, but his tools – symbolising his bond with the craft and the guild and guaranteeing the quality of his products – were confined to the specific production and commercial area of the house.

Spatial constraints could have had a profound effect on the manufacturing process and retail practices for particular goods. Wheelwrights, for example, needed more space to manufacture their goods than other craftspeople, and the finished goods themselves were also too large to be sold in the shop. So in the case of the two wheelwrights in our sample, Jan Parcheval (1559)[94] and Cornelis Veyts (1559),[95] the production and possibly also the retailing of carriages and wheelbarrows was done in the workplace (*werckhuus*), and the wood was stored upstairs in the attic, in the courtyard and on the street. The latter was actually not allowed, because it disturbed traffic and cluttered the streets.[96] In Cornelis Veyts's inventory, the workplace where the wood and the artisan's tools were stored is even described by the appraiser as *winckel ofte werkhuus*, indicating that the space was much more of a workplace that was also used as a retail space. The stacks of wood and cut planks on the street immediately made clear what type of craft these two gentlemen were practising and informed the passers-by of the quality of the wood that was used.

In the case of the coopers, the manufacturing of barrels, tubs and casks was done within the boundaries of the shop. The inventory of cooper Geraert Coop (1568),[97] for example, clearly mentions a small table, a small closable desk, three three-legged stools (*driestael*), a workbench, some tools and several barrels, with one tub standing in front of the door. The other rooms in his house did not contain any tools, stock or raw material, or references to or traces of the production process. In the inventory of fellow cooper Stevin De Groote (1572)[98] were parts or components of barrels and tubs (such as hoops) stored in rooms other than the shop such as the upstairs room above the front room, the back room and the attic, but all the finished goods and all the tools and specialist items needed for the cooper's trade were kept solely in the shop. Even in the small and humble abode of cooper Jan Sheerlippens (1561),[99] where the inventory mentions only two rooms (kitchen and front room), and where the tools, stock and raw materials of the cooper were located in the front room together with his household goods, the appraiser differentiated clearly between the goods. The newly made goods were labelled: eight *nieuwe cuupkens* and two *nieuwe coelvaten*, to indicate that they were the cooper's own products destined to be sold at some point in time. And the hoops and tools of the artisan were mentioned thereafter.

The two examples we have of painters offer peculiar cases. The first example is the inventory of well-known painter and engraver Marcus Gerards,[100] painter of the famous city map of Bruges. Gerards was also a devout Protestant, so in 1568, he fled to London to escape the death penalty imposed on him by the ferocious Council of Troubles. His goods were seized by the Council of Troubles and the Duke of Alva; they were inventoried and valued to be publicly sold.[101] His inventory is therefore the only one in our sample that was constructed in a very unusual and specific context. It mentions five rooms: the hall, the kitchen, a sleeping room, a room above the hall and the back room. In terms of Gerards's profession, the appraiser could find three panel paintings with unidentified themes in his hall and one map. Given the period, this could well have been the famous city map Marcus Gerards made for the city of Bruges only six years before, though more detailed information about the map in his hall is missing.[102] Intriguingly, his painting materials and tools were found not in a room at the front of the house, but in a room above the hall and in the back room. One would suppose that this was not in accordance with the guild regulations considering visibility of production, but the only thing that the painters' guild required was that painters sell their works in the open, either from the fronts of their shops or within public view.[103] After all, it was important for painters to work in good light (preferably northern light). And that light could have been better in a room other than the one at the front of the house. The guild regulations of the Bruges guild of Saint Luke even stated that: 'degene vanden voorseiden ambochte, die wercken op cameren of achterwaert vande strate, ende gheenen tooch en hebben binnen haerlieder werchuuse, dat die zullen moghen houden eenen tooch daert hemlieden ghelieven zal'.[104] So painters were allowed to work in a room that was not directly visible or open to public view and to sell their products elsewhere. Parish records reveal that the Bruges painter Peter Claeissin lived in a house on Jan Mireal Street, while he had a shop together with Adriaan Eyeman in another part of town.[105] The most important thing was that the retail sale of paintings was done in the open and within public view, at home in the shop or elsewhere in the city. And although Marcus Gerards did not have a shop attached to his house (perhaps the shop was located elsewhere in the city? Or perhaps he worked only on commission?), he did have some paintings (and a map) on display in his hall. Perhaps these paintings were used as a business card or signboard of his profession and were therefore displayed in the room closest to the street? In the inventory of painter Pieter de Clievere (1541),[106] no signs of a retail space were found either, though it seems that his floor was used as a sort of display room as well, because it contained no fewer than two painted cloths, three other (cloth?) paintings in frames and a panel painting of Saint John the Baptist in the Wilderness on top of a cupboard. These were not the only paintings De Clievere owned, however, because in the second room, two panel paintings were displayed on a cupboard. This large number of paintings owned by a household was rather exceptional in Bruges at that time, so we would suggest that De Clievere kept some of his produced paintings to himself as a way to show his skills and expertise to potential buyers.

In general, we can safely conclude that in all the houses of these producer/retailers, professional activity was confined to the retail area or the workplace. No tools or specialist instruments of the crafts were found anywhere else in the house than in the shop or workplace (werckhuus). In houses where the functions of working, selling and living were combined, there was often a spill over of raw materials, stock and parts from the commercial environment into the domestic area, but it seems that most craftspeople were eager to keep this spill over to a minimum and that they were careful not to store tools and finished products in domestically furnished living areas. The tools of a craftsperson symbolised a bond with the craft and guild and externalised the craftsperson's status as a master; therefore, tools were preferably kept in the business area of the house. Tools refer to the master's skills and ability to perform the trade. Craftspeople (or master guildsmen) were only allowed to use the tools inherent to the craft after they had proven (by means of a master's proof) that they knew the tricks of the trade and were therefore capable of starting their own businesses.[107] So the tools of a craftsperson not only represented his participation in the trade but also symbolised his master status, his skills and his trustworthiness in using them to manufacture high-quality goods.[108]

Another similarity between all the aforementioned shops of producer/retailers was the absence of any piece of decoration or furniture except for the furniture that was used by the craftsperson during production and retail. It seems that the shops all had basic interiors. In contrast to the shops of the retailers of cloth and linen discussed before, not a single shop displayed decorative items (except of course in the case of the painters, but here the paintings should be seen as saleable goods) or was equipped with seating to accommodate customers. In the end, it was the skills and reputation of the artisan, symbolised through the tools of the craft and safeguarded by the location of the shop in the house, combined with the intrinsic qualities of the commercial stock that had to entice and convince potential buyers of the integrity of the craftsperson and to proceed to a purchase.

Category 4: Bakers

In the later Middle Ages, there were several types of bakeries active in a city. In addition to 'ordinary' bread bakers, pastry bakers were also members of the bakers' guild.[109] But in our sample are only the inventories of bread bakers. The bakers' shops did not differ much from the shops of the other producer/retailers. The three bakers in our sample, Adriaan Stalpaert (1569),[110] Charle Raison (1542)[111] and Quinten Lucas (1567),[112] all had a retail space or shop in the house and a *backhuus*, a bakehouse, or a separate building with an oven. The bakers were obliged by the city government to have their ovens in fireproof buildings to prevent any form of fire hazard.[113] These bakehouses were equipped not only with ovens but also with all the other necessary tools bakers needed to bake their bread.

The loaves of bread were sold in the shop. Remarkably though, these shops seem to have contained a lot of furniture such as chairs, benches, desks, chests and cabinets. Baker Raison's shop, for example, included one desk or counter (*contoir*), a bench with storage space underneath (*lys*), several baskets, two chests and a balance with weights. Stalpaert's shop, in turn, contained only two chairs and a balance; Lucas's shop had several baskets, a balance and a cabinet to put the bread in. So although the shops themselves were not decorated with paintings or mirrors, there was seating that would suggest possibilities for longer visits or stays in the shops.[114] To some extent, it would be counter-intuitive. This could mean several things: chairs and benches were present in a baker's shop, because people would buy bread on a more regular basis than, for example, a new hat, so the human interaction between buyer and seller of the bread was deemed more intense; or the seller of bread did not have to do anything more than hand over the bread to the customers in his shop and was perhaps in need of a place to sit down when there was no one to be served; or people had their dough already prepared themselves and came to the bakery to have it baked. The actual experience of the buying of bread (and other goods) is in need of more research, so more answers to these questions will become possible.

Category 5: Textile Trades

The fifth category comprises people who were producing goods or semi-finished goods at home, but were not selling them direct to the end user (or the consumer). In our sample, they were all employed in various branches of the textile industry of the city, ranging from dyers and weavers to shearers and silk *reeders*. The textile trade had for a long time been one of the strongholds of the Bruges economy. In the words of Stabel, Puttevils and Dumolyn, 'it was textile manufacture that provided Bruges with an industrial foundation'.[115] But the economic climate for textiles changed drastically between the fourteenth and sixteenth centuries; the traditional luxury cloth industries, which dealt with heavy materials, had to make way for the increased importance of lightweight woollens or cloth that was 'very similar in appearance to the traditional luxury cloths, but somewhat cheaper and of medium quality'.[116] In her research on dress and clothing in sixteenth-century Bruges, Isis Sturtewagen found a whole array of these light textile products in the inventories of middle-class Bruges citizens, made by the so-called Nouvelle Draperie Légère.[117]

The textile production from the late thirteenth and early fourteenth centuries was 'organized within the framework of guilds and the small-scale entrepreneur, usually a guild master, became the pivotal figure in the industry'.[118] People of different social and economic backgrounds were working in the textile industry, ranging from wealthy entrepreneurs such as drapers to middle-class guild masters and relatively poor wage-earning skilled or unskilled workers.[119] Almost every stage in the production of textiles was carried out by a different branch of the textile industry with occupations ranging from shearers, combers, and fullers to dyers, spinners and weavers. Most of these guildsmen were not producing directly for the customer (and end user of the textiles), but most likely for another guildsman, merchant or entrepreneur.

In our sample, we have several guildsmen who were actively involved in the textile industry who worked at home but did not sell their products directly to end users (in contrast to the producer/retailers we discussed earlier). Most of them were subcontracted by an entrepreneur or wealthy guildsman. But some were at the head of their own company, like the drapers. The *zydereeders*, dyers, tapestry weavers, shearers and say, fustian and cloth weavers in our sample were all working in some room at home. So although they did not invite potential customers in, their occupation did occupy certain rooms in their homes, making it worthwhile to question (and measure) the impact of employment in the textile industry on the rest of the domestic environment (and vice versa). And just as with the producer/retailers, we are well aware that there were differences between the trades, even among the guildsmen within the same trade – more often than not depending on personal wealth and the size of the house.

Joos van Cuevele (1562)[120] was a silk twiner (*zydereeder*) and lived in the Goezeputstraat in Bruges. Silk twining is a process of literally twisting the silk threads to create stronger silk yarn. It was preparatory work that was carried out prior to the process of weaving or dying the yarn (usually done by somebody else).[121] In Van Cuevele's house, the activity of silk twining was performed in the workhouse (*werckhuus*), where the tools of the trade were found, namely mills, spools, bobbins, chairs and workbenches. Because he had no fewer than five workbenches and several mills, he likely employed some journeymen or workers as well. The finished silk yarn, however, was stocked elsewhere – in the room next to the hall at the front of his house. So the room where the finished (or semi-finished) goods were stored was clearly separated from the work floor. In the room at the front of the house, the appraisers found a basket filled with twined silk of different colours and another eight baskets with silk and several bobbins. In the other ground-floor room (*vloer*), Van Cuevele kept some tools and raw materials such as raw silk, blank bobbins and some sticks that were used *ter neeringhe vanden zydereeders*[122], a balance or scale and some weights. In the other rooms of the house, no stock or tools were found, except for some *zydewinden*, or silk spools, in the kitchen. So it seems that the production of the silk yarn took place at the back of the house in a separate space, large enough to hold the necessary tools and equipment, whereas the finished goods were kept in a room at the front of the house. The presence of a balance, several bobbins, silk and finished goods might indicate that merchants, entrepreneurs and other guildsmen were received there.

The situation is somewhat different for dyers. The location of their activity seems to have been highly dependent on the size of their houses. To a certain extent, this has to do with the fact that dyeing is a rather space-consuming activity and perhaps even more than others, an activity in which a lot of filthy kettles and jugs are needed (for heating, decanting and fermentation, and vats with water, potash and dyestuffs), as is apparent from the description of the activity by textile historian John Munro.[123] The relatively wealthy dyer Jan Lenaert (1540),[124] who lived in a six-room house, had a separate workplace (*werckhuus*) where his kettles with dyestuffs and water and his tools were stored and used. Consequently, he was well able to separate the production area from the rest of the house even more adequately than his fellow craftspeople. Dyer Joos Vlamync (1546),[125] on the other hand, had to keep his kettles and barrels with dye and water and his tools in his kitchen and in two other cellars (though it is uncertain whether the latter were attached to the house where he lived or were rented elsewhere in the city). His house consisted of merely three rooms, of which two were labelled 'small',[126] so he had no choice but to house his tools and equipment in his living quarter. Dyers Jacop de Clercq (1560)[127] and Jacop vanden Sip (1585),[128] in turn, practised their occupation in a room labelled as floor, but stocked the raw materials upstairs in the attic.

What they all had in common though – and also with most of the other craftspeople in our sample – was that there were no other furnishings or objects found in the rooms where the guildsmen performed their trade, except for items that were related to the trade itself. In the case of the shearers (*droogscheerders*), the situation is rather similar; the house size determined where the activities of shearing and carding could take place. Adam Coeman (1566)[129] and Cornelis Oudemarc (1572)[130] both performed their trade in a room called the floor (*vloer*) at the front of their houses. Both men owned the necessary tools for the trade of shearing, such as shears and one or two shearer's workbenches that were adapted to the specificities of the trade and had a padded, slanted top and small hooks along its two ends for securing one section of the cloth.[131] Furthermore, Oudemarc had a spinning wheel, teasels for carding, two reels, a press, a scissors block and several cabinets in his workplace as well. The press was usually used in the final stage of the process, when the finished cloth was pressed and then folded and packed for delivery.[132] Intriguingly, in both cases, the rooms that fulfilled the task of workspace also contained two types of seating furniture: a *preeckstoel* and a woman's chair (*vrouwenstoel*). The first type of chair was, according to literature, brought to church and used for praying at home. But the chair could have had other functions or served other ends as well. It was small and usually foldable,[133] so it was an ideal piece of seating furniture to be used in a workplace where space was limited and it might well have been used by the craftsperson while performing activities. The other type of chair is the woman's chair. It is as yet not completely clear what this gendering of a chair exactly means, but scholars assume that the chair was probably smaller in size and used predominantly by women when performing their daily tasks.[134] So the presence of a woman's chair in the workplace might point to a particular female participation in the trade.

The third shearer, Pieter Douchet (1562),[135] had a much larger enterprise. His tools and equipment were concentrated in two separate spaces in his dwelling: in the floor room, where he stored two special workbenches and nine shears (together with a balance and some teasels); and in a detached workplace (*werckhuuse*), where he had no fewer than four looms, three spinning wheels (in the back room of the workhouse) and another loom and several baskets. The presence of all these different types of tools might indicate that he was combining three activities of the textile trade (shearing, spinning and weaving) and was employing other skilled or unskilled workers to do part of the job. His main employment of shearing (which was also the final stage after weaving) was done at the front of the house – in the floor – whereas other activities were done at the back in a building that was detached from the first. Though the second building was mainly used for production and manufacturing, it also contained rooms that were equipped with household goods such as clothing, accessories, beds and chairs. But the tools and the equipment of trade were, again, never mingled with these household objects. Perhaps the journeymen or workers were receiving room and board as part of their wage?

The last group of craftspeople in the textile industry were weavers of all kinds of fabrics. Our sample consists of four weavers (which are identified as such), each producing a different type of fabric: cloth weaver Cornelis de Corte (1568),[136] fustian weaver Laureins De Doncle (1568),[137] say weaver Richard Janszuene (1561)[138] and tapestry weaver Antheunis De Sant (1542).[139] What all these weavers had in common was that they had only one loom in their possession and that this loom, with all its accessories, was positioned in a room at the front of the house. Only say weaver Richard Janszuene had some combed and uncombed wool in his back room as well. That the production of the weaves was done (or had to be done) at the front of the house, visible to passers-by and guild officials, is not surprising. The guilds of the tapestry weavers, for example, were often confronted with severe abuses and fraudulent businesses. Some weavers had dared not to weave characters and landscapes into their tapestries, but had painted them with wet paint on the warp.[140] In this way, inferior work was produced that brought the reputation of the trade into disrepute. The famous edict or general ordinance of Charles V that was published by the general authorities in 1544 codified all the statues and regulations of the tapestry trade. The edict was specifically intended to safeguard the quality of the weaves and tapestries produced in Flanders, Brabant and Hainaut and had to restrict abuses and other trade- and quality-related problems.[141] So transparency of manufacturing techniques to safeguard the quality of the product and the reputation of the guild was important for the guilds in the textile trade as well.

The last category is somewhat different from the earlier ones. In our sample, Jan de la Meire (1569)[142] was a draper. The profession of draper is somewhat peculiar.

It is not a real producer/retailer type, because the draper only buys the raw materials from suppliers and gives them to his subcontractors or workers, who process them to finished or semi-finished goods that the draper then sells to fellow entrepreneurs or guildsmen.[143] Draper Jan de la Meire lived in the Ganzestrate in Bruges in large premises that consisted of no fewer than ten rooms (a workhouse included). The floor of his house was occupied by an array of tools and equipment, including six shears, two workbenches, nine teasels, a barrel with some shorn wool, two iron combs, a balance with lead weights, a large press, two spinning wheels, several barrels and baskets with wool yarn, and thirteen reels of yarn. Judging by the nature of these tools and raw materials, we can deduce the particularities and tools of different trades all engaged in textile and wool processing that were performed in that single space, such as carding, combing, spinning and shearing wool. Because there were also four woman's chairs in that space and one woman's sofa chair with a cushion, we could suppose that women were also performing some of these tasks.[144] Spinning, combing and carding are seen by many scholars as typical female (and unskilled) occupations.[145] In contrast to what we have seen so far, not only raw materials such as wool but also some of the tools were scattered all over the house. In the front room of the house, De la Meire stored some Spanish wool and three packets of an unidentified type of wool; in the attic (*upperzoldere*), a number of new teasels were kept, and in a room called *middelcamere*, the draper kept seventeen reels or bobbins of yarn, two barrels with bobbins and three combs, two baskets and fourteen pairs of teasels. Also in the back room, the draper stored two piles of Spanish wool and several reels. But he also had a detached workhouse that, according to the appraisers' description, was located at the back of the house. And this was a place of production that was used for manufacturing only. There, the appraisers found two looms with cloth weaves, four baskets and several reels. So contrary to shearing, carding and spinning, the activity of weaving was assigned to the space at the rear of the house.

The tools in the draper's rooms also inform us that instead of purchasing the finished product from masters, the draper himself engaged in the process of cloth production by employing skilled or unskilled workers in his house.[146] The workforce was set to work in rooms that were separated from the living quarters of the draper and his family, but the tools and raw materials were stored in all kinds of rooms, even in rooms that were used by family members. The work places were equipped only to perform the tasks of the trade and were therefore not furnished with additional furniture or decoration. These household goods were reserved for the domestic living rooms of the draper's house.

Similarities and Differences: The Broader Picture

Whether retail and manufacture were combined in the same space or not, it was deemed important that the production of goods, the raw materials and the goods themselves were visible to potential buyers as well as to guild officials. Most shops and workplaces were therefore situated at the front of the house. Several guild regulations consider the presence of ample light as an important requirement for shops, because it was used as a convenient tool to prevent fraudulent, or *secretelic*, practices. One statute of the guild of the joiners, for example, illustrates this point clearly by stating that '*niemande secretelic wercken en mach*'.[147] The guild of the coopers underlines the importance of ample light in the shop and workplace *omme de volcke ook niet te bedrieghene*.[148] By producing and selling goods in adequately lit spaces at the front of the house (or outdoors as in the case of the painters), it was possible not only to safeguard the manufacturing process but also to sell the products within public view. Therefore, it seems that in sixteenth-century Bruges, the guilds had *not* yet relinquished the idea that the problem of product quality should be solved by tying together product quality, trade mark and master status in the front room of the masters' house – where the product was made and sold under the sign or banner of the guild.[149]

Quite the contrary even, and we would dare to say that shop design – or, better, the physical layout and organisation of the broader retail area, not the decorative design of the shop – and the ways in which goods were displayed were also used by as a way to 'solve' the issue of product quality and information asymmetries, guaranteeing and representing both the intrinsic quality of the goods and the skills of the artisan. So product quality was not only communicated to customers or merchants by means of collective hallmarks[150] (especially not in the context of the shop); it was also done by shop design and infrastructure, the visibility of tools and equipment and the display of the commercial stock. The scale (*balanse*), for example, was an item that was present in all kinds of shops: it was used to sell products by weight and to showcase the credibility and professionalism of the seller/artisan perhaps even more clearly than the goods themselves. On the basis of a rather small sample size, guilds expert Bert De Munck asserted that the emergence of shops went hand in hand with either specialization within the sector (some masters specializing in retail, others producing exclusively for large entrepreneurs) or the gradual separation of work floor and shop within the house (the work floor moving towards the back of the house).[151] In most cases, the work floor was situated at the front of the house, like the shop, but in some instances, the production was indeed performed at the back of the house, often by skilled or unskilled employees, while the finished goods were stored in a room at the front. Was this evidence of a gradual evolution towards an increasingly wider separation between production and retail? At the moment, it is hard to prove because our sample size is rather small. More research should be undertaken to propose well-founded statements to challenge these debates.

Nevertheless, what Walsh concluded for the eighteenth-century shop fits the sixteenth-century shop perfectly well too: she argued that 'quite clearly eighteenth-century shops were not places of "primitive barter", dark and disorganized, where goods were "left to sell themselves". Instead they were geared up to active and effective selling, using the available methods of enticement to their fullest extent'.[152] Though the shops of sixteenth-century Bruges were not as fully furnished with seating furniture, paintings and mirrors as the eighteenth-century shops Walsh studied, their infrastructure was also consciously designed and furnished (with tools, instruments and finished goods) to convince potential buyers of the product quality of the goods on display and of the craftsperson's trustworthiness, professionalism and skill. So the retailing of goods in sixteenth-century Bruges still happened within the context of the 'old model' of intrinsic qualities.

An interesting similarity between nearly all shops seems vital in pinpointing the character of the retail space as part of a dwelling (and indirectly also of the rest of the home). That similarity is the virtual lack of any type of decoration and of any reference to religious or devotional practices. Although 'guilds were a type of brotherhoods in which devotional practices and egalitarian ideals took centre stage next to economic benefits and calculation',[153] no statues or devotional paintings were found in the shops studied. Most of the artisans had these decorative and devotional objects elsewhere in the house, but clearly not in the shop or workhouse. The only exceptions to the rule were the two cloth sellers discussed earlier and a shearer and a dyer. But the latter two used their workspace also as a living space due to the limited sizes of their homes. Looking at the ratios for paintings in sample periods 4, 5 and 6 (table 4 and graph 5), it follows that it was not likely that paintings would have appeared in shops or workplaces (ratio<1).[154]

This is quite intriguing, because each guild normally had a patron saint that was related to the trade itself. Moreover, late medieval urban life was full of references to religion and devotion, so we would expect to find at least one reference to the guild patron (or to Mary or Christ) in the workplaces and shops of Bruges artisans. But it seems that devotional life was either reserved for the domestic area in the house or was

Table 4. Ratio of Paintings in Shops or Floors

SAMPLE PERIOD	RATIO SHOP	RATIO FLOOR
1528–1549	-	0.53
1559–1574	0.38	0.13
1584–1600	-	0.83

Source: Database of inventories © IB, JDG & IS

Graph 5. Proportions or the Number of Paintings per Space compared to the Total Number of Paintings for the Sample

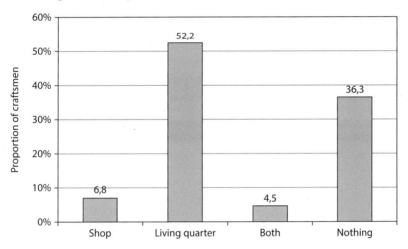

Source: Database of inventories © IB, JDG & IS

to be practised in places where members joined together, such as guilds' houses, chapels and guild altars in churches.[155] This should not come as a surprise though, because it has already been acknowledged that artisans were obliged to cease their activities and even close their workplaces and shops on Sundays and holidays. Clearly then, there was no room and no time for devotion and religion inside the shop and during commercial activities. Hence, at least in Bruges, private devotion, as well as decoration in general, and religion were explicitly reserved for the domestic environment of the house.

Even more telling, Bruges shops were often without heating and lighting equipment. Only one shop contained a hearth, and this was both used for the trade and for cooking the food of the artisan and his family (based on the utensils). So in this, we can follow the finding of Blondé and Van Damme that heating – when present – 'appears to have been functional and seems not to have constituted any aspired level of comfort or luxury in shop premises'.[156] A fully equipped fireplace, used for cooking or just for heating, was clearly reserved for the domestic living spaces further back in the house.

Moreover, our evidence urges that the current theory about the lack of boundaries between 'commercial' and 'private' spaces indoors, in other words, that the economic and domestic functions of the urban household were inextricably intertwined and that there were few private domestic rooms,[157] should be nuanced. Although in some cases, there was indeed some sort of spill-over effect of especially raw materials from the business area to the domestic area, in all other cases, it was a matter of course that tools and finished goods were never to be mingled with household goods. Even when in cases of space constraints finished goods were stored in rooms of the house other than the shop or workhouse or when pieces of (household) furniture were put in the shop, the mixture of the two types of goods (commercial goods and household goods) was kept to an absolute minimum (as is also apparent in the description of the appraisers). So 'from the perspective of material culture, there was a clear demarcation between "the shop" and "the home"'.[158] The fact that there was at least a psychological boundary (but in most cases also a clear physical one) between the spaces of work and the spaces of home might also explain why the house searches Decuelaer discussed felt intrusive to the affected guildsmen and their families.[159] Furthermore, common law had always prohibited infringements of private property. Representatives of the law were not even allowed to enter houses. Only at the end of the Middle Ages were changes made in Bruges.[160] Looking at it from a legal perspective, this could also be the reason why guild statutes state that artisans have to work in their front room, implying that there was even a legal demarcation between (semi-public) workshops and the – we might say 'private' – domestic spaces of the house. Though the house itself and the family honour were important in constructing and representing the guildsman's honour and social and political status, they were clearly not part of his commercial activity and his daily pursuits.[161]

Although houses might contain shops, the latter were usually treated as separate spaces. Shops as retail and production spaces seem to have operated by their own rules and values, which were far removed from the values that were expressed and materialised in the domestic quarters of the house. Moreover, from an economic point of view, sustaining an exclusively commercial environment would also have helped to ban the sales of unregulated goods and other fraudulent activities.[162] So in fact, it was especially the key values found in the guild regulations of most guilds at that time – visibility, integrity, product quality and transparency – that defined the social behaviour of buyers and sellers as well as the architecture and spatial organisation of the retail space – although strategies of enticement were not shunned either. The places of retail and manufacture reflected above all the requirements, responsibilities and values that artisans shared as members of guilds and as members of the community of Bruges. The evidence is convincing of both the existence of an exclusively commercial environment inside the house and of the existence (or at least a certain awareness) of the specificity of private domestic space.

But the shop or the retail space on the ground floor was only one site where public life met the domestic practices and material culture of the household. Houses could contain different types of these transitional sites, especially the larger ones. Another site in the house where business was welcomed was the office (*contoor*). It was a room where business matters were discussed, where accounts, invoices and family papers were made and preserved, and where books of all types were read and contemplated. In the next chapter, we will move therefore to supposedly one of the most exclusive, private, most gendered and at the same time one of the most formal spaces in the interior: the *contoor*.

THE MERCHANT IN THE *CONTOOR*

Introduction

'Work in the house, or rather the house as a place of work, is a theme that is often evoked but rarely investigated by historians of the pre-industrial period'.[1] The truth of such a statement was already proven in the previous chapter, which showed the growing importance of the late medieval shop at the expense of the market stall, a subject that has so far barely been touched upon. Furthermore, we have also seen that most artisans not only sold their products from their shops but also produced finished and semi-finished goods in a workshop or workhouse at home. So studying these traces of interaction between the functions of production and habitation has been shown to be worthwhile when studying the character of domestic space. And although we have found that these commercial spaces were more or less spatially and socially separated from the rest of the house (on the micro level of the house itself), most artisans and retailers still used their homes as what historians Franco Franceschi and Rafaela Sarti have labelled an 'instrument of work'.[2]

But houses were often involved in the world of commerce and trade in a different way. Even though taverns, inns and headquarters of companies remained important meeting places, as well as the stock market ('Beurs') in Bruges,[3] for national and international merchants and traders, many Bruges merchants and artisans also managed their businesses from home. Even when business transactions were not always concluded on the spot, the business administration and management of the accounts still required a special space in the merchant's house. Franceschi therefore supposed a strong organic link between the spaces of work and habitation, especially in the houses of merchants.[4]

Many humanist-inspired Renaissance treatises on architecture, the consumption practices of acquisition and the management of the household, such as the *Libro dell'arte di mercatura* (1498) by Benedetto Cotrugli, ascribed a fundamental role to the home in the running of a company.[5] Besides advice on the necessity of a central location and the representative powers of the exterior of the house, the increasing diffusion of a particular domestic space was discussed in this context as well, in other words, the setting up of the studiolo, or study. Plenty of books and articles have been written about that specific type of room, which was by no means new in Italian *palazzi* but began to occupy an important place in the Italian merchant's home during the Renaissance period.[6] Some scholars have even labelled this room 'the quintessential Renaissance space [...] designed to accommodate the secular scholarly pursuits associated with the rise of humanism', and with a renewed cult of *studious leisure*, a 'signature space in an age increasingly obsessed with the fashioning and presentation of the self' and with an increasing culture of consumption.[7] In other words, according to this research, the study as a room became a personal environment used primarily for the display of especially inner virtue, erudition, intellectual capacities and taste,[8] but also a room that played a role in trade: a room that fully meets the requirements of a humanist scholar-entrepreneur.

It soon became clear, however, that the actual use and character of this room could change according to the wealth and status of the owner and the owner's daily pursuits.[9] Moreover, although the visual imagery of the period tends to stress the contemplative, religious and private aspects of the room, treating it as a retreat from public (and even domestic) life, the study could also function, directly or indirectly, as a social space 'in which intellectual ideas are engaged with and exchanged', just like some of the objects that were on display.[10] Some studies, like those of the members of the Medici family in Florence, were even open to public view and treated as a kind of tourist attraction because of the unique collection of objects they housed,[11] whereas other study rooms were more humble and often had more practical uses.[12] So in some cases, business activities were performed within the study as well, but in other cases, other rooms were used as offices and at least the Italian version of these were, according to Dora Thornton, often small in size and not well suited for any other purpose than 'to settle correspondence, weigh coins and compile memoranda.'[13]

Comparable to the Italian situation, the *Medieval Dutch Dictionary* makes a clear distinction between *contoor* (i.e. office, derived from the Latin *computare*) and *studoor* (i.e. study, derived from the Latin *studium* or *studere*).[14] So strictly speaking, the *contoor* would match the meaning of the businesslike office, whereas the *studoor* would represent the humanist study. Intriguingly then, when scanning through the Bruges sources, it seems that the Middle Dutch word for 'study', *studoor,* was, like the Italian word for 'office', virtually non-existent. What we do find in these Bruges sources are references to rooms that were labelled solely as *contoor*. But the inventory of such a *contoor* shows a different type of room from the one Thornton described as the small, cramped offices in the Italian Renaissance merchant houses. So how then should we interpret the Bruges *contoren*? If the functionalities of both a businesslike office and a scholarly study were combined in the *contoor*, then this space was, even more than other spaces, a threshold between 'outside'-focused and 'inside'-focused occupations; it would have been a place where the public life of business and commerce and the private world of reading, study and contemplation were deliberately combined. So it is important to study this type of room precisely because we have to question the functionality and the social and spatial connectivity of this room with the rest of the domestic space. Other commercial spaces like the shop and workshop were consciously isolated from the rest of the house and household because of transparency and concerns about product quality imposed by the craft guild, but these spaces were also vital in establishing the image of credibility and status of the artisan or merchant. Was the *contoor* a consciously – socially and spatially – isolated space as well? And if so, for what reasons?

Most scholarly research, however, has focused on the functions the Italian Renaissance *studioli* performed. For the Low Countries, similar research efforts to understand and question the existence or use of such specific rooms, presumably named after their function (infra), are practically non-existent.[15] Indeed, although it has long been assumed that the Italian studiolo was the precursor of the later *Kunstkammer* and Wunderkammer, there seems to be a gap in our knowledge about the links between rooms like the Bruges *contoor* and the room types used for displaying and preserving collections of art and naturalia, objects from nature, that appear in early seventeenth-century inventories in the Low Countries.[16]

If the Bruges *contoren* were indeed part of the Renaissance culture of self-fashioning, not only creating and externalising an image of the merchant as an erudite scholar but also and perhaps even more so of the merchant as a business person, then traces of this purpose must be found in the interiors of these rooms, in the objects and constellations of objects that were on display (such as decorative items including paintings, intellectual tools such as maps and books and businesslike materials such as account books, money chests and writing desks). These items were not just emblematic of a culture of consumption and collecting, as Maria Ruvoldt and others argue.[17] As we saw in the previous chapter on shops and workshops, material objects such as the scales, shears and looms of craftspeople are to be seen not only as repositories of monetary value but also as things that were imbued with meaning. Objects such as paintings, mirrors, maps, account books, quills and books that were both in use and on display in the *contoor* should therefore be seen as the tools used in practising the trade of commerce and as a means to express the owner's status as a business person as well as an emblem of the owner's ideal self. The focus must therefore be on the objects that were kept in this specific type of room and not just on the intellectual activities that were performed there;[18] every item in this type of room was a messenger to the degree that it appears to have carried meaningful messages for the user of the room and for occasional visitors. Or as Sven Dupré puts it, some items were more functionally used in performing tasks and rituals in that room or outside it; other objects did not have an immediate practical use but needed to be spoken about.[19]

The *Contoor* in Bruges

That a *contoor* was not commonly found in the domestic geography of Bruges houses is clear from the fact that only ten inventories out of a total sample of 502 contained references to a room labelled *contoor* (or its diminutive, *contoirke*).[20] Only two citizens owned two *contoren*: the front *contoor* and back *contoor* in the house of gilder Adriaen Claeyssins (1569)[21] and the *contoirken* and the *contoorcamere* of widow Anna van der Moere (1596).[22] Most of the *contoren* were located in houses that contained a large number of rooms; house sizes in these inventories range from six to sixteen rooms. So it would follow that the amount of space available in a house was a clear determining factor in making the choice whether spaces with a presumed particular functionality – such as the *contoor* – were to be created. In some cases, the *contoor* was probably very small and perhaps a kind of simple pop-up wooden construction that could be placed in another room.[23] This might explain why the *contoor* of Pieter Hendrick Winkelmans (1595) was, according to the appraiser, located *inside* the hall (*zaal*) and why the *contoor* of Anna van der Moere, widow of Lieven Step (1596), was described as "t contoirken nevens de sale".[24] In the first case, Winkelmans's space in the hall was probably reduced in size by the construction in it of a second room that had to be more or less separate from the first one. In the second case, the *contoor* is probably some sort of small annex to the hall, perhaps not a fully defined room on its own but more of an extension of the hall. The woodcut of such a small, wooden construction from the work of the French writer and printer Gilles Corrozet (fig. 4) may be a good illustration of this pop-up construction (1559). In the painting by Quentin Metsijs of Erasmus of Rotterdam (1517), the humanist is probably seated in a similar small room with wooden panel walls (fig. 5).

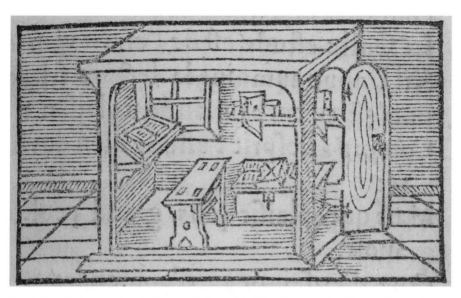

Fig. 4. Detail of a woodcut 'le blason de l'estude', Gilles Corrozet, Les Blasons Domestiques contenantz la décoration d'une maison honneste, et du mesnage estant en icelle, invention joyeuse et moderne, Paris, 1559, © Bibliothèque nationale de France, Rés. Ye-1380, 33

Fig. 5. Erasmus working in a room with wooden shuttering, Portrait of Erasmus of Rotterdam, Quentin Metsijs, 1517, Oil on panel, transferred to canvas, Gallerie Nazionali di Arte Antica, © Roma (MIBACT) - Bibliotheca Hertziana, Istituto Max Planck per la storia dell'arte/Enrico Fontolan

The Italian studiolo was situated in the most private quarters of the palazzi and in the case of the Florentine or Venetian urban elites, mostly in the direct vicinity of the sleeping room.[25] It was a room that was more or less detached from the rest of the house (and therefore from the other rooms), providing their users with the necessary privacy, peace and tranquillity to immerse themselves in reading and studying, offering the users a chance to invite people of their own choice into the space.[26] Most of the studioli were therefore located upstairs, away from the hustle and bustle of everyday life. But some of the Bruges *contoren* were located downstairs.[27] Although the description of the precise location of three *contoren* is rather vague, all the other six *contoren* were clearly situated downstairs at ground-floor level. This downstairs position had something to do with the role this type of room fulfilled in the commercially oriented character of the house.

Furthermore, judging from the sources, it would seem debatable whether these *contoren* were detached from the rest of the house, because in the inventories, they were often added together with other rooms (other than sleeping rooms) such as the hall, kitchen, *salette*, dining room, front room and workshop. Looking more closely at the sequence of the rooms, it seems that the *contoren* were either added together with other rooms (like the *contoor* in Winkelmans's hall) or their exact location was presented as if it was not entirely clear where the room was precisely located. Indeed, in some cases, it seems as if the *contoor* was floating between upstairs and downstairs, lacking a more precise location. That this type of room had a somewhat peculiar position in many houses would seem plausible.

In what follows, we will discuss the *contoren* we have found for Bruges separately to fully grasp their location, layout and functionality. We will start our discussion with the *contoren* that were clearly part of the business environment of the house.

The *Contoor* as Office and Treasury

Marie van Cleven was a silk twiner (*zydereeder*) and lived in a seven-room house in the Steenstraat in Bruges.[28] An inventory of her possessions was made in 1559 because of a debt. The presence of tools such as silk mills, bobbins and raw silk reveals that Marie van Cleven conducted her activities of silk twining downstairs at the front of the house, in a space that was labelled as the floor (*vloer*). The activity of silk twining was limited to this space, however, because there were no tools for twining or other silk-working activities present elsewhere in the house. Only on the upper floor did she store some woodwork that was used during production. The house of Van Cleven also contained what was described as a *contoircamerken*, a small room that was mentioned in the inventory right after the back room and before the upper-floor room. Where this *contoor* was actually positioned in the house is difficult to establish: Could it possibly be an office on the landing – between two parts of the stairs? Or a room on a mezzanine floor? But the fact is that Marie used this small room as a storage space for her precious finished goods (bobbins of twined silk), raw materials (*rauwe zijde*) and a scale as well as for storing her household valuables such as a silver salt cellar and two (probably also silver) spoons. In no other room of her house were silver objects found. So although the size of the room was allegedly small (e.g. the diminutive form in *camerken*) and its location uncertain, it was the most valuable room in her house.

We see a similar situation in the house of fellow silk worker Jan De Burggrave (1564),[29] who did not use his *contoor* downstairs as an annex to his commercial space as Marie van Cleven did, but he did use it as a treasury for his valuable silver and hollowware. The finished and raw silk was confined to his workhouse and the room downstairs. Pewter and silver objects were both considered by many citizens as their personal bank accounts. The intrinsic value of both types of objects is rather high (and more or less remained high) depending on the quality of the raw materials, so in times of need, pewter and silver objects could be either melted or pawned for money in pawnshops.[30] When times were good and opportunity arose, the salt cellar, jugs, plates and dishes could be put to use in the dining room or front room (or other places to which guests were invited), impressing the guests by representing the wealth of the family. So it seems that both silk workers used their *contoren* for no other purpose than as a treasury and safe. And although the *contoren* were in both cases probably located somewhere downstairs and were spatially (in the case of Jan De Burggrave) and functionally (in the case of Marie van Cleven) linked with their professional activities and with commerce, it seems that the spaces were not meant to be accessed by anybody other than Marie and Jan themselves.

However, Marie van Cleven was not the only one who used her *contoor* as an annex to her commercial or manufacturing space in the house. Gilder Adriaen Claeyssins (1569)[31] inhabited a house with at least eight rooms, situated in the Langestraat in Bruges. He was one of the few citizens who had not one but two *contoren* in his house, both serving different purposes and occupying different locations in the dwelling. His *voor contoor* or 'front' *contoor* was indeed probably situated at the front of the house and served the purpose of the type of office Thornton described earlier,[32] in other words, a place where correspondence and accounts were settled and money was weighed (a quite literal interpretation of the Latin *computare*, or counting). The only objects the space contained (according to the inventory) were *bourgouische daelders*, or silver coins, and a small chest with *rentebrieven*, or interest letters. No pieces of furniture were mentioned nor decorative items such as paintings, mirrors or statues, though paintings, individual chairs, mirrors and luxury textiles were found in abundance elsewhere in his house. It was a room that, at least functionally, was used in the daily transactions the gilder had to perform while doing his business at the front. His other *contoor*, situated at the back of the house, was used more as a treasury for storing his expensive raw materials (purses with forged gold) and boxes with finished or semi-finished goods such as pieces of gilded or golden jewellery and rosaries. The collection was complemented by only one silver object, a silver water jug, probably owned by the gilder himself. So like Marie van Cleven's *contoor*, both Adriaen's front and back *contoren* were functionally (and perhaps also spatially?) part of his commercial space (administration and storage), though, unlike the shop, they were themselves not part of the retail or production space itself.

Intriguingly, although both spaces in Adriaen's house have been given a spatial specification in the inventory (*voor* and *achter contoor*), their exact location in the home and especially their orientation towards other rooms is still unclear. Both rooms were mentioned at the end of the list of rooms in the inventory, without any indication of their interconnectedness with the other rooms of the house (not even with his shop). It was as if both rooms were indeed part of the house, but at the same time, they did not entirely fit in. The tasks that were performed there – storing precious materials or managing payments and debts – could be considered as requiring a certain degree of isolation from household activities that were performed elsewhere. In all likelihood, the storage of precious objects and the act of managing business was not something that was meant to be open for public view nor for other household members to see. The interior of these rooms, therefore, was kept simple and focused on the performance of this specific but important task.

One of the two *contoren* of Anna van der Moer, widow of Lieven Step (1596), combined two functions: storing valuable household objects such as hollowware, a mirror and textiles and operating as an office where money could be weighed and letters and other papers were to be kept. In contrast to the former *contoren*, this room was situated much more accurately in space. In fact, this small *contoor* (*contoirke*) was positioned next to the hall (*zaal*). The hall was a reception room (with a table, some seating furniture and two paintings) and a storage space (with a container filled with candlesticks and a box for grain). From its contents, this room may have been situated at the front of the house, and so, then, was the *contoirke*. The other *contoor*, however, was probably situated upstairs and was used only for storage, because it comprised only two large chests and a smaller wooden box.

In general, it seems that when the *contoor* was used only as an office or a room where accounts were handled, correspondence was done and where money was kept and counted, the room was situated downstairs at the front of the dwelling, lacking any kind of decoration or seating but focused on the job. The lack of seating would suggest that the space was not designed to accommodate people, or at least not for long hours. Though there is no evidence of receiving people, the *contoor* as a workplace or office is probably situated at the front, because people (clients, for example) could still access the space if necessary without disturbing the family and the rest of the household.[33] So in a sense, the area was easily accessible but at the same time remained relatively isolated from the rest of the house. In this way, the *contoor* certainly was 'a solution to various logistical problems that affected the businessman: the need for seclusion and the necessity of storing confidential documents'.[34] In other cases, the *contoor* was literally an annex to the commercial space of the shop or workshop and was used to store valuable raw materials or finished goods, like the *contoren* in the houses of gilder Claeyssins and silk twiner Marie van Cleven. And even here, the room was isolated from the rest of the house as well, treated as a safe and treasury, nobody other than its users being able to enter.

In houses where one would expect to find a *contoor* but where this type of room was not specified in the inventory for whatever reason, the objects that were associated with a *contoor* such as account books and scales for weighing money were mostly found in the front room or room next to the floor, in other words, at the front of the house (fig.6). Say weaver Richard Janszuene (1561), for example, did his bookkeeping 'inde voorcamere daer men zeide dat richard zyn mesaaige hielt' or in his front room where he also carried out his work.[35]

The *Contoor*: More than an Office?

In some cases, the *contoor* also offered the business person a comfortable place to undertake longer periods of work and a place to keep a collection of books. In this sense, it was more compatible with the image we have of the Italian Renaissance studiolo as a place for study, though the differences prove to be more important than the similarities.

Fig. 6. A Hanseatic merchant portrayed in his office, Portrait of the Merchant Georg Gisze, Hans Holbein the Younger, 1532, Oil on wood, © Staatliche Museen, Berlin, bpk / Kupfer-stichkabinett, SMB / Dietmar Katz

The *contoor* of Spanish merchant Fernando de Castere (1568)[36] did not get a precise location from the appraiser in the inventory, but based on the sequence of the rooms, it was located near the *salette*. This could be important, because as we will see in the next chapters, the *salette* became the reception room par excellence in the second part of the sixteenth century, designed and furnished to accommodate family and visitors comfortably. De Castere's *salette* contained no fewer than six luxurious Spanish chairs and several benches with cushions, a table with a tapestry table cover, a painting and judging from the hearth equipment, a well-functioning fireplace. Though it was not specified as such, we may suppose that the *contoor* was situated next to it. This room, in turn, was a well-equipped working room where De Castere could manage his business and correspondence. Just like the other *contoren* discussed above, the practical nature of the room is reflected in many of its objects such as the scales for weighing money, utensils used for writing (writing desk or *schrijflade*, penknife to cut paper, sand and scissors) and answering correspondence (seal with coat of arms of the family) and a *silvertresoor*, a cupboard for storing precious silver objects. But unlike the other *contoren*, his *contoor* also comprised some rather peculiar objects such as the two *geleyerse* or majolica saucers, three brushes, a small chest with some shirts, a mirror, a portrait of his wife Claudine Lem, a Latin Bible, a book by the Roman writer and stoic philosopher Seneca and a *plakaatbook*, a book with a collection of official open letters, marked by a stamp.

The two *geleyerse* or majolica dishes De Castere owned could be seen as evidence of a wish to decorate the space with exclusively refined crockery and a desire to have either something fashionable or familiar displayed.[37] Though we do not know the exact quality of his majolica dishes, majolica in general not only stood for refinement and taste but also represented high status and wealth; only the wealthiest class in Bruges owned specimens of this glazed earthenware. Moreover, most of the majolica or tin-glazed earthenware that was found in Bruges was owned by the wealthier Hispano-Bruges households in particular.[38] In her study on tableware, Inneke Baatsen offers a possible explanation by saying that these families used this material to establish a specific identity. Not only did the possession of these luxuries mean high status and prosperity but also implied a certain connection with (international) trade.[39] I would like to add that the possession of a certain type of majolica also indicates the strong commercial link between the Spanish nation, its home country and the Bruges market (infra). Originally, most of the majolica earthenware was indeed imported into the Low Countries from abroad; first from Valencia in Spain and later on also from local production centres in northern Italy. As we will see in the second part of this book, the nations of Castile and Biskaje were important commercial players in the city of Bruges even when the economy went downhill.[40] Through the port of Sluis, they traded goods with their homeland of Spain but also with the New World and other overseas regions. As a result, they

Fig. 7. Spanish-Moorish plate, 15th century, anonymous, Bruges, © Musea Brugge / OCMW Brugge, O.OTP0008.XXI, www.artinflanders.be

came into contact with Antwerp, which in the meantime, had become not only the commercial centre but also the main production centre for tin-glazed earthenware (*geleyers werck*) in the Low Countries (fig. 7).[41] Thanks to these commercial ties with Antwerp and their existing ties with homeland Spain, these Hispano-Bruges households had the ideal opportunity to come into contact with novelties such as majolica from Valencia, Italy and Antwerp. So in the case of the dishes in De Castere's *contoor*, we tend to agree with Baatsen's conclusion: 'the majolica added to both the merchant's social and cultural capital, which in turn increased his credibility as a man in and of this world, up-to-date with the newest fashion and firmly connected to foreign trade'.[42] So the fashion for collecting and displaying valuable objects was not only an expression of humanistic and scholarly ambition[43] but also fitted the image merchants wanted to propagate.

De Castere's two majolica dishes were not the only items found in the Bruges *contoren* that could fit with this desire to articulate the image of the entrepreneur as a man of the world. Guillaume van Damast (1566)'s[44] four exotic knives and the world map, or *mappa mundi*, in the *contoor* of silk trader Domenicus Vaerheil (1567)[45] could also be seen as objects of knowledge and commerce and therefore assisting in drawing a picture of the business person's connection with contemporary knowledge of geography and trade[46] – just like the globes in seventeenth-century *Kunstkammers* that also reflected the involvement of Antwerp's merchant-collectors in global trade networks.[47] Like the seventeenth-century art and naturalia

collectors, it seems that these merchant-entrepreneurs attached a similar importance to the dissemination of their constructed identity.[48] But in contrast to these
Kunstkammers, the *contoren* were probably not open to a wide public, and what our
Bruges merchants had on display was not a large commodity collection in the sense
of a group of related objects like the art or minerals collections of seventeenth-century connoisseurs-collectors. The fact that they were able to have at least one dish
of majolica or an exotic knife on display was thought to be convincing enough. Furthermore, what they had on show was not something that could be described as a
'marvel of nature', such as gemstones, seashells, dried sea creatures, plants, flowers or
insects.[49] What we find in the *contoren* of Bruges was therefore not (yet?) a type of
consumption that pursued natural knowledge, investigating the world and engaging
with nature. Instead, it was intended primarily to symbolise the economic and social status of its owner. The only direct references to nature (i.e. to flora and fauna)
we can find in the inventories are the birdcages with or without exotic birds and the
kynchoorne or seashell (*Buccinum undatum*) that was kept in the small room, called
the *garderobe*, belonging to Jan Blaeuvoet (1563).[50]

However, in the inventory of the same Jan Blaeuvoet, we did find traces of a
particular way of engaging with nature – alchemy.[51] In his *contoor* were nine *fiolen*,
or small glass bottles, and a *distilleerclocke*. The latter probably referred to the so-
called alembic, which was a frequently used distillation device.[52] Bruges archaeolo-
gists have also found such alembics and related glass containers in a cesspool in the
Spanjaardstraat (near the nation house of the Castilians).[53] The alembic was used,
for example, to distil alcohol, water and hydroliths, liquids with a concentration of
flavours and fragrances and volatile essential oils.[54] The oldest alembics are made of
glass, but in the late Middle Ages, alembics of pottery and stoneware came into use
– copper and brass were used only after the Middle Ages. Intriguingly, Blaeuvoet's
was said to be made of lead or was used in relation to lead. In any case, if he wanted
to extract a fluid through the distillation process, the alembic was to be heated to
the evaporation point. At that temperature, steam is formed, which after cooling in
the dome, would flow via the spout into the reservoir as a liquid.[55]

By the mid sixteenth century, alchemy was of widespread interest and no longer
the preserve of a small group of initiates.[56] Indeed, the forerunner of chemistry was
even commodified and commercialised during the sixteenth century so that alchemical knowledge had become more accessible and widely dispersed. For novices and
practitioners alike, it was not that difficult to find a variety of theoretical alchemical
literature and practical books in the vernacular; books, as well as recipes and skills,

could easily be purchased from a variety of people. This commercialised practical alchemical knowledge was by no means limited to metallurgy or the transmutation or multiplication of metals (forging lead into gold and the production of noble metals), but was also about medicine and brewing (alcoholic) liquids.[57] Blaeuvoet chose to practise the art of alchemy – or to have it all stored – in one specific room, a room that stood separate from all the others. In his large house of eleven rooms, all filled with a tremendous number of objects, he chose to do this in a small, almost unfurnished room that had no potential of inviting people in. Where exactly his *contoor* was located in the house is not entirely clear. In the inventory, it was drafted right after the collections of silverware, clothing, hollowware and linen, whereas all the other rooms were summarised prior to these collections of goods. So it seems that the role of the room in the whole of the house was again not entirely clear to the appraiser either. But it was perhaps this insulating character of the room that convinced Blaeuvoet to perform his alchemical processes exactly there.

In four other inventories in our sample, we came across references to other *lode clocken*, though it is uncertain whether these were also used in the process of distillation. Only in the case of teacher Domen Vleedorp (1550)[58] did the appraiser find *twee looden clocke omme water te deselen*. Although the meaning of the last word is not entirely clear, these devices were probably used to distillate water as well, which Vleedorp chose to do in his kitchen rather than elsewhere in his house.

In Blaeuvoet's room, the *fiolen* or glass bottles could then have served as receptacles in the distillation process or as containers for storing the liquids. Besides the alembic and other elements of the distilling process, he also had two *goutgewichten*, small scales for weighing money or gold, stored in his *contoor*. Perhaps these scales that could weigh smaller objects very accurately were even used in the alchemical context as well. The fact is, of course, that a lot of objects that should have been there in the context of alchemy were not listed in the inventory after all, so we probably only have a glimpse of Jan Blaeuvoet's alchemy room. The other objects in his room were mostly used for storage, such as the two cupboards with several drawers (one cupboard had gilded drawers), the iron chest, a certain number of barrels and four little baskets. However, many objects of his household were included in the list of items that had already been sold or were about to be sold (*venditie*). And these items were not listed per room or location, so it might be possible for the *contoor* to have comprised more items than the few objects that were assigned to it. The mirror that was added to the list of the *venditie*, for example, could have been such an example.

An item that, according to scholarly literature, was often found in studies was indeed the mirror. According to Paula Findlen, the object was thought to be suitable in a study, because it 'made visible the dialectic between knowledge and self-knowledge'.[59] And it was commonly used in contemporary literature and art to warn those looking into it to 'know themselves', in other words, it was a visual stimulant to encourage contemplation and self-consciousness.[60] But mirrors had more practical uses as well, especially in the context of reading and writing when managing business administration. The *Roman de la Rose*, for example, offers a thorough description of the properties of mirrors, 'which have such marvelous powers that they magnify small letters and illuminate ancient, faded script so that it could be read more easily'.[61] So it was believed to be an aid to one's reading; a mirror was not only used as an optical glass in reading, it also reflected incoming rays of daylight, creating an extra light source, which was welcome in a period when only candles, fireplaces and oil lamps produced it.[62]

Another pleasing effect of a mirror hanging in a small but well-furnished room is that it reduces the feeling of being trapped in a small and often crowded room by making the room feel more spacious. Furthermore, it allows a person to see everything reflected in the mirror[63] – ideal when one has stored one's collection of valuable items in there. But apart from their practical uses, mirrors were often exclusive and costly luxury items as well – especially the more expensive and also more complex *christallijne* mirrors produced according to the Venetian glass-making technique.

Consequently, mirrors were only rarely found in the living quarters of the people in our sample. Until the end of the sixteenth century, only a small proportion of the population owned a mirror, and it seems that these objects have been favoured most by a wealthier audience. When calculating the general ratio of mirrors – and thus the likelihood that mirrors would have been located in a specific room – it appears that the *contoor* yields a relatively high ratio of 3.1. But other rooms, such as the dining room (4.3), the sleeping room (5.4) and the *salette* (3.2), yield even higher ratios. So the *contoor* was certainly not the only place where mirrors were displayed, and mirrors also occurred frequently in other spaces.

The type of mirror displayed in the *contoren* is hard to say, because appraisers did not give a precise description of the mirrors they found. In the case of Vander Moer, the square mirror was probably stored there as one of many other precious items the widow had put away safely in her *contoor*. De Castere's mirror, on the other hand, was grouped together with his writing equipment and seals, probably referring to its role in a particular writing context. But in the case of De Castere, we would suggest that the mirror also had another function, a function that it shared with the two majolica dishes mentioned before; in other words, it emblematised his success as a business person and his image as a man of the world, fascinated by the pleasure and benefit of the 'natural magic' of optical manipulations. Mirrors were indeed expensive and exclusive objects at that time, and the technique of producing crystal-glass mirrors was still new to the Low Countries. Though transparent crystal glass was mentioned as early as the early sixteenth century, it took until 1537 before Lucas van Helmont developed a local industry and was making 'verre cristallin l'in-star de Venise' in Antwerp.[64]

In contrast to mirrors, many more *contoor* owners had books stored and displayed in their rooms. In fact, it seems that books were the most defining items of this type of room. When we calculate where or in what type of room there was the highest possibility to find any type of book, the *contoor* seems to yield the highest ratio (11.9) along with the dining room (2.8), the front room (2.4) and the *salette* (1.7). So the *contoor* was not the only location in the house where books were kept and potentially read, but when this room was available in houses, it was certainly the most preferred one.

The collections of books that were listed in the inventories under study are not extensive, which does not mean that some Bruges canons, wealthy international traders and political leaders were not able to have impressive private libraries at the time.[65] But their inventories were not part of our sample. Spanish merchant Jan I Pardo, for example, had an extensive library, evidenced by a book list found in the family archive of the Pardos (1560).[66] The list contains no fewer than twenty-eight book titles, ranging from books in the vernacular, medieval scholastic literature and holy lives to contemporary Spanish religious books. Canon Jacob de Heere (1546–1602), in turn, donated no fewer than 120 individual books in his will.[67] But these large collections of books were rather the exception than the rule, especially for middle-class households of Bruges. Most people who were interested in books had only a handful of them.

Unfortunately, however, only in exceptional circumstances is the subject of the book known. Fernando De Castere, for example, had in his *contoor* a collection of twenty-four small printed books in Latin, French and Spanish (including a Latin bible), a book by Seneca (referring to Stoic philosophy) and a book with *plakkat-en*. But the title identification usually does not go much further than that. What is striking, then, is that appraisers did make the effort to make a distinction between printed books and manuscripts, a practice that was still prevalent in the seventeenth century.[68] Guillaume van Damast, for example, had three manuscripts and an undefined number of printed books, while Domenicus Vaerheil had *diverssche gheprente boucken*, or printed books in his *contoor* as well as one paper book – probably a notebook. Printed books and booklets were, in general, easier to obtain from a bookseller than the handwritten manuscripts were. Due to the rapid development of book printing, such printed books were also accessible to a wide audience. Though the epicentre of sixteenth-century book printing and bookselling was set in Antwerp (for example, in the famous Officina Plantiniana or the printing business of Christophe Plantin),[69] several successful booksellers and printing companies such as Hubertus Goltzius's Officina Goltziana remained in Bruges.[70] Though these booksellers had several internationally and locally written books on offer, ranging from treatises and humanistic literature to recipe books, dictionaries and religiously inspired literature and bibles,[71] most books in the inventories are religious in nature, like bibles and books of hours (the latter type was particularly found in the fifteenth-century sample period). But this should not come as a surprise; since the fifteenth century, the so-called Devotio Moderna movement, originating in the Netherlands and neighbouring parts of Germany, promoted a type of affective piety that had become popular in vernacular as well as in Latin devotional literature – so private, often solitary, devotion within the home became widespread.[72] In this sphere, the demand for religious texts increased enormously. In particular, devotional texts in the vernacular began to flourish in the late fifteenth and early sixteenth centuries, an increase that was already apparent in the time of handwritten manuscripts and which was subsequently stimulated by the rise of the printing art.[73] Although books were easier to obtain thanks to the printing press, they were still seen as a symbol of the ability to read. The more varied a collection was – in theme but also in language – the more it became a status symbol for its owner (fig. 8).

Similarities and Differences: The Broader Picture

In general, it seems that the *contoor* was a rather small room, functionally and spatially set apart from the other rooms in the same house (often even by the appraiser). In some instances, the *contoor* was more or less an annex of another room (in most cases of the hall), but it was always built as a separate space (it was a hall with a

Fig. 8. Saint Hieronymus in his Study, Albrecht Dürer, 1514, Kupferstichkabinett,
© Staatliche Museen, Berlin, bpk / Gemäldegalerie, SMB / Jörg P. Anders

contoor and not just a large hall). And whether the room was located at the front
of the house or somewhere upstairs, it was deliberately intended to harbour certain
activities and certain items, keeping them apart from the rest of the household. This
was perhaps also the reason why few pieces of furniture were found in these rooms.
The only pieces of furniture found there were several types of cabinets and chests to
store things, along with an occasional chair or writing desk for the merchant to read
and write comfortably.

Despite the room's label as *contoor* – specifically referring to the act of counting
and to the act of doing business in general (from the Latin *computare*) – specialisation was not the rule. Though the activities of reading, counting and writing were
central to this space, several other items convey the range of interests encompassed
by this type of room. For the group of middle-class and urban elitist owners of *contoren*, the room 'answered a range of needs'.[74] It could be used as an office or writing
room, as a storeroom or treasury for household or commercial valuables, or as a
place where a merchant could read, study and pray. It was place where owners could
immerse themselves in contemplation, but where they could also articulate their
status as trustworthy, honourable and competent entrepreneurs.

More importantly, and even for this period, 'objects displayed in a study were
expressions of the self'.[75] In scholarly literature on Italian Renaissance *case*, the room
where business entered the realm of the home is immediately connected with the
growing interest in the creation of collections and with the humanistic love for the
exotic and the cult of erudition.[76] However, we are inclined to link it to yet another
facet of the owner's ideal self: the objects in the *contoren* were meant to portray
and even strengthen the owner's status as a trustworthy, honourable and competent
business person. So the objects in the *contoor* were not intended to represent the
ideal of the humanist scholar, but rather expressed the image of an educated entrepreneur, fully fitting within the commercial climate of the city. Indeed, in the case of
the Bruges *contoren*, clear tangible and visual associations were made with the world
of business and commerce. The objects on display had to represent the necessary
virtues of organisation, rigour and credibility a merchant-entrepreneur (merchant
and artisan) had to master to manage a business. The majolica dishes and the mirror
in the room of Fernando De Castere, the *mappa mundi* of Domenicus Vaerheil, the
alchemy installation of Jan Blaeuvoet and the books of Guillaume van Damast were
all signifiers of this social and economic status. These luxury items were not only
expensive and therefore exclusive, they also exemplified the knowledge and expertise these people had regarding the world, trade and perhaps also nature. In this but

also in their correspondence, they consciously engaged with the outside world – although it was not necessarily staged for outsiders to see. Like shops and workshops, *contoren* were therefore part of the business space of a house but, like the shop and workshop, physically and functionally set apart from the domestic living quarters.

In the Bruges *contoren*, a rarefied atmosphere of retreat from the everyday was thus created. Merchants and artisans retreated into their *contoor*, experiencing the room 'through the power of the objects it contained'.[77] To underline the study's similar metamorphic powers, Ruvoldt cites an oft-quoted passage from the works of Niccolò Machiavelli in which, on the threshold of his study, he strips off his mundane, everyday clothes and puts on the robes of court and palace.[78] In doing this, he passes into the world of study and contemplation. Though we are less convinced of the spiritual atmosphere of the *contoor*, several black garments were found in some Bruges *contoren* too, as well as clothes brushes and water pots used for personal hygiene. Black as a colour for clothing was strongly associated with formality and with officials and urban elites. And it is considered as a given that traders and city elites were quite often completely dressed in black in portraits as well, especially in the second part of the sixteenth century.[79] So although we cannot be completely sure about their usage or the reason why these garments were kept there, it seems that these special garments (or at least clean garments) were worn by the merchants when they resided in the *contoor* (and perhaps also outside in the city), because the clothes conferred upon their wearers a sense of awareness of the tasks that await them, enhancing their retreat from the everyday, perhaps also sharpening concentration and their diligence.

This type of room was, in most cases, specifically tailored to fulfil the needs of the sixteenth-century Bruges business person. As a working room, the *contoor* formed a strategic location in terms of doing administration and the act of conducting business. It was a small room, spatially isolated at home, but functionally and materially oriented towards the outside world, although it was also socially exclusive. The *contoor* was the least common space encountered in inventories and was especially present in the inventories of the wealthier citizens. This means that people made a conscious decision whether such a room was built (or created) or not. Having enough space was, after all, an important precondition to be able to differentiate between spaces. In the next chapter, we will move from the least common space in a house to a room that was present in nearly all houses, small or large: the kitchen.

AT THE HEART OF THE HOME: ROOMS AT THE HEART OF DOMESTIC CULTURE

Judging from historical documents such as the registers of the city's aldermen, it seems that the kitchen was not only frequently present in Bruges houses, it was also a label that was used by appraisers and officials to distinguish a particular room from another already early in time. Moreover, it is also apparent that it was the first room to be explicitly referred to by its function rather than its location.[1] The semantic origin of the word 'kitchen' underlines this functionality, because it clearly refers to a type of household function: cooking. The Middle Dutch word *cuekene* goes back to the vulgar Latin *cucina*, referring to food preparation.[2] The specific naming of the kitchen as a specialist room somehow mirrored a material process that had originated in the medieval period. The development of improved ventilation systems and the relocation of the central fireplace to the side wall enabled the furnishing of a semi-demarcated or separate 'fireplace' for cooking purposes.[3] Originally, the space where the only central fireplace was located was multifunctional in nature, because it was used for a lot of different functions at the same time. People needed the fire for cooking and boiling food, but it was also the preferred place to sleep and socialise, especially in winter, because it was also the warmest and brightest place in the house. But by relocating the central hearth to the side wall and by connecting it to a chimney, it had the advantage of reducing the amount of smoke in the room, making it more pleasant and healthy to reside in and to connect other rooms, upstairs or next door, to this central chimney as well, creating secondary hearths in the same house.[4]

To equip a room with a fireplace is important, because the presence of a hearth meant that the room could be lit and heated, enabling some particular household functions and daily tasks to be performed there. Moreover, the creation of secondary fireplaces suggested that these functions no longer *necessarily* had to be done in one and the same room. Hence, in theory, when enough space was available in a dwelling, some functions such as sleeping, eating and socialising could easily be relocated to other heated spaces.

Historiography has surely become used to defining the kitchen as 'a room predominantly used for cooking and work'.[5] Antony Buxton categorises kitchens in Tudor houses as service areas, like butteries, cellars and services houses, primarily ded-
icated to the preparation of food for cooking and storage.[6] Inspired by architectural
treatises such as that of Italian Renaissance theorist Leon Battista Alberti[7] and influenced by a new genre of kitchen scenes produced by the 'new school' by the likes of
painters Pieter Aertsen (1508–1575) and Joachim Beuckelaer (ca. 1535–1574), the
kitchen was indeed considered by many scholars as a 'backstage' private place where
all types of meals were prepared, especially by women and servant maids.[8] Indeed,
in the kitchen scenes by Aertsen and Beuckelaer, but also in the works of Martin van
Cleve, Jan Steen and Pieter Cornelisz van Rijck, the kitchen is depicted as a space
clearly defined by its cooking facilities and utensils.[9] In these paintings, a prolifera-
tion of foodstuffs, kitchen utensils and tableware and an eye-catching hearth were
deliberately put at the centre of attention. The often satirical, allegorical or moral messages painters tried to convey were deemed only identifiable (and therefore
made accessible) when the scenes were placed in an environment recognisable to
contemporary viewers (see infra).[10] Consequently, painters had to consider the in-
gredients of their painted constructions. But even if painters borrowed their ingre-
dients from the material culture of their clients to use as props to make their painted
scenes familiar to the viewer and to make the underlying message accessible, it remains to be seen whether these scenes were not mere constructions of snapshots of
material culture rather than depictions of everyday experience.[11] Indeed, how familiar and how general were these painted kitchens in reality? To what extent did they
represent an actual interior? The kitchen on the panel painting previously attributed
to Jan II Van Coninxloo (ca. 1489–after 1546), for example, depicting a scene from
the life of Saint Benedict when performing the *Miracle of the Broken Sieve* (1552) is
situated in an elite household, given the huge and diverse amount of copper, brass
and metal cooking utensils and a maidservant in the front (fig. 10). The setting and
especially the combination of the objects, makes it very realistic, and we can easily
imagine that it was recognisable to contemporaries. In contrast, painters Aertsen
and Beuckelaer often introduced classical architectural features in their kitchen interiors, such as Dorian mantelpieces and classical columns, which were probably
not familiar to the majority of city dwellers. We have argued elsewhere that these
kitchen scenes were probably not mere representations of reality but should be interpreted as topos of that time, 'a phenomenon of cultural, not material reality'.[12] So
paintings are useful for this kind of research only to a certain extent: they probably

Fig. 9. Kitchen scene of staff preparing food. The Four Elements: Fire, Joachim Beuckelaer, 1570, Oil on canvas, London, © The National Gallery

do not communicate what a kitchen actually looked like (first of all because there was no such thing as *the* kitchen), and they probably do not depict all the household functions a kitchen actually contained either. What they depict is a scene that was set in a recognisable environment (a kitchen where one could cook food given the cooking utensils and the fireplace) and that, by necessity, had to be neatly and methodically arranged. Painters such as Aertsen and Beuckelaer used the primary function of kitchens (i.e. preparing food) to tell their story, because they wanted to raise the issue of the affluent and opulent lifestyle of citizens by emphasising abundance (including the presence of one or more servants); in other words, they had no regard for other possible functions of rooms like kitchens (fig. 9).

Previous research on the use of the kitchen space in the sixteenth-century Low Countries has yielded interesting results for the city of Antwerp. A first systematic analysis of the post-mortem inventories of the period 1560–1570 by Carolien De Staelen and a follow-up study by Inneke Baatsen, Bruno Blondé and myself have demonstrated that no fewer than 83 to 90 per cent (on average) of the sampled

Fig. 10. Kitchen interior with hearth, furniture and utensils. The Miracle of the Broken Sieve, Jan II van Conincxloo, 1552, left panel of diptych, Oil on panel, Brussels, © Royal Museum of Fine Arts, www.artinflanders.be

households had at least one kitchen.[13] Households without kitchens mostly oc-cupied small one- or two-roomed dwellings.[14] So the larger the house, the more room was available and the more likely it was that a kitchen was present. Following Gwendolynn Heley's definition of room use – 'the function of a room was dictated by available space, linked to wealth in some cases, and to occupational and domes-tic requirements'[15] – one might also assume that the more space was available, the more specialised kitchens would have become. However, research has proven that this is not always the case. It appears that some people had more than one kitchen, often a small and a larger one. In this case, the latter was characterised by a mixture of daily functions, ranging from sleeping (or at least the presence of a bed) and cooking to eating and entertaining. The smaller kitchen, on the other hand, was mostly equipped for food preparation only.[16] So the so-called *pronkkeukens* or more luxurious and highly furnished spaces with a mixture of functions were, therefore, no prerogative of the seventeenth-century northern Netherlands, but already exist-ed in sixteenth-century Antwerp.[17] So even though there was no shortage of space and service rooms such as the *bottelarij* took over some of the kitchen's functions, it seems that some people in Antwerp were nonetheless eager to organise the kitch-en as the heart of the household with a clear social function. In this case, most of the actual cooking was transferred to the smaller kitchen, although cooking utensils still remained present in the *groote keuckene* as well. Some of the larger kitchens in the houses of the upper layer of middle-class society in Antwerp developed, there-fore, from a more or less functional storage and cooking room into a comfortable, well-furnished social space.[18] Could this be defined as a form of functional speciali-sation but then on a micro level? And was this a unique Antwerp phenomenon? In Bruges, domestic space was much more easily available than in densely populated Antwerp, and at the end of the sixteenth century, no fewer than 88 per cent of the sampled households had at least one room that was labelled kitchen.[19]

The Kitchen in Bruges

The kitchen of the wealthy Winkelman family discussed earlier was clearly predom-inantly used as a cooking area where the preparation of different kinds of food took place. Specific items of hearth equipment such as roasting spits, kettle hooks and waffle irons were kept there, ready to be used when cooking occurred. The rest of the cookware such as kettles, pans and pots, but also bottles and a sieve, were stored in the nearby *bottelarij*, or storage space. However, these cooking utensils were not the only objects that were found by the appraiser in this specific room in the house. Several pieces of storage furniture such as a pewter cupboard (*tinschaprade*) and a small cupboard for storing sugar (*suuckerschaprayken*), several pieces of seating furniture such as chairs and benches, a table with tablecloth and a counter were mentioned as there as well. Moreover, the Winkelman family's kitchen was also used as one of the repositories of table linens and decorative textiles, as witnessed by the substantial number of bankers (*banc cleren*), fireplace rugs (*schoucleren*) and dishcloths (*droochcleren*). The eight chairs, the foot stool with rug and the benches suggest that the kitchen was a room where the members of the household could enjoy comfortable seating and perhaps even a meal. Is this evidence of a more multifunctional kitchen rather than a specialised workplace?

In general, we could distinguish between two general types of kitchens in the Bruges samples: specialised kitchens that were fitted for cooking and food preparation only and multifunctional kitchens where other household activities were carried out except for cooking, such as sleeping, dining and sitting.[20] According to the theory of functional specialisation, we should find ever more specialised kitchens in sixteenth-century Bruges. But results indicate quite the opposite: we even found a reversed evolution from a greater emphasis on specialised kitchens in the fifteenth century to a mere 45 per cent at the close of the sixteenth century. So while both treatises and paintings promoted a higher degree of specialisation of domestic space, the data yielded by the inventories suggest otherwise.

During the sixteenth century, the proportion of small houses (two to three rooms) with a kitchen had risen enormously – from 44 per cent to 77 per cent. Smaller houses were thus ever more likely to have a room labelled 'kitchen' as well. The kitchens in the dwellings of people of the middling ranks in Bruges (four to five rooms) were relatively more specialised than the kitchens in smaller houses. This should not come as a surprise of course, because these households had more spatial opportunities to have their dinner elsewhere in the dwelling. In larger multi-storey houses (six rooms or more), the frequency of specialised kitchens declines in favour of kitchens with dining facilities. So for these households, the reverse rule seems to apply: the more rooms a family had, the higher the chance that their kitchens were also used for dining. More rooms allowed for a more complex partitioning of domestic space, so wealthier families inhabiting larger houses were probably able to organise formal dinner parties elsewhere in the house, such as in a dining room or *salette*, but most probably still ate their less formal meals in the kitchen. These households usually employed several members of staff as well, which might also explain why these larger houses had eating facilities in the kitchen.

In all of the kitchens we studied, people were able to cook, albeit sometimes under different circumstances, using different types and qualities of cooking utensils. But in some kitchens, various non-specialised household activities could take place, including sleeping, sitting and socialising, and it could also be used as a storage space. In the remainder of this chapter, we will question to what extent kitchens were equipped to house any of these functions and whether these spaces were connected with other domestic spaces where some of these or other household functions were performed.[21]

Sleeping in the Kitchen

Throughout the sixteenth century, there was a sharp decline in the number of kitchens that were used for sleeping (or at least in the number of kitchens where beds were present). From 51 per cent in the fifteenth century, and even 65 per cent in the early sixteenth century, to 38 per cent at the end of the sixteenth century. Even in multifunctional kitchens, it seems that sleeping facilities were slowly disappearing from the kitchen. This trend is especially visible in the last two decades of the sixteenth century. Spatial constraints or spatial opportunities could offer some explanation of why some people would sleep in their kitchens; in smaller houses, the kitchen was often the only heated room in the dwelling. But these spatial constraints alone cannot sufficiently explain why people were less inclined to sleep in the kitchen. Of course, seasonal patterns undoubtedly also played a part in people's choice of where they wanted to sleep. In the winter, people would have preferred warmer locations near a fireplace, whereas in the summer, people would have searched for more airy spaces. But notwithstanding these possible seasonal variations in sleeping patterns, perhaps we have to look for more cultural motivations. These motivations might also explain why we found room labels such as *slaapcamere* in sixteenth-century Bruges, while authors Loughman and Montias have claimed that 'it was only after about 1700 that independent bedrooms generally emerged; until then, most rooms had sleeping facilities'.[22] Indeed, why was one particular room with a bed labelled as a 'bedroom', whereas other rooms with beds were not? We will dive into this subject in the next section on sleeping rooms.

Sociability in the Kitchen

Depictions of the kitchen in sixteenth-century kitchen scenes by, for example, Beuckelaer and Aertsen, hardly show beds, chairs or benches, except for the stool that was used by the kitchen maid while she stirred the boiling stew or plucked a chicken. And the tables were mainly used to display food items. Only in the painting *Peasants by the Hearth* (ca. 1560)[23] was the kitchen depicted as a place of (exuberant) sociability, with several stools and a set table, a place to gather round the fire, play a game and have some drinks and some food. But perhaps this scene was an example of what Paul Vandenbroeck has labelled 'inverse self-definition'?[24] In his view, it was painted for an urban bourgeois audience and meant to illustrate a situation that was not preferred.[25] In the more modest dwellings where the kitchen with its hearth was the main room of the house, the presence of seating such as stools and simple chairs might not come as a surprise. But among the seating are different types of chairs, benches and small stools, all of them further defining the function and character of the Bruges kitchen.

Differences in seating furniture reveal a lot about the function of the furniture itself and the use of the room in general. In wealthy Antwerp kitchens, for example, appraisers have found examples of luxurious Spanish chairs, chairs that were fashionable and luxurious at that time and therefore rather expensive.[26] This means that at least some kitchens also performed a more sociable or display function besides food preparation. Small benches and stools, on the other hand, were multifunctional in use and could be used as chairs as well as small tables. They were also easy to move from one room to another. They often had a limited height and were therefore ideal to use in performing manual work (such as spinning or weaving) or during cooking. Stools were also cheap and therefore within reach for a larger group of people. Reclining chairs and sofa chairs, on the other hand, were often much sturdier and heavier and therefore required more effort to move. They had a more permanent character, and thanks to their shape, armrests and backrests and later stuffed seating, they were also increasingly more comfortable for their users.

Although benches remained vital pieces of furniture in many interiors, they lost their dominant position as the favoured piece of seating furniture in most households. De Staelen labels this trend the 'individualisation' of seating furniture; chairs underwent a growing popularity at the expense of multi-person benches. For the kitchen in particular, this evolution was visible as well. Though they were still present in the cooking area, the mean number of larger benches declined during the sixteenth

Table 5. Types of Chairs in Kitchens per Sample Period

SEATING	1438–144	1450–1510	1528–1549	1559–1574	1584–1600
Stools, small benches (schabelle)	47.6%	5.3%	6.3%	6.9%	9.9%
Chairs	9.1%	20.6%	30.4%	40.3%	36.4%
Large benches (lijs)	6.4%	4.7%	11.3%	9.8%	11.1%
Spanish chairs	0.0%	0.0%	0.0%	0.0%	0.0%
Sofa chairs (leunstoel, zetel, kuipstoel)	0.0%	12.3%	38.9%	36.5%	51.8%

Source: Database of inventories © IB, JDG & IS

century, whereas the mean number of chairs increased. So small benches as well as the larger *lijs* benches were increasingly replaced by chairs. Replacing the larger benches with more movable chairs and stools also made the room much more flexible in use. In table 5, we see the shares of each type of seating in kitchens per sample period.

In the first sample period, the proportion of stools and small benches in kitchens is still rather high, especially compared with the percentages in the following sample periods. Nearly half of all the stools in people's houses were thus located in their kitchens. But throughout most of the sixteenth century, it seems that most of these small seats were located elsewhere in the domestic space and not in the cooking area. They were probably still used as kitchen aids during cooking, but other seats in the kitchen were replaced by other types of seating furniture. Indeed, an increasingly high proportion of chairs was found in kitchens, from only 9 per cent in the first sample period to around 40 per cent in the second half of the sixteenth century. And it was not just these simpler, still rather easy-to-move chairs that were found more often in kitchens; reclining chairs and sofa chairs also occurred more frequently. In the last sample period (in the final two decades of the sixteenth century), nearly half of the total number of reclining chairs in houses were found in the kitchen.

In smaller houses, people often dined in their kitchens, because they had no other place to eat, whereas in larger houses, the more formal dinner parties were held in other rooms such as dining rooms or *salettes*, and the more informal meals were probably still held in the kitchen. The reclining chairs and sofa chairs may have participated in this dining culture, though they may also have played a part in the context of leisure time. Nonetheless, the mean number of this type of chair per kitchen was rather low. So either leisure time in the kitchen area was limited to certain guests and household members (and possibly members of staff) who could take their place on the few individual comfortable seats, or there was still some kind of a supper hierarchy and the highest in rank was to be seated in the most comfortable chair in the kitchen.[27] Wouter De Dorpere (1590), for example, had several types of seating furniture in his kitchen.[28] In addition to his five chairs, there were a sofa chair and a *dronckaertstoel*, probably a rocking chair,[29] as well as a small table. The kitchen of Joos Minne (1567), in turn, was also equipped with five chairs and two sofa chairs, all round his kitchen table.

The more exclusive and luxurious chairs, the so-called Spanish chairs and *saelstoelen*, or hall chairs, were, however, entirely absent from the kitchen. Both these types of chair were a novelty in the sixteenth century, because some of these chairs were upholstered – a new feature of individual seating furniture, though not yet entirely replacing cushions and other textile furnishings.[30] Upholstered seating gradually became more popular not only because it breathed comfort thanks to stuffing and leather- or textile-covered fixed seats, but their symmetrical design, attractive materials and, above all, their meticulous workmanship bestowed a distinctive splendour on their owners.[31] Upholstered chairs were therefore first and foremost meant as luxury furniture, comfortable to sit on and also highly decorative. Not unexpectedly, these luxurious leather- or textile-backed chairs with or without armrests made sitting for longer periods of time easier, which was especially convenient during dinner parties and other social events. They were luxury objects, status objects even, predominantly present in the wealthier households of Bruges. In the fifth sample period (1559–1574), these chairs appeared only in the richest of households; in the sixth sample period (1584–1600), some people of the middling groups could afford these types of chairs as well, but the majority of owners were still part of the highest wealth category. The luxurious character of the hall chair also becomes clear when we look at its diffusion across the domestic space. Hall chairs were most often positioned in rooms labelled *camere*, front rooms and the *salette*. The same compelling results were obtained for the Spanish chair; the dining room and the *salette* were most preferred. In both cases, the kitchen was clearly not a preferred place for locating these types of chairs, suggesting that with regard to sociability and the performance of status, there were still other rooms that were better equipped to fulfil these functions. So in general, people were increasingly able to sit comfortably in the kitchen and join each other for dinner or leisure near the fireplace, but the most exclusive pieces of seating furniture (if present) were still reserved for other places elsewhere in the house.

In Antwerp, the kitchen (and especially the *pronkkeuken*, or the grand or display kitchen) was often a space where lots of decorative objects were found. The mantelpieces and tables, for example, were often decorated with finely woven cloths or tapestries, whose functional use (protecting furniture from burns and stains) was subordinate to their decorative value.[32] This also indicates that in these display kitchens, the focus was not on cooking; otherwise, the valuable textiles would have dripped with fat and would have smelled of food and smoke. More importantly even, paintings also appeared in the kitchen, albeit in smaller numbers compared to rooms such as the Antwerp front room.[33] According to Merwin Corbeau, kitchens in seventeenth-century Dutch houses developed into display rooms as well, 'aesthetically enhanced by decorative items'.[34] In Bruges, however, kitchens were remarkably less sumptuously decorated than in Antwerp[35] – they were even one of the least preferred areas to be furnished with decorative items.[36]

Bruges kitchens were characterised by the appearance of a combination of practical cooking utensils and items divorced from an immediate practical function in terms of cooking, such as paintings, holy water fonts, mirrors and decorative textiles. This is not to say that these objects were not used in a pragmatic way at all.[37] As we will see in the second part of the book, the rather small number of paintings, devotional statues and holy water fonts should be interpreted as part of a context of devotional practice. Paintings were used and appreciated because of their ability to affect family morality and as aids in contemplation and private prayer. The presence of the holy water fonts might underline this practice in kitchens even more clearly. The holy water fonts were probably filled with consecrated water that people could acquire from their local priest. According to Donal Cooper, they could then sprinkle the water over devotional images to increase their efficacy.[38] He concluded that 'in this way, the laity appropriated the liturgical practice of the clergy to frame the sacred within their own homes'.[39] These *sperrewatervaetkens*, or holy water fonts, were certainly not positioned only in the kitchen, but their presence clearly hints that liturgy and devotion were of some meaning in everyday service rooms like kitchens as well. Bruges citizen Jan Crocket (1540) even had in his kitchen a *preicstoel*, or prie-dieu, a functional aid for the performance of individual domestic piety or a small chair used for people to kneel and pray (fig. 11).[40]

Hence, the low number of paintings, statues and other decorations in Bruges kitchens indicate that these items were not primarily used to impress occasional visitors by their appearance, but they were also used by the kitchen maids, cooks, occasional kitchen dwellers and children as devotional items to help express their

Fig. 11. Prayer bench, 15th century, Bruges, © Musea Brugge / OCMW Brugge, O.OTP0035.VII, www.artinflanders.be

piety while working or simply residing in the kitchen. At the same time, the low numbers of paintings in kitchens may also point to the fact that, in general, people did not prefer to have these items displayed in busy, crowded, often dirty and populous spaces like the kitchen but were more inclined to have them in other rooms.

The low occurrence of decorative objects such as paintings and sculpture in kitchens does not necessarily mean that these rooms were not aesthetically appealing to household members and the occasional visitor. Instead, kitchens still expressed the status of the household using its own vocabulary. Indeed, pewter, copper and metal pots, pans, bowls, plates and dishes in all numbers were stored in the kitchen. In some kitchens, glasses and shining pewter tableware were deliberately put on display on open shelves or so-called *tin schapraden*. This made it easier for the cook or maid to find the necessary dishes and pots, but it also showed the range of cooking utensils and tableware the household owned. To the contemporary eye, an apparent abundance of objects such as textiles and silverware, but also pewter and hollowware, were all signs of prosperity.

Dining Room and Salette

Alison Smith argues that in larger houses, larger social gatherings would have occurred in the central hall, but that for their meals, hosts chose a location 'according
to the number of people to be served, the time of year, and probably also the time
of day'.[41] As we saw in our discussion about the Bruges kitchen, people could have
enjoyed their meals in the kitchen as well as in other rooms, because tables and
chairs were positioned in plenty of other types of rooms as well. But in the case
of Bruges, there is still a noticeable difference from other cities such as, for example, sixteenth-century Antwerp and seventeenth-century Amsterdam.[42] Indeed, in
the Bruges sample, we found no fewer than fifty-five *eetcamere*, or dining rooms –
rooms with labels that explicitly referred to the function of eating. Like *slaapcamere*,
or sleeping rooms, and *cueckene*, or kitchens, this label therefore suggested a specific
function, in this case focused on and equipped to facilitate a dinner party.

Dining rooms existed in all social classes and all sample periods except for one.
Only in the last sample period (1584–1600) is the label *eetcamere* completely missing. Antoon Viaene has argued that this might be the result of a linguistic shift that
occurred around the middle of the sixteenth century; the *salette* would then have
replaced the *eetcamere* as a label for a convivial space to eat.[43] According to Viaene,
the *salette* was, therefore, a more fashionable way of labelling a dining room.[44] However, something more was going on than just a linguistic shift, because the *salette* as
a room label showed up only in the more spacious and wealthy houses. So the *salette*
seems to have been a more exclusive 'brand' for indicating the spaces of domestic
conviviality.

It is immediately apparent from the sources that the dining room was the most
decorated and most luxurious room in many types of houses and throughout most
of the sixteenth century. It was a room where it was highly likely to find paintings,
mirrors, board games, decorative textiles (cushions, table covers, cupboard covers,
tapestry and *carpette*) and the most comfortable and luxurious types of seating furniture (hall chairs, chairs, reclining chairs). Of the inventories with a dining room,
93 per cent had at least one table in this room, and all had several pieces of seating
furniture. Near the fireplace, it was therefore the ideal place to have a dinner party,
to celebrate conviviality and enjoy precious leisure time. Some dining rooms were
also used as places for displaying armour and different kinds of tableware (in cupboards, cabinets and so-called *glazenberden*, cases for storing and displaying glasses), and these rooms were often places where specific types of outer garments were

stored and where household textiles such as napkins, tablecloths and towels were kept clean and spotless in chests. Interestingly, the room often also housed large and sumptuously dressed beds. Only in seven cases was the hearth used not only as a heating source but also as a cooking fire, as indicated by the several cauldrons, kettles and roosting spits found there.

The name *salette* is a diminutive and refers to a small hall or *zaalkin*.[45] Each *salette* we found in the inventories was – like the dining room – equipped with serviceable pieces of furniture, including a table and seating (new types of upholstered chairs like hall chairs and Spanish chairs were more commonly found here than in any other rooms), pieces of hearth equipment (but only meant to stir up the fire like bellows and fire tongs and not for cooking a meal), burners, candles and decorative objects such as paintings, mirrors and statuettes. Table 6 presents an overview of the types of furniture and furnishings in the *salettes* of our samples. We did not take into account the exact number of pieces of furniture per inventory but only considered the types of furniture that were present; objects that could hint at the ability of the room to effectuate certain household functions. The last *salette* in the table was situated in the house of widow Anna van den Berghe (1596).[46] The lack of decorative textiles and decorative elements is somehow remarkable but is fully in line with the rest of her inventory. The only decorative item the appraiser found in her house was a small mirror, but this item was registered together with other loose items belonging to the widow without a reference to the mirror's original location. It is apparent from this table that the range of furniture remains relatively limited to tables and seating (with an occasional cupboard in some of the inventories), which stands in contrast to most of the dining rooms. Almost every *salette* was decorated with items such as paintings, statues or mirrors, and the furniture was often ornamented with luxurious fabrics. The *salette* of François Verbrugghe[47] (1586) nicely illustrates this: his *salette* offered room for a small group of people to enjoy each other's company around an extendable table or to enjoy the beautiful sound of the present harpsichord. Guests and household members were able to choose between five hall chairs, six benches and six stools to sit on, some of which were cushioned. The room was decorated with no less than ten paintings and a cupboard.

Compared to the dining room, the *salette*, in general, served far fewer secondary functions such as storing textiles and tableware, sleeping or presenting a venue for cooking. It seems that this was a trend that started with the dining room and continued throughout the entire second half of the sixteenth century. The wealthier the household, the fewer secondary functions the dining room fulfilled. So the *salette*

Table 6. Furniture and Furnishings in the Salette

N	YEAR	TABLE	SEATS	HEARTH EQUIPMENT	DECORATION	DECORATIVE TEXTILES
1	1563	X	X	X	X	X
2	1568	X	X	X	X	
3	1568	X	X	X	X	X
4	1584	X	X			X
5	1585	X	X	X	X	
6	1585	X	X	X	X	X
7	1585	X	X		X	X
8	1586	X	X	X	X	X
9	1586	X	X		X	X
10	1596	X	X	X		

Source: Database of inventories © IB, JDG & IS

– and therefore also its furnishing – seems to have been even more specialised in function than the dining room. The *salette* was equipped only to serve the function of a reception room, a place where guests were received and entertained. In three out of the four inventories of the less wealthy households, the *salette* also contained a furnished bed. In these inventories, the *salette* was sometimes also furnished with less exclusive furniture such as hall chairs or Spanish chairs and with more small benches and stools. But notwithstanding this difference in quality and grandeur, it still fulfilled similar functions as its namesake in the wealthier households. The *salette* was most probably a relatively small room in which space was scarce, so also for practical reasons, it could not be open to everything and everyone at any time of the day. In the houses of the city elites, the *salette* was thus a room where guests were invited to experience the splendour and social status of the family. In some houses then, the *salette* took over one particular function of the dining room, while other functions were transferred to other spaces.

The house of Ghysbrecht Colve (1586) offers an interesting illustration of the latter theory.[48] His *salette* was one of the eleven rooms that were mentioned in the inventory and was situated on the ground floor, near the kitchen. It contained a cupboard with a painting of the Crucifixion and two metal candlesticks with candles, a large bench, a table, six smaller benches, four hall chairs, a painting on the mantelpiece, four other paintings, two metal burners and two portraits of Ghysbrecht and his wife. Beds were located in the sleeping room, the room above the bedroom and the maids' room. Kettles, pots and pans and hearth equipment used for cooking were kept in the kitchen itself and some more on the *plaetse*, or courtyard. Ghysbrecht Colve's armour (his black harness, *ponjaert* or dagger, helmet and gloves) was put on show in the room labelled *zaale*, which was used as an entrance lobby through which one passed to enter the living rooms, situated at the front of the house in the Vlamingstrate in Bruges. But the *zaale* was not only an entrance lobby, it was also furnished with a table and comfortable chairs and benches, so guests could be received there as well. It seems that where they were received depended on the status of the guests and their link with the household, the occasion of their visit and the time of day.

The presence of a *salette* was thus clearly related to the size of the house; much like the parlour in Tudor houses, it seems that 'the larger the house, the more likely that it would contain one'.[49] This rather exclusive character probably changed in the course of the seventeenth century. Even though *salettes* still mainly occurred in the higher wealth categories, they are also found in the more modest households of seventeenth-century Brussels.[50] Nevertheless, the *salette* remained a more private or socially exclusive space, with less evidence of everyday activity. The room itself was equipped with particular objects, intended to serve only a handful of functions. Due to the presence of other spaces, this room did not have to be very flexible in use and did not have to be quickly transformed when the occasion arose. In the many households that did not have a *salette* as a reception room, the 'public' functions of the *salette* were accommodated within other rooms such as the kitchen.[51]

Conclusions

Throughout the sixteenth century, kitchens came to function more as venues for dining as well as for cooking, as increasingly more objects serving as dining facilities such as tables, seating, table linen and tableware were found in these domestic spaces. At the same time and especially during the second part of the sixteenth century, beds more or less disappeared from the kitchen area, even in the smaller houses where space was presumably scarcer. Perhaps the combination of cooking and eating was more accepted in daily routines even among the higher social classes than the combination of sleeping in spaces where food was prepared and consumed? This would suggest a change not only in food and dining culture but also in the rituals of sleeping. Kitchens were not only used as a place to enjoy a good meal but also as a place to rest, to enjoy the warmth of the fire and the company of others. In larger houses, the evidence suggests that there was a segregation of sociability: informal meals with family members or staff took place in the kitchen, whereas more formal dinner parties, peer entertainment or more select socialising took place first in the dining room and later in the even more exclusive *salette*.

The Elusive Realm of Sleep: Sleeping Rooms

Roger Ekirch was one of the first scholars to question sleep patterns and sleep rituals in the pre-modern period or, as he has so eloquently put it in his work, to enter 'the elusive realm of sleep in early modern British society'.[52] According to him, historians have so far neglected sleeping rituals and the history of nightlife altogether because of a lack of sources; only the subject of dreams has yet attracted comprehensive scrutiny.[53] In the discussion of this realm of sleep, Ekirch therefore left the study on the cultural interpretation of dreams behind and drew attention 'to the relationship between the public leisure pursuits of the upper classes, incidences of broken sleep and habits of bed-sharing'.[54] However, Ekirch's most important finding is the so-called 'segmented sleep' or bimodal sleep, which he describes as 'the age-old pattern of "first" and "second" sleep'.[55] The scholar found evidence in a wide variety of sources that until the close of the early modern period, 'people on most evenings experienced two major intervals of sleep bridged by up to an hour or more of quiet wakefulness'.[56] According to him, this was not something people were worried about; on the contrary even, this routine was considered common, and people used this time as a precious opportunity for leisure, contemplation and prayer. Gerrit Verhoeven recently questioned this theory at least for the late modern period, with historical evidence from eighteenth-century criminal records of the local criminal court in Antwerp. Contrary to Ekirch's hypotheses, Verhoeven found that most eighteenth-century Antwerp residents slept fewer hours than first expected, slumbered in a monophasic way (and were not familiar with a bimodal sleep pattern) and rarely if ever took a nap during the day.[57] The author therefore suggested that the transition from pre-modern (two-phase) to modern (single-phase) sleep patterns was probably situated in the later Middle Ages or Renaissance rather than the eighteenth or nineteenth century.[58] But detailed research on this earlier period is unfortunately lacking.

Whether people's sleep was interrupted sometime at night or not, it was still credited by many contemporary writers such as the sixteenth-century Dutch physicist Levinus Lemnius (1505–1568) as a physical and psychological medicine.[59] Quiet, restful sleep was considered to be healing for body and mind. Sleep was considered one of the six 'non-natural things' in the theory of Greek physician Claudius Galen that could have benefitted or harmed the health of an individual 'depending on their proper or improper applications'.[60] The works of Galen were revitalised during the Renaissance period, because they fitted well into a general and growing concern for health and longevity. The Galenic treatises and other works by classical medical authors such as Hippocrates and Aristotle were printed in Latin translation, and some treatises were even translated into the vernacular and therefore accessible to a wide readership.[61] All authors of medical treatises agreed that it was of the utmost importance to ensure a good and tranquil sleep. And this should take place in a designated and suitably equipped room. Sixteenth-century English physician William Bullein, for example, advised that the chamber must be 'clean, pleasant smelling and pleasing to the sight'.[62] Heavy odours or vapours and noise had to be minimised, because that would disturb the senses and thus a good night's sleep. As some treatises such as those by Alberti and Palladio emphasised, the disturbing smells and smoke originated in kitchens, referring to the dirt and discomfort of the room,[63] this might have been an important reason why people (who had enough room) were less likely to sleep in their kitchen. What Ekirch did not discuss, however, but what cannot be ignored in a study of bedtime rituals and sleeping culture either, is the spatial context of sleep. Perhaps the scholar found it too hazardous to speak of a true sleeping environment in a period when people could sleep almost anywhere in the house.

Many authors have already stated that beds could be placed almost anywhere in the house and that people often had more than one bed.[64] The wealthier one was, the more beds one had. The mean number of beds per household was always higher in the wealthiest households (though there was also a larger variation in this social class, with households owning no fewer than thirty beds, and others 'merely' owned eight). Furthermore, we see a general rise in the mean number of beds per household throughout the entire sixteenth century. Historian Mark Overton and his team noticed a similar rise in the level of bed ownership in Kent and Cornwall. They noted that the average number of beds per household rose during the seventeenth century.[65] From this, they deduced that either more servants were living in especially the wealthier households or that bed sharing by the members of a household (or by staff, children and lodgers) was becoming less common – again especially, or first, in

Table 7. Ratios of Beds in Rooms

ROOM	RATIO 1438–1444	RATIO 1450–1510	RATIO 1528–1549	RATIO 1559–1574	RATIO 1584–1600
BACK ROOM	1.4	1.3	1.7	1.6	1.5
DINING ROOM	0	1.2	1.7	1.08	
FRONT ROOM	1.6	1.9	1.4	1.7	2.8
KITCHEN	0.1	0.2	0.4	0.5	0.2
ROOM	1.7	1.5	1.9	1.8	1.8
SALETTE				0	0.5

Source: Database of inventories © IB, JDG & IS

the wealthier households.[66] The latter already suggests a tendency towards personal-isation or individualisation in early modern bed culture.

Looking at the spread of beds and bedding throughout dwellings (table 7), apart from specifically labelled bedrooms or *slaapcamere*, back rooms, front rooms, dining rooms and 'rooms' yielded high ratios – and so were preferred places to sleep – throughout the sixteenth century. So beds were nearly everywhere. The ratios in the table indicate the likelihood to discover beds in these rooms – the higher this number is above one, the more likely it was that one or more beds were found there.

In some rooms, however, it was unlikely that people would have put themselves to rest; these rooms were service rooms such as pantries, butteries, *garderobes* and cellars (only yielding ratios between 0 and 0.2), shops and workshops (ratios around 0), floors (ratios between 0 and 0.3) and even kitchens. So if these rooms were present in a house, it was unlikely that they would have contained a bed; thus, these were not likely places where people would sleep.

Rooms where beds were definitely present were bedrooms (fig. 12). In our samples, we found a total of twenty-six bedrooms; two inventories that mention this room label twice, each time with a distinction according to size (large bedroom and small bedroom). Looking at graph 6 below, the room label seems most in use in the second part of the sixteenth century. However, the frequency of the room label *slaapcamere* must be put in perspective, because it represents only twenty-six occurrences out of a total of 1,654 individual rooms (with or without a particular label). So it means that the room label was not commonly used by appraisers, suggesting that separating the act of sleeping in a separate room was not really fully established yet (or at least not in every household or social layer).

Fig. 12. 'The Great Bed of Ware', carved oak bed, probably from Ware, Hertfordshire, UK, about 1590. © Victoria and Albert Museum, London

Graph 6. Absolute Number of Bedrooms per Sample Period

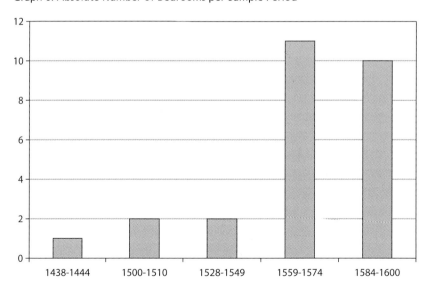

Source: Database of inventories © IB, JDG & IS

Graph 7. Inventories with Room Label *slaapcamere* per Social Group

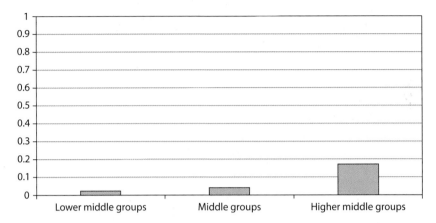

Source: Database of inventories © IB, JDG & IS

Furthermore, bedrooms were predominantly found in the larger houses of the more wealthy middle groups of Bruges society, suggesting that the availability of space was a decisive factor (graph 7).

Canon Jacob Vrombert's house (1502) contained no fewer than eight rooms, of which two were labelled *slaapcamere*: 'slaapcamere van den meester' and 'cleene slaapcamere'.[67] These were certainly not the only rooms in his house where beds were located. The appraisers found another dressed bed with curtains (probably a fixed bed or alcove) in the dining room as well, and one in the room of the servant girl. The smaller house of bonnet maker Stevin Sremont (1541)[68] contained a sleeping room as well, but here again it was not the only room where beds were located. Also his front room contained a bed, as well as his back room. François Claissone's inventory (1559)[69] was full of beds. His sleeping room contained only one well-made *ledikant*, or bedstead, and a smaller *lysecoetske* probably for children or infants, but the four rooms upstairs also contained at least one bed each, as did the front room downstairs. So bedrooms were probably not identified as such simply because they contained a bed and not even because they contained a well-dressed bed, because other rooms in the same households could have contained such a furnished bed as well. However, what these sleeping rooms with beds distinguished from other rooms with beds is the fact that these rooms were used by specific people. So not only the amount and the quality of the bed sheets, the bed curtains and the mattresses reflected the social status of its users, but also the room itself was dressed in such a way that the appraisers were capable of distinguishing a sleeping room from another room with beds.

Interestingly, contrary to what the room label would have us believe, the bedrooms were not at all equipped just with a bed and its appurtenances. Indeed, most of these bedrooms were dressed with chairs, tables, lecterns, sofa chairs, storage furniture, paintings, mirrors and pieces of clothing as well, suggesting complementary household functions of dressing, study, leisure, sociability and conviviality all in the same room. Why were they performed in a room other than the dining room or front room? And how can this all link with social culture in this period and with the tendency of people to withdraw (if possible) from the kitchen to sleep?

In the pre-modern period, it was common for people to sleep together either in separate beds all positioned in the vicinity of the same fireplace or even in the same bed.[70] Servants, for example, were often put to rest in the same room as their employers. In Bruges, we see that the mean number of beds per household increased during the sixteenth century, especially in the wealthier households, suggesting that bed sharing by the members of a household was becoming less common. Interestingly, in contrast to unlabelled or otherwise labelled rooms with beds, the mean number of beds in bedrooms was much lower (1.47 in bedrooms versus 3.2 in other types of rooms), suggesting that sleepers in bedrooms were allowed more 'privacy' compared to sleepers in the other rooms. So although the bed in the bedroom could still be used by more than one sleeper,[71] it was not likely to be accompanied by other beds used by servants, visitors or other family members.

The results suggest that bedrooms had a predominantly private character, but were also equipped to do other activities than just sleeping. Indeed, most of these rooms contained elaborate seating furniture such as chairs and benches and tables as well. Jan Antheunis even had a *verkeerberd*, or board game, somewhere near the fireplace and in the vicinity of the two sofa chairs.[72] Some bedrooms housed a *glazenberd*, or glass cupboard, full of glasses and a *tinschaprade*, or a pewter cabinet with several types of pewter dishes, wash basins and a salt cellar, all ready to use in a convivial and sociable context. The bedroom of Stevin Sremont (1541), for example, housed no fewer than three *lysen*, or large benches, and two tables.[73] It all hints at a sociable character of bedrooms showing similarities with the bedroom, or *camera*, in many Italian Renaissance instances of *case*, which was also renowned for its role in the domestic sociability of the house, because it was equipped and often used to entertain friends and important guests or even as a place to discuss business matters.[74] In contrast to the reception room, or the *sala* or *portego*, the *camera* was only accessible by invitation, so the host could decide if and when and for whom this room was made semi-public or semi-private. So instead of being a strictly private space, it was rather a socially exclusive room.

Furthermore, most Bruges bedrooms not only housed seating furniture and tables but were also furnished with paintings, textiles and mirrors. Indeed, most bedrooms in our sample contained at least one devotional object, be it a statuette, holy water font, image or painting. The bedroom of François Claissone (1559),[75] for example, was decorated with a painting and a crystal (*cristalijn*) mirror, which was a highly appreciated novelty in the sixteenth-century domestic interior. The painting was positioned on the cupboard, probably situated near the well-furnished bedstead. The bedroom of Jan Atheunis (1560),[76] was decorated with a mirror and its pavilion as well, complemented with some *bescreven cleeden*, or canvas paintings, and a devotional statue of Jesus Christ. The smaller and humbler bedroom of innkeeper Jan Bleys (1585),[77] was provided with two paintings, of which one depicted the Virgin Mary. These decorative and often also devotional objects were not only intended for the eyes of visitors but also fulfilled an important role in the private devotion and perhaps even in the sleeping rituals of the bedroom users as well.[78]

In the second part of this book, we will see that paintings in sixteenth-century Bruges fitted within a strong devotional culture. Devotional paintings and statuettes in bedrooms – and often very near or even *in* the bed – were indeed ideal charms or amulets to ward off evil spirits and misfortune from the chamber and the area around the bed and to put sleepers under the protection of Jesus, Mary or any other saint. All kinds of saints painted in biblical scenes protected the couple or the person in the bed or could ensure that the marriage was quickly fruitful. Devotional images were also used as a sort of prayer book, or *Andachtsbild*, for people when they were performing their evening or morning devotions. Gleaned from the objects, it would appear that bedrooms were also ideal places for private worship and devotional practices.

Other objects underline this exclusive and personal aspect of the character of a bedroom's interior even more; people often kept some of the most valuable furnishings and emotionally laden items in their bedrooms (fig. 13).[79] Not only did the marital bed itself often embody a strong symbolic value, symbolising the matrimonial union between the couple and representing the wealth of the household,[80] but other objects could have had a place in the intimate, personal world of the owner as well. Canon Jacob Vrombert (1502),[81] for example, had his personal sword rack in his master's bedroom and his ceremonial clothes in the adjoining small bedroom,

Fig. 13. In the bed of the abbot a small diptych is hanging as a charm to ward off all evil. Portrait of Abbot Christiaan de Hondt, Master of 1499, c. 1500, Panel, 30 x 14 cm, Antwerp, © Royal Museum of Fine Arts, www.artinflanders.be

while Achilles Van Den Berghe (1567)[82] even had his own portrait in his bedroom. François Claissone (1559)[83] kept a small chest covered in leather with personal accessories in his sleeping room, and Jan Bleauvoet[84] and his wife (1563) had their box with letters and their personal jewellery stored there.

Conclusions

The chairs, tables, paintings, hearth equipment, books, games and cupboards that were found in bedrooms point to activities people residing in these rooms immersed themselves in during the evening, at night or during the day; these activities included reading and leisure or prayer and contemplation in all calmness and tranquillity, far removed from the hustle and bustle of the household. The presence of candles and chandeliers, but also of fireplaces and burners, would have made it easier and more comfortable to perform these activities, though sixteenth-century physician Andrew Borde warned people that 'while waiting for bedtime one should not stand or sit too close to the fire as its heat dried the blood and made stiff the nerves and joints of man'.[85] Bedrooms were not as private as we understand them today; they were 'public' to a limited extent: a social space restricted to the householder's family and close circle of intimate friends and visitors.[86] Indeed, it was probably exactly this seemingly private character of the bedroom that automatically created a certain distance from 'others' and from other rooms. Furthermore, and perhaps more importantly, sleepers in bedrooms had more chance of getting their revitalising and much-needed sleep in a quiet and peaceful environment.

Similarities and Differences: The Broader Picture

'Simple dichotomies like "frontstage" and "backstage" or "public" and "private" are too crude to capture the usages of rooms and their contents'.[87] Bedrooms, for example, blurred such distinctions, because they were both a private place for sleeping and praying and a semi-public place where a select number of guests could be entertained. Thresholds were not only constructed between the outside of the city and the inside of the home, but also between spaces – between the commercial spaces of shop or workshop and the home, but also within the domestic living space itself. In the more spacious houses, social boundaries were raised between particular rooms: some rooms were not accessible to everyone or at any time of the day. The bedroom, *contoor* and *salette*, for example, were only accessible on certain occasions and for certain people. So we are more inclined to speak of a 'social specialisation' of spaces than of a 'functional specialisation', and of a 'differentiation' of functions across spaces. But of course, much depended on the size of the dwelling and the amount of available space. Wealthier households could easily rearrange their domestic environment in such a way that some daily functions were transferred to other spaces. The act of sleeping in larger households was transferred to a bedroom, storage to service rooms and large and more formal sociable events to the dining room or *salette*.

Interestingly, if more space was available, domestic space could be used to structure household practices according to their everyday or exceptional character, and as such, a hierarchy was created between different rooms in the more spacious dwellings. This was certainly the case for sociable practices; the kitchen clearly functioned as a space for everyday conviviality, whereas the dining room and later the *salette* were ranked as the most suitable rooms for exceptional convivial activities. A room often forgotten in this hierarchy is the bedroom. If set apart from the other rooms, it was characterised as a space for resting, private leisure and private devotion but also for sociability in a limited group. It was certainly one of the most valuable rooms in terms of the financial value of the objects located there. Not only did people often use their bedrooms to store precious items such as jewellery, money and important documents, the bed furniture in itself was very costly, and the sheets, blankets, cushions and mattresses were also worth quite a lot of money.[88]

PART 2

DOMESTIC OBJECTS IN CONTEXT

INTRODUCTION

The first part of the book was devoted to the spatial context in which the domestic material culture was set. Emphasis was put on the relationship between people and spaces, objects mainly figured as parameters to uncover the daily activities that were performed in different kinds of domestic spaces. The second part of the book examines the associations of household objects and domestic activities by putting these objects in their original use context. In the Bruges inventories, a wide range of objects was listed, relating to all kinds of domestic activities, responding to household needs, and they were obtained locally or from a distance and employing diverse technologies.

The field of material culture research – and more specifically research on the material culture of the home – has benefitted greatly from the different 'turns' the disciplines across the humanities have experienced throughout the last few decades: the 'material turn', with its attention to the 'materiality' of things and the 'spatial turn', in which 'spatiality' was 'simultaneously a social product (or outcome) and a shaping force (or medium) in social life' (discussed in the general introduction).[1] The volume *Everyday Objects*, published in 2010 by Richardson and Hamling, has proven seminal in foregrounding the study of the materiality of household objects.[2] *Everyday Objects* could even be considered a strong representative of this new strand of scholarship, taking the first steps in combining both 'turns' by relating objects, spaces and people to one another and connecting individuals to wider social and cultural events through their environment of materiality, a new kind of 'turn' that was already instigated by scholars writing about city palaces in Renaissance Italy.[3] The authors of *Everyday Objects* proposed an integrated and multidisciplinary approach characterized by a specific methodological interest in the use of artefacts as source materials, and especially aimed towards a type of historical analysis that gives as much space to materiality as has previously been given to economic or political forces, kinship or gender.[4]

Although the study of everyday life generated some strain on existing sources and methodologies in history and historiography, the methodological gaze did not go to artefacts and objects as sources alone; the value of archival documents to uncover the dialectic relationship between the spatial context and the meaning of objects did not entirely lose attention either. Some years before the publication of *Everyday Objects*, Evans already argued that probate inventories would 'easily' allow research on the functions and multiple meanings of objects.[5]

In this part of the book, we intend to revalue the use of archival sources to study domestic culture by focusing on the textual assemblages of objects in inventories to deduce cultures of use.[6] Some objects – for instance a 'chimney cloth' – betray their spatial and contextual arrangement in a discursive way, while other objects are sporadically linked to specific places such as the linen in the wardrobe, the candlesticks on the chimney mantle, armour and weapons in large chests, washing basins and bathtubs in specific bathing ensembles linked to the kitchen. Yet, most importantly, even the mass of unlocated objects in such room-by-room listings can be approached in a spatial way by taking the 'word distance' between the objects into account. Concretely, this means that we can deduce the location of objects in a particular room – their relation towards each other and thus their spatial context – by assessing the sequence of the objects listed in that same room. Of course, to do this for a broad data sample, the methodology necessitates a complex data architecture designed for taking into account the specificities of the sources and to ensure that all the bits and pieces of information could be captured. It is necessary, therefore, not only to insert the objects mentioned in each inventory into a database but also to take into account their material typologies and their position in the lists as a whole. To achieve this, only inventories that list the material culture in a systematic room-by-room approach were included for this part of the research.

In the following chapters, particular object clusters are discussed: in the first chapter, attention goes to panel and canvas paintings; in the second chapter, the main role is played by household textiles, decorative textiles, seating and sleeping furniture. All these objects were both part of an increasing spectrum of decorative and ornamental furnishings and of an ever more varied array of utilitarian objects and furniture that was put to use in people's houses.

DEVOTION ON DISPLAY?
PAINTINGS IN DOMESTIC INTERIORS

Introduction

On 3 May 1583, Joncvrouw Petronella Heve, widow of a former alderman and governor of the Bogardenschool,[1] Remeeus Ommejaeghere, died from effects of the plague.[2] Petronella had clearly outlived her second husband, who had died several years before, and her estate was managed by their eldest son, Jacob Ommejaeghere. The estate refers to grandchildren as well, so Petronella was probably old when she died. Except for some jewellery, crystal buttons and a silver rattle, which were already donated to Jacob and his children, all the household goods were publicly sold by stockholder Guillaume Bibau. But the inventory of Petronella's estate was accompanied by her last will and testament. Along with his children and his natural sister Cathelijne, Jacob inherited the major part of the property. His other sibling, his half-sister Jozijne de la Faulx, born to a previous marriage with Loys de la Faulx,[3] inherited far less. Sums of money as well as objects such as pieces of garment were bequeathed to kith and kin. But one particular object immediately attracts the eye: an object whose value was not expressed in money, but which was bequeathed with the explicit wish that it stay in the family. A *tafereel, daer zy inne gheschildert staet*, or a painting in which the deceased was depicted, was bequeathed to Petronella's eldest son Jacob, who in turn passed it on to his eldest child after his death. The painting was not sold publicly by the stockholder, but became an heirloom, proving the emotional and communicative value of this decorative object.

That paintings were important in Petronella's life (not only at home but also in church) is also proven by the family portrait that – to this day – hangs in the Church of Our Lady in Bruges, attributed to Bruges painter Pieter Pourbus by art historians Weale and d'Hulst. The painting has survived the test of time and was, in due course, donated to the church in Bruges (fig. 14).[4] For the first time, the person who had left this estate was given a face.

Fig. 14. Left and right panels of the altar-piece of Remi Ommejaeghere and Petronella Herve, Pieter Pourbus, 16th Century, oil on panel, © Bruges Church of Our Lady, www.artinflanders.be

The painting is described by Pourbus specialist Paul Huvenne as part of a founder portrait, meant to serve as an altarpiece in church. It was probably part of a triptych (although the central panel is missing) – with Petronella and their daughters on one wing and husband Remeeus and their sons depicted on the other wing, without any patron saints.[5] Petronella is depicted in the company of her three daughters, of whom we only know Cathelijne and Jozyne from their mother's inventory and will; Remeeus is portrayed together with three sons, of whom their eldest, Jacob, was probably positioned right behind his father. Two of the three sons and one daughter are depicted as if they are looking directly towards the viewer; whereas the eldest son, Jacob, and the other two daughters follow the gaze of their parents to what is depicted on the central panel. Perhaps these children were still alive, like their parents, when the painting was done? We know for certain that Jacob, Cathelyne and Jozijne were still alive when their mother died. The other children were not mentioned in Petronella's will – probably because they had already died at the time it was created.

From her inventory, we know that Petronella owned no fewer than eighteen paintings, a statue of Our Lady and an unspecified alabaster statue. These paintings were probably intended for display at home, shown and also used within a certain social and spatial context. What exactly was the use value, function and location of these paintings and statues in Petronella's house? What do we actually know about the purpose of images (panel paintings, painted canvases and prints alike) within the setting of a late medieval dwelling? And to what extent was the situation in Bruges different from that in neighbouring Antwerp?

In historiography, and especially for the southern Low Countries in the late medieval and early modern period, research has focused mainly on how many paintings certain social groups were willing or able to acquire (or at least for particular urban contexts such as Antwerp) and where, how and from whom they could buy these goods. Yet we are still in the dark as to *why* these images were bought or passed on from generation to generation, as was the case with Petronella Heve's portrait (i.e. the desire for goods that lay behind demand),[6] how they were appropriated and used by citizens of all sorts and how displaying certain images related to social and cultural practices. As Colum Hourihane summarises the main argument of the chapter by Thomas Dale, 'the meaning of these works [of art] comes not from their placement within a category but from understanding their purpose and how they worked with other media and objects'.[7] Studying paintings from this new angle, we argue not to follow the lines of the 'old debates' or what Michael North and David Ormrod described in the 1980s as 'the earlier formalist and connoisseurial approaches to the discipline',[8] 'dominated by assessment of success in technique, quality and aesthetics as well as a concern with the maker's biography and oeuvre'.[9] A detailed assessment of the nature and quality of form, technique and style as well as the meaning of iconography is certainly necessary,[10] but we aspire to go further down the line of framing contemporary paintings in their original context, so transcending the interest in the business of art, the dynamics between production and consumption, and the experience of making, buying and selling.[11] This of course does not mean that we lose sight of the supply side, because there is an important interaction between supply and demand. However, the demand side of the art market in Bruges was only rarely the subject of research, though the recently published volume on Pieter Pourbus and fellow sixteenth-century painters working and living in Bruges already offers a little more insight into the impact of supply-side evolutions on the demand and possession of paintings.[12] Brecht Dewilde's study in this volume is the only exception to the rule, though his study of the ownership of art was only a by-product of his research on the Claeissens painter family.[13] Most attention is still paid to the workshop practices of painters and to the mechanisms of the art trade.[14] It is certainly worthwhile then to consider ownership patterns of these workshops' potential clients; in other words, we will focus on private ownership of paintings, not on the fraternities, guilds or religious institutions that were also valuable clients. An important side note to this is that our research is based on inventories, which means that at least some of the paintings could be in family possession for generations (such as the portrait of Petronella), so iconographic preferences may be somewhat distorted.

In this book, we consider images as pieces of material culture that were constantly in action; – in interactions between individuals and objects, objects and spaces and between objects themselves. In this chapter, we will confront the material characteristics of the images we find in the inventories with wider social and cultural practices.[15] Indeed, the attitude of users[16] towards images as decorative objects and their role in the *performative* space of the dwelling may uncover underlying socially and culturally driven motivations for consuming these particular decorative objects.

Fifteenth-century paintings in private ownership have already long been situated in the context of either churches or private religious practice.[17] Following the principles of the *Devotio Moderna* – promoting a type of affective piety that had become popular in vernacular as well as Latin devotional literature – private, often solitary, devotion within the home became widespread.[18] Domestic space was customised for religious purposes, and the production of devotional objects such as prayer books, books of hours and rosaries increased 'the capacity of ordinary people to create a devout visual and even aural environment in their own homes, should they wish to do so'.[19] But panel paintings were in general rather expensive, because most were painted on commission. However, scholars such as James Bloom, Filip Vermeylen, Maximiliaan Martens, Carolien De Staelen and Dan Ewing observed a gradual change in the production and consumption of paintings from the end of the fifteenth century onwards; an increasingly higher production of paintings was intended for a larger, open and more anonymous market.[20] Furthermore, a new type of consumer emerged at the end of the sixteenth and in the course of the seventeenth century, a new elitist and intellectual consumer, or a *collector-connoisseur*, who acted as a patron and appreciated and measured art as part of a collection.[21] So for some people, the meaning and function of art must have changed. Although both changes were most visible and most tangible in Antwerp[22] – in contrast to the Bruges art market, the Antwerp market was characterised by its centre-specific manufacturing and marketing conditions[23] – art historians such as Maximiliaan Martens and Maryan Ainsworth say that the Bruges guild of St. Luke (the guild of the *image-makers* that joined panel and cloth painters, mirror makers and saddlers) changed its commercial strategy at the end of the fifteenth century as well and even more explicitly during the course of the sixteenth century, due to the changing market equilibrium.[24] Instead of consciously limiting speculative and serialised production, the guild adopted a more lenient stance towards free market sales as more and possibly cheaper paintings were unloaded on the open market.[25] More-over, it was specified by the city aldermen in a charter of 1466 that not only were panel painters allowed more space to sell their products, but also cloth painters, whose cheaper work on canvas or linen was first and foremost intended for a larger and more anonymous market, were officially allowed to display and sell their work in public. Although these measures for the most part legalised common practice – canvas painters had already been employed in Bruges for a longer period of time[26] – it might also indicate an increased demand for canvas paintings and a gradual change in the consumption behaviour of citizens.[27] A wide range of artistic and ma-terial quality of such objects that came on the market suggests, according to Jeanne Nuechterlein, that a broad cross section of society used them.[28]

In the first part of the sixteenth century, the Bruges art market was relatively comparable to the Antwerp one: a relatively high number of painters were active in Bruges, and many of them produced both for the local open market and for export to the Iberian peninsula.[29] Others were active in producing paintings ordered by the many urban and religious institutions, brotherhoods and guilds that were impor-tant buyers of art, certainly in this first half of the sixteenth century.[30] In the second half of the sixteenth century, the effect of the expansion of the Antwerp art market, combined with periods of economic downfall, caused a drop in demand from insti-tutions. Fewer painters were active in Bruges, and an increasing number of Antwerp paintings were sold in Bruges as well. Some workshops, such as the Claessens work-shop, still held an important part of the market, but had to specialise in certain gen-res to do so.[31] However, as we will see in this chapter, over the long run and generally speaking, the number of households owning paintings and the number of paintings per interior were relatively stable throughout the sixteenth century. So the market changed, but the ownership of paintings did not seem to have changed along with it. Or were there more subtle shifts that were characteristic of the Bruges context?

What's in a Name?

Using probate inventories to study the material characteristics and use value of im-ages has to be done with caution. On the one hand, there is the notorious *word-mat-ter* problem, a problem concerning the interpretation of terminology that each researcher in the field of material culture studies is faced with.[32] Spanish merchant Fernando de Castere and his wife, for example, owned five paintings, each of them labelled by the appraiser as *tafereel*.[33] In the inventory of 1568, they were classified not by the name of the painter or artist, but by the support or the medium. The term *tafereel* is probably derived from the Middle Dutch word *tafele*, meaning a wooden tablet or a long, thin, flat piece of timber, and therefore presumably refers to the wooden support of a panel painting.[34] *Een tafereelkin met de figuere van besitteghe*, or a portrait of the owner of the inventoried items, could be illustrative. However, the precise meaning of the term *tafereel* is not straightforward at all times and could sometimes confusingly refer to a wooden or polychrome retable as well. Retables were indeed sculpted reliefs made from a wooden tablet. Equally problematic is the term *beilde* and the French word *image*, primarily found in the fifteenth-century sample. Both terms may refer to any type of decorative item, be it a statuette, a painting or a retable. References to the objects' material make-up do not appear frequently, but sometimes it was noted that the *beilde* was framed in a wooden *cassyn*, or frame. In those instances, we may safely label these objects as paintings. The distinction between a crucifix or a painting of the Crucifixion was not always easy to draw either, but we will argue that, in most cases, a *crusifixe* refers to the sculptured religious cross instead of the painted image.

Wooden panels (or *tafelen* or *berderen*) were not the only media depicting painted images. Cloth or canvas paintings were produced by that other important branch of the guild of the image-makers, the cloth painters, called *cleerscrivers* in Bruges. In a charter of 1466, the city aldermen stated that cloth painters – whose cheaper work on canvas or linen was mainly intended for a larger, anonymous market – were allowed more space to sell their products and to display and sell their work in public.[35] In the inventories, cloth paintings were described in two different ways: *bescreven cleed*, literally 'painted cloth,' referring to the name of the guild and their profession, or *tafereel up douck*, 'painting on cloth,' referring mainly to the medium of the painted image, such as linen or canvas. A note of caution is due here, because it is often difficult to recognise the type of support of the registered paintings from the scant amount of detail that was given. Only when the painting is literally described as *tafereel up doeck* or *beschreven cleedt* do we know for sure that the support is canvas or cloth.[36] Because of price and size differences between wooden panel paintings and cloth paintings, it may be assumed that in most cases, appraisers would have clearly distinguished between canvas and panel paintings. Inventories were, after all, first and foremost drafted to provide an overview of the resale values of former household goods.

Throughout the sixteenth century, the terminology used to refer to a painting did not change much. The terms *tafereel* and *berd* used for panel paintings, *beilde* for paintings and statuettes, and *bescreven cleed* or *tafereel up douck* for cloth paintings continued to be commonly used in all types of inventories. In contrast to the nomenclature used in Antwerp documents, the concept of *schilderie*, referring to a wooden panel (*schild*) as well as to the technique of painting, did not occur in the Bruges sample.[37] The French term *image* was used only occasionally in the sixteenth-century sample, but seems to have prevailed especially in the fifteenth century. This was due to the fact that the documents of the mid-fifteenth-century sample (particularly the inventories of the burghers of illegitimate birth) were written in French. According to the *Dictionnaire du Moyen Français*,[38] *image* means 'apparence d'une personne, qui la rend reconnaissable', or a picture of a person who is recognisable, or more specifically 'représentation d'une divinité'. The few *images* that were enlisted in the mid-fifteenth-century sample indeed exclusively depicted the Virgin Mary.

Appraisers often used the adjectives *cleen*, or small, and *groot*, or large, to describe the size and length of paintings, but the suffix *–kin* was even more commonly used to indicate smaller paintings. An evolution in size throughout the sixteenth century cannot be easily discerned from the available source material. Both large and small paintings are found in each sample period and in every social class, though the suffix *–kin* is more often used than the reference to a 'large' work.

One of the consequences of the genesis of the source material is that certain objects were not mentioned because of their low intrinsic and low resale value, whereas others received a more than detailed description. Prints are a common example of this. These objects were cheap and of low quality and therefore simply not worth mentioning, and certainly not in great detail. Their existence is, however, apparent from certain contemporary paintings.[39] In contrast, paintings of wealthier citizens were more likely to be described in greater detail.[40] Appraisers working in wealthier households possibly needed to differentiate more between objects of the same type, because of the often larger number of paintings and the often greater variety of locations where the items may have been kept. But other more financially and commercially inspired motives may have played an equally important role as well.

The few price data we have for paintings in Bruges were not found in the inventories but in the account book of *stochoudere*, or second-hand dealer, Guillaume Bibau, who wrote down the prices and buyers of all the second-hand goods he sold for each estate between 1567 and 1568.[41] Bibau was one of the four official second-hand dealers of Bruges in this period.[42] In his account book, every resale value of each household object originating from an estate of deceased citizens (153 estates for that period) was set out in great detail. In this respect, the prices in his book are the *resale* values of goods (like in the inventories) and not the original prices of new, unused products. Browsing through the resale accounts, a range of household objects can be recognised, ranging from pewter cutlery and silver dishes to wooden beds, wardrobes and innumerable pieces of luxurious or worn-out clothing. Some pieces of artwork, such as mirrors, statuettes of Mary and paintings were sold as well, covering different sizes and diverse subject themes. Most of the *taferelen*, however, were not further specified and no further details were given except for their resale values. Of the more than forty-nine paintings (forty-nine different entries, but more paintings in number) that were mentioned in Bibau's account book, only seven were mentioned by theme: 'Suzanna', two banquet scenes (or Last Suppers?), the mythological figure of 'Pyramus', 'Saint Magdalene', a Crucifixion scene and 'the Adoration of the Magi'. Interestingly, the data from the Bibau's account book indicate a correlation between the level of detail in the description of the painting and its resale price.[43] In the commercially oriented case of the *stochoudere*, the incentive to describe more highly valued and higher-quality paintings more accurately must have been significantly high.

Possessing Paintings in Fifteenth- and Sixteenth-Century Bruges

In the fifteenth century, Bruges was 'a really exceptional center since it combined the presence of a court with that of a rich commercial bourgeoisie, an exceptionally large community of foreign merchants, and an extraordinarily well-to-do and broad middle class'.[44] But the Burgundian dukes left the city at the end of the fifteenth century and relocated their court to Malines and Brussels; many foreign nations left the city in the course of the sixteenth century in search of better prospects in the city of Antwerp, and many artisans and local merchants followed in their wake.[45] Nevertheless, a certain continuity of local art patronage remained viable among elites and institutions, and from the second part of the fifteenth century, even among the middling groups of society. Moreover, as will be discussed later, the nation of the Castilians, the largest of the foreign nations in Bruges in the sixteenth century, kept a foothold in the city until well into the seventeenth century as well. These

Graph 8. Inventories with Paintings per Sample Period and Social Group

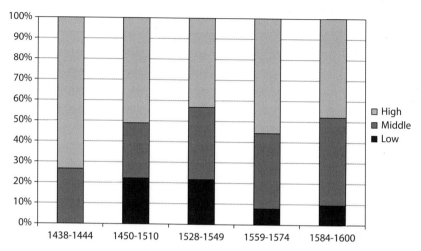

Source: Database of inventories © IB, JDG & IS

international merchants, most of whom had already lived in Bruges for generations, converted a large part of their productive capital into cultural capital. So local luxury industries were expected to last for another certain period of time because of a relatively strong local market and the concentration of capital in the hands of the upper middle classes, even in a city past its prime.[46]

In the inventories, there are few images in the sample from the first half of the fifteenth century. As we discussed earlier, burghers of illegitimate birth were in general relatively poor (situated in the lower social strata of Bruges society), and only a few wealthier households were included in the sample. The few *images* that were mentioned in these inventories were indeed mainly owned by the small number of wealthier people; the *ymaige de nostre dame* or the painting of Our Lady, for example, was owned by the relatively wealthy single man Hannequin Rugheman (1439).[47]

Graph 8 shows an overview of the number of inventories of households as a percentage that have at least one painting.

For this early fifteenth-century sample, it is not surprising that no other types of paintings or other decorative objects were mentioned, not even in the wealthier inventories. The production and commercialisation of the cheaper canvas paintings was probably still limited by the craft at that time and most panel paintings were produced on commission, hence especially consumed by an elite and well-to-do audience.[48]

In the second sample period (1450–1510), paintings were found in the estates of all three social groups; even among the lowest social group about 30 per cent of the estates included at least one painting. The same more or less holds true for the first sample period of the sixteenth century (1528–1549), with a slight increase in estates with images in the middle groups. The increase in the ownership of artwork during the second sample period could be explained by the higher production of cheaper ready-made images. The 1440s, 1450s and 1460s marked the apex of the attraction of immigrant artisans to the Bruges labour market, with a rise in the number of new masters entering the Bruges guild of painters in the fifteenth century.[49] Most of the new masters were immigrants, among them some of the most famous talents such as Petrus Christus and later Ambrosius Benson.[50] Both were very active in the production of especially standardized devotional images.[51]

Comparing the data of the 1450–1510 and the 1528–1549 samples with the samples of the second and last part of the sixteenth century, it is striking that the percentage of estates with images of the lowest social group decreases, whereas the share of the middling groups and higher middling groups slightly increases. The difference in ownership patterns between the social groups tends to be much larger in the fourth sample period, suggesting a kind of social polarisation, an effect of the economic situation in the city. The 1550s and the 1560s especially were characterised by inflation and struggling luxury industries, leading to an economic contraction phase that was felt particularly keenly by the lower social groups of society.[52] It is not surprising then that these groups chose to invest their already shrunken budgets elsewhere or preferred to buy cheap prints instead of panel or canvas paintings.

Our data – even though they do not include guild, governmental and religious institutions – suggest that the city of Bruges was, for a long time, still able to maintain a decent clientele for painters throughout the sixteenth century. Furthermore, the ownership of paintings was certainly not a prerogative of the more wealthier social groups alone. Even some people of the lower middle groups were able and willing to own paintings that were, commercially speaking, valuable enough to be documented by the appraiser. But how many paintings did people own on average? To what extent can we see these social differences in the average number of paintings people owned?

In table 8, we calculated the mean number of paintings for each social group per sample period. The first sample period (1438–1444) is not part of this calculation, because the table focusses on the sixteenth century. The most interesting aspect of this table is that the average numbers per social group for the first sample periods in

Table 8. Average Number of Paintings per Household per Social Group (inventories with paintings; n = 228)

SAMPLE PERIOD	LOWER MIDDLING GROUPS	MIDDLING GROUPS	HIGHER MIDDLING GROUPS
1450–1510	3	2.5	3.5
1528–1549	1.4	2.2	2.4
1559–1574	1.7	1.96	4
1584–1600	1.7	3.4	10.2

Source: Database of inventories © IB, JDG & IS

Table 9. Weighted Average of Paintings per Household (total number of inventories; n = 502)

SAMPLE PERIOD	WEIGHTED AVERAGE
1450–1510	2.86
1528–1549	2.05
1559–1574	2.21
1584–1600	3.43

Source: Database of inventories © IB, JDG & IS

the table did not differ much. But further on in the century, however, these proportions change slightly; the wealthier social groups on average owned more paintings than the lower social strata, and the differences increase towards the end of the sixteenth century.

To have a global picture of the average number of paintings inventory holders owned, we calculated the weighted mean for each sample period, taking the weight of each social group in the total number of estates per sample period into account. Table 9 represents the weighted mean number of paintings for each sample period. The data suggest a slight increase in the mean number of paintings per household throughout the period, even though the differences between the sample periods are not very large.

Admittedly, whether these mean numbers are low, mediocre or high can only be examined by making a comparison with other cities, such as the well-documented city of Antwerp. Because it is not always clear how authors have calculated their mean numbers of paintings per household, caution is needed when comparing numbers.

For the period from 1532 to 1567, Maximiliaan Martens and Natasja Peeters calculated an average number of 5.2 paintings per Antwerp inventory (n=415).[53] The social composition of their inventory sample was different from ours – Martens and Peeters's Antwerp sample was composed of *arresten*, or economic confiscations, and not of the wealthier post-mortem inventories and confiscation records – which makes it even more interesting to note a 'tendency toward collections focused on paintings, already noticed in 1532–1548 [...] became even clearer in the 1560s,'[54] suggesting higher numbers of paintings per inventory even in the less well-to-do households, an evolution we did not find in Bruges. This becomes even more obvious when compared with other cities such as Metz. The mean number of paintings per inventory in seventeenth-century Metz was 5.5 – lower than the figure for Antwerp, but still higher than that for Bruges.[55] So the difference between the Antwerp and Bruges averages is undeniably substantial. Most of Bruges's citizens did not have significant collections of paintings in their homes, but there were some exceptions especially towards the end of the sixteenth century. The wealthy citizen Pieter Hendrick Winkelmans, for example, who died in 1595, left behind no fewer than eighteen paintings scattered over *only* five of the sixteen rooms of his house, suggesting a concentration of paintings in particular spaces.[56] The woman we discussed before, Petronella Heve, owned eighteen paintings as well. François Verbrugghe owned no fewer than twenty unidentified paintings in 1586, dispersed over three rooms: the floor, a room facing the street and his luxurious *salette*.[57] This suggests that at least a certain segment of the wealthier citizens of Bruges were influenced by the changing consumer culture of the Antwerp art market. However, because only twenty-one inventories (of a total of 502 in our total sample) had more than three paintings, large collections were the exception rather than the rule in Bruges, even towards the end of the sixteenth century.

Canvas and Panel Paintings

In Bruges, the guild of the image-makers combined into one organisation the panel painters, the cloth or house painters, mirror makers, glass painters and the saddlers and collar makers.[58] Throughout the fifteenth and sixteenth centuries, the panel painters were most numerous within the corporation, especially when compared to cloth painters. Reading the articles in the statutes and regulations of the guild and browsing through the litigations between panel and cloth painters, it becomes clear that panel

Graph 9. Evolution of Support (Panel/Cloth) per Sample Period per Social Group

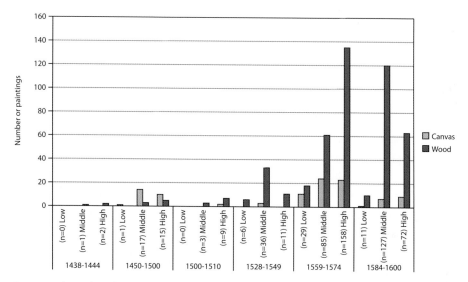

Source: Database of inventories © IB, JDG & IS

painters initially had (or claimed to have) more rights and liberties concerning the use of materials and paint and the sale of their products than canvas painters.

Following a dispute, the court concluded in 1463 'dat de voorseiden cleederscrivers niet ne zullen moghen wercken up hueren clederen met eenigher olievarwen'.[59] So the cloth painters were not allowed to use oil paint, which was to remain a monopoly of the panel painters. Though one could easily paint oil on cloth or linen – the technique even became widely accepted after 1540 – the *cleerscrivers* had to work with cheaper pigments and rapidly drying aqueous media, supporting the idea of the supposedly less prestigious role canvas paintings played in Bruges.[60] Were canvas paintings indeed considered less qualitative alternatives to wooden panel paintings? Quality and price differences between canvas paintings occurred as well. A judgement from 1458 stated that a cloth painting of more than two ells in length should be on new linen, whereas old linen could be used for smaller works, provided the fabric had no holes or stains.[61] Images painted on lesser-quality cloth were attached to a frame and a wider *cassin*, thus hiding the crumpled ends of the stretcher under the wooden framework.[62]

Only for the second sample period, from 1450 to 1500, is it noticeable that canvas supports made up the greater share of supports for each social group of the sample. But for all the other sample periods, a completely different picture emerges; canvas paintings were present in the households of the middle and wealthier social groups, though only in relatively lower numbers. The increasing social distribution of the originally more expensive panel paintings could be explained by a growing supply thanks to the increased production of this type of painting. Increased production lowers prices for consumers, consequently lowering the threshold for more people to buy these items. The wider ownership of panel paintings was therefore not necessarily due to an increase in the standard of living, but perhaps also to the greater affordability of these goods.

So graph 9 suggests that canvas paintings were not appreciated just by the poorer layers of society. But the graph also suggests that canvas paintings were not as popular as one would expect when following the assertion by Diane Wolfthal that Bruges was formerly the most important centre for canvas painting in the Netherlands.[63]

A conflict of 22 June 1545 between the *cleerscrivers* and the panel painters may lift a corner of the veil.[64] Exact lengths and heights of paintings were never mentioned in the inventories, nor in the statutes of the guild of Saint Luke.[65] But the conflict in 1545 reminded guild members of regulations that were not included in the original guild statues, but are illustrative of the importance of complying with a certain standardisation of the dimensions of canvases. Two members of the sub-guild of the *cleerscrivers*, Arnoud Boudins and Matthys van Assenede, were summoned to account for their professional negligence on the subject of the size of their products. Both men were accused of selling cloths with incorrect dimensions: 'twee sticken vander iije soorte die te cort waren elc een vierendeel' ('two pieces [of cloth] of the third type that were too short, each of them one *vierendeel* [too short]') and were obliged to pay a fine to the guild. As was stated in the document, it was clear for the dean of the guild that both artisans had violated the statute about standardisation that was granted to the *cleerscrivers* by the image-makers and approved by both parties in 1515. Five different types, or *soorte*, of cloth were defined in the document, each with its own fixed measurements: a *groote soorte*, or the large type, of nine *ellen* long and four *ellen* wide; the *soorte daer naer* or the second type, of six *ellen* long and four *ellen* wide; the third type of five *ellen* long and eleven *vierendeel* wide; the *ghemeene soorte*, or the common type, of four *ellen* long and nine *vierendeel* wide; and the *cleene soorte*, or the smallest type of cloth, of eleven *vierendeel* long and seven *vierendeel* wide.[66] To put these measurements into perspective, we have recalculated the old measures of length to modern standards, knowing that one Bruges *el* is approximately seventy centimetres. So the largest canvas painting of nine ells long and four ells wide is, when converted, approximately 6.3 m long and 2.8 m wide – a painted cloth that could easily cover a wall. The smallest canvas painting had to be eleven *vierendeel* (or a quarter of one *el*) long and seven *vierendeel* wide; recalculated to modern standards, it had to be 1.9 m long and 1.2 m wide. So one could wonder whether the often large dimensions of canvas paintings could explain their fairly low number in the inventories, an observation that complements the findings of art historian James Bloom. He found that linen paintings had gradually developed as decorative objects in their own right, not from panel paintings but from tapestry *cartoons* that were generally executed first on linen or paper.[67] The author continues by arguing that canvas paintings first participated in a fifteenth-century culture of substitute acquisition as cheaper but durable substitutes for the more expensive tapestries, and because of their thematic variety and despite their alleged lower quality, paved the way for the further development and commercialisation of panel painting. The conflict discussed earlier between the *cleerscrivers* and the image-makers exemplifies, among other things, that linen paintings could have been very long and very wide indeed, just like tapestries, ideal for covering a wall or part of a room.[68] Seventeenth-century author Karel van Mander recites in his book the work of cloth painter Rogier of Bruges and states that 'in desen tijdt had men de maniere om te maken groote doecken met groote beelden in, die men gebruycte om camers mede te behanghen als met tapijtserje',[69] thereby arguing that cloth painting figured as both a substitute and a complement for tapestry.

Wolfthal described Bruges as the centre of canvas painting in the fifteenth century and stated that 'approximately forty percent of all painters in Bruges specialized in canvases, as compared with only four percent in Antwerp over the years 1509 to 1530'.[70] At the end of the sixteenth century, Bruges citizen Zegher van Male even declared that there had been large numbers of *cleerscrivers* in Bruges throughout the sixteenth century.[71] Bruges canvases were even sought after by a particular group of wealthy citizens, although not so much for their own use. Indeed, in his lamentation, Zegher van Male already suggested the substantial export of canvas paintings to other places in Europe (the Iberian peninsula, the Italian city states and Germany) during the sixteenth century.[72] The presence of an extensive international quarter in the city where most nation houses were located must have facilitated commercial opportunities for Bruges (cloth) painters. Although most international merchants left Bruges at the beginning of the sixteenth century for the commercial hub of Antwerp – the nations of Genua, Florence and Lucca moved in 1516, and the Portuguese consulate set off for Antwerp even earlier (1511) – the nation of the

Castilians (and to a lesser extent also the Basque traders and merchants of Navarre) stayed in the city even when the Spanish wool staple disappeared from Bruges in 1586.[73] These Spanish merchants would have formed the ideal intermediaries for the export trade in wool and textiles such as linen, but certainly also for the export of paintings from Bruges to the commercial cities of Castile.[74]

The exact size of the export of paintings to the Iberian peninsula is difficult to measure.[75] In all likelihood, it was nothing like the large aggregates of Mechelen paintings that were produced for export throughout Europe and the Americas between 1540 and 1680.[76] But perhaps the larger Bruges canvases were meant to serve other purposes than the small canvas paintings of Mechelen? In this respect, we support the hypothesis that cloth paintings of Bruges gained popularity in Castile (and other places on the Iberian peninsula) as a kind of ersatz product of the larger, heavier and more expensive tapestries and were not considered as substitutes of the generally more expensive wooden panel paintings.[77] Hilario Casado Alonso found evidence of a strong demand from a growing group of Spanish elites, clergy and members of the urban oligarchy for these and other Flemish luxury products.[78] The research of other authors interested in the trade and cultural networks of the Hispano-Flemish world, including experts Didier Martens and Karel Jan Steppe, clearly signposts the importance and viability of the luxury market of Bruges for the consumption of decorative objects in Castile as well, because many paintings preserved in Spain are attributed to renowned or anonymous sixteenth-century Bruges painters.[79] So Spain remained an important market for Bruges art well into the second half of the sixteenth century, when the Antwerp art trade also took over a large part of this market.[80]

Jacques van Heede's written record of the tax of 2 per cent collected by Gheraert Gramaye, *recepueur qual(ifier)*, on all the goods that left the ports of Bruges, Damme and Sluis for the Iberian peninsula (mainly Castile and Portugal), and from there on to the West Indies and other colonised areas, is preserved in the national archives of Brussels.[81] The accounts were arranged by date and by ship. For each ship, the merchants are mentioned with their goods (specified by quantity and by type of packaging) and the value of the goods (sometimes individually valued, sometimes per batch of goods). Besides wool, textiles, soap and in some cases even items of furniture, merchants such as Franciso del Peso, Melchior de Vega, Jehan Gailso Descallado and many more exported *fardeaux* or *pacquets* of *poinctures*, or packages of paintings, from Bruges to Spain or Portugal. Not only were the paintings themselves exported but also some raw materials for producing canvas paintings in Spain or elsewhere, such as canvases and paintbrushes – the latter transported in barrels.

Though not many details of the exported paintings can be derived from the registers described above, the results undeniably provide a glimpse of canvases that were produced in Bruges and exported by members or associates of the Spanish nation to the Iberian peninsula in particular. Merchants like Jehan Gailso Descallado and Cesar Cremona were trading in *taferelen* as well as canvas paintings. But the *taferelen*, or panel paintings, were packed differently for shipping than the canvas paintings and were traded in much smaller quantities than the canvas paintings.

Yet luxury products reached the Spanish market also through other channels such as the annual fairs of Medina del Campo in Castile-Léon. The city of Burgos, for example, because of its important role as a centre for the wool trade with Bruges in the early sixteenth century, was an important centre for art transactions as well.[82] From the sixteenth century, however, trade in the direction of the Iberian peninsula proceeded along two paths; Bruges still played its part but was ever more clearly accompanied by the new and fast-growing commercial city of Antwerp. Nevertheless, the cultural exchange between Bruges and Castile was still encouraged throughout the sixteenth century thanks to the strong commercial ties between the two centres.[83] Intriguingly, members of the Spanish nation in Bruges owned both panel and canvas paintings alongside tapestries themselves, though presumably with a slight preference for the oil on panel paintings and tapestries. Wealthy merchant Vélasco de Béjar, for example, owned four images painted in oil paint – one of the Three Wise Men, one of Saint Jerome, one of Christ and one of Saint Anne – and only one canvas painting painted in aquarelle, depicting the seven known planets.[84] It seems that living closer to the production centres of tapestry enabled these wealthy merchants to decorate their walls with the *real thing* and only to a lesser extent with the painted canvases.

Paintings and Iconographical Themes

Spanish merchant Fernando de Castere's collection of paintings is rather exceptional, because all five paintings were labelled in the inventory with their iconographic theme. Except for the one little painting with the portrait of his wife Claudine, the iconography is overall religious. Another remarkable exception to the rule is the inventory of noblewoman Barbara de Ourssin, widow of Jan de Fonteine, whose household goods were registered by court clerk Jan Gheeraerts in 1587.[85] The couple owned an extraordinary and excessive number of twenty-one paintings, several sculptures and a couple of maps, which were all meticulously described by the appraiser. Barbara's collection of paintings is therefore particularly intriguing, because it is also rather exceptional, not only because it was fairly extensive in number but also because a lot of detailed information about the paintings was written down by the appraiser. One of the paintings – a portrait of a *joncvrouwe*, or a lady – was even dated 1550, which means that it was more than thirty years old when it was registered in the inventory. Besides landscapes, maps, devotional images and statuettes, de Ourssin owned several portraits of which the sitters were meticulously identified as emperor Maximilian, family member Philibert de Ourssin and a certain Gheeraert Bossilion. Intriguingly, she possessed some of the newly emerging genre paintings with rather 'modern' or innovative pictorial subjects such as 'a person who plays the violin', a 'beheading of St. Jan by Herod's daughter', a *schilderie* (the only occasion the term *schilderie* is used in the samples) of a 'huus van plaisancen' or country house, an *effegie* of 'Lady Justice' and a painting of a 'jester with a golden chain'.[86] The detailed description of the art collection of the Bruges noble household not only reveals the richness and variety of the collection, but it may also reveal something about the knowledge and the attentiveness of the appraiser or of the people who accompanied him during the process. Indeed, the data from the inventory suggest that the appraiser or the other people in the room actually recognised some of the sitters in the portraits and thought it important to have it registered. They were able to accurately describe the figures and scenes on most of the paintings and were attentive to technical details such as the types of frames for the paintings, the types of paintings (the appraiser uses several different terms to indicate a certain type of painting) and the support (paper, cloth or panel). Unfortunately, however, the de Ourssin collection is truly an exception to the rule, because no other household of the samples owned so many paintings and other works of art that were so accurately described. For the whole period under study, the subjects of the paintings in the inventories are only rarely known (graph 10).

To some extent, it would seem remarkable and even counter-intuitive to know so little about what is depicted in a painting, because appraisers must have had good reason to distinguish objects from each other by defining (and thus identifying) them during the registration process of an inventory. Conversely, Martens and Peeters found other numbers for Antwerp; for the period from 1532 to 1548, the subject of no fewer than 89.5 per cent of the paintings was identified, though the percentage of 'unknowns' increased from 10.5 per cent in the 1540s to 39.7 per cent in the period from 1566 to 1567.[87] Both scholars assume that the increase in the number of

Grafiek 10. The Subject of Paintings

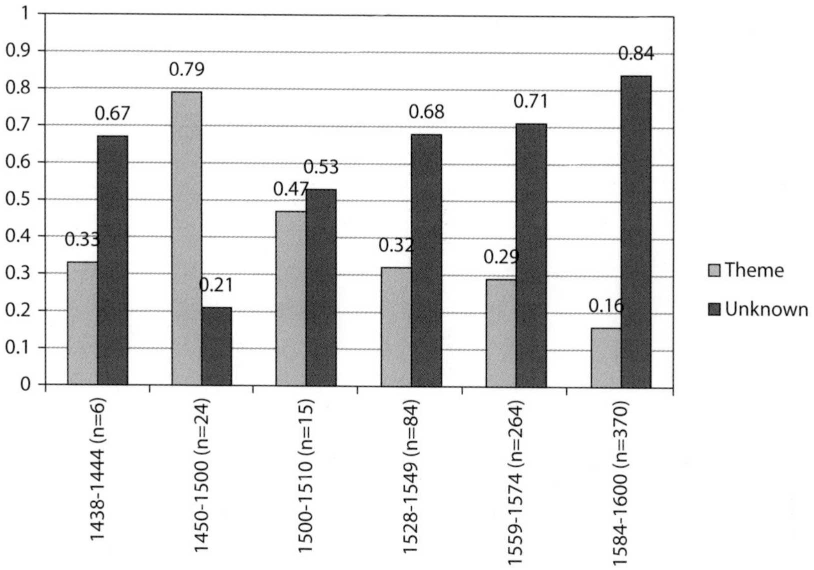

Source: Database of inventories © IB, JDG & IS

unidentified paintings 'is linked to an expansion of the number of works of low quality and workshop copies that flooded the Antwerp local market in the 1560's, which the clerks glossed over without carefully identifying them'. In *stochouder* Guillaume Bibau's account book, we found indeed that the more detail a painting was described in, the higher its resale value. Evidence of the workshop practices of several Bruges painters, for example Adriaan Isenbrant, indeed suggests that multiple cheaper copies of certain paintings were brought on the market.[88] So following the hypothesis of Martens and Peeters, all this is evidence of a reorientation of the art market towards the production of cheaper paintings and copies. Bruno Blondé, in turn, goes much further and suggests that a large number of unidentifiable paintings would be an indication of a declining economy and a crisis in the art market.[89] Although some Bruges workshops – for example, of the more famous artists-artisans such as Lancelot Blondeel (1496–1561) and his pupil and son-in-law Pieter Pourbus (1523–1584) or Ambrosius Benson (1518–1550) and Adriaan Isenbrant (1480–1551)[90] – still produced high-quality products, commissioned especially by institutions,[91] foreign merchants and by local elites,[92] the proportion of lower-quality and thus cheaper paintings surely must have flooded the market and even grew in the course of the sixteenth century.

Graph 11. Iconography on Paintings per Sample Period

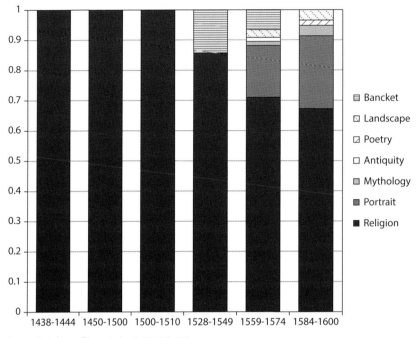

Source: Database of inventories © IB, JDG & IS

Still, some of the iconographical themes of paintings were recognised and re-corded by the appraiser. Graph 11 shows a simplified overview of the standardised iconographic themes of the identified paintings throughout the sample periods.[93] Admittedly, classifying these subjects into categories is not an easy task. Confusion about the theme of a painting can be caused by a lack of additional information pro-vided by the appraiser or by a thematic generalisation; a *Wildernesse*, for example, could be a landscape or a devotional painting referring to the biblical scene with Saint John in the wild. In some cases, it is difficult to distinguish between actual likenesses of the portrait's owner or family members on the one hand and 'portraits' of humanlike figures such as *tronies* on the other hand. In a similar way, a *bancket* could refer to the biblical scene of the Last Supper, but equally well to a profane banquet or a family dinner.[94]

Graph 11 shows all the different themes of the paintings in the inventories of our sample. What is interesting is the larger subject diversity towards the end of the sixteenth century. And there is not only a larger variety in secular themes. Also

Table 10. Breakdown According to Theme per City (Antwerp and Bruges)

THEME		OLD TESTAMENT	NEW TESTAMENT	DEVOTION	ALLEGORY, HISTORY, MYTHOLOGY	PORTRAIT	GENRE	TOTAL
CITY	ANTWERP	12.00%	16.30%	24.30%	8.00%	22.60%	16.70%	100.00%
	BRUGES	8.90%	32.50%	45.50%	1.60%	8.90%	2.40%	100.00%
TOTAL		11.70%	17.70%	26.10%	7.50%	21.50%	15.50%	100.00%

Source: Database of inventories © IB, JDG & IS and Database of inventories © Carolien De Staelen

the variation in religious scenes increased as well, besides Mary and Jesus scenes, scenes from the Old Testament, such as Holofernes and Judith and (the daughters of) Lot emerged, as well as specific religious scenes such as the Adoration of the Magi, which were popular and widely copied in Antwerp as well.[95] Only in the last two sample periods, in the second half of the sixteenth century, did 'new' and secular subjects such as mythology, antiquity, landscapes and portraits – referring to a rather humanistic ideology of rediscovering and revaluing ancient culture, nature and the self – become popular in Bruges, though they were still limited in number. So genre paintings, landscapes, portraits, nudes and ancient mythologies, numerous in Antwerp inventories of the period, seem to have appeared only infrequently in the Bruges domestic interiors under study, and then only at the end of the century. The iconography for the most part was still cast in a tradition of devotional art until the end of the sixteenth century. Brecht Dewilde also concluded that the iconography that was popular in the first half of the sixteenth century, that of the small devotional painting, was even reintroduced by the workshops of Gillis and Pieter II Claeissens in the second part of the sixteenth century as a kind of new old style of paintings. It was a conscious marketing strategy but also in response to a constant demand for this type of painting. Most people in Bruges retained an rather conservative taste for paintings.

The difference in taste and in production and consumption in Bruges and Antwerp in the same period becomes even more apparent in table 10. We have calculated the share of each theme for each city separately (in percentages and omitting the category of 'unknown'), using the data from the analysis by Carolien De Staelen for Antwerp.[96] The table presents the breakdown of iconographic themes that were described in the inventories. It confirms the observation that most paintings in Bruges

Table 11. Iconography and Social Group (1559–1574)

SOCIAL GROUP	RELIGION	UNKNOWN	PORTRAIT	LANDSCAPE	*BANCKET*	ANTIQUITY	MYTHOLOGY
Low	2	14	1	0	0	0	0
Middle	15	79	1	0	3	0	0
High	43	103	12	2	7	1	1

Source: Database of inventories © IB, JDG & IS

Table 12. Iconography and Social Group (1584–1600)

SOCIAL GROUP	RELIGION	UNKNOWN	PORTRAIT	LAND-SCAPE	*BANCKET*	ANTIQUITY	MYTHOLOGY	POETRY
Low	1	15	0	0	0	0	0	0
Middle	26	168	10	1	0	0	0	1
High	15	124	5	1	0	0	2	0

Source: Database of inventories © IB, JDG & IS

had a strong devotional theme and character, whereas in Antwerp, the market was much more diverse and the emphasis was both on religious paintings as well as on genre paintings and portraits.

When we look at the data on iconography for each social group (table 11 & table 12), it is clear that the variety in iconographic themes was most pronounced in the group of the wealthier middle groups, especially for the 1559–1574 sample period.

This means that the 'newer' and probably secular subjects such as mythology, landscape, antiquity and portrait were mainly owned by wealthier citizens. For the last sample period, from 1584 to 1600, this difference seems to be less pronounced but still exists. This could mean two things: the wealthier citizens of Bruges were wealthy enough and willing to purchase paintings of which some were painted according to the latest 'fashion' and brought into Bruges by many Antwerp painters and art dealers; and less affluent families were either treasuring paintings that had already long been in the family or were buying more 'traditional' themes, some as cheaper copies on wooden panels.

Devotion on Display

Diana Webb already asserted that 'isolated on the gallery wall, such images cannot now tell us in what physical setting they were originally located or used, or indeed by whom'.[97] Hence, the old formalist and connoisseurial debate on the reception and use of art neglects the object's role in the daily pursuits of its owner and primary viewer.[98] Let's put these paintings back in their original spatial domestic context using 2D historical documents.

To determine the potential locations of paintings in dwellings, we have studied only those inventories in which the household goods were recorded room by room. Of the total sample of inventories, we were able to examine a corpus of 309 inventories with room indications. The largest share of paintings was located in a room which was merely labelled as such, 'room' (table 13).

Some of the percentages in this table are very low, because of the low appearance of paintings in certain rooms or because certain rooms were only found in a couple of houses. Nevertheless, some general conclusions can be made. Throughout the long sixteenth century, paintings could be found nearly everywhere, except for the service rooms, though heated rooms were preferred, and there was a slight concentration of paintings in the more luxuriously furnished and heated rooms where visitors could be received and where family members could retire. We have labelled these rooms 'reception rooms', because they contained at minimum some seating furniture and heating and/or light fixtures. For the first and second sample periods (though not many inventories of these samples had room indications), the floor (*vloer*), the dining room (*eetcamere*), the kitchen (*cueken*) and some unspecified rooms (*camere*) were the focal points of paintings in different sorts of dwellings. The dining room remained an important site for displaying paintings in the third and fourth sample periods as well, in addition to the floor, the front room (*voorcamere*) and the lower room (*neercamere*). Interestingly, the back room (*achtercamere*) and the sleeping room (*slaepcamere*) were also deemed important places to display paintings. The *salette*, or parlour, as a room label appeared in the inventories only from the second half of the sixteenth century and increasingly often at the end of the century. As we have discussed, the *salette* seems to have replaced the dining room as a label for a comparable room with similar functions, in other words, a comfortably furnished and heated room with chairs and/or benches, a table and often also some storage furniture. In our fifth and sixth sample periods, paintings

Table 13. Percentage of Paintings in Rooms

	1438–1444	1450–1500	1500–1510	1528–1549	1559–1574	1584–1600
Back Room	0.0%	16.7%	10.0%	1.2%	5.9%	14.6%
Floor	66.7%	16.7%	10.0%	5.4%	1.9%	6.5%
Room	33.3%	16.7%	0.0%	26.8%	43.0%	35.7%
Kitchen	0.0%	16.7%	0.0%	3.5%	5.2%	4.0%
Dining Room	0.0%	33.3%	40.0%	34.0%	7.0%	0.0%
Sleeping Room	0.0%	0.0%	10.0%	3.6%	3.2%	4.9%
Front Room	0.0%	0.0%	10.0%	14.3%	17.6%	12.2%
Lower Room	0.0%	0.0%	20.0%	0.0%	0.0%	1.6%
Casteelkin	0.0%	0.0%	0.0%	1.8%	0.0%	0.0%
Mezzanine	0.0%	0.0%	0.0%	1.8%	0.0%	0.0%
Nette room	0.0%	0.0%	0.0%	1.8%	0.0%	0.0%
White room	0.0%	0.0%	0.0%	3.6%	0.0%	0.0%
Unknown	0.0%	0.0%	0.0%	1.8%	0.6%	3.0%
Shop	0.0%	0.0%	0.0%	0.0%	0.6%	0.0%
Office	0.0%	0.0%	0.0%	0.0%	1.9%	0.8%
Cellar	0.0%	0.0%	0.0%	0.0%	0.6%	0.0%
Attic	0.0%	0.0%	0.0%	0.0%	0.0%	0.0%
Salette	0.0%	0.0%	0.0%	0.0%	8.5%	13.0%
Chapel	0.0%	0.0%	0.0%	0.0%	0.6%	0.0%
Middle Room	0.0%	0.0%	0.0%	0.0%	2.6%	1.6%
Corridor	0.0%	0.0%	0.0%	0.0%	0.0%	0.8%
Servants Room	0.0%	0.0%	0.0%	0.0%	0.0%	0.8%

Source: Database of inventories © IB, JDG & IS

were displayed in the front room, floor and back room as well. Graph 12 (detail of graph 11) further underlines the preference of users to display paintings in these so-called reception rooms.

On a micro level, the location of decorative objects and especially their proximity to other objects in the same room could hint at particular symbolic meanings and use values.[99] We have therefore calculated the spatial context of the largest group in the category of religious paintings, images of Mary, and the largest group of secular images, portraits, for the last three sample periods in an attempt to revive the actual use context of these types of paintings.

Graph 12. Paintings in Reception Rooms

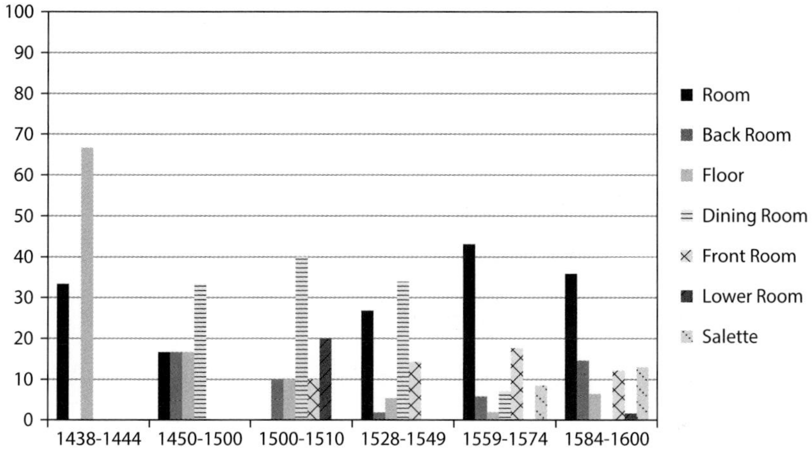

Source: Database of inventories © IB, JDG & IS

Marian images were most popular among religious iconography, followed by all types of saints. Most inventories simply cited an 'Our Lady' without specifying any more details about the scene. The popularity of this Marian imagery was part of a larger trend in the production of religious art, which started in the fifteenth century. The late medieval laity were increasingly encouraged to focus on their inner spirituality and take charge of their own prayers and devotions.[100] As a result, an increasing proportion of them acquired devotional objects for that purpose. Panel paintings, prints and canvases, as well as statuettes and tabernacles were produced that intensified the Marian devotion.

In these paintings, Our Lady was made the central figure of the scene, thereby building a bridge from the sacred realm of prayer to the here and now of the audience and creating a strong sense of immediacy. Jeanne Nuechterlein attests that a new visual iconography that was rapidly gaining popularity in fifteenth-century Netherlands – that of the Virgin in a fully developed domestic interior – was specially attuned to the lives of the (more well-off) urban citizens, the targeted public for buying these objects.[101] These images were used as a so-called *Andachtsbilder*[102] in different ways: as a medium between the sacred and the mundane during prayer (after all, in Christian orthodoxy, Mary was considered the moderator between God and his worshippers), as a constant reminder of one's religious responsibilities and as a permanent divine presence in the home, protecting all those in that same

space. In the words of Jacqueline Musacchio, 'certain devotional images could sanc-
tify a room, and their presence required certain behavior'.[103] So 'the purpose [...] was
not to communicate a particular message but to cultivate a certain experience'.[104]
Jessica Buskirk supplements the latter view by stating that 'unlike earlier German or
Italian traditions of the Andachtsbild, which are dominated by emotionally charged
scenes of the Pieta or Christ as Man of Sorrows, the majority of small, devotional
early Netherlandish paintings are tender, but not obviously heartrending, images
of the Madonna and Child.'[105] Indeed, the Virgin was evoked representing the two
essential qualities of motherhood: the image of a woman both authoritative and
nurturing. For Florence, Musacchio therefore found a strong link between domestic
devotional art – the image of Our Lady or Madonna and Child in particular – and
the importance of marriage and the family.[106] Remarkably, even in a period of religious uncertainty and the spread of Calvinistic propaganda reacting against the
material culture of holiness and thus against pictures of saints and all other signals
of the sacred, religious imagery and especially the image of Mary and other saints
remained strongly present in Bruges interiors.

Because 'like books, paintings offer an indication of the cultural and religious
environment in which the owners lived',[107] a comparison between the ownership
patterns of Calvinists and Catholics would be meaningful. However, distinguishing
between the two religious groups is unfortunately difficult, if not impossible, for
our case, because we do not have information about the religious preferences of the
inventory holders. That there were city dwellers with a preference for the Calvinistic teachings is clear from Ludo Vandamme's prosopography of people who were
mentioned in the Duke of Alva's documents of the Council of Troubles around the
Wonder Year 1567.[108] Unfortunately, there are preserved only seven inventories of
confiscated goods from Bruges citizens who were accused of heresy by the Council
of Troubles, and these inventories were heavily affected by moisture and mould and
therefore difficult to read. But because scholars studying the Reformation in Bruges
assert that there was only a 'presence of a broad middle group of "protestantized
Catholics", sympathetic to some but not all aspects of reform',[109] we do not expect
to find major differences in material culture. Guido Marnef has done this comparative exercise for Antwerp, where the impact of the Calvinist and other Reformation
teachings has been much more pronounced.[110] Bearing in mind that some paintings that Calvinists possessed might have been inherited from Catholic parents
or relatives, Marnef found that New Testament scenes were much more common
among Catholics and that stories from the Old Testament were more popular with

Calvinists. In our sample, we find most Old Testament scenes (i.e. eight paintings of Abraham, Lot, Moses, Adam and Eve) in the fifth sample period (1559–1574) and only two in the last sample period 1584–1600 – in other words, around the period of the short-lived Calvinist Republic from 1578 until 1584. But it is not clear whether these paintings were owned by Calvinists or Catholics. And none of the inventory owners of our samples were examined by Ludo Vandamme in his prosopography.[111]

For the 1528–1549 sample period, it was clear that Marian images occurred mostly in the dining room and unidentified rooms labelled as 'room'. In the next sample period, 1559–1574, the Marian images all occurred in unidentifiable rooms; the last sample period, 1584–1600, places these images in sleeping rooms and again in unidentifiable rooms. Interestingly, all the paintings of the Virgin Mary were painted exclusively on wooden panels. So the preference for a medium that was much firmer and less subject to wear and tear was still retained. Another change lies with the imagery of saints (e.g. Saint John, Saint Salvatore, Saint Anne and Saint Francis). They were much more widespread among the rooms of dwellings and were displayed in so-called frontstage rooms (or potentially public rooms) such as the dining room, the floor and the front room, as well as in so-called backstage rooms such as the back room and the kitchen. In the sample period of the middle of the sixteenth century, they were all painted on wooden panels, but towards the end of the century, most were painted on canvas. The latter were predominantly hung in the back room and kitchen. Other religious subjects such as the crucifix or the Crucifixion scene, scenes of Christ, Old Testament scenes and parables were, however, mostly situated in the front rooms. So it seems that people felt the need to have the more personalised pictures of saints in the more private spaces of the house – just like the Marian image – whereas the more general biblical pictures were rather displayed in the more public spaces – just like portraits. In the painting of Lucas Cranach the Elder, a wooden image of the Madonna and Child kept a watchful eye over Cardinal Albrecht of Brandenburg in his very own study (fig. 15).

As discussed before, the secular portrait that hung in the office of Spanish merchant Fernando de Castere is an example of a new genre of painting that became popular in the sixteenth century. Of these 'new' genres, the portrait was certainly the most numerous in the inventories. This type of panel painting was originally considered an overtly elitist piece of art, only to be found in the palaces of city elites and the nobility. But by the middle of the sixteenth century, however, the portrait as an artistic 'genre' had become popular among the middling groups of citizens and

Fig. 15. Painting of Madonna and Child in the study of the Cardinal. Cardinal
Albrecht of Brandenburg as St. Jerome, 1526, Lucas Cranach the Elder, German,
1472-1553, Oil on wood panel, 45 1/4 x 35 1/16 inches, SN308, Bequest of John
Ringling, 1936, © Collection of The John and Mable Ringling, Museum of Art, the
State Art Museum of Florida, a division of Florida State University

lower city elites as well.[112] Indeed, art historian Till-Holger Borchert argues that from the fifteenth century onwards, portraiture was no longer an exclusive privilege of the high nobility and that these paintings were adopted as a means of representation by increasingly larger segments of society.[113] Some of Bruges's famous painters, such as Pieter Pourbus, even specialised in painting portraits for and of merchants and their family members. For them, it represented their status as a respectable member of Bruges society.

Although portraiture is considered rather new for that period, it showed an interesting connection between continuity and change of which the portrait of Petronella Heve is an fascinating example. Most scholars have claimed that the devotional diptych was popular during the fourteenth and fifteenth centuries, but gradually grew out of fashion and experienced its swansong in the second part of the sixteenth century,[114] but it seems that the idea behind the devotional diptych was not entirely abandoned.[115] Lorne Campbell found that in diptychs, the heraldic conventions of externalising hierarchy were followed, because the most important character was pictured on the right wing (from the perspective of the sitter) and the lesser individual was positioned on the left.[116] On devotional diptychs, the portrait of the donor of the painting is therefore on the right wing (from the perspective of the audience) and the saint or the figure of Christ on the left wing. Comparing this to the several portraits of couples in the inventories, it seems that the husband was always mentioned first by the appraiser, so was presumably pictured or displayed left of his wife (from the perspective of the appraiser). It is therefore not far-fetched to assume that these portraits of couples had the same message of representing not only status but also the *liaison* or marriage into which the couple had entered – the more so because many portraits have the heraldic symbols of the families of the sitters depicted at the rear, such as the portraits of Petronella and her husband Remeeus Ommejaeghere that are displayed in the Church of Our Lady in Bruges. Portraits of couples were therefore not only a firm claim of their place in the social and commercial network of the city but also a symbol and the celebration of their marriage and their household.[117] This is probably also the reason why Petronella wanted to keep the portrait in the family by donating it to her son and heir, and why Fernando preferred to have the picture of his wife hung in his office. The pendant portrait as a genre was still in transition in this period – from serving a predominantly religious purpose towards a more secularised representation of family lineage and status (fig. 16 & fig. 17).

Fig. 16. Left and right panels of altarpiece of Juan Pardo and his wives Anna Ingenieulandt en Maria Anchemant, Bruges, © Musea Brugge, www.artinflanders.be

Fig. 17. Pendant portraits of Christoffel Ghuyse and Elisabeth Van Male, Pieter Pourbus, 16th Century, Bruges, © Musea Brugge, www.artinflanders.be

Some portraits were painted according to the principles of devotional diptychs, but not every portrait was meant to be hung as a pendant of another one. The origins of these single portraits could just as well lie with the devotional diptych. But as they detached from the devotional diptych, a new type of portraiture emerged, appropriating the frontal view of the sitter, which was previously exclusively used for saints and the Holy Face.[118]

Using Erving Goffman's theory on the performance of identity in everyday life,[119] Peter Burke describes the portrait as a system of signs representing social status, attitudes and values.[120] In this view, the portrait not only represented the consumption preferences of urban elites but also communicated identity: a desired image of themselves. Goffman argues that even in ordinary situations, individuals have a tendency to present themselves and their activity to others. Through this 'impression management', they guide and control the impression others form of them, doing (or not doing) certain kinds of actions while sustaining their performance. What is more, the roles individuals performed were staged in a certain space or a particular material context.[121] Portraits perfectly fitted in as the material props that could be used in this 'impression management' process. Merchants and other well-to-do citizens used portraits to show off – but often in a subtle way – hereby displaying wealth, status and their self-proclaimed savoir faire. The portraits of Jacquemyne Buuck and her husband Jan van Eyewerve exemplify this; they depict both spouses in their expensive and matching outfits in front of their commercial habitat along the Vlamingstraat.

When charting the spatial dispersion of portraits in interiors, the results seem to underline the argument Burke and his followers made: portraits were primarily intended to communicate the social and economic status of the sitter to the outside world. Notwithstanding the fact that portraits were by definition very personal in nature, representing a self-image or the image of family members, they were displayed in the most public areas of the house; some were displayed in the *salette* (in the 1559–1574 and 1584–1600 sample periods), others in originally unidentified rooms that were well equipped to receive guests (in the 1528–1549, 1559–1574 and 1584–1600 sample periods). This means that these rooms included several different types of seating furniture, storage furniture and heating amenities. Charles de Fonteyne (1591), for example, who inhabited a house of six rooms, owned two portraits: one double portrait of himself and his wife hanging in his *salette* and one portrait displayed upstairs.[122]

Most scholars working on the location of paintings in a dwelling limit themselves to study the macro level of domestic space: the level of the room.[123] But paintings as decorative objects were part of a specific material context; each room contained several objects at the same time, and these objects were usually arranged in both a pragmatic and a meaningful way. So to understand the significance of the use of objects and the changes therein, we need to place these goods in their original spatial context.[124] One could argue that this kind of information would be missing in the sources and that it would be difficult to reach that micro level of detail, but in fact in some of the inventories, it was often literally stated where exactly paintings were located. When it was not, we could deduce the location of some artworks in a particular room by looking at the sequence of the objects that were listed in that same room.[125] One of the most surprising findings is that it was often stated in inventories that *taferelen* or *beilden* were located on top of or directly above a *trezoor*, or a cupboard (see graph 13). Furthermore, in several cases, candlesticks were placed on the same cupboards. This combination of a devotional painting, candlesticks and statuettes all together displayed on a cupboard might suggest the creation of some kind of domestic altar. The cupboard seems to have played an important role in this setting, acting as the stage for a devotional object ensemble, and it retained this role in the second part of the sixteenth-century as well. A dispute between craftspeople brought before the aldermen of Bruges in 1466 illustrates even more so the potential use of the cupboard as an altar table within a domestic setting. Since the 1455 concordat between joiners and carpenters, the joiners had been forbidden to make church furniture, because that was the privilege of the carpenters. Therefore, they were not allowed to make church altars. But there was a way of circumventing this prohibition; as a result of a dispute, the following was stated: 'maer es ende wort hemlieden (joiners) wel gheoorlooft elre te makene, in cameren of zalen, dreschoor- en <u>outaerwijs</u> ende anders, verhemelt ende onverhemelt, zo hemlieden dat commen zal te werckene, zonder dangier'.[126] So joiners were allowed to produce *outaerwijs dreschooren* or altar-like cupboards. The dispute between the joiners and the carpenters and the permission for the joiners to produce altar-like cupboards clearly refers to a need and actual demand for such pieces of furniture and underlines the credibility of such a custom.

The Annunciation by the Antwerp painter Joos van Cleve (fig. 18) illustrates this well. Joos Van Cleve's painting is intriguing, because it puts three types of images together in one view: a more formal triptych, a coloured print or woodcut and a medallion (or a mirror?). It reminds us of the fact that different types of images

Graph 13. Location of Paintings in Rooms per Sample Period

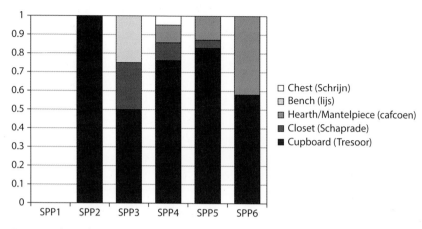

□ Chest (Schrijn)
▨ Bench (lijs)
▧ Hearth/Mantelpiece (cafcoen)
▦ Closet (Schaprade)
■ Cupboard (Tresoor)

Source: Database of inventories © IB, JDG & IS

Fig. 18. Religious painting displayed on a cupboard. Next to the bed a colored print is nailed to the wall. The Annunciation, Joos Van Cleve, c. 1525, Oil on Wood, New York, © The Metropolitan Museum of Art, CC0

could be displayed and 'used' in one room, though not necessarily at the same time and in the same way. In this case, they were probably all used or intended as an *Andachtsbild*, or a devotional image, but perhaps used during different moments in time or during different stages of private devotion. The triptych is clearly positioned on top of a cupboard that is dressed with a white cloth – mimicking a miniature altar, establishing religious decor, but only when needed, because the triptych could easily be closed. Opening and closing paintings with shutters implies a specific activity associated with prayer.[127] The print, on the other hand, was nailed to the wall. It was something that was visible at all times, sanctifying the room as a whole and as a profound reminder of virtuous behaviour. However, this type of image cannot be found in the inventories because of their poor state of preservation and also because of their low resale value. The print in this painting by Van Cleve is the image of the Old Testament prophet Moses holding the Ten Commandments, perhaps reminding beholders of their duties to have a fruitful and devout life. The medallion hanging against the bed frame could have been a painting as well as a mirror – it is not easily detectable from the image. Nevertheless, it was something that was cherished and held close to the body when asleep. In the chapter on the sleeping room, we have seen that there was a dear connection between sleeping, sleeping furniture and private devotion before, during or after sleeping.

Another place that was preferred as a display for paintings was the mantelpiece. Judging from the data on the graph, it seems as though the mantelpiece as a location for paintings gradually took over the role of the cupboard. Looking at the iconography of late fifteenth- and sixteenth-century miniatures and paintings, it seems that during this period and despite the radiating heat of the fire, people seemed to be particularly attracted by the fireplace and organised their seating furniture precisely near it. On calendar miniatures of, for example, illuminator Simon Bening, family members and staff are enjoying the warmth of the fireplace during their work, dinner or leisure time. Also during summer, when the warmth of the fireplace was no longer needed, people tended to cover up their fireplace with wooden planks or rugs but still took their places before them. But besides this reuniting, social character of the hearth, it fulfilled or was assigned an important symbolic character as well.

In fifteenth-century burgher houses, a lot of mantelpieces of the most important hearths were often decorated with sculpted figures or themes from courtly love poetry or folk morality such as the unequal lovers (fig. 19).[128] Some of these figures were also polychromed, increasing the decorative splendour of the mantelpiece even more. From the early sixteenth century onwards, the use of sculpted figures

Fig. 19. Ornament of a Mantelpiece, head of a man, 15th Century, Bruges, © Musea Brugge, www.artinflanders.be

was becoming less common, and they were gradually replaced by sculpted chimney stones (*haardsteen*) and other ornaments that had much in common with a new taste for ancient architecture.[129] So the dominant theme of the sculptures changed, but fireplaces still remained important architectural features for the propagation of a rich and meaningful imagery.

Moreover, people tend to decorate the mantelpiece of the fireplace with other, mobile objects such as paintings, prints, statues and rugs, turning hearths into the centrepiece of the room. However, these decorative objects were not exclusively placed there to embellish the fireplace, but were intended to induce a certain behaviour or mediate certain messages as well. Because of its centrality in the interior of the room, it is not surprising that the fireplace was used as a stage for *Andachtsbilder* to remind people of their religious duties. Furthermore, because these pictures and statues were usually placed above eye level, it was as if the saints and religious figures on the images were watching over the people in the room and the activities that took place there. According to Amanda Vickery, this location was popular for this type of imagery not only because of its centrality in the room but also because the hearth made the connection between different worlds.[130] On the one hand, this connection strengthened the message of the religious images, because it referred to the connection between the earthly world and the spiritual world, but it was, on the other hand, also necessary as a boundary to protect the soul of the house from evil spirits.[131] Interestingly, portraits of family members could be interpreted in a rather similar way. When the portrait was hung in a central location in the room – above the fireplace, for example – the sitter in the painting was fully present in the room where the painting was staged.[132] And more importantly, the subject fully participated in every social event that took place in that same space and perpetuated the memory of the deceased. It is interesting then that none of the portraits was located on a cupboard, which would mean that the cupboard was, as it were, reserved for the display of especially devotional images, underlining once again its devotional function.

Conclusions

In Bruges, the artistic production of the sixteenth century was formed in the mould of the artistic tradition of the fourteenth and fifteenth centuries, especially in terms of iconography. Painters kept to a certain style that was recognisable for their customers, who preferred religious themes in addition to the more modern 'Renaissance' styles blown over from Italy and Antwerp. Scholars have labelled this iconography of panel and cloth paintings and tapestries as merely 'provincial', not to say 'old-fashioned',[133] but it rather seems to have been an interesting coping strategy of the Bruges market: specialising in familiar themes for the panel paintings and investing in the production of substitute products – the canvases – of the otherwise more expensive tapestries.

However, Bruges was certainly not a 'closed market'; some of the painters working in Bruges (for example, Jan Provoost, Gerard David and Albert Cornelis) bought a craft membership at the Antwerp guild of Saint Luke already after the start of the sixteenth century or sold their products in the Antwerp Pand, thereby increasing their economic viability, their market share and the number of potential buyers. And vice versa, there was an increasing presence of Antwerp painters and art dealers in Bruges, especially from the second half of the sixteenth century, who sold their products directly on the Bruges market. These new, predominantly secular iconographic genres were especially popular among the more well-to-do citizens and among the merchants who identified themselves with their Antwerpian colleagues.

Whether or not paintings were located on or above a cupboard or mantelpiece, these images were outwards expressions of both the family's social and cultural status and their religious devoutness. The paintings thus combined the function of display with taking part in the private devotion of each of the family members. Marian images moved to the more private rooms of the house, their places taken over by a less personal iconography. Though new iconographic themes (such as portraits, banquet scenes and landscapes) appeared in some Bruges households (especially in the more well-to-do households), paintings were definitely 'consumed' and used differently in Bruges than in Antwerp.

There were undeniable changes and transformations in the painting industry and in the variety of visual themes produced and sold in Bruges, but the specific local context of Bruges left a clear impression on the local industry and on the material culture of citizens. We would therefore argue that locality is an important factor in the study of material culture, consumption patterns and local market strategies as well. Instead of focusing on the already much-discussed art market of Antwerp, the study of Bruges has proven to be a necessary undertaking to fully understand the contemporary appreciation of objects such as paintings and to acknowledge the importance of locality and diversion in the study of well-known economic and cultural tendencies. In contrast to what one would expect when studying art ownership patterns of citizens in a sixteenth-century Renaissance city with a presumed humanistic culture, paintings convincingly played their part in the devotional culture of many citizens. So 'luxury' objects such as paintings were clearly put to use in a daily context, a characteristic they seem to share with luxury textiles and tapestries.

FOR PUBLIC ELEGANCE AND PRIVATE COMFORT:[1] TEXTILES AND FURNITURE

Introduction

In his classic *The Civilization of the Renaissance in Italy*, Jacob Burckhardt noted that 'we read in the novelists of soft, elastic beds, of costly carpets and bedroom furniture, of which we hear nothing in other countries'.[2] In other words, he observed a wider interest in cleanliness and comfort in Italian households, which he described as 'unique at the time' as well as unique for Renaissance Italy.[3] Although the idea of achieving comfort or 'the self-conscious satisfaction with the relationship between one's body and its immediate physical environment'[4] is believed to be discussed and debated in contemporary literature only from the seventeenth century onwards,[5] the actual awareness of the associations between body, material culture and environment (i.e. comfort but also discomfort) can indeed be situated much earlier.[6] Danièle Alexandre-Bidon argues that, given the frequent use of references to the experiences of 'comfort' in contemporary literature, the notion of comfort and discomfort must already have been present in the minds of medieval city dwellers.[7] Heating, light, access to water, protection against draught, but also spatial and social order, for example, were considered comfortable conveniences; most medieval rooms were indeed organised and equipped in such a way as to maximise these basic comforts.[8] Although a lot of goods such as heating facilities, candles, bed textiles and cushions were used to reach a certain level of domestic comfort, they were also frequently used as a means to some other end.[9] Putting cushions on chairs meant far more than offering guests a comfortable seat during dinner. In Desiderius Erasmus's booklet, *Goede, manierlijcke zeden*[10], the preparing of the chairs and benches for dinner was an integral part of the ritual of organising a dinner party, because, as Erasmus's readers learned, more than promoting physical comfort, these cushioned chairs and benches externalised underlying social relations, enmities and friendships among the diners and exemplified the status and social knowledge of the host.[11] Which seat was equipped with a cushion and which was not, and for whom the comfortable chair was intended, were vital questions in the game of domestic sociability. Comfort was therefore always linked to status and wealth. Indeed, the ability to reach a certain degree of domestic comfort and to use it as a means to other ends (such as privacy, sociability and self-fashioning) depended on wealth, and it represented the status of the entire household. That is also the reason why, according to Frank Trentmann, comfort was a dynamic 'driver of consumption'.[12] Textiles, more than any other household goods, served to reach many instances of domestic comfort and the inherent or indirect goals of privacy (bed curtains), sociability (cushions, upholstered chairs and tablecloths) and self-fashioning (tapestry and bed curtains).[13]

Comfort and the Textile Environment

Household textiles and their role in daily life have long played the role of the least favourite topic of textile historians. It was only in the contribution to Beverly Lemire's volume on the *Power of Fashion* that textile historian Giorgio Riello attempted to redirect the focus of textile historians from the history of costume, dress and attire to the history of the so-called 'flat textiles'; textiles that were, according to him, 'produced [not only] to decorate but also organize and govern domestic life'.[14] He argues that our historical and methodological understanding of textiles has been too heavily influenced by dress and especially by the concept of *fashion* as the ever-changing material base of dress and the prerogative of scholars working on dress and clothing in the past. Surely, then, there is an urgent need to pose the question whether the *fashionability* of tailored fabrics penetrated the realm of domestic textiles[15] and whether it was even deemed important by contemporaries that furnishing textiles had to be fashionable at all. Much depends on the role textiles played within the domestic culture of the sixteenth century and how and for what purpose members of households created a so-called *textile environment*.[16]

Textile products such as cushions, bed curtains, table rugs and tapestries were all used in the structuring of the household and its inner workings precisely through its connection with furniture and morphological elements such as walls and chimneys. In other words, it was textiles and furniture that defined a person's home – more than bricks and mortar – and shaped the desired social and domestic environment. Indeed, textiles were used to soften hard wooden benches, protect people from draught or keep them safe, warm and cosy, but also served to express standards of material comfort, wealth and social status.[17] According to Giorgio Riello, the combination of both textiles and furniture therefore captures social and cultural practices that were less transient than those associated with dress and attire, but also less structural than architecture and buildings.[18]

This chapter aims, therefore, to focus precisely on the complementarity between decorative textiles and pieces of furniture such as chairs, tables and beds – influencing the 'relationship between one's body and its immediate physical environment'[19] – and morphological features such as walls and chimneys to look for evolutions throughout the period under study in the creation of domestic comfort and uncover related social practices of creating or maintaining privacy and sociability.[20] By focusing on this complementarity, we put the decorative textiles in context, which allows us to learn more about the motivations behind purchasing, using and consuming them. The chapter consists of four different components or sub-themes, all of which make the connection between textiles and furniture and the broader domestic environment.

In the first part, the connection is made between seating furniture, on the one hand, and cushions, seat covers and upholstery, on the other, as a proxy to studying changes and evolutions in the relationship between the body and material culture – focusing on posture, social behaviour and sociable life. In this respect, we will start from the idea that comfortable seating acted as an invaluable means to express deference as well as status. Second, beds and especially bedding such as curtains and *saarges* are put centre stage. The bed was an important piece of furniture, because it was seen as 'the most important space of textile use and display'.[21] Beds could tell a lot about the households who owned, displayed and used them, because it was mainly social standing and hierarchy that determined the shape, the material, the decoration and the location of the bed.[22] The high economic value of a bed had to do not only with the quality of the wood, but mainly with the quality of the bed textiles.[23] The bedding of some beds included bed curtains as well, not only colouring the interior but also granting the bed status and prestige and dividing it from the rest of the room. Bed curtains were certainly not reserved only for the richest of households, because they could be made from the simplest, most basic and therefore cheaper fabrics such as say (*saai*[24]) just as well as from the most expensive and colourful fabrics such as silks and satins. In all cases and regardless of the quality of the material, bed curtains had the ability to improve physical comfort and to create a private space amidst the rest of the room. In this section, we therefore ponder on the unique ability of bed curtains not only to protect the sleeper from draught and cold but also to create a certain level of privacy and at the same time display the household's wealth and status. Third, the interaction between the body and its environment (i.e. the room itself) is made tangible through the study of tapestry. Tapestry has long been considered the luxury textile par excellence for princes, kings, dukes, popes and counsellors, because it was often very expensive due to the capital intensive production process and the use of rare raw materials.[25] Though many historians of tapestry advocate going beyond the surviving pieces of tapestry, they eventually limit the subject of their study to tapestry hangings, almost ignoring the production, distribution and consumption of all other woven objects. Some do give examples of tapestry cushions and bench rugs, but it is not clear whether they see these as mere secondary tapestry products or as simply other products made from tapestry besides hangings. But tapestry as a fabric or a weave did come in various forms and qualities, especially in the fifteenth and sixteenth centuries.[26] Notwithstanding price and quality differences, it appears that tapestry woven for textile wall hangings, table rugs, cushions and cupboard covers was popular among different social groups in sixteenth-century Bruges. Perhaps tapestry owes its popularity to the fact that even the lesser-quality pieces of tapestry had similar propensities to the more expensive and exclusive ones? Or perhaps tapestry is favoured, because it goes well with the market for garments that were made from new and fashionable textiles, marked by 'a renewed fascination with contrasting textures'?[27]

In the fourth and last part of the chapter, the relationship between decorative textiles and furniture is approached in a different way. Instead of considering the visible and decorative features of textiles, we question the value of decorative textiles by looking at storage furniture and the ways sheets, blankets and cushions were presumably hidden from view. One may assume that the design, wood type, quality and location of chests and cabinets was often decisive in the decision to store a particular type of textile in a particular type of container at a specific location.[28] Hester Dibbits found, for example, that in several seventeenth- and eighteenth-century Dutch communities, the linen cupboard took an increasingly prominent place in the interior and in social life, proving, for one thing, the multifaceted role of decorative textiles in daily life.[29] In this part of the chapter, two types of storage furniture are discussed, two types of chests that were specifically named after their function to treasure textiles and garments: the *garderobe* and the *cleerschaprade*. Because of their specialised name and because it appears that they were owned only by the more well-to-do, the question arises to what extent this particular piece of furniture was really intended for *private* storage or whether it performed a role in the self-fashioning of its owners.

The Seat of Authority? The Design and Social Character of Seating Furniture

Furniture and Textiles

In his book on the Englishman's chair, John Gloag concisely summarises the value of the study of seating furniture: 'seats of almost any kind, fixed or movable, reveal the posture and carriage of the men and women for whom they were made, and chairs show more faithfully than any other article of furniture the importance accorded to dignity, elegance and comfort'.[30] The design, furnishing and related social character of seating furniture is therefore the subject of this subchapter. For our study it is instructive to question whether or not seats were upholstered or cushioned, whether these cushioned chairs and benches were intended for more than one person or had a rather individual character, to learn where they were located in the house and how they were positioned as regards each other and other objects to measure underlying social practices.

One of the most common features for increasing the comfort of seating furniture and adjusting the posture of the sitter was cushions. When calculating the social diffusion of cushions, it seems that they were relatively expensive objects since they were concentrated in the wealthier households of our sample. This view is shared by Jeremy Goldberg following Mark Overton et al. for later medieval and early modern England; data on Kent suggest that by the seventeenth-century cushions (of all kinds of fabric) were a common item of furnishing, whereas this was not the case for the less prosperous county of Cornwall.[31] In Bruges it appears from table 14 that a lot of households of the more wealthier social group (higher middling groups) possessed cushions but they owned them only in rather small numbers.

To put these numbers into context and to consider what function these cushions might have had in the interior, we have calculated the relative number of seats per sample period and per social class. We calculated the number of seats starting from the idea that all types of benches (*banc, lijs, siege, scabelle banc*) represent at least two potential seats, whereas all types of chairs and sofa chairs represent only one seat.[32] The results are presented in table 15.

Looking at the results of this calculation, it is striking that cushioned seats (or the cushioned backs of these seats – depending on how they were actually used) were certainly not the standard in most households and that choices had to be made as to where to put a cushion. The chance of coming across a cushioned seat was

Table 14. Mean Number of Cushions per Household

SAMPLE PERIOD	SOCIAL GROUP	SUM OF CUSHIONS	MEAN OF TOTAL HOUSEHOLDS	MEAN OF HOUSEHOLDS WITH CUSHIONS	MEDIAN
1450–1500	Low	0	0.0	0.0	0
	Middle	14	0.7	4.7	4
	High	74	6.7	12.3	4
1528–1549	Low	7	0.6	3.5	3.5
	Middle	22	0.6	3.1	2
	High	13	2.2	3.3	3
1559–1574	Low	7	0.1	1.2	2
	Middle	34	0.4	1.2	2
	High	107	2.5	2.9	2
1584–1600	Low	1	0.0	0.2	1
	Middle	89	1.4	3.2	2
	High	80	5.7	5.7	3

Source: Database of inventories © IB, JDG & IS

Table 15. Comparing Sum of Cushions with the Total Number of Seats per Sample Period and per Social Class

SAMPLE PERIOD	SOCIAL GROUP	SUM OF CUSHIONS	NUMBER OF SEATS
1450–1500	Low	0	5
	Middle	14	174
	High	74	182
1528–1549	Low	7	42
	Middle	22	283
	High	13	62
1559–1574	Low	7	332
	Middle	34	814
	High	107	1112
1584–1600	Low	1	115
	Middle	89	942
	High	80	482

Source: Database of inventories © IB, JDG & IS

much higher in houses of the wealthier social groups (High), while in the lower middle groups (Low), it was already quite exceptional to encounter a single cushion. So comfortable seating in terms of a soft and perhaps slightly elevated seat or back was certainly not commonplace.

For the 1528–1549 period, the dining room, the front room and unidentified rooms were types of rooms where the chance of encountering cushions was highest. For sample period 1559–1574, the same types of room pop up: the dining room, the *salette* and the back room. But the sleeping room in this case appears also to have been a preferred place to display cushions. Interestingly, the least likely place to find cushions was the kitchen. The same results also apply to the last sample period, 1584–1600; the *salette*, the front room and the back room yield higher ratios, whereas the kitchen continues to be of little significance. In general, therefore, cushioned seats were usually found in the more luxuriously furnished spaces that appeared to have had the potential to receive guests.

Cushions or cushion covers were made from a variety of textiles such as colourful cloths, light woollens such as say and serge and luxurious silks (especially in the later part of the sixteenth century), but the majority had a tapestry cover (graph 14). Although people had fewer and fewer cushions in their houses, the cushions they did have were probably made from tapestry.

Graph 14. Fabrics and Cushions

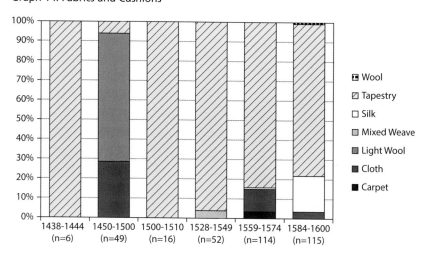

Source: Database of inventories © IB, JDG & IS

Other sorts of textiles that were used to decorate and soften seating were bankers or rugs to cover benches (*banccleed*). These rugs were especially popular in the first sample period and became less important during the sixteenth century. In the first sample period, they were made of woollen fabrics, cloth and tapestry; in the later sample periods, they were made only of tapestry.

Continuity and Change

Although a longitudinal detailed study of the character and design of Bruges's seating furniture throughout the fifteenth and sixteenth centuries is difficult because of a difference in language that is used in the inventories of the first sample period (the inventories of the burghers of illegitimate birth were drawn up in French and not in the Middle Dutch of the later inventories) and because some benches were not recorded because they were fixed to the walls, it is still possible to observe gradual changes in the shape, design and use of the seats and in the posture of the sitter. As we have just seen, cushioned seats were not omnipresent in domestic interiors, so one might question how 'possessions and ideals of comfort remained part of a civic culture that continued to be oriented towards public display and posterity'.[33]

Generally, there were two types of seating furniture, each with several derivatives: chairs and benches. Small, one-person benches and stools with hard wooden surfaces were easy to handle and easy to move to wherever they were needed. In the painting of *Jesus with Martha and Mary*, for example, a three-legged stool is used as a raised platform for a tub, containing foodstuffs (image 20). The stools and small benches were designed to be used only for a short period of time or were repurposed as seating for children or young servants when needed. Therefore, they were not meant to be comfortable, and none of them was mentioned in our inventories as having a cushion or rug. Most smaller benches and stools even lacked a backrest, which meant that sitters constantly had to control their muscles when sitting upright without support for their backs, necks and heads.[34] Sofa chairs (*zetele*), barrel chairs, basket makers' chairs and reclining chairs, on the other hand, still forced sitters to sit upright, but in contrast to the stools and one-person benches, they allowed them to adopt a more comfortable pose due to armrests and backrests. The chairs were generally bigger, heavier and less easy to handle, and so designed to be sat in for longer periods of time. But despite their size, they were not necessarily luxurious or expensive – wickerwork and barrel chairs, for example, were by far the cheapest form of seating.[35]

Fig. 20. A woman is preparing food using a driestael or a three-legged stool. Detail from Christ in Bethany, in the house of Martha and Mary, Anonymus, 16th Century, Oil on Canvas, Bruges, © Musea Brugge, www.artinflanders.be

One-person benches (*schabelle* or *schabelle bank*) or small stools and triangular seats (*driestael*) (fig. 20) were the most common seating furniture in the fifteenth century, alongside benches with or without storage space underneath the seat, such as the *lys*. Small benches were scattered throughout the domestic spaces and occurred mainly in the floor and in the kitchen, where they were used in the process of food preparation. None of these smaller benches were cushioned or dressed with a banker.

Other pieces of seating furniture that were better equipped to be sat on for longer periods of time (at least in comparison with stools and one-person benches) were the so-called *quayères*. Though it is difficult to infer from the inventories what these pieces of furniture looked like, these were probably the large, massive, throne-like armchairs, often with storage space underneath the seat, we see in contemporary

Fig. 21. Armchair, made in France, c. 1580, Walnut, © Victoria and Albert Museum, London

paintings and illuminations.[36] Because of their size and weight (i.e. to a certain extent deducible from the preserved copies in the Victoria and Albert Museum in London; fig. 21),[37] they were certainly not intended to be moved very often and were therefore placed in areas where people would sit for longer periods of time.

Some scholars locate these chairs on the dais of a great hall or some other important and commanding position, often in the context of supper.[38] The master or mistress of the house then had the privilege of sitting on the 'seat of authority' while other diners had to be satisfied with less comfortable benches and stools.[39] Although the *quayère* was indeed a rather prestigious piece of furniture (and perhaps even more expensive than other types of seating because of its raw materials such as oak)[40] and wealthier people often possessed more than one chair, even less wealthy, single persons of the lower social strata in Bruges were able to afford at least one such chair.

To find the exact furniture arrangement around the chair, we have looked for combinations of chairs with other pieces of furniture that were all in close vicinity, in other words, mentioned by the appraiser precisely before or after the chair and in the same room. For the fifteenth-century sample of Bruges, only five contexts (in five different inventories) out of thirty-one contexts with chairs appear to match the theory of the supper hierarchy. The dining room of Willem van Nokerhoud (1444), for example, contained a table with one *quayère* and six

Fig. 22. A throne-like chair is standing next to the canopied bed. The Annunciation, Master of FVB, c.1480, Copper plate Engraving, Amsterdam, © Rijksmuseum

stools.[41] The other two dining rooms in the sample (with a table) both had stools and benches as seats for sitting at the table but no chair. The upstairs chamber of Guillaume Serveur (1444), the room called *bouge* of Elisabeth, wife of Henry le Hollandre (1438), and the kitchen of Tanne, wife of Lampsin Bousse (1439), all included a set of one table with one chair, or *quayère*, and two benches, or *lys*.[42] The benches were probably positioned on each side of the table with the single chair at the head of it.

However, it appears from our data that most of the high-backed chairs were placed next to a bed, a practice that is also noticeable in contemporary paintings and illuminations. As we discussed earlier in the chapter on panel paintings, a new visual iconography was rapidly gaining popularity in the fifteenth century southern Low Countries, in other words that of the Virgin in a fully developed domestic interior.[43] Most of these Annunciation scenes were situated in a room that would resemble some sort of a bedchamber. The centre panel of the *Annunciation Triptych* by Rogier van der Weyden (1434)[44] is an example of such a scene set in a bedchamber-like interior with a fully made-up canopied bed and a throne-like chair standing next to it. The engraving on paper of the Annunciation (ca. 1480)[45] by the anonymous early Netherlandish engraver Master FVB (active ca. 1480–1500) shows a similar setting (fig. 22). In both artworks, the Virgin Mary is depicted praying on a prayer stool in front of her bed, suddenly disturbed by the archangel bringing her the news of the imminent birth of her son. Next to the bed is a wooden throne-like chair.

The *Livre des métiers*, a schoolbook written in Bruges during the second half of the fourteenth century, containing texts in Middle Dutch with French translations, mentions that 'neffens d'bedde, eenen setel' is needed.[46] The habit of placing a chair next to a bed was also made explicit in a late fifteenth-century contract between Catherine de Saint-Genois (abbess of Flines) and sculptor Ricquart to make a wooden altarpiece for the abbey church.[47] The contract stipulated a detailed list of requirements the artist had to observe. In the middle section of the altarpiece, beneath the Crucifixion of Christ, the Birth of Christ had to be depicted. In this scene, the Virgin had to be seated on 'un lit richement orné et garni de rideaux entr'ouverts'.[48] Further on, we read a more detailed description of the precise setting of the bed 'et par la costé du quavech de ladicte couche, au lez dextre, par devant, sera fourmé la manière d'une quayère appoyoire, de telle façon que on les fait en Brabant et en Flandres et en plusieurs aultres lieux'.[49] The bed and the high chair were thus meticulously described and compared with recognisable, everyday examples. A lot of the chairs we come across in the inventories of the first sample period are indeed situated near a bed. Elisabeth, the rich widow of Arnoud d'Honde (1438), had no fewer than three chairs, of which one was mentioned as standing next to the *grand lit*. The two other chairs described as 'old' were supposedly moved by the widow to a room that served as a storage space for old furniture and the armour of her late husband.[50]

The fifteenth century data suggest that the chairs could have performed different functions in different settings; as the seat of honour at the (dinner) table, but also as a prop next to a bed, for example as a standard for hanging clothes when preparing to go to bed or as a prayer stool. In some rare cases, the chair fulfilled a role in a reception room (such as the floor or front room) as one of the seats in front of the fireplace. But these chairs were only rarely discovered in rooms such as the kitchen. Interestingly, though these high chairs, or *quayères*, were the seats of honour on certain occasions, they were only rarely cushioned or dressed with a banker. Even in paintings, we hardly ever see throne-like chairs dressed with cushions. Notwithstanding the fact that this type of chair is equipped with backrests and armrests, it remains an unyielding, vertical kind of chair. The back of the sitter remains completely vertical, 'with the result that the head is thrown off balance, the back left unsupported, and the sitting posture becoming penitential as the flat seat is not shaped to the body or tilted and is in the wrong height from the ground'.[51] So at times when these chairs were seen as the most privileged seats in the room, fulfilling an important role in the context of social hierarchy, representing rank and position, they were granted this role because of their uniqueness (there was often only one such chair in the room), their size and sturdiness and the fact that the sitter could sit upright for a longer period of time, but certainly not because these chairs were comfortable in terms of offering softer seating.

In contrast to these spartanly dressed chairs, lager benches such as the aforementioned *leson* or *lys* were often furnished with a loose piece of cloth employed as a seat covering called a banker, or *banquier*. Moreover, cushions of different types of fabric and colour were put on benches to soften the hard wooden surface of the seat and back as well. The rich inventory (1438) of Margriete, the wife of Jehan de Steenackere, describes how the outhouse or the small house in the backyard (*maisoncelle derriere au jardin*) was filled with smaller benches and stools standing around the table and near the bathtub and with one larger bench, or *lys*, offering extra seating for family members or potential visitors.[52] According to the information from the inventory, the bench was not furnished with textiles, but Margriete and her husband had the ability to do so when the occasion arose, because the large chest, or *escring*, standing next to the *lys* held several bankers and red and blue cushions.

Cushions and bankers were not the only devices used to improve the position of the sitters; in some cases, a footstool was sometimes put in front of the bench as well. In this way, the feet of the sitters were raised, the muscles of the pelvis and the back could relax and the sitter would sit much more comfortably. But the footstool was still only rarely used to improve seating comfort around the middle of the fifteenth century. It was only throughout the second half of the century that the use of footstools in front of benches seems to have increased.

A footstool could easily be replaced by a narrow footboard, illustrated in the interior of the Annunciation scene by the Master of Flémalle (ca. 1427–1432),[53] where we see a large bench in front of the fireplace. The bench is furnished with a green banker covering the seat and the back of the bench and a large yellow, goldish cushion. A narrow wooden footboard attached to the front of the bench could support the feet and legs of the sitter, improving ergonomics and allowing the sitter to enjoy the warming heat of the fire for a longer time. A similar bench with a rotating back and a footboard on one side is depicted on another painting by the same artist; the right panel of the Werl altarpiece depicts Saint Barbara, who is seated on a large bench that is dressed with red cushions and a red banker (fig. 23).[54] When the radiating heat of the fire became too warm to bear, the sitter could easily rotate the backrest of the bench and sit on the other side of the bench facing away from the immediate fire.

Fig. 23. Saint Barbara sitting on a bench before the hearth. The bench is decorated with a red coloured banker and some red cushions on the seat. Werl Altarpiece, right panel of St. Barbara, Robert Campin, 1438, Tempera on Panel, Madrid, © Museo del Prado

The variety in seating furniture clearly increased in the course of the second half of the fifteenth century. In the second sample period (1450–1500), we find a larger amount and a more diversified array of seating furniture. It seems that both the throne-like chairs and stools or small one-person benches had developed into a new type of seating; in the inventories of this sample period, we find *stoelen*, or chairs. Though it is difficult to know what these chairs looked like, it was certainly not a term meant to describe seats similar to small benches or stools, because these had their own terminology: *schabelle(bank)* or *banxke* for one-person benches and *driestael* or *drievoete stoelen* for three-legged stools. Some households had *schabellen*,

Fig. 24. Joseph sits on a barrel-shape chair. Holy Family at Supper, Hours of Catherine of Cleves, c. 1440. MS M.917, pp. 150–151. © The Morgan Library & Museum, New York

driestaelen and *stoelen* all at the same time and in the same room. Nor does it mean that the throne-like chairs, or *quayères*, no longer existed in this period either. The *zetele* (and perhaps also the *leunstoel*, or reclining chair) was probably a derivative of the previously discussed throne-like chair as the Middle Dutch term *zetel* has a similar meaning to the English medieval 'chair' or 'seat of authority'.[55] Some of the *zetele* were described as *opstaende zethele* or *hoghe zetele*, which refers to the high back of the seat. When calculating where these seats would have been situated, the results suggest that the *zetele* could have appeared in many different rooms (back room, dining room, room, kitchen and front room). Looking more closely at the material contexts of this type of chair, it is telling that most of these seats were still located near a bed, just like the *quayère*. Some others were found near a table with small benches and three-legged chairs suggesting a hierarchical supper context, such as the *setele* in the back room of the house of Jehanne, the widow of Jacob Jooris (1476).[56] The table was accompanied by two benches, three three-legged stools and one turned *setele* cushioned with two red cushions.

Another type of the regular wooden *setele*, and new in this period but remaining present in the interior throughout the whole of the sixteenth century, is the *cuupsetele*, or barrel chair. As the name suggests, this type of seating furniture is made from barrels or was made following the principles of barrel making.[57] How and by whom they were made is not entirely clear. Even the ordinances of the craft of the barrel makers do not provide any information on the production of these chairs.[58] According to Berend Dubbe, the chair was manufactured by removing a piece of the barrel so that the remaining part formed the backrest. The *cuupsetele* thus had low armrests and a curved back because of the barrel shape.[59] On the miniature 'Holy Family at Work' in the book of hours of Catherine of Cleves (ca. 1440), Joseph is seated on a primitive example of a barrel-shape seat (fig. 24).[60]

Not only were the shape and construction of the *cuupsetele* different from those of the *zetele*, but the function of this type of chair also seemed different from that of the 'original' or 'fifteenth-century' throne-like chairs. When calculating their relative dispersion over the rooms, they would have occurred mainly in the kitchen – an interesting development and very different from the use context of the fifteenth-century *quayre*. In most cases, these barrel chairs standing in the kitchen – often but not always in the company of reclining or wickerwork chairs and benches – were also cushioned. Perhaps these more comfortable chairs not only represented the growing social importance of the kitchen as a locus of sociability and conviviality but also materialised the need for comfortable seating during the prolonged act of preparing food.[61]

The long, often decoratively crafted benches, or *lys*, were still popular during the second half of the fifteenth century, as were the regular benches, small benches and stools. The latter occurred especially in rooms where flexible seating furniture was often needed such as the dining room and the floor (*vloer*), whereas the former were spread across the house with the exception of the kitchen. Interestingly, the larger benches were still more often seen than the chairs and sofa chairs (*zetele*) fitted with cushions.

During the first half of the fifteenth century, people who could afford cushions preferred to have them put on benches such as the *lijs* or *schabellebanck*, rather than on individual, throne-like chairs. The latter chairs were, in most cases, literally used as seats of authority and propagated status and prestige through their sturdiness and size. Throughout the second half of the fifteenth century, we see a larger variation in these status chairs, made of a variety of materials such as wooden barrels, wickerwork and oak. The chairs were therefore increasingly less expensive and more in reach of a larger group of consumers. Some of these 'cheaper' chairs were often equipped with cushions, in contrast to the 'original' *quayres*, but these cushioned chairs seem to have functioned in a wholly different context – in the kitchen near the pots and pans and the simmering soup or in situations where it was necessary to have a comfortable seat for hours in a day.

Significant changes in the design and use of seating furniture and its connection with textiles occurred during the second half of the sixteenth century. So-called *saelstoelen* and *spaansche stoelen* were from then on part of the array of seating furniture in the more well-to-do households. In addition, the number of the plainer, individual seats also increased. Both the more luxurious chairs and the simpler ones were increasingly adorned and softened with cushions, such as the hall chair of Joos Themmerman (1584) standing in a room labelled *camere*, which was furnished with a tapestry cushion.[62] Others were decorated with larger pieces of tapestry such as the two *tapytschee zaelmakers stoelen* in the dining room of Jan Baptist Lommelin (1569).[63] Both types of chairs represented, as it were, an evolution in the design of individual seating furniture, because they were probably lighter and more graceful than the previously discussed throne-like chairs. Some of the *saelstoelen* and *spaansche stoelen* were also upholstered – a new feature of individual seating furniture, though not yet entirely replacing cushions and other textile furnishings.[64] Upholstered seating gradually became more popular not only because it breathed comfort thanks to stuffing and leather- or textile-covered fixed seats, but their symmetrical design, attractive materials and, above all, their meticulous workmanship bestowed a distinctive splendour on their owners.[65] Upholstered chairs were therefore first and foremost meant as luxury furniture, comfortable to sit on and also highly decorative. In England, one of the first well-known and appreciated upholstered single chairs was called the 'farthingale chair', referring to the hooped dress or farthingale worn by women during the sixteenth century.[66] It was a broad-seated chair presumably made to accommodate the hooped dress or farthingale,[67] a feature that was not necessary in the Bruges context, because Flemish women did not wear such wide, hooped dresses.[68] Wealth and status began to be expressed through the light design and the comfort of chairs rather than their sturdiness and size.

Fig. 25. Backstool fitted with leather, 1660-1700, © Victoria and Albert Museum, London.

Not unexpectedly, these luxurious leather- or textile-backed chairs with or without armrests made sitting for longer periods of time easier, which was especially convenient during dinner parties and other social occasions. They were luxury objects, status objects even, predominantly present in the wealthier households of Bruges. In the fifth sample period (1559–1574), these chairs appeared only in the wealthier households; in the sixth sample period (1584–1600), some people of the middling groups could afford such types of chairs as well, but the majority of owners were still part of the highest wealth category. The luxurious character of the hall chair also becomes clear from its distribution across the domestic space. Hall chairs were most often positioned in rooms labelled *camere*, middle rooms, front rooms and the *salette*, with a dazzling ratio of nineteen. The same compelling results were obtained for the Spanish chair; the dining room and the *salette* were preferred.

Spaensche stoelen were by definition upholstered, but not exclusively with leather (fig. 25). Originally, the chairs were most likely covered with Spanish leather, but soon other materials were in use. In all likelihood, the Spanish chair appeared first in Antwerp at the beginning of the sixteenth century – the first records date to 1520.[69] According to Ria Fabri, an expert on the subject, these chairs were first imported from the Iberian peninsula and were distributed from Antwerp to the rest of the southern Low Countries.[70] But Bruges was also named as an early consumption centre for this type of chair.[71] This early presence of Spanish chairs in Bruges should come as no surprise, of course, because the city had long been the second home of many Iberian traders and merchants. The chairs could easily have been imported from the Iberian peninsula to Bruges directly through the port of Sluis or imported from neighbouring Antwerp, though they might have been produced locally as well (as was eventually the case in Antwerp). Indeed, in all likelihood, the prefix 'Spanish' referred more to the style of the chair than to its production centre (or the origin of its leather seat).[72] However, we cannot seem to find any evidence of a local production of this type of chair in Bruges, compared to the abundant references to this craft in the Antwerp sources – Antwerpian Gabriel Duvael who left an inventory in 1588 was even a *Spaansch stoelmaecker.*[73] So Spanish chairs were perhaps difficult to access for most Bruges citizens, and the possession of this type of seating furniture was therefore limited to the families of Spanish merchants and the Bruges well-to do –people with money and easy access to the Antwerp or Spanish market.

Indeed, looking at ownership details, only nine households out of our total sample of 502 households owned a Spanish chair. This low figure is even more noteworthy when compared with the numbers in Antwerp. Carolien De Staelen's research has shown that no fewer than ninety-five Antwerp households out of a total of 205 in the period between 1566 and 1599 owned at least one Spanish chair.[74] Furthermore, most of the chairs in Bruges were in the possession of Spanish families; Fernando de Castere, for example, owned no fewer than seven Spanish chairs, and Marie Pardo, wife of Fernando de Matanca, had four Spanish chairs in her son-in-law's room.[75]

To conclude, during the sixteenth century, individual chairs were increasingly decorated with fabrics be it cushions or upholstery. It was no longer only the master of the household who sat on the only throne-like chair in the room, but guests and other household members could take a seat on individual – and often cushioned or upholstered – seats as well, be it in the context of dinner or in the context of work and leisure. This is not to say that differences in domestic and social hierarchy were no longer made visible. The specification of *men's* and *women's* chairs (*mannenstoelen* and *vrouwenstoelen*), for example, probably indicated notable differences in size.[76] In some other cases, only one upholstered chair was equipped with armrests, whereas the other upholstered chairs in the same space were not. Moreover, whereas the throne-like chair of the early and mid-fifteenth century was certainly not comfortable in terms of offering its user a soft seat, from the sixteenth century onwards, the most prestigious pieces of seating furniture in the room were the chairs with a fabric or leather decoration, such as luxurious upholstered Spanish chairs. So comfort became a vital part in the game of exemplifying social status.

The second part of the sixteenth century was, however, marked not just by changes in individual seating facilities; the nature of multiple seating furniture also changed. Not only did the number of benches per household decrease, benches of all kinds were increasingly less furnished with cushions or bankers, which was in stark contrast to the period before. Even in the poorer households, the median number of benches decreased over time, in favour of individual chairs.

Show Me Your Bed and I'll Tell You Who You Are!

A complete set of sleeping furniture – in other words, a wooden bed frame (*coetse* or *ledikant*) and its accompanying appurtenances such as a mattress (*bedde*), sheets, blankets, cushions and on some occasions also curtains – was one of the most expensive goods in households.[77] Nevertheless, there were great price and quality differences between different types of beds. These differences may be attributed to the type of bed (*coetse, wentelcoetse, lysebedde, ledikant*, box-beds, fixed beds) as well as to the number of sheets and blankets and the type of textiles used to cover the bed.[78] In most cases, the bed was dressed with a mattress of different fillings and qualities, sheets, a blanket (*saarge*), two pillows, a bolster and in some cases also some curtains and a *rabat*.[79] But some beds in the Bruges inventories were not fully made up or were only soberly dressed, indicating that these beds were either not in use at the time the inventory was made or that the users of these beds held lower ranks in the household's social hierarchy (for example, servants or temporary lodgers).[80] Hence, the variations in the type of wood, in size and in workmanship of the bed frame and in the use of textiles was quite great, but it was, above all, social standing that determined the shape, the material, the decoration and the location of the bed.[81] In this regard, the marriage bed was generally larger, was furnished more richly with fabrics and was closer to the fire than, for example, the beds of children, maidservants, apprentices or occasional visitors.[82] We have also explained in a previous chapter that in some households, the marital bed was located in a specific and suitably equipped room, the sleeping room. Notwithstanding the assumed necessity of bedding and textiles related to sleeping and the fact that beds were basic and almost indispensable household goods, we could question the use value of these textiles and whether this changed throughout the period.

That the marriage bed fulfilled an important role in the household and that this was also noticeable from its size and decoration is apparent from the inventory of widow Cathelyne de Berg (1569).[83] Her house contained at least four rooms; an unidentified 'room', a kitchen, floor and an attic. All the rooms on the ground floor were equipped to cook, eat, work, receive visitors and sleep in. But the bed with the most opulent textiles, the *coedste met gordynen rabat ende tapytsche saerge*, or the bed with curtains, a *rabat* and a blanket made from tapestry, was not placed in one of the most frequently used rooms of the house but was stored away in the attic together with some pieces of clothing, a table and some cushions. A more 'sober' bed, without the curtains but still with a tapestry blanket, was positioned downstairs in the unidentified 'room' – a room that had the potential to receive and entertain guests. Perhaps Cathelyne thought it no longer necessary or even appropriate to put her marriage bed in the centre of her home? Or is this an illustration of a gradual move of the bed from the more public spaces of the house to the privacy of a separate bedroom? The fact remains that beds derived a lot of their value from their symbolic meaning as well. They were a frequent gift in wills from mothers to their daughters or aunts to their nieces or from mistresses to their domestic servant girls.[84] Bedlinens were also vital parts of a dowry,[85] because clean sheets, blankets and cushions were considered indispensable for a good night's sleep.[86] So in general, the bed was a strong symbol for marriage, the household and the creation of a home.

The bedding of some particular beds included bed curtains as well, colouring the interior, but also granting the bed status and prestige and dividing it from the rest of the room.[87] Curtains protected the sleepers from draughts and cold. Draped around the bed, they made sleeping far more comfortable in houses where cracks and crevices were omnipresent. Nonetheless, when looking in the inventories, we see that not every bed was dressed with curtains. Moreover, throughout the period, we see little change in the total number of beds with curtains per sample period, with only a slight increase throughout the entire sixteenth century. So despite the comforts these textiles could offer, the majority of beds were not dressed with curtains. Antony Buxton came to a similar conclusion in his study of non-elite households of the market town of Thame in Oxfordshire in the seventeenth century. He calculated that only 14 per cent of the total sleeping furniture in the Thame inventories consisted of curtained and canopied bedsteads.[88]

Table 16. Mean Number of Beds with Curtains per Sample Period

SAMPLE PERIODS	NUMBER OF HOUSEHOLDS	NUMBER OF BEDS (COETS)	BEDS WITH CURTAINS	MEAN OF BEDS WITH CURTAINS PER HOUSEHOLD
1438–1444	69	81	16	0.23
1450–1500	33	132	11	0.08
1500–1510	10	23	3	0.13
1528–1549	57	111	27	0.24
1559–1574	221	493	115	0.23
1584–1600	112	293	67	0.23

Source: Database of inventories © IB, JDG & IS

Table 17. Mean Number of Beds per Household for Two Sample Periods

SAMPLE PERIOD	NUMBER OF HOUSEHOLDS	BEDS WITH CURTAINS	MEAN PER HOUSEHOLD
1438–1444	69	16	0.23
Low	35	3	0.09
Middle	25	4	0.16
High	9	9	1.00
1559–1574	221	115	0.52
Low	80	14	0.18
Middle	94	56	0.60
High	47	55	1.17

Source: Database of inventories © IB, JDG & IS

In each sample period, it is clear that each household owned on average at least one bed (with bedframe and mattress) (table 16), but also that not every household owned a bed with curtains. The mean numbers per sample period are somewhat misleading, however, because the mean number of beds with curtains per household is reduced by the small number of curtained beds in the lowest social groups. In table 17, we therefore break the calculation down per social group for sample period 1 (1438–1444) and sample period 5 (1559–1574).

Differences between the two sample periods are notable, but it is also clear that the higher up the social scale, the more likely that people owned at least one bed with curtains. This is not surprising, because fabrics required a certain investment, an investment the lower social groups were not always able to make. So our image of the late medieval curtained bedstead is probably more coloured by the contemporary imagery of wealthier beds and households.

Scholars have discussed two other important motivations behind the use of bed curtains, which could shed light on their absence or presence: curtains would increase the privacy of the sleepers, creating a private, secluded micro space within the macro space of the room[89] and the use of opulent curtains would lend the bed and the family a certain prestige.[90] The quality of the fabric (and perhaps also the quality of the colouring) might have been an important tool in the representation of status. However, it appears that in the Bruges sample, curtains were only exceptionally made from expensive silks such as *tûle* and *caffa*, or taffeta. Indeed, we have found only four cases of silk curtains out of a total of seventy-five cases in which the type of fabric was known. One pair of curtains, a canopy and a *rabat* were of the more luxurious *caffa* or a silk, which Isis Sturtewagen describes as patterned silk velvet, with floral or geometric patterns. It could be both of a single colour or multicoloured.[91] These particular textiles were part of a set of the bed furniture of the wealthy Hispano-Bruges Marie Pardo, who lived in a large house near the Borse, the city's stock exchange (1597).[92] Unfortunately, the *caffa* textiles were lumped together with all the other textiles of the household, which makes it nearly impossible to link them to a specific bed in a specific room in her house. So these bed garments were categorised separately from their furniture, though the bedding that was on the bed during appraisal was registered together with the furniture. It suggests that these *caffa* textiles were not used at all times and brought out only on special occasions.

Most curtains, however, were made from less expensive say (*saai*) (64), and a few from other fabrics such as cloth (1), linen (5) or serge (1). Say was a light woollen fabric, produced in the southern Low Countries on a large scale (and often imported from England or the Northern Netherlands)[93] and therefore available to a wide range of consumers. Say was much lighter than tapestry and cloth (the latter was used to make warm outer garments) and probably also more permeable, permitting the passage of air and light when necessary, ideal for curtains that were used for protecting sleepers during the night. Say curtains were certainly not the most exclusive or expensive ones,[94] especially not when compared to silk, so the argument of using high-quality, expensive curtains to show off status might be true for the higher elites in society, but was less valid for the middling groups of Bruges urban society.

Say was also an important fabric used in dress, but its popularity declined during the sixteenth century, because some say was submitted to fulling and thus no longer showed the weave structure. Sturtewagen has shown that surface textures on the fabrics for garments were purposely sought after precisely because of a certain fascination with the reflection of light.[95] But while the fabrics used in the clothing trade became much more diversified – from the mid sixteenth century, a whole array of light textile products was encountered, made by the so-called Nouvelle Draperie Légère, together with a variety of mixed weave fabrics of wool, silk or cotton[96] – say remained the main fabric for bed curtains even at the end of the sixteenth century.[97] So the fashionable new fabrics were not used in the creation of the textile environment of the bed. In the context of dress, the outer garments were still dominated by the more 'traditional fabrics' such as cloth and say, whereas silk and the new light woollens were predominantly used 'for the layer of garments underneath', so the garments people wore when at home.[98] In other words, in terms of fabric, there was a discrepancy between fabrics used for dress worn at home and fabrics used as decorative bed textiles.

In the first sample period (1438–1444), the few beds with curtains we found were nearly always placed in rooms with a public character. But the use of bed curtains changed, however, throughout the sixteenth century. The share of beds with curtains in rooms with a public character declined tremendously to nearly one half. It seems that the wealthier one was, the less likely it was that the dweller would situate a bed with curtains in a room with a public character. There were, of course, still higher middle-group households who intentionally put canopied and curtained beds in rooms into which people could be invited (such as the dining room, the *salette* or the front room), but at the same time, it appears that there was a move away from potentially 'public' spaces (spaces with plenty of seats, a table, a hearth, decoration, etc.) towards the privacy of the inner home. It follows the trend on the sleeping room; in houses where there was enough space, people were inclined to create a separate room for sleeping that was more private than others and only occasionally open for visitors. Sarti, Thorton and Currie saw a similar trend in the larger Renaissance houses of Florence and Milan; there were more rooms with a bed separate from the one used for receiving guests 'to create a relatively private personal space',[99] a trend that was also similar to what Carolien De Staelen witnessed in sixteenth-century Antwerp: a growing separation between reception and sleeping functions.[100] So canopied or curtained beds might just as well have stayed prestigious and linked with marital life, but the marital bed itself was placed less and less often in the more public spaces of the house. Perhaps the physical act of sleeping itself (and all it entails such as dressing and undressing oneself, smells and sounds of sleeping) was no longer associated with public life and the eyes of outsiders?

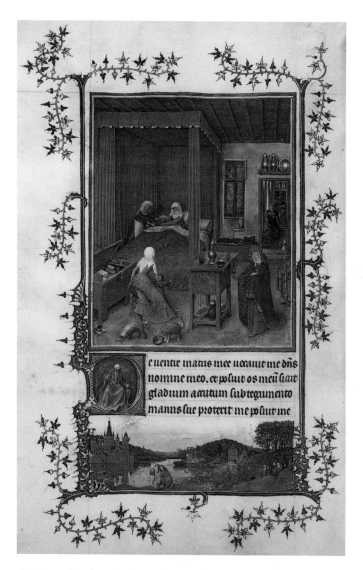

Fig. 26. Bed with red curtains. The Birth of John the Baptist (miniature from the Très Belles Heures de Notre-Dame), Jan van Eyck, c.1422. Body colour on parchment. © Museo Civico d'Arte Antica, Turin, Italy

A phenomenon comparable to the fact that the physical act of eating was becoming less the subject of discussion, whereas dining practices, manners and the social character of the dinner party were growing in importance.[101]

Fig. 27. Bed, 17th century (with 19th century details and textiles), Bruges,
© OCMW Brugge, www.artinflanders.be

To conclude, beds were omnipresent in many households throughout the fifteenth and sixteenth centuries, but only a minority of these beds were decorated
with curtains or a *rabat* (fig. 26 & fig. 27). Besides protecting the sleepers from
cold, curtains were also used to denominate the most important bed(s) for the more
important people of the household. Throughout the sixteenth century, especially
in the wealthier households, these curtained beds were less and less present in the
more public spaces. This might point to a growing importance attached to privacy
and the controlled or semi-accessibility of private spaces or might indicate that the
majority of middle-class people were not able or keen to retain in their domestic
space a special 'status' bed used only for performative or conspicuous purposes. As

in the previous section on seating furniture and comfort, it seems that the function of textiles such as curtains somehow changed. And choices were made as to which bed would be equipped with curtains and in which type of room this bed would be situated. Perhaps the character of how to showcase status and the ability to provide for comfort changed?

Keeping Up Appearances? Tapestry in the Domestic Interior

One of the merchants of the Spanish nation, Vélasco de Béjar, also related to the Hispano-Bruges Pardo family, died in 1555 and left an inventory and a will, which were drafted and preserved by the notary of the Spanish nation, Pedro de Paredes.[102] Vélasco and his wife, Catalina Coquill, owned several tapestry hangings of different styles, sizes and provenance, all described in great detail. Their house had two dining rooms, one on the street side and one facing the courtyard. The walls of the two dining rooms were completely covered in tapestries. Even the windows of the larger dining room facing the courtyard were fully dressed in tapestries as well. Each separate piece of hanging was meticulously described in size and design; sometimes even the background colour of the tapestry was mentioned. All of these hangings were of the *verdure*, or foliage, type. Not only the walls of these rooms were decorated with lively weaves; even the bed in the larger dining room was covered with a large and colourful tapestry bedspread. More precisely, it was *eene grote tappytse saerdse groote feullaige dienende inde groote eidcamere jeghen het hof rondomme met lysten of boorden vier ellen en half hoogh ende drie ellen en half breed dienende op tbedde van tgroote lydechampt*, or a large tapestry bedspread with foliage and decorative framework, located in the large dining room facing the courtyard, four ells high and three and a half ells wide, to cover the bed of the large bedstead.[103] Besides the *chambers*, or the tapestry ensembles that filled the rooms to the brim with tapestry, Vélasco de Béjar and his wife possessed other tapestry bedspreads and several bench rugs as well, also of the *verdure* type. Some of the bankers were described as *met personaigen*, without further specification. Furthermore, they owned no fewer than twenty-four cushions or four sets of six cushions with the same theme; six had a rose in the centre, six the coat of arms of Vélasco's parents-in-law, or the *wapenen vande overledene vader ende joncvra moedere*, another six a red heart in the middle of the cushion and six tapestry cushions with no further specification. Two pieces of tapestry were labelled *velu*, hand-knotted with high pile, and the base colour of these tapestries was defined as violet and red, respectively.[104] So Vélasco de Béjar and his wife owned tapestries in many guises, from opulent wall hangings covering entire rooms to tapestry cushions and colourful tapestry bedspreads. One could easily state that de Béjar's ownership of tapestries to some extent resembles the lavishly decorated *chambres* of kings and dukes or the high urban elites. Hangings were important pieces of decoration, because they were 'markers of wealth, power and distinction' and because 'tapestries functioned as eloquent expressions of their owners' ambitions, accomplishments, policies, threats, faith and taste'.[105] However, this case of tapestry ownership and tapestry use was rather exceptional in Bruges, especially for the middling classes. The majority of the references to tapestry in the Bruges inventories are about objects – utensils even – made from *tapisserie*, items such as cushions, bedspreads and table covers.

Until recently, however, scholars were primarily focused on the most imposing of hangings, the sumptuous silk weavings with gold and silver thread (tapestries that were also best preserved) and used only on special occasions.[106] Moreover, the study of tapestry and the definition of the 'tapestry' article has long been centred around surviving hangings.[107] Guy Delmarcel unintentionally stresses the dangers of a study of just these remains, by referring to them as 'archaeological remains of the art of tapestry' although he himself is guilty of using only surviving hangings as a source material to base his study on.[108] Meanwhile, scholars have started to realise that tapestry came in various forms and qualities, especially in the fifteenth and sixteenth centuries.[109] The well-known tapestry hangings themselves varied greatly in size, quality and price in this period – from expensive Brussels tapestry hangings to lower-end *verdure* tapestry from Oudenaarde[110] and also Bruges – and were supplemented by other forms of tapestry that themselves varied greatly in quality and price, such as woven pillow covers, bench, table and chimney rugs and woven bedding.[111] Even the duke of Burgundy himself, Philip the Bold, ordered a *chambre*, or an ensemble of tapestry goods, in 1410, which included not only wall hangings but also bench covers, couch covers and tapestry squares.[112]

Especially because there was 'space in the medieval trade for the production of tapestry of varying degrees of quality'[113] and therefore for cheaper variants of the product – such as those made out of wool instead of silk – tapestry-producing centres, including Bruges, set out to produce a more standardised and therefore cheaper mass product attainable for a larger group of potential consumers already in the late fifteenth century. Guy Delmarcel and Erik Duverger both specify that the shops and workshops of tapestry weavers in the city of Bruges had a wide selection of figured carpets, verdures, cushion covers, banking and tablecloths and bedspreads displayed, all ready-made for on spec sale (fig. 28–30).[114] Indeed, both authors agree that one of the reasons why only few pieces of Bruges tapestry are still preserved today had to do with the fact that late fifteenth- and sixteenth-century Bruges weavers produced tapestry predominantly intended for daily use.[115]

The cushions, bankers, bed curtains and upholstery of seats discussed in the previous sections were not the only types of textiles that granted specific pieces of furniture a particular place or a special role in the spaces and rituals of daily life. Other types of household textiles, such as textile wall decorations, table rugs and cupboard covers were all part of the same 'textile environment' of the interior. We know that most bed curtains were made from light woollen fabrics such as say, with some exceptions, but most of the other textile objects in the interior were made from tapestry.

Graph 15 unmistakably emphasises the large presence of tapestry in the interior as it shows for each object type the most common type of fabric used (when the fabric was mentioned in the inventory). Tapestry and carpet were put into two different categories. Tapestry was woven and could be made from different types of fabric such as silk and wool. Carpet, or *carpette*, was probably also a certain type of weaving, but differed somehow from tapestry and intended to cover objects, not walls.[116] So it was appreciated because it had the look of a woven fabric, but was cheaper than tapestry. Many bedspreads and table covers were made from *carpette*. The two fabrics did not differ much in resale value, although some pieces of tapestry were clearly much more expensive than any type of carpet. Textile expert Peter Stabel proposes that carpet was thus a different type of tapestry, not necessarily of lesser quality.[117]

Although the precise type of fabric is not always specified by the appraiser, the relative preponderance of tapestry objects is undeniably clear. The categories of *canopy* – which comprises canopies or covers of mirrors and which were predominantly made of silk – and of *cupboard covers* are both exceptions to the rule, together with the aforementioned bed curtains, which were primarily made from say. Cupboard covers were made from lighter fabrics, such as say, linen and cloth. These kinds of fabrics were much lighter than tapestry and easier to fold and handle than the stiffer woven fabrics. And because devotional paintings were often displayed on top of a cupboard, we may assume that the focus was on these images and not on the fabric underneath. Moreover, as we have seen, many such cupboards with devotional paintings and candlesticks mimicked church altars, so the cloth on top of the cupboard might also mimic the altar cloth the priest used for drying his hands during Mass.

Fig. 28. Bruges-styled verdure of wool and silk, fragment, Bruges, © Musea Brugge, www.artinflanders.be

Fig. 29. Bruges-styled tapestry hanging of wool and silk, Bruges, © Musea Brugge, www.artinflanders.be

Fig. 30. Cushion cover with the arms of Sacheverell, Silk and wool, with silver and silver-gilt thread, Sheldon Tapestry Workshops (maker), Warwickshire (possibly, made), 1600-1620 (made), © Victoria and Albert Museum, London

Graph 15. Fabrics and Decorative Textiles

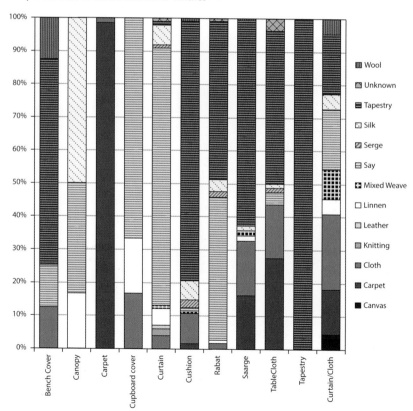

Source: Database of inventories © IB, JDG & IS

Graph 16. Fabrics of Cushions

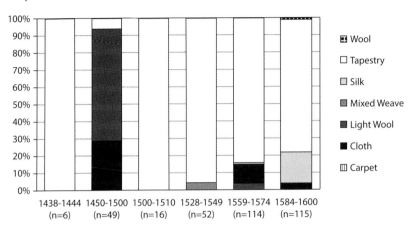

Source: Database of inventories © IB, JDG & IS

Bench covers and *saarges*, or bedspreads, were in the majority of cases, made from tapestry, but the number is particularly striking in the case of cushions.[118] Nearly 80 per cent of all the cushions of which the material was mentioned were labelled as *tapijtse kussens*, or cushions made from tapestry. The same applies to bankers or bench covers – approximately 80 per cent of which were identified as tapestry.

Table covers in particular were made either from tapestry or from *carpette*. The table covers in graph 16 were of a more decorative nature and used to decorate tables – not for covering the table during dinner. Sometimes, plain white linen or cloth tablecloths were spread over the decorative table covers to protect the fabric from stains and greasy hands.[119] According to Marco Spallanzani, these rugs to cover tables had a purely ornamental function.[120] Coloured table covers were mentioned only in the inventories from the fifth sample period (1559–1574) onwards, so from the second part of the sixteenth century. They were often stored in the *bottelarij*, or the pantry, in larger houses, together with other table furnishings, cutlery, dishes and plates. When in use, we could find coloured table covers especially in the dining room and the *salette*, both rooms where guests could be invited for dinner. But table covers were also used as a decorative feature for tables in sleeping rooms and front rooms.

In general, it seems that when people wanted to cover furniture to embellish the wooden structures of chairs, benches, beds and tables, tapestry was the preferred medium. It was as if items of furniture were 'dressed' in it. Though objects of say

Table 18. Tapestry Objects per Household

SAMPLE PERIOD	SOCIAL GROUP	NUMBER OF HOUSEHOLDS	NUMBER OF HOUSEHOLDS WITH TAPESTRY OBJECTS	SUM OF TAPESTRY OBJECTS	MEAN
1450–1500	Middle	20	1	1	1.00
	High	11	2	4	2.00
1500–1510	Middle	5	2	7	3.50
	High	2	2	12	6.00
1528–1549	Low	12	2	7	3.50
	Middle	34	16	41	2.56
	High	6	4	18	4.50
1559–1574	Low	80	9	19	2.11
	Middle	94	17	34	2.00
	High	47	34	161	4.74
1584–1600	Low	33	7	9	1.29
	Middle	65	33	153	4.64
	High	14	13	114	8.77

Source: Database of inventories © IB, JDG & IS

and cloth, such as bed curtains, *saarges* and cupboard covers were often colourful and therefore visible as well, many art and textile historians have stated that tapestry could be used more easily to communicate subliminal messages of status, family lineage and taste and figured well in a newly developing taste for luxurious-looking, colourful fabrics with contrasting and light-reflecting textures obvious in the domain of dress.[121] Cushions, tablecloths, bench covers, wall decorations and spreads were in general all attractive to the eyes of the observer and were to be used, felt and experienced by visitor and host alike.

Nearly all households of the wealthier middle groups owned at least one piece of tapestry (table 18). The mean number of tapestry objects even increases for the wealthiest group throughout the sixteenth century, whereas the number for the middling groups remains more or less steady. We know that from the late fifteenth century onwards, a lot of tapestry-producing centres were embarking on the production of a more standardised and therefore cheaper mass product attainable for a larger group of potential consumers. So thanks to the local production of on spec goods, people started to buy and use the fabrics that were previously only within the reach of the court and a rich elite. At the same time, however, these middle-class consumers had to satisfy themselves with lesser-quality varieties of fabrics, because high-end and high-quality silk and tapestry were still available only to the richest in society.

In this context, there is a certain similarity to the ownership of silks in clothing. Earlier on, owning and wearing silks such as velvets, brocades and satins were the prerogative of the elites. According to Jeroen Puttevils, the market for silks was a limited one, 'dominated by the luxurious consumption of silks by the urban high nobility'.[122] But the genesis of a 'local silk production made it possible, in theory at least, to offer luxuriously looking but at the same time reasonably affordable fabrics [...] to an increasing group of people'.[123] So a cheaper silk fabric that was woven from half satin and half silk (i.e. Bruges satin) became increasingly popular among the middling social groups to use in dress but also in accessories. So it was the best of both worlds, because the fabric was cheaper and therefore easier to afford, but it still retained the 'luscious look of real silk satin'.[124] And here as well, Sturtewagen concludes that 'during the sixteenth century the number of half silk and silk objects mentioned in the inventories increases considerably, although surely, this middling class consumption should not be over-estimated compared to the expenditure of the court'.[125] Silk was therefore no longer the prerogative of the higher elites and came within the reach of other social layers of society – which, to some extent, also explains the flood of sumptuary legislation 'that swamped large parts of Europe during the late Middle Ages and the Early Modern Period, but remained largely absent in the Low Countries'.[126]

So the middling groups clearly owned lower-quality but equally splendid tapestry objects, though the number of tapestry wall hangings was limited. Tapestry objects were mainly used as functional objects or props, such as cushions and bedspreads, and only rarely as wall decoration. People had good alternatives or substitutes for the more expensive tapestry hangings, such as larger canvas paintings (see previous chapter), so there was no need to invest in expensive tapestry hangings. But the question remains why people would prefer to have tapestry as the most important fabric of their textile environment.

Though Bruges harboured several ateliers, it was certainly not the main centre for tapestry production in the Low Countries at that time. Brussels, Oudenaarde, Arras and Tournai produced far larger quantities of tapestry and were widely known for quality in both fabric and design.[127] Antwerp acted as an important distribution centre for the marketing of tapestry from other urban centres.[128] But especially in the fifteenth century, the Bruges tapestry industry was thriving and was even attractive to foreigners, because several foreign masters bought citizenship and membership of the Bruges guild.[129] Guy Delmarcel claims that most tapestry coming off the Bruges looms was specifically characterised as a type of millefleurs tapestry with a central coat of arms or central cartouche with figures set on a densely flowered ground, on the one hand, and as figurative sets characterised by 'the direct simplicity of their drawing', on the other hand.[130] Delmarcel asserts furthermore that the Bruges market was also an export market with a large Spanish outlet, especially for heraldic tapestries and with a preference for 'a more traditional presentation', similar to their taste for paintings.[131]

Although tapestry objects were easily the most visually alluring interior objects, references to these objects in inventories were mostly brief, without much detail of the iconography or weaving structure. We have found only sixteen references to the iconography or the aesthetic layout of the weave out of a total of 740 entries (individual entries, so without exact numbers). Four references included cushions with armorial illustrations and a tapestry tablecloth representing a coat of arms. Two bedspreads were *ghefigureerd*, or had a figurative design, and one bedspread was labelled as a *verdure*, or a design with foliage, flowers or animals.[132] In addition, there were nine more references for thirty-two individual pieces of tapestry, where more information on the design of the weave was revealed. François de la Vega (1545) owned tapestries with greens, flowers and animals (*verdures*) and displayed them in his dining room.[133] Cornelis van Praet (1561), who lived near the Koningsbrug by the river, displayed six pieces of tapestry in his dining room, together with a tapestry tablecloth to cover the large square table and two tapestry or embroidered cushions that were part of his textile environment as well.[134] In general, the tapestry objects that were given most attention in the inventories were owned by the upper social layers of Bruges society – such as the many foreign merchants eager to buy luxury products to furnish their own homes and to export to their home countries – and were mainly used as wall hangings. These were probably also the most expensive ones, with a high resale value. So the appraiser and the family of the deceased had every reason to note these objects in great detail.

Indeed, the only inventories that do give more information on the iconography and even sometimes the provenance of the tapestry hangings and other tapestry objects were nearly all of members (or spouses of these members) of the Spanish nation. This higher degree of detail in the description of objects in these inventories may be due to the fact that most were drawn up by a notary appointed by the nation itself and not by the appraisers working for the city. Jacquemyne van Steeland (1583) was married to Pedro de Oroses, consul and bailiff of the nation of Biscaye in

Bruges, and owned three pieces of tapestry, again of the *verdure* type, with coats of arms.[135] Though we do not know where she bought her tapestries or who delivered them, judging from the iconography of the tapestry described, it seems likely that she bought tapestry that was Bruges-made or had a clear Bruges-like iconography. The tapestries were displayed in a room above the hall, or *inde tweetste camere boven de zaele*, where a bed with yellow curtains, a green rug on the chimney, benches and a wardrobe were found as well – probably not the most public and luxurious room in the house. Also members of the wealthy Pardo family possessed a large collection of tapestry hangings. Jozijne Pardo, married to Adriaen De Bosch, died in 1574 and left behind an impressive legacy. *Tapisserie* was one of the object clusters in her inventory, following the silverwork and preceding all the linen. Jozijne Pardo and her husband clearly loved the more fashionable tapestry collections in addition to the more traditional (and often less expensive) *verdure*, because their inventory comprised no fewer than *zes sticken van bruesselsche tapitserie met personnageyn*, or six pieces of figurative Brussels tapestry, and *vijf sticken van tapitserie van feuillage*, or five pieces of *verdure*. Besides these hangings, Jozijne owned many tapestry cushions, all bearing a coat of arms.[136]

As explained above, the Spanish nation in Bruges had its own notary and therefore its own system of administration. In the archives of that organisation, we could find five more inventories, of which copies were not found in the city archives, but which yield important information on the ownership of decorative textiles, especially tapestry. Jasper de Caestre, son of Diego de Canuna, native of Burgos in Spain and bailiff of the Spanish nation, died in 1569. He and his wife did not own any woven tapestry hangings, but they did own tapestry cushions and bedspreads and *cinq pieches de tapyts dhispagne de cuyr dore*, or five pieces of Spanish tapestry or gold leather, which were displayed in the hall.[137] This is quite unusual for Bruges – only two other inventories refer to gold leather hangings, of which one was from a descendant of a renowned Hispano-Bruges family.[138] The production of locally produced gold leather on a larger scale began only at the end of the sixteenth and the beginning of the seventeenth centuries in Mechelen, the main production centre for this luxury product in the southern Low Countries.[139] So Jasper de Caestre's gold leather hangings were probably imported from Spain as well, because most of the gold leather that was consumed in Europe was mainly produced in Spanish urban centres and, from there, exported to other European regions and to the colonies.[140]

In general, it seems that the vast majority of the tapestry hangings in the inventories had a *verdure* theme, though some were specifically labelled as made in avant-garde Brussels or according to the Brussels figurative style. However, the absence of provenance data makes it difficult to determine where the hangings were produced, distributed and bought. But because Bruges tapestries were sought after in overseas Spanish regions[141] and they were exported by Bruges ships from Sluis,[142] it does not seem implausible that many of these hangings were Bruges-made goods. Of the other tapestry products we know very little in terms of iconography, except for some cushions with coat of arms. In all likelihood, it would have been a mixture of figurative scenes and foliage potentially combined with coats of arms (i.e. the Bruges style) – themes that, in principle, did not differ much from the iconography on the expensive tapestry hangings in the court rooms of the people from the upper layers of society.[143]

What did differ, however, was the way tapestries were used; the more expensive wall hangings that covered the walls of palaces had to play an important but also active role in the events that took place in front of them. James Bloom even found that, in some contexts, tapestry hangings with specific themes were often replaced by other hangings that would fit the event and the company better.[144] Given the limited number of tapestries in the houses of the urban middle classes and given that most tapestries there was made into usable objects such as cushions and bedspreads, we believe that the ownership and display of tapestry in itself was deemed important to invoke its ability to represent status, taste and affluence – and above all, to embellish the interior with bright colour.

A Colourful Interior

That interiors were colourful seems beyond dispute. Colourful wall hangings and murals must have embellished the walls of many houses,[145] whereas decorative textiles were invaluable in vivifying the whole of the interior. Adding to this the different types and colours of the woods of the benches, chairs, tables and chests, the shining surfaces of brass and copper chandeliers, pewter dishes and metal pots, the paints of pictures and statuettes, the interior certainly became a true collection of a wide spectrum of colour.

In terms of colour schemes, Giorgio Riello's argument that textiles historians focus almost exclusively on dress applies once more. Most literature on the use of colours in late medieval society tends to concentrate on the colours in the clothing of the urban middling and higher social groups.[146] Based on city accounts, portraits, dyers' manuals and probate inventories, interesting findings were made. Isis Sturtewagen noticed, for instance, that black was, by far, the favourite colour in Bruges, followed in popularity only by various shades of red, and to a lesser extent, blues and greys, brown, green and white.[147] The colour black was predominantly used for outer garments worn outside the home, whereas more colourful dress was worn closer to the body and thus most probably at home.[148] Consequently, because we mostly find vibrant colours in most interiors (especially blue-, green- and red-coloured textiles) rather than black, the indoor outfits of the citizens fit perfectly well with the colour of their interiors. Moreover, Sturtewagen found only few changes in the use of colour during the fifteenth and sixteenth centuries, in contrast to the use of fabrics and the decoration of garments.[149] But as can be seen from the pie charts (graph 17), the colour spectrum for interior textiles was completely different from that of dress, and it showed a major shift throughout the fifteenth and sixteenth centuries in colour preferences from blue and red to predominantly green and red. Instead of a 'shift to the Dark side',[150] we see the growing popularity of green and the declining importance of the colour blue. Raymond Van Uytven argued that blue as a colour for interior textiles gained attractiveness only from the fifteenth century onwards.[151] So its popularity in Bruges was probably relatively short-lived and lasted only half a century. In contrast, the role of different shades of red seems to have remained unchanged over the two centuries. Violet, yellow and white became popular during the sixteenth century as well, though still in very small numbers. The colour black, increasingly popular for clothing, was no more than a rarity in the case of interior textiles.

Carolien De Staelen observed the same evolution in the colour scheme for the decorative textiles in the Antwerp inventories.[152] Her findings underline the idea that this shift was not a unique Bruges phenomenon and that explanations should probably be set in a broader context. The shift from blue to green in the colour of predominantly cushions, curtains and bedspreads is also noticeable in contemporary paintings. On fourteenth- and early fifteenth-century paintings and miniatures, bed curtains are predominantly blue, whereas the curtains of late fifteenth- and sixteenth-century beds were bright or dark green (and on some occasions even red). For the importance of black as a colour of attire, Sturtewagen proposes the hypothesis that it was not so much the colour of black that came into fashion, but the symbolic values of authority, modesty and decency, seriousness and competence – ideal for 'formal' outer garments – attached to it that became important.[153] Van

Pie charts (17). Evolution of Colours of Decorative Textiles

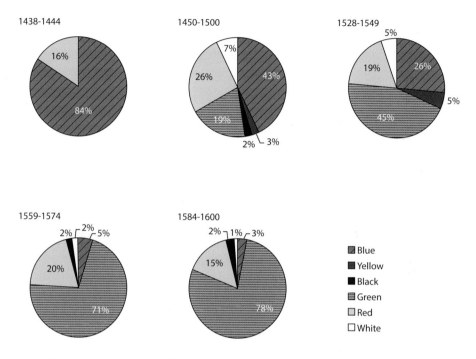

Source: Database of inventories © IB, JDG & IS

Uytven argued for a symbolic language of colours as well, especially for the colour green.[154] His findings argued that the colour green was often associated with loyalty, love, newness, joy and fertility, which would be the main reason why green was used for bed hangings in paintings and in courtly literature.[155] Van Uytven's argument will certainly be valuable for textiles in paintings, but as Jeanne Nuechterlein warns us, caution is needed when props in painted scenes are compared with objects in reality, because they often have a symbolic layer that did not necessarily correspond to real life experience.[156] Nevertheless, the popularity of the vibrant colours of blue, green and red as colours of the interior and of domestic life, as opposed to the popular colour black of outdoor clothing, might underline a separation between the life indoors and outdoors.

Curtains and cushions occur in the earliest sample periods and remain present in the interior of many Bruges citizens' houses throughout the whole period under study. However, their colour palette changed. In the fifteenth-century samples, curtains were always coloured blue. In the first part of the sixteenth century, curtains changed to blue, green and red, but in the second part of the sixteenth century, the colour blue disappeared completely. The colour palette of cushions shows a similar pattern, though the evolution is less obvious. In the fifteenth-century samples, blue cushions were clearly more frequent than in sixteenth-century samples. But the opposite applied for the colour green. The colour palette of *saerges*, or bedspreads, was more variegated already from the beginning of the period and, besides blue and green, also included different reds, yellow, black and lots of white. The latter ones, the white bedspreads, were often specified as 'Spanish', probably referring to the type of wool that was used to make them.

The shift cannot immediately be explained by a shortage of dyes or any other problem on the supply and production side either, because according to Isis Sturtewagen citing Judith Hofenck de Graeff, 'different shades of green were achieved by over-dying woad (i.e. the fermented leaves of the woad plant were used to produce the colour blue) with yellow; sometimes mixed with red, resulting in brownish green tones'.[157] So the colours or dyestuffs in blue and yellow were still needed to produce the colour green. And also black colours were always obtained by a combination of red and blue dyeing. In Bruges, the craft of the blue dyers had the exclusive right to dye textiles blue using the raw materials woad and indigo. The red dyers were allowed to dye fabrics in different shades of red.[158] These shades of red were produced using different types of raw materials, one more expensive than the others.[159] The rarer the raw material, the more it granted prestige to the wearer or the owner of the dyed fabric. But unfortunately, no further details of the shades or qualities of the colours were given for the flat textiles.

Furthermore, the yellow dyestuff that was used for dying yellow and green was collected from both the locally cultivated weld (*Reseda luteola*) and since 1500, also from the fustic or dyer's mulberry (*Maclura tinctoria*) that was imported from the New World.[160] When combined with other dyestuffs and mordants, a range of yellow and greenish colours could be produced.[161] Perhaps the greater availability of the latter raw material made it easier and cheaper for dyers to produce more greens? And perhaps this more extensive palette of colour variations made the colour more attractive for consumers?

Exposing or Storing Textiles: The *Garderobe* and the *Cleerschaprade*

Different types of objects were used to store the colourful textiles, such as chests, cupboards and wardrobes, but only two types of storage furniture, the *garderobe* and the *cleerschaprade*, were specifically named after their function of storing textiles.[162] Presumably, the names of the two types of furniture were sometimes interchangeable, as De Staelen found in her research: the Antwerp canon Simon Moors, had a 'groote garde robe ofte cleerscappraye' (1598).[163] It was not used just for storing pieces of clothing, but also for keeping household textiles such as napkins, sheets and tablecloths.

In the households of the fifteenth-century Bruges samples, the presence of a *cleerschapprade* is still rather an exception. The single woman Christine De Gheits (1438) was the only one to own an *amaires a mettre habis* in the first sample period (1438–1444).[164] The same goes for clergymen Jan Badereau (1460), who was the only owner of a *cleerscaprade* in the second sample period (1450–1500).[165] This type of furniture appeared most often from the fourth sample period (1528–1549) onwards and especially in the samples of the second half of the sixteenth century, which corresponds to the greater variation in furniture pieces in households throughout the sixteenth century. The *cleerschaprades* were generally located in rooms where storage furniture for textiles was needed: the ratios were highest for the back room, sleeping room, front room and hall. In the sleeping room, they were mainly used to store sheets, blankets, pillows and curtains, besides pieces of clothing. The *cleerschaprades* that were located in the halls were all used in the context of maintenance, laundry and general storage of different types of goods. The *cleerschaprades* in the front rooms were probably also used to store the textiles when these were not in use or were used to store extra pieces of household textiles and frequently used clothing. It is, however, difficult to know whether these pieces of storage furniture also had a performative function, comparable with the linen cupboards and cabinets in the seventeenth- and eighteenth-century Dutch households Hester Dibbits described earlier.[166] Some *cleerschaprades* were described as large, so they must have drawn the attention of visitors, especially in rooms people had to pass through when entering the house, such as the hall at the front of the house, or where they were received by the host, such as the front room. The pieces of furniture were never described as decorated or furnished in the inventories, but perhaps their size and appearance

Fig. 31. Cabinet,
16th Century, Bruges,
© Musea Brugge,
www.artinflanders.be

were more important and much more telling than their decoration and craftsman-ship; the larger the *cleerschaprade*, the more textiles it could contain (fig. 31).

Like the *cleerschaprade*, the *garderobe* was relatively unknown in the earlier sam-ple periods and more common from the second half of the sixteenth century on. The term was used to denote both a small room used to store household goods and a piece of storage furniture (probably a type of chest). One could suggest that both varieties of the *garderobe* fulfilled a similar function: both were used to store deco-rative textiles such as cushions, table covers and clothing.[167] Jan Baptiste Lommelin (1569), for example, owned a *garderobe* as a piece of furniture where he kept two green silk and embroidered curtains that were remade and used as a table cover.[168] The *garderobes*, especially in their spatial form, were reserved only for the wealthier social groups.

People were most likely aware that certain chests, trunks and other kinds of furniture were often the repositories of valuable or frequently used objects.[169] This is illustrated not only by the locks and reinforced straps on chests and trunks of all sizes but also by the fact that when goods were seized or confiscated in case of debt, chests, coffins and trunks were often immediately locked and sealed by the bailiff. In this way, goods could not leave the house unnoticed, and they were kept togeth-er in the chest (preventing the estate from decreasing in value). The unfortunate servant girl of canon Jacob Vrombert (1502), for example, lost some of her personal possessions, because her master's chests, which contained some of her own possessions, were already sealed by the bailiff during appraisal without her noticing:[170] an interesting but unfortunate example of the effectiveness of the chest's function of concealing and protecting goods. Both the *garderobe* and the *cleerschaprade* were used to conceal and protect the most expensive textiles (flat textiles and clothing), but at the same time, also hinted at their precious content and the related status of the household.

Conclusions

According to Giorgio Riello, the combination of textiles and furniture captures social and cultural practices that were less temporary than those associated with dress and clothing but also less structural than architecture and buildings.[171] Throughout the sixteenth century, a changing interconnection between furniture and flat textiles as a proxy for the importance accorded to taste, elegance and posture and gradual changes in the nature of sociability and comfort could be noticed. It was a shift inherent of a prevailing civic culture; a culture that entailed a different kind of sociability from before, but also a culture in which design, posture, comfort, taste, touch, colour and variety were all deemed increasingly important. Tapestry as a fabric or weave, for example, represented first and foremost status, affluence but also taste and knowledge about what was fashionable. People used tapestry not only because it represented status but also because it had an important aesthetic appeal as well, because it added visual interest and it satisfied a taste for colour and texture. In other words, it was the design and the aspirational look of goods and the behaviour associated with them that were deemed most important for the urban middling groups, in this case more important perhaps than the intrinsic value. This civic culture did therefore not go as far as what De Clercq, Dumolyn and Haemers labelled 'vivre noblement', or emulating the lifestyle of the ennobled elite.[172] The urban middle groups seem to have had their own use culture of luxury objects, fostering their own civic identity and social status.[173]

GENERAL CONCLUSIONS

Thanks to ground-breaking research projects and publications, especially about late medieval and early modern Britain and Renaissance Italy, research into the material culture of the home has slowly gained scholarly recognition as a missing link in studies on social, economic, political and religious developments of European societies. Yet despite this progress, historians studying material culture in the past have considered and used probate inventories too often as almost 'random' lists of objects found in the houses of people who had their belongings inventoried and publicly sold. It was often easier to reconstruct and interpret inventories and connect them to social class, gender, life cycle, cultural identity, political power or to grand narratives of modernisation, industrious revolution and so on than link these lists to real objects, daily lives and practices, let alone appreciate the materiality of the assemblages of objects and therefore assess the mechanisms by which materiality interacts with social organisation. However, while it is true that objects never 'speak directly for themselves' (not even in the context of visual representations such as paintings or prints), archival materials such as inventories do contain vital information about the domestic contexts in which the objects once gained meaning. As post-mortem and confiscation inventories offer 'information about past domestic objects and spaces, which also bear the traces of embodied existence',[1] these sources allow research on the functions and multiple meanings of objects, as they can be inferred from their spatial arrangements. Furthermore this research has proven that inventories are also highly revelatory for the domestic geography of houses, the prevailing social culture and the interconnectivity between people, objects and spaces. Indeed, especially when they are taken together in large numbers and scrutinised for the minutiae and details they contain, probate inventories 'can help us to paint a reasonably detailed picture of domestic spaces and domestic objects'.[2]

Inventories have not only enlightened us about the tendencies in material and domestic culture and about the creation of domesticity in sixteenth-century Bruges, but they have also offered a clear view on the impact of the economic upwards and downwards movements on the standards of living of citizens and the city's position within the network of trading towns. Inflation and a reorientation of the Bruges economy from the international market to the regional or local market, especially in the second half of the sixteenth century, affected the standards of living of especially the lower social groups and middling groups of Bruges society. Indeed, while Bruges merchants and entrepreneurs and some members of the middle groups still enjoyed the relative economic growth that characterised especially the first half of the sixteenth century in Bruges (mainly because of a strong position in the regional market and a relatively good position in parts of the international trade), this was by no means the case for all members of society.

The presence of the nation of the Castilians (and to a lesser extent, the Basque traders and merchants of Navarre) probably significantly contributed to the survival of especially the Bruges luxury industry in the sixteenth century. Merchants of the nation were eager consumers of the products of this luxury industry, but they also exploited the Bruges's harbour of Sluis and exported especially canvas paintings as desired substitutes for the famous large Flemish tapestries and even tapestries themselves. Even though they were respectable players on the international market, and therefore present on the Antwerp market as well and eager to convey that image through their material culture, the community thrived in Bruges until the end of the sixteenth century. Although they were expected to have integrated well into Bruges society, they maintained a particular material culture that was still firmly linked with their original homeland. Spanish furniture and majolica were uniquely found in the houses of these merchants, along with objects such as tapestries and paintings that were probably produced in the city itself or imported from or via the Antwerp market.

The size of the dwelling, the internal organisation of domestic space and the furnishing of the rooms clearly varied according to the social status of its inhabitants. The social polarisation that arose in sixteenth-century Bruges therefore had an impact on the interiors of its citizens: the wealthier middle groups (merchants, wealthy craftspeople, most members of the Spanish nation and city officials) could afford to acquire and use 'new' decorative objects (or high-end substitutes) such as mirrors, tapestry, fashionable iconography and individual upholstered chairs. They were therefore also able to participate in the new 'trends' within social culture, valuing virtues such as comfort, privacy and sociability, and to organise their domestic spaces to reach these goals. The room type of the *salette* that appeared in houses at the end of the sixteenth century provides an interesting illustration. It was a small, well-decorated and socially exclusive room intended to receive and entertain guests. The room only occurred in the more spacious houses of the wealthiest families that were able to use the *salette* only on particular moments in time for particular people and for only a handful of activities. The lower and middle middling groups, however, were often able to buy and use only the cheaper variants of decorative objects or substitutes and were, depending on the size of the dwelling, able to organise and use the available domestic space thoughtfully, but only within the boundaries of spatial constraints. Kitchens were therefore often used as both cooking area and dining room, because no other location for eating was available in the smaller houses. Nevertheless, each member of the urban community (of course with the exception of the poorest) managed to create their own home and a specific domestic material environment. This broad social embedding of material and domestic culture in late medieval and early modern Bruges was even striking.[3]

Innumerable studies have searched for that distinguished boundary between public and private space in late medieval and early modern houses.[4] Late medieval dwellings are often suspected of being predominantly 'public', harbouring little 'private' space, mainly due to the presence of labour activity within their walls. Domestic space was thus long considered as mere public space and the economic and domestic functions of the urban household were considered to be inextricably intertwined. However, our Bruges evidence strongly nuances the current theory about the lack of boundaries between 'commercial' and 'private living' spaces indoors. The evidence put forwards is convincing for both the existence of an exclusively commercial environment inside the house (shop, workshop and office) and of the existence and the awareness of a separate domestic sphere. Furthermore, thresholds were not only constructed between the commercial spaces of shop or workshop and the living area but also between spaces within the home. Evidence suggests that these internal spatial boundaries were usually more of a social and temporal character. Bedrooms, *contoren*, dining rooms, *salettes* and kitchens, for example, were to be used on certain moments in time and by certain people. It follows that it probably was not so much a *functional* specialisation of space that occurred in sixteenth-century houses (though a more diversified use of space throughout the period was visible), because even specialised room labels translated into multiple room functions (such as the kitchen), but it was rather a *social* specialisation of spaces in the houses of especially the wealthier social groups. The smaller the dwelling, however, the less differentiated domestic space was and the less this social and temporal differentiation could be sustained. The private–public dichotomy was thus much more layered than previously assumed and did not necessarily entail an inside–outside division. The public life of the city was sometimes drawn inside the physical structure of the house when customers, clients, visitors or business associates were served or entertained, or when goods purchased elsewhere were brought into the house to be stored, used or displayed. But houses were also places of family memories, religious contemplation and private devotion. Thus, the everyday world of people in late medieval and early modern cities was not limited to the public life on the streets. To fully grasp the construction of people's social identities and their experience of daily life, the specificities of citizens' domestic life are therefore just as important to consider as the particularities of their public life.

In the most recent and common interpretation of social and economic life between the fifteenth and seventeenth centuries, 'the transformation of the world of goods and changing attitudes towards the acquisition, display and consumption of everyday and 'luxury' objects within the home has become central'.[5] However, these transformations of the world of goods occurred at different speeds. There were, for example, large differences noticeable in the material culture of two of the largest urban centres in the southern Low Countries: Bruges and Antwerp. Decorative objects such as paintings and tapestries, for example, used in Bruges domestic interiors figured in a different cultural framework than in contemporary Antwerp. Through a close reading of object assemblages, we discovered that in Bruges, religious paintings were often put on house altars and used for private prayer. In Antwerp, on the other hand, such paintings were preferably displayed on the walls and functioned more exclusively as decorative items.

Material and spatial practices connected to the home actively created and amplified divergences, tensions and boundaries between urban social groups, men and women and between household members alike.[6] In addition, they provoked materiality dynamics, in which objects or combinations of objects were not passive indicators for changed behaviour, but in themselves active vectors of behavioural change. Further research into the dialectic relationship between the spatial context and the meaning of objects and therefore a refined approach towards defining the social and cultural functions of the home is urgently needed, and a close integration of materiality studies and social analysis may provide the key to unravel the important link between social dynamics, spaces and objects.

APPENDIX 1: INVENTORY HOLDERS WHO WORKED AT HOME

RETAILERS					
YEAR	NAME	OCCUPATION	ROOM NR.	SOCIAL CLASS	SOURCE
1469	Margriete, Ingel Potters wijf	Mercer/grocer	2	B	Arrest
1480	Luuc van Slinghelande	Mercer	5	C	Arrest
1502	Wouter van Gheldre	Herring seller	3	A	Arrest
1530	Pieter van Steenkiste	Mercer/grocer	6	C	Arrest
1562	Fernand de Vlime	Cloth seller	3	B	Arrest
1563	Ruebrecht Hanevil	Mercer/grocer	5	C	Arrest
1564	Margriete wijf van Jacob Obbelaere	Linnenseller	4	C	Inventory
1584	Christoffel de Valcken	Mercer	4	B	Arrest
PRODUCER RETAILERS					
YEAR	NAME	OCCUPATION	ROOM NR.	SOCIAL CLASS	SOURCE
1464	Clais de Man	Tailor/cloth seller	3	C	Arrest
1540	Colyn Beghaert	Candlemaker	2	B	Arrest
1540	Yserael Negheman	Belt maker	4	B	Arrest
1541	Adriaen van Male	Stocking maker	4	B	Arrest
1541	Stevin Remont	Bonnet maker	4	B	Arrest
1541	Jan Maertin	Bonnet maker	9	B	Arrest
1559	Cornelis Veyts	Wheelwright	2	A	Arrest
1559	Jan Parcheval	Wheelwright	4	A	Arrest
1561	Jan Sheerlippens	Cooper	2	A	Arrest
1560	Jan Duivelinc	Shaft maker	6	B	Arrest
1568	Sander Collet	Shaft maker	4	B	Arrest
1568	Gheeraert Coop	Cooper	3	B	Arrest
1571	Silvester Van Pamele	Hatter	5	C	Arrest
1572	Steven de Groote	Cooper	6	C	Arrest
1583	Rombaut De Doppene	Turner	4	A	Arrest

PRODUCERS RETAILERS (REST GROUP)					
YEAR	NAME	OCCUPATION	ROOM NR.	SOCIAL CLASS	SOURCE
1566	Jeronimus van Trier	Silversmith	4	B	Inventory
1541	Pieter De Clievere	Painter	2	A	Arrest
1541	Jan de Clerc	Organbuilder	2	A	Arrest
FOOD PRODUCERS/RETAILERS					
YEAR	NAME	OCCUPATION	ROOM NR.	SOCIAL CLASS	SOURCE
1542	Chaerle Raison	Baker	4	B	Arrest
1567	Jhannekin Vlamincx wijf van Quintin Lucas	Baker	?	B	Inventory
1569	Adriaen Stalpaert	Baker	3	A	Arrest
PRODUCERS (TEXTILE INDUSTRY)					
YEAR	NAME	OCCUPATION	ROOM NR.	SOCIAL GROUP	SOURCE
1540	Jan Lenaert	Dyer	7	C	Arrest
1542	Antheunis De Sant	Tapestry weaver	3	B	Arrest
1546	Joos Vlamync	Dyer	4	A	Arrest
1559	Marie van Cleven	Silk Reeder	7	C	Arrest
1560	Jacop de Clerc	Silk dyer	3	B	Arrest
1561	Richard Janszuene	Say weaver	6	C	Arrest
1562	Joos De Cuevele	Silk Reeder	9	C	Arrest
1562	Pieter Douchet	Shearer	8	C	Arrest
1566	Widow Adam Coeman	Shearer	4	C	Arrest
1568	Cornelis De Corte	Cloth weaver	3	B	Arrest
1568	Laureins De Doncle	Fustian weaver	3	A	Arrest
1569	Jan de la Meire	Draper	10	C	Arrest
1572	Cornelis Oudemarc	Shearer	2	B	Arrest
1585	Jacop Vanden Sip	Dyer	5	B	Arrest
1585	Pieter Gehysock	Draper	3	A	Arrest

Social Group A = Lower Middling groups; B = Middling groups; C = Higher Middling group

APPENDIX 2:
INVENTORIES WITH '*CONTOOR*'

SAMPLE PERIOD	YEAR	SOCIAL GROUP	HOUSE SIZE (NUMBER OF ROOMS)	NAME	OCCUPATION	NUMBER OF CONTOORS
2	1476	A	/	Thomaes van Thottenay	English Merchant	1
5	1559	C	7	Marie van Cleven	Silk reeder	1
5	1563	C	11	Jan Blaeuvoet	Unknown	1
5	1564	B	6	Jan De Burggrave	Silk weaver	1
5	1566	C	7	Guillaume van Damast	Unknown	1
5	1567	C	8	Domenicus Vaerheil	Silk dyer	1
5	1568	C	16	Fernando de Castere	Spanish Merchant	1
5	1569	C	8	Adriaen Claeyssins	Gilder or Goldsmith	2
6	1595	B	13	Pieter Hendrick Winkelmans	Unknown	1
6	1596	B	14	Anna van der Moere	Unknown	1

Social Group A = Lower Middling groups; B = Middling groups; C = Higher Middling group

NOTES

General Introduction

1. Pero Tafur, *Travels and Adventures, 1435–1439*, trans. and ed. M Letts (London: Routlegde, 2004), 198–200, also in Jean Wilson, *Painting in Bruges at the Close of the Middle Ages: Studies in Society and Visual Culture* (Philadelphia: University of Pennsylvania Press, 1998), 1.

2. Marc Ryckaert et al. (eds.), *Brugge, de Geschiedenis van een Europese Stad* (Tielt: Lannoo, 1999), 63 & 66.

3. Peter Stabel, 'Selling Paintings in Late Medieval Bruges: Marketing Customs and Guild Regulations Compared', in *Mapping Markets for Paintings in Europe, 1450–1750*, ed. Neil De Marchi and Hans J. Van Miegroet (Turnhout: Brepols, 2006), 89–105; Heidi Deneweth, 'Brugge zoekt en vindt alternatieven', in *Brugge*, ed. Valentin Vermeersch (Antwerp: Mercatorfonds, 2002).

4. Wim Blockmans, 'The Creative Environment: Incentives to and Functions of Bruges Art Production', in *Petrus Christus in Renaissance Bruges*, ed. Maryan W. Ainsworth (New York, Metropolitan Museum of Art), 11–20.

5. Raymond van Uytven, 'Stages of Economic Decline: Late Medieval Bruges', in *Production and Consumption in the Low Countries, 13th–16th Centuries* (Abingdon: Routledge, 2001), 259–269.

6. Heidi Deneweth and Ludo Vandamme, 'Bruges in the Sixteenth Century', in *Vergeten Meesters. Pieter Pourbus en de Brugse Schilderkunst van 1525 tot 1625*, ed. Anne van Oosterwijk (Bruges: Snoeck, 2017), 10.

7. Deneweth, 'Brugge zoekt en vindt alternatieven', 87.

8. Deneweth and Van Damme, 'Bruges in the Sixteenth Century', 10.

9. Deneweth, 'Brugge zoekt en vindt alternatieven', 87.

10. Ibidem, 86–99; Wilfried Brulez, 'Brugge en Antwerpen in de 15de en 16de eeuw', *Tijdschrift voor Geschiedenis* 1 (1970): 15–37.

11. Heidi Deneweth, *Huizen en Mensen. Wonen, verbouwen, investeren en lenen in drie Brugse wijken van de late middeleeuwen tot de negentiende eeuw* (PhD diss., Vrije Universiteit Brussel, 2008), 347.

12. Deneweth and Van Damme, 'Bruges', 16–17.

13. Ibidem.

14. Ludo Vandamme et al., 'Bruges in the Sixteenth Century: A Return to Normalcy', in *Medieval Bruges, c 850–1550*, ed. Andrew Brown and Jan Dumolyn (Cambridge: Cambridge University Press, 2018), 447–448.

15. Heidi Deneweth, *Goede muren maken goede buren. Verbouwingen en buurtleven in Brugge, 1500–1800* (Bruges: Van de Wiele, 2020), 23–24.

16. Ludovico Guicciardyn, *Beschryvinghe van alle de Nederlanden anderssins ghenoemd Neder-Duytslands*, trans. C. Kilianus (Amsterdam, 1612). Also cited in Deneweth, *Goede muren*, 27: '(Bruges was) A very beautiful, powerful and large city', 'the houses (in Bruges) are more beautiful than in any other city'.

17. Vandamme et al., 'Bruges in the Sixteenth Century', 482–483.

18. Ibidem, 445. Although Deneweth also found that some streets and neighbourhoods suffered from various stages of abandonment and decay, which the city authorities tried to hide by building or restoring mainly the facades of houses. See Deneweth, *Goede muren*, 42–43.

19. Jonathan Barry and Christopher Brooks (eds.), *The Middling Sort of People: Culture, Society and Politics in England, 1550–1800* (Basingstoke, Palgrave Macmillan, 1994).

20. Paula Hohti Erichsen, *Artisans, Objects and Everyday Life in Renaissance Italy: The Material Culture of the Middling Class* (Amsterdam: Amsterdam University Press, 2020), 32.

21. Bruno Blondé and Wouter Ryckbosch, 'In Splendid Isolation: A Comparative Perspective on the Historiographies of the Material Renaissance and the Consumer Revolution', *History of Retailing & Consumption* 1, no. 2 (2015): 105–124.

22. Tara Hamling and Catherine Richardson, *A Day at Home in Early Modern England: Material Culture and Domestic Life, 1500–1700* (New Haven: Yale University Press, 2017), 4–5.

23. Paula Hohti, 'Conspicuous Consumption and Popular Consumers: Material Culture and Social Status in Sixteenth-Century Siena', *Journal of the Society of Renaissance Studies* 24, no. 5 (2010): 654–670. See also Mariët Westermann, '*Wooncultuur* in the Netherlands', *Nederlands Kunsthistorisch Jaarboek*, 51 (Zwolle: Waanders, 2000), 10–11.

24. Peter Arnade, Martha Howell, and Walter Simons, 'Fertile Spaces: The Productivity of Urban Space in Northern Europe', special volume, *Journal of Interdisciplinary History* 32, no. 4 (2002): 515–548.

25. Paula Hohti, 'Domestic Space and Identity: Artisans, Shopkeepers and Traders in Sixteenth-Century Siena', *Urban History* 37, no. 3 (2010): 373.

26. Alexa Griffith Winton, 'Inhabited Space: Critical Theories and the Domestic Interior', in *The Handbook of Interior Architecture and Design*, ed. Lois Weinthal and Graeme Brooker (London: Bloomsbury Press, 2013), 41.

27. Lynne Walker, 'Home Making: An Architectural Perspective', *Signs* 27, no. 3 (2002), 823, also cited in Griffith Winton, 'Inhabited Space', 41.

28.   Arnade, Howel, and Simons, 'Fertile Spaces', 517. Henri Lefebvre, *La Production de l'espace* (Paris: Éditions Anthropos, 1974). See also Megan Cassidy-Welch, 'Space and Place in Medieval Contexts', *Parergon*, 27, no. 2 (2010) for a discussion on the use of the theory of Lefebvre in studies on the medieval period.

29.   Griffith Winton, 'Inhabited Space', 47.

30.   Erin Campbell, Stephanie Miller, and Elizabeth Carroll Consavari, 'Introduction', in *The Early Modern Italian Domestic Interior, 1400–1700*, ed. Erin Campbell, Stephanie Miller, and Elizabeth Carroll Consavari (Aldershot: Ashgate, 2013), 1.

31.   Yair Mintzker, 'Between the Linguistic and the Spatial Turns: A Reconsideration of the Concept of Space and Its Role in the Early Modern Period', *Historical Reflections* 35, no. 3 (2009): 37.

32.   Leif Jerram, 'Space: A Useless Category for Historical Analysis?', *History & Theory* 52 (2013): 400.

33.   Ibidem, 400–401.

34.   Ralph Kingston, 'Mind over Matter? History and the Spatial Turn', *Cultural and Social History* 7, no. 1 (2010): 111–121, cited in Jerram, 'Space', 410.

35.   Thomas Gieryn, 'What Buildings Do', *Theory and Society* 34, 2002, 35–74, cited in Jerram, 'Space', 417.

36.   Daniel Roche, *A History of Everyday Things: The Birth of Consumption in France, 1600–1800* (Cambridge: Cambridge University Press, 2000), 83–84.

37.   Matthew Johnson, *English Houses, 1300–1800: Vernacular Architecture, Social Life* (Harlow: Pearson, 2010), 2; Matthew Johnson, *An Archeology of Capitalism* (Oxford: Oxford University Press, 1996), 171–172. See also Ann Matchette, 'To Have and to Have Not: The Disposal of Household Furnishings in Florence', *Renaissance Studies* 20, no. 5 (2006): 704.

38.   Edward Soja, *Post-Modern Geographies. The Reassertion of Space in Critical Social Theory* (London: Verso, 1989), 7.

39.   Blondé and Ryckbosch, 'In "Splendid Isolation"', 109; Marta Ajmar-Wollheim, Flora Dennis, and Ann Matchette, 'Introduction. Approaching the Italian Renaissance Interior: Sources, Methodologies, Debates', *Renaissance Studies* 20, no. 5 (2006). For example, the exemplary Mario Praz, *An Illustrated History of Interior Decoration, from Pompeii to Art Nouveau* (London: Thames and Hudson, 1964). See also Peter Thornton, *The Italian Renaissance Interior, 1400–1600* (New York: Harry N. Abrams, 1991).

40.   Lisa Jardine, *Worldly Goods: A New History of the Renaissance* (London: W. W. Norton, 1998).

41.   Richard Goldthwaite, 'The Empire of Things: Consumer Demand in Renaissance Italy', in *Patronage, Art and Society in Renaissance Italy*, ed. F. W. Kent and P. Simons (Oxford: Oxford University Press, 1987), 153–175; Ibidem, *Wealth and the Demand for Art in Italy, 1300–1600* (Baltimore: John Hopkins University Press, 1993). For a discussion of Goldthwaite's

claims, see also Bruno Blondé, 'Shoppen met Isabella d'Este. De Italiaanse renaissance als bakermat van de consumptiesamenleving?' *Stadsgeschiedenis* 2, no. 2 (2007): 139–140.

42.   Elizabeth Currie, *Inside the Renaissance House* (London: Victoria and Albert Museum, 2006), 8–10.

43.   Ibidem, 11; Elisabeth Cohen and Thomas Cohen, 'Open and Shut: The Social Meanings of the Cinquecento Roman House', *Studies in the Decorative Arts* 9, no. 1 (2002): 61; Campbell, Miller, and Consavari, 'Introduction', 2.

44.   Cohen and Cohen, 'Open and Shut', 63.

45.   Marta Ajmar-Wollheim and Flora Dennis, 'Introduction', in *At Home in Renaissance Italy*, ed. Marta Ajmar-Wollheim and Flora Dennis (London: Victoria and Albert Museum, 2006), 12.

46.   *De Re Aedificatoria*, 1450 (published in 1486).

47.   *Trattato di archittettura*, 1465.

48.   *Due dialoghi … del modo di disegnare le piante delle fortezze secondo Euclide*, 1557.

49.   James Lindow, *The Renaissance Palace in Florence: Magnificence and Splendour in Fifteenth-Century Italy* (Aldershot: Ashgate, 2007).

50.   Ajmar-Wollheim and Dennis, 'Introduction', 14; Evelyn S. Welch, 'Public Magnificence and Private Display. Giovanni Pontano's *De splendore* (1498) and the Domestic Arts', *Journal of Design History* 15, no. 4 (2002); Guido Guerzoni, 'Liberalitas, Magnificencia, Splendor: the Classic Origins of Italian Renaissance Lifestyles', in *Economic Engagements with Art*, ed. Neil De Marchi and Craufurd D. W. Goodwin (Durham, NC: Duke University Press, 1999), 332–378.

51.   Ajmar-Wollheim and Dennis, *At Home*, 15.

52.   Veerle De Laet, *Brussel binnenskamers. Kunst- en luxebezit in het spanningsveld tussen hof en stad, 1600–1735* (Amsterdam: Amsterdam University Press, 2011); Ria Fabri, 'De "inwendighe wooninghe" of de binnenhuisinrichting', in *Stad in Vlaanderen. Cultuur en Maatschappij, 1477–1787*, ed. J. Van der Stock (Brussels: Gemeentekrediet, 1991): 127–140.

53.   Jan d'Hondt et al. (eds.), *Huizenonderzoek & stadsgeschiedenis: handelingen van het colloquium op 28 november 2008 in Brugge* (Bruges: Levend Archief, 2009); Deneweth, *Huizen en Mensen*.

54.   Carolien De Staelen, *Spulletjes en hun betekenis in een commerciële metropool. Antwerpenaren en hun materiële cultuur in de zestiende eeuw* (PhD diss., University of Antwerp, 2007).

55.   Witold Rybczynski, *Home: A Short History of an Idea* (New York: Penguin Books Ltd, 1987), 75; Philippe Ariés, *Centuries of Childhood: A Social History of Private Life* (London: Vintage, 1965), 385.

56.   Westermann, '*Wooncultuur* in the Netherlands', 13–33.

57.   Rybczynski, *Home*, 75.

58.   Irene Cieraad, 'Introduction: Anthropology at Home', in *At Home: An Anthropology of Domestic Space*, ed. Irene Cieraad (Syracuse: Syracuse University Press, 1999), 1–12; Hilde Heynen,

'Modernity and Domesticity: Tensions and Contradictions', in *Negotiating Domesticity: Spatial Productions of Gender in Modern Architecture*, ed. Hilde Heynen and Baydar Gülsüm (London: Routledge, 2005), 1–29; Anton Schuurman, 'Is huiselijkheid typisch Nederlands? Over huiselijkheid en modernisering', *Low Countries Historical Review* 107, no. 4 (1992): 745–759. See also Britt Denis, 'In Search of Material Practices: The Nineteenth-Century European Domestic Interior Rehabilitated', *History of Retailing and Consumption* (2016): 4.

59. Matthew Johnson, *English Houses 1300–1800: Vernacular Architecture, Social Life* (London: Pearson, 2010); Chris King, 'The Interpretation of Urban Buildings: Power, Memory and Appropriation in Norwich Merchants' Houses, c. 1400–1660', *World Archaeology* 41, 3 (2009): 471–488; Ursula Priestley and P. J. Corfield, 'Rooms and Room Use in Norwich Housing, 1580–1730', *Post-Medieval Archaeology* 16 (1982): 93–123.

60. Jeremy Goldberg and Maryanne Kowaleski, 'Introduction', in *Medieval Domesticity: Home, Housing and Household in Medieval England*, ed. Jeremy Goldberg and Maryanne Kowaleski (Oxford: Oxford University Press, 2008), 1.

61. Goldberg and Kowaleski, 'Introduction', 2.

62. Ibidem, 2.

63. Felicity Riddy, '"Burgeis" Domesticity in Late Medieval England', in *Medieval Domesticity*: *Home, Housing and Household in Medieval England*, ed. Jeremy Goldberg and Maryanne Kowaleski (Oxford: Oxford University Press, 2008), 17; Felicity Riddy et al., 'The Concept of the Household in Later Medieval England', in 'The Later Medieval English Urban Household', ed. Sarah Rees-Jones et al., *History Compass* 4 (2006): 5–10.

64. Goldberg and Kowaleski, 'Introduction', 4; Danièle Alexandre-Bidon, 'Le confort dans la maison médiéval. Une synthèse des données', in *Cadre de vie et manières de'habiter (xiie-xvie siècle)*, ed. Danièle Alexandre-Bidon, Françoise Piponnier, and Jean-Michel Poisson (Turnhout: Brepols, 2006), 129–144, 129–130.

65. Tara Hamling and Catherine Richardson, *A Day at Home in Early Modern England. Material Culture and Domestic Life, 1500–1700* (New Haven: Yale University Press, 2017). See also Cavallo, 'The Artisan's Casa', 66.

66. Jeanne Nuechterlein, 'The Domesticity of Sacred Space in the Fifteenth-Century Netherlands', in *Defining the Holy: Sacred Space in Medieval and Early Modern Europe*, ed. Andrew Spicer and Sarah Hamilton (Aldershot: Ashgate, 2005), 72.

67. Goldberg and Kowaleski, 'Introduction', 3.

68. Amanda Vickery, *Behind Closed Doors. At Home in Georgian England* (New Haven: Yale University Press, 2009), 3.

69. De Staelen, *Spulletjes*.

70. Luxuries are defined here as goods that are not needed to survive. This means that a small wooden painting or a cloth wall hanging could be seen a luxury as well, although it is not necessarily expensive.

71. Filip Vermeylen, *Painting for the Market. Commercialization of Art in Antwerp's Golden Age* (Turnhout: Brepols, 2003), 147–149; Arnout Balis, 'De nieuwe genres van het burgerlijk mecenaat', in *Stad in Vlaanderen*, ed. Jan van der Stock (Brussels: Dexia Nv, 1991), 240; Jan Lampo, *Vermaerde coopstadt: Antwerpen in de Middeleeuwen* (Leuven: Davidsfonds, 2000).

72. Lopez, Robert S. 'Hard Times and Investment in Culture', in *The Renaissance. Medieval or Modern?*, ed. Karl H. Dannenfeldt (Boston, D.C.: Heath and Company, 1959), 57.

73. Ibidem, 56–57; Goldthwaite, Richard, *Wealth and the Demand for Art in Italy, 1300–1600* (Baltimore: John Hopkins University Press, 1993).

74. Van Uytven, Raymond, 'Splendour or Wealth: Art and Economy in the Burgundian Netherlands', *Transactions of the Cambridge Bibliographical Society* 10, no. 2 (1992): 102.

75. Ibidem, 104.

76. Deneweth, Heidi, 'Een demografische knoop ontward? Brugse bevolkingscijfers voor de vroegmoderne tijd', *Handelingen van het Genootschap voor Geschiedenis te Brugge* 147, no. 1 (2010): 3–48.

77. Deneweth, 'Brugge zoekt en vindt alternatieven', 91. Blockmans, 'Fondans en melancolie de povreté', 31; Deneweth, *Huizen en Mensen*, 151–170.

78. Deneweth, *Huizen en Mensen*, 151–170.

79. Deneweth, 'Een Demografische Knoop Ontward?', 35–37.

80. Van Damme, Ludo, *De Socio-Professionele Recrutering van de Reformatie te Brugge, 1566–1567* (Master's Thesis, Leuven University, 1982); Deneweth, 'Een Demografische Knoop Ontward?', 37.

81. Deneweth, 'Een Demografische Knoop Ontward', 47; Baatsen, Inneke, *A Bittersweet Symphony. The Social Recipe of Dining Culture in Late Medieval and Early Modern Bruges (1438–1600)* (PhD Dissertation, University of Antwerp, 2016), 26.

82. Jerram, Leif, 'Space: A Useless Category for Historical Analysis?', 400–419.

83. One exception to the rule is the sixteenth-century ground plan of an unidentified Antwerp house. It is a paper ground plan of the ground floor of the front part of the house. Each room was named and measurements were given. According to De Staelen, this house was rather large compared to other Antwerp houses, since this one measured no less than 48m in depth and the facade was 12.33m wide, whereas the façades of other houses were often only 5 or 6m wide. Given the presence of a warehouse in it, it was probably inhabited by a wealthy merchant and was therefore not very representative of the rest of the Antwerp built

environment. See: De Staelen, *Spulletjes*, 102–107 and City Archive Antwerp, ICO, 13/7h, grondplan van gelijkvloers met kamerbenamingen en afmetingen.

84. Gwendolynne, Heley, *The material culture of the tradesmen of Newcastle upon Tyne 1545–1642: The Durham probate record evidence* (Durham: Durham University, 2007).

85. According to Sara Pennell, access analysis was developed as an analytical tool for modelling urban planning and settlement layouts, but it has been adapted by Bill Hillier and Julienne Hanson to present 'genotypes' of building structures and also to suggest how a building works to interface the relationship between the occupants and those who enter as visitors. See: Sara, Pennell, 'Pots and pans history: the material culture of the kitchen in early modern England', *Journal of Design History* 11, no. 3 (1998): 201–216.

86. Kate, Giles, 'Seeing and Believing: Visuality and Space in pre-modern England', *World Archaeology* 39, no. 1 (2007): 105–121; J., Ayres, *Domestic Interiors: The British Tradition 1500–1850* (New Haven: Yale University Press, 2001).

87. Luc, Devliegher, *De huizen te Brugge* (Tielt, 1975).

88. Deneweth, *Goede Muren*, 13–19.

89. Vickery, *Behind Closed Doors,* 3.

90. De Staelen, *Spulletjes*; De Laet, *Brussel Binnenskamers.*

91. Giorgio, Riello, 'Things Seen and Unseen. The Material Culture of Early Modern Inventories and their Representation of Domestic Interiors', in *Early Modern Things. Objects and their Histories, 1500–1800,* ed. Paula Findlen (Basingstoke: Routledge, 2013), 125.

92. Ibidem, 125; See also: Anton, Schuurman, 'Probate Inventories: Research Issues, Problems and Results', in *Probate Inventories: a New Source for the Historical Study of Wealth, Material Culture, and Agricultural Development*, Wageningen, ed. van der Woude, Ad and Anton Schuurman (Wageningen: Wageningen Landbouwhogeschool, 1980), 21; Overton, Mark, 'A Computer Management System for Probate Inventories', *History and Computing*, 7, no. 3 (1995): 135–142.

93. Riello, 'Things Seen and Unseen', 127.

94. Ibidem, 127.

95. Daniel Lord, Smail, *Legal Plunder. Households and Debt Collection in Late Medieval Europe* (Cambridge: Harvard University Press, 2016), 19.

96. Katherine Anne, Wilson, 'The household inventory as urban 'theatre' in late medieval Burgundy', *Social History* 40, no 3 (2015): 335–359.

97. Gilliodts-Van Severen, *Coutumes des Pays et Comté de Flandre: quartier de Bruges* (Brussels, 1871–1885, vol. 1), 482–485. See also: Baatsen, *A Bittersweet Symphony*, 37.

98. Riello, 'Things Seen and Unseen', 135.

99. Ibidem, 127. See also the remarks made by Daniel Lord Smail: *Legal Plunder*, 67.

100. Smail, *Legal Plunder*, 67.

101. Mark, Overton, Jane, Whittle, Darron, Dean and Andrew, Hahn, *Production and Consumption in English Households, 1600–1750* (Abingdon: Routledge, 2004), 13.

102. Lena Cowen, Orlin, 'Fictions of the Early Modern English Probate Inventory', in *The Culture of Capital: Property, Cities and Knowledge in Early Modern England* Turner, ed. S; Henry (Abingdon: Routledge, 2002), 53. See also: Daniel Lord, Smail, 'Persons and Things in Marseille and Lucca, 1300–1450', *The Oxford handbook of history and material culture* (New York: Oxford University Press, 2020): 7.

103. Riello, 'Things Seen and Unseen', 135.

104. Adrian B., Evans, 'Enlivening the Archive: Glimpsing Embodied Consumption Practices in Probate Inventories of Household Possessions', *Historical Geography Volume*, 36 (2008): 40.

105. Ibidem, 40–41.

106. Smail, *Legal Plunder*, 10.

107. Ibidem, 9.

108. Rachel P., Garrard, 'English Probate Inventories and Their Use in Studying the Significance of the Domestic Interior, 1570–1700', *A. A. G. Bijdragen* 23 (1980): 55–81.

109. Evans, 'Enlivening the Archive', 44.

110. Martha C. Howell, *Commerce before Capitalism in Europe, 1300–1600* (Cambridge: Cambridge University Press, 2010), 145–207; Julie De Groot, 'Zorgen voor later? De betekenis van de dienstperiode voor jonge vrouwen in het laatmiddeleeuwse Gent herbekeken.', *Stadsgeschiedenis* 6, no 1 (2010): 1–15; Ann Matchette, 'To have or to have not. The disposal of household furnishings in Florence', *Renaissance Studies* 20, no 5 (2006): 704; Patricia Allerston, 'Consuming problems: worldly goods in Renaissance Venice', in *The material renaissance,* ed. Michelle O'Malley and Evelyn, Welch (Manchester: Manchester University Press, 2010), 12.

111. Smail, *Legal Plunder*, 4–5.

112. De Staelen, *Spulletjes*, 26–27; Heidi Deneweth, Jan D'hondt, and Kathleen Leenders, *Een huis in Brugge. Vademecum voor de historische studie van woningen, eigenaars en bewoners* (Bruges: Levend Archief, 2001), 128–132.

113. Orlin, 'Fictions of the Early Modern English Probate Inventory', 51–83.

114. Peter Stabel, 'Markets and Retail Circuits of the Late Medieval Countries. Economic Networks and Socio-Cultural Display', in *Fiere e Mercatie. Nella Integrazione delle Economie Europee Secc. XIII-XVIII*, ed. Simonetta Cavaciocchi (Florence: Le Monnier, 2001), 808–809.

115. The so-called *bastard goods* are described in detail in the accounts of the Brugse *schout* for a number of years: General State Archive Brussels, Rekenkamers, 13773 and 13774, 1438–1444. See also: Myriam Carlier, *Kinderen van de minne? Bastaarden in het vijftiende-eeuwse Vlaanderen*, part of Verhandelingen van de Koninklijke Vlaamse Academie van België voor Wetenschappen en Kunsten, 3, 2001. We would like to thank Peter Stabel who kindly made

these inventories available in transcribed and digitized form. He has used these sources in several of his publications himself, for example in Peter Stabel, 'Militaire organisatie, bewapening en wapenbezit in het laatmiddeleeuwse Brugge', *Belgisch Tijdschrift voor Filologie en Geschiedenis* 89, no 3 (2011): 1049–1073.

116. Inneke Baatsen, Julie De Groot and Isis Sturtewagen, 'Single Life in Fifteenth-Century Bruges. Living Arrangements and Material Culture at the Fringes of Urban Society' in *Single Life and the City, 1200–1900,* ed. Julie De Groot, Isabel Devos and Ariadne Schmidt (Basingstoke: Palgrave Macmillan, 2015), 180.

117. Carlier, *Kinderen van de Minne*, 139–142.

118. Julie De Groot and Peter Stabel, 'The domestic interior in mid-15th-century Bruges. Between representation and material reality', 6, paper presented at the international conference 'Art, Art History and History' at the University of Antwerp, 2011.

119. Jan Dumolyn, *De Brugse opstand van 1436–1438* (Heule: UGA, 1997).

120. De Groot and Stabel, 'The domestic interior in mid-15th-century Bruges', 6–7.

121. Deneweth, D'hondt and Leenders, *Een huis in Brugge*, 120–122.

122. Catharina d'Hooghe, *De huizen van het Zuidproosse te Brugge van ca. 1400 tot 1920* (Brussels: Algemeen Rijksarchief en Rijksarchief in de Provinciën, 68, 1997); Jan Anseeuw et al., *Achter Brugse Muren: op zoek naar Materiële cultuur in Brugge, 1500–1800* (Bruges: Levend Archief, 2014), 14–19.

123. Deneweth et al., *Een huis in Brugge*, 48–49. See also: A. Schouteet., *De Klerken van de Vierschaar te Brugge met Inventaris van hun Protocollen* (Bruges, 1973).

124. Schouteet, *De Klerken van de Vierschaar*.

125. Anseeuw, *Achter Brugse Muren*, 17.

126. Gilliodts-Van Severen, *Costumen*, 72–76. See also: Isis Sturtewagen, *All Together Respectably Dressed. Fashion and Clothing in Bruges During the Fifteenth and Sixteenth Centuries* (PhD Dissertation, University of Antwerp, 2016), 264.

127. Gilliodts-Van Severen, *Costumen*, 74–76.

128. We consulted the registers of the following clerks: Beernaerts (1530–1532), Berlot (1560–1563), Bisschops (1569–1585), Coolman (1541–1545), De Queester (1561–1562), De Rouf (1589–1603), Digne (1550–1584), Gheeraerts (1566–1602), Ghislin & Smout (1528–1549), Mommcngy (1541–1561), Pancoucke (1560–1562), Philipet (1583 1585), Plocquoy (1543–1560), Smet (1531–1539), Telleboom (1559–1560) and Vandevelde (1585–1600).

129. Anseeuw, *Achter Brugse Muren*, 12–13. See also: A. Schouteet A. and J. De Groote, *Index op de boedelbeschrijvingen en –rekeningen (Staten van goed)* (Bruges, 1973).

130. Gilliodts-Van Severen, *Costumen*, 30 and 82.

131. De Groot, 'Zorgen voor later', 1–15; Kim Overlaet and Inneke Baatsen, 'Zilveren lepels in het zestiende-eeuwse Mechelen: luxueus eetgerei of betekenisvolle gedinckenisse?', *Tijd-Schrift. Heemkunde en lokaal-erfgoedpraktijk in Vlaanderen*, 11 (2015): 16–29, Martha C. Howell, 'Fixing Movables: Gifts by Testament in Late Medieval Douai', *Past and Present*, 150, 1 (1996): 3–45.

132. Baatsen, *A Bittersweet Symphony*, 43. See also: Daniel Lord Smail, *Legal Plunder*, especially the chapter on Credit and Coin, 89.

133. Guido Marnef, Guido and Hugo De Schepper, 'Raad van Beroerten (1567–1576)', in *De Centrale Overheidsinstellingen van de Habsburgse Nederlanden (1482–1795)*, ed. Erik Aerts et al. (Brussels: Algemeen Rijksarchief, 1994), 469–477.

134. Ludo Vandamme, *De socio-professionele recrutering van de reformatie te Brugge, 1566–1567* (Master's Thesis, Catholic University of Leuven, 1982).

135. The social stratification that was used in this research was established at the University of Antwerp. Additional information can therefore be found in the dissertations: Sturtewagen, *All Together*, 265; Baatsen, *A Bittersweet Symphony*, 62; De Groot, *At Home*.

136. Hamling and Richardson, *A Day at Home*, 9.

137. Gregory Clark, 'The Consumer Revolution: Turning Point in Human History or Statistical Artefact?', *Munich Personal RePEc Archive*, paper n° 25467, 1–22.

138. Thera Wijsenbeek-Olthuis, *Achter de Gevels van Delft. Bezit en Bestaan van Rijk en Arm in een Periode van Achteruitgang (1700–1800)* (Hilversum: Verloren, 1987), 102–114.

139. De Staelen, *Spulletjes*; Bruno Blondé and Veerle De Laet, 'Owning paintings and changes in consumer preferences in the Low Countries, seventeenth-eighteenth centuries', in *Mapping Markets for Paintings in Europe 1450–1750*, ed. Neil De Marchi and Hans Van Miegroet (Turnhout: Brepols, 2006) 68–84; Overton et al., *Production and Consumption*, 23; De Laet, *Brussel Binnenskamers*, 51–52.

140. Deneweth, 'Een demografische knoop ontward?'; Deneweth et al., *Een huis in Brugge*, 41–47.

141. John Michael Montias, 'Quantitative Methods in the Analysis of 17th Century Dutch Inventories', in *Economics of the Arts: Selected Essays*, ed. Victor A. Ginsburgh and Pierre-Michel Menger (Amsterdam: Elsevier, 1996), 1–26.

142. Overton et al., *Production and Consumption*, 18.

143. De Laet, *Brussel Binnenskamers*, 51–52.

144. Ingrid De Meyer, 'De Sociale Structuren te Brugge in de 14e eeuw', *Studiën betreffende de sociale strukturen te Gent, Brugge en Kortrijk in de 14de en 15de eeuw* (Heule, 1971), 7–78.

145. Vandamme, *De Socio-Professionele Recrutering*, 336–342.

146. Heidi Deneweth, 'Moving up or down the housing market. Real Estate and Social Change in Bruges, 1550–1670', paper presented at the Tenth European Social Science History Conference in Vienna, 2014, 5.

147. Ibidem

148. We would like to thank Heide Deneweth for making available the *penningkohieren*.

149. But it excludes those object categories like clothing, silverware, professional tools and merchandise since the presence of these object types depended on source typology.

150. The sources on which this book is based offer interesting data for a study of family life in late medieval and early modern Bruges, though we believe that this would result in a different kind of book.

151. For a similar approach see also: Tara Hamling and Catherine Richardson, *A Day at Home in Early Modern England. Material Culture and Domestic Life, 1500–1700* (New Haven: Yale University Press, 2017), 5.

152. Rafaella Sarti, *Europe at Home. Family and Material Culture, 1500–1900* (New Haven: Yale University Press, 2004).

153. See for a reflection on the primacy of luxury objects in the study of material culture: Catherine Richardson and Tara Hamling (eds.), *Everyday Objects: Medieval and Early Modern Material Culture and Its Meanings* (Aldershot: Ashgate, 2010).

154. For example: James Lindow, 'For Use and Display: Selected Furnishings and Domestic Goods in Fifteenth-Century Florentine Interiors', *Renaissance Studies* 19, no 3 (2005): 634–646.

155. Ria Fabri, "Van een gestocken tresoirken tot een rare schrijffcabinet" of Antwerpse kasten van de laat-16de tot de vroeg-18de eeuw: typologie en gebruik', in *Opgeruimd staat netjes. Bergmeubelen van eind 16de tot begin 20ste eeuw,* Exhibition Catalogue Stedelijk Museum Vander Kelen – Mertens (Leuven: City of Leuven, 1997).

156. Campbell, Miller and Consavari, 'Introduction', 6; Antony Buxton, *Domestic Culture in Early Modern England* (Woodbridge: The Boydell Press, 2015), 9.

157. Johnson, *English Houses*, 138.

158. Griffith Winton, 'Inhabited Space: Critical Theories and the Domestic Interior', 41.

159. Maria Ruvoldt, 'Sacred to Secular, East to West: The Renaissance Study and Strategies of Display', *Renaissance Studies* 20, no 5 (2006): 640.

160. Sarah Van Borm, *Hiëronymus in Huis. Religie en Studie in de woningen van het Mechelse kapittel, 1495–1554,* (Master's Dissertation University of Antwerp, 2015); Ria Fabri, '"Van een gestocken tresoirken tot een rare schrijffcabinet".

161. Elisabeth Currie, *Inside the Renaissance House* (London: Victoria and Albert Museum, 2006), 79.

162. Some decorative objects are therefore not discussed in these chapters. Alabaster statues, wood-en tabernacles, prints and maps are all fascinating bits of the visual culture of contemporary

consumers as well, but would lead us too far when discussing the characteristics of the interior and the interaction between objects, spaces and people. This does not mean, of course, that a study of these objects would not contribute to a better understanding of the material culture of this period. But we chose to study objects that were present in larger quantities in the interiors of many different citizens.

163. James Bloom, 'Why Painting?', in *Mapping Markets for Paintings,* ed. Neil De Marchi and Hans van Miegroet, 17–31.

164. Colum Hourihane, 'Introduction', in *From Minor to Major. The Minor Arts in Medieval Art History, The Index of Christian Art: Occasional Papers,* ed. Colum Hourihane (Pennsylvania: Penn State Press – Princeton University, 2012), XVII.

165. Ibidem, XVII.

166. Marina Belozerskaya, *Luxury Arts of the Renaissance* (Los Angeles:Getty Publications, 2005), 13–14.

167. Wim De Clercq, Jan Dumolyn and Jelle Haemers, 'Vivre Noblement: Material Culture and Elite Identity in Late Medieval Flanders', *Journal of Interdisciplinary History* 38, no 1 (2007): 1.

168. Larry Silver, 'Art and Minds: Scholarship on Early Modern Art History (Northern Europe)', *Renaissance Quarterly* 59, no 2 (2006): 372.

169. Ibidem, 372.

170. Anne-Laure Van Bruaene, *Om beters wille. Rederijkerskamers en de stedelijke cultuur in de Zuidelijke Nederlanden (1400–1650)* (Amsterdam: Amsterdam University Press, 2008).

171. Hamling and Richardson, 'Introduction', 11–12.

172. Hamling and Richardson, 'Introduction', 2.

Introduction: Crossing the Threshold

1. CAB, Staten van Goed, SVG-1ᵉ reeks-1595.

2. Chris King, 'Domestic Buildings. Understanding Houses and Society', in *The Routledge Handbook of Material Culture in Early Modern Europe,* ed. Catherine Richardson, Tara Hamling and David Gaimster (London: Routledge, 2017), 116.

3. Vickery, *Behind Closed Doors*, 3.

4. King, 'Domestic Buildings. Understanding Houses and Society', 115.

5. Ibidem, 116.

6. Pennell, 'Pots and Pans History', 202.

7. Vandamme et al., 'Bruges in the Sixteenth Century', 450–451.

8. Ibidem, 450.

9.   Vickery, *Behind Closed Doors*, 29; De Staelen, *Spulletjes*, 105; Annik Pardailhé-Galabrun, *La Naissance de l'Intime. 3000 Foyers Parisiens XVIIe-XVIIIe siècles* (Paris: Presses Universitaires de France, 1988), 255–257.

10.   Lena Cowen Orlin, *Locating Privacy in Tudor London* (Oxford: Oxford University Press, 2007), 108; See also: Buxton, *Domestic Culture in Early Modern England*, 87.

11.   Ursula Priestley and Penelope J. Corfield, 'Rooms and room use in Norwich housing, 1580–1730', *Post-Medieval Archaeology*, 16 (1982): 93–123; King, 'Domestic Buildings', 118; Deborah Krohn, 'Picturing the Kitchen: Renaissance Treatise and Period Room', *Studies in Decorative Arts* 16, no 1 (2008/2009): 20–34; Guido Guerzoni, 'Servicing the Casa', in *At Home in Renaissance Italy*, 146–152; Currie, *Inside the Renaissance House*, 13–14; Heley, *The Material Culture of Tradesmen*, 293.

12.   Matthew Johnson, *English Houses 1300–1800. Vernacular Architecture, Social Life* (London: Pearson, 2010); Buxton, *Domestic Culture*, 89–90.

13.   King, 'Domestic Buildings', 121.

14.   King, 'Domestic Buildings', 121; Sarti, *Europe at Home*; Aynsley, J. and C. Grant, *Imagined Interiors: Representing the Domestic Interior since the Renaissance* (London: Victoria & Albert Museum, 2006).

15.   Currie, *Inside the Renaissance House*, 13.

16.   De Staelen, *Spulletjes*, 109.

17.   De Laet, *Brussel Binnenskamers*, 115.

18.   Vickery, *Behind Closed Doors*, 13.

19.   Lorna Weatherill, *Consumer Behavior and Material Culture in Britain 1660–1760* (Abingdon: Routledge, 1988), 8.

20.   Erving Goffman, *The Presentation of Self in Everyday Life* (New York: Anchor Books, 1959).

21.   Wheatherill, *Consumer Behavior*, 9.

22.   Ibidem

23.   Weatherill, *Consumer Behavior*, 9–11; Wilson, 'The household inventory as urban 'theatre', 335–359.

24.   Overton, *Production and Consumption*, 135.

25.   Katherine A. McIver, 'Let's eat. Kitchens and dining in the Renaissance pallazo and country estate', in *The early modern Italian domestic interior, 1400–1700. Objects, spaces, domesticities*, ed. E.J. Campbell E.J. et al. (Farnham: Ashgate, 2013), 159–173; Inneke Baatsen, Bruno Blondé and Julie De Groot, 'The kitchen between representation and everyday experience. The case of sixteenth-century Antwerp', in *Trading Values in Early Modern Antwerp,* ed. Christine Göttler et al. (Leiden: Brill, 2014), 162–184.

26. Guerzoni, 'Servicing the Casa', 146–152; Baatsen et al., 'The Kitchen between Representation and Everyday Experience', 166–167; McIver, 'Let's Eat', 159; Orlin, *Locating Privacy in Tudor London*, 105–107.

27. Overton, *Production and Consumption*, 134.

28. Orlin, *Locating Privacy*, 108.

29. Riello, 'Things seen and unseen', 125–150.

30. Ibidem, 133.

31. Ibidem, 135.

32. John Loughman and John Michael Montias, *Public and private spaces: works of art in seventeenth-century Dutch houses* (Zwolle, Waanders, 2000).

33. The exceptional high percentage of the functional room labels of the lowest social group in the second sample period is probably due to the low absolute number of rooms in that sample. The sample consists of only 6 rooms of which most were named after a room function (4).

34. Baatsen, *A Bittersweet Symphony*, 209–210.

35. Vickery, *Behind Closed Doors*; Pardailhé-Galabrun, *La Naissance de l'Intime*, 255.

36. Loughman and Montias, *Public and private spaces*, 26.

37. Riello, 'Things Seen and Unseen', 139.

38. Baatsen, De Groot and Sturtewagen, 'Single Life in Fifteenth-Century Bruges', 181; Overton et al., *Production and Consumption*, 122–131.

39. Orlin, *Locating Privacy in Tudor London*, 109.

40. De Staelen, *Spulletjes*, 94–95; Pardailhé-Galabrun, *La Naissance de l'Intime*, 255–256.

41. Baatsen, *Bittersweet*, 210.

42. Bruno Blondé and Roland Baetens have tried to construct a typology of three house types in Antwerp (one-room-dwelling, middle-class house (*burgerhuis*) and patrician house), which Carolien De Staelen has used in her research on material culture as well. However, because of Bruges's different demographic, geographical and economic constellation, and because we think that typologies are not representative for the actual late medieval and early modern situation, we will not use that typology in this research. See: Roland Baetens and Bruno Blondé, 'Wonen in de Stad: Aspecten van de Stedelijke Wooncultuur', in *Stad in Vlaanderen. Cultuur en Maatschappij, 1477–1787*, ed. Jan Van der Stock (Brussels: Dexia nv, 1991), 63–64; De Staelen, *Spulletjes*, 96–97.

Connecting the House to the Street? The Shop and Workshop

1. Portrait of Jan van Eyewerve and Jacquemyne Buuck, Pieter Pourbus, 1551, Oil on oak panel, 97,7 x 71,4 cm
    Groeninge Museum, Bruges.
2. A. Vandewalle and K. Van Damme (eds.), *Hanzekooplui en Medicibankiers: Brugge, wisselmarkt van Europese culturen* (Oostkamp: Stichting Kunstboek, 2002).
3. Many thanks to Isis Sturtewagen for her analysis of the clothing of both spouses.
4. Paul Huvenne, *Pieter Pourbus, Meester-Schilder 1524–1584* (Bruges: Gemeentekrediet and City of Bruges, 1984), 211–215; Van Oosterwijk (ed), *Vergeten Meesters*, 194–197.
5. Flemish Art Collection Website, Flemish Primitives; http://vlaamseprimitieven.vlaamsekun-stcollectie.be/en/collection/portrait-of-jacquemyne-buuck, consulted on 09/08/2020.
6. Portrait of Cornelia Pietersdr. and Portrait of Dirck Ottensz., Cornelis Engelbrechtsz, 1518, Oil on panel, 56.5 x 34.5 cm, Koninklijk Museum voor Schone Kunsten, Brussels.
7. Van Oosterwijk (ed), *Vergeten Meesters*, 96.
8. Peter Stabel, 'From the Market to the Shop. Retail and Urban Space in Late Medieval Bruges', in *Buyers and Sellers. Retail Circuits and Practices in Medieval and Early Modern Europe*, ed. Bruno Blondé, et al. (Turnhout: Brepols, 2006), 96–97.
9. Ibidem, 97.
10. David Clark, 'The Shop within?: An Analysis of the Architectural Evidence for Medieval Shops', *Architectural History*, 43 (2000): 58–87.
11. Hareld Deceulaer, 'Pret-à-porter, gender en gezondheid. De veelvuldige betekenissen van huiszoekingen bij kleermakers en oudekleerkopers in het laat-16de-eeuwse Antwerpen, in *Werelden van Verschil: Ambachtsgilden in de Lage Landen,* ed. Catharina Lis and Hugo Soly (Brussels: VUB Press, 1997), 136.
12. For a discussion of these traditional thoughts and theories see: Ilja Van Damme, *Antwerpse klanten en kleinhandelaars tussen continuïteit en vernieuwing ca. 1648 – ca. 1748* (PhD Dissertation, University of Antwerp, 2006), 199.
13. Vickery, Amanda, *Behind Closed Doors,* 3.
14. Clé Lesger, *Het Winkellandschap van Amsterdam. Stedelijke structuur en winkelbedrijf in de vroegmoderne en moderne tijd, 1550–2000* (Hilversum, Verloren, 2013), 19.
15. Ilja Van Damme, *Verleiden en Verkopen. Antwerpse Kleinhandelaars en hun klanten in tijden van crisis (ca. 1648–ca.1748)* (Amsterdam: Aksant, 2007), 22; Ibidem, 'Pendelen tussen revoluties en tradities. Recent Historisch Onderzoek naar de Kleinhandel in de Late Middeleeuwen en de Nieuwe Tijd (ca 1450 – ca 1850)', *Stadsgeschiedenis* 2, no 1 (2007): 54–55.

16. Claire Walsh, 'Shop Design and the Display of Goods in Eighteenth-Century London', *Journal of Design History* 8, no 3 (1995): 157.

17. Van Damme, *Antwerpse klanten en kleinhandelaars*, 31.

18. D. Davis, *Fairs, Shops and Supermarkets: a History of Shopping* (Toronto and London: University of Toronto Press, 1966), 3–53.

19. Michael J. Winstanley, *The Shopkeeper's World, 1830–1914* (Manchester: Manchester University Press, 1983), 58.

20. Van Damme, *Verleiden en Verkopen*, 105; Walsh, 'Shop Design and the Display of Goods', 157.

21. Van Damme, 'Pendelen tussen Revoluties en Tradities', 54.

22. To name just a few: Van Damme, *Verleiden en Verkopen*; Bruno Blondé et al. (eds.) *Buyers and Sellers: retail circuits and practices in medieval and early modern Europe* (Turnhout: Brepols, 2006); Jan-Hein Furnée and Clé Lesger (eds.), *The landscape of consumption: shopping streets and cultures in Western Europe, 1600–1900* (Basingstoke: Palgrave MacMillan, 2014); Anneleen Arnout, *Streets of splendor. Shopping culture and spaces in a European Capital City (Brussels 1830–1914)* (Abingdon: Routledge, 2019).

23. Jon Stobart, 'Shopping Streets as Social space: Leisure, Consumerism and Improvement in an Eighteenth Century Town, 1660–1840', *Economic History Review* 55 (2002): 31–50; Nancy Cox, *The Complete Tradesman. A Study of Retailing, 1550–1820* (Aldershot: Ashgate, 2000).

24. John Benson and Laura Ugolini, 'Introduction. Historians and the Nation of Shopkeepers', in *A Nation of Shopkeepers. Five Centuries of British Retailing*, ed. John Benson and Laura Ugolini (London/New York: Tauris Publishers, 2003), 9.

25. Blondé et al. (eds.), *Buyers and Sellers*.

26. Benson and Ugolini, 'Introduction. Historians and the Nation of Shopkeepers', 4.

27. Stabel, 'From the Market to the Shop', 79.

28. Arthur Van de Velde, *De ambachten van de Timmerlieden en de Schijnwerkers te Brugge: hun wetten, hun geschillen en hun gewrochten van de XVe tot de XIXe eeuw* (Ghent: A. Siffer, 1909), 76.

29. Ibidem, 80

30. Arthur Van de Velde, 'Het ambacht der stoeldraaiers, zeef-en waslichtmakers, te Brugge', Société D'Emulation de Bruges, *Mélanges* (1909): 8–9.

31. Stabel, 'Markets and Retail Circuits of the Late Medieval Countries, 797–817.

32. Van de Velde, 'Het ambacht der stoeldraaiers, zeef-en waslichtmakers, te Brugge', 8–9.

33. Bert De Munck, 'Guilds, Product Quality and Intrinsic Value: Towards a History of Conventions?', *Historical Social Research, Special Issue: Conventions and Institutions from a Historical Perspective* 36, no 4 (2011): 107.

34. Deceulaer, 'Pret-à-porter, gender en gezondheid'

35. Ibidem, 113.

36.   Evelyn Welch, *Shopping in the Renaissance. Consumer Cultures in Italy, 1400–1600* (New Haven: Yale University Press, 2005), 4–5. See also: R. K. Marshall, *The Local Merchants of Prato: Small Entrepreneurs in the Late Medieval Economy* (Baltimore: John Hopkins University Press, 1999).

37.   Welch, *Shopping in the Renaissance*, 4–5.

38.   Leon Battista Alberti, *De Re Aedificatoria: On the Art of Building in Ten Books,* trans. J. Rykwert, N. Leach and R. Tavernor (Cambridge: Cambridge University Press, 1988), 152. See: Welch, *Shopping*, 125.

39.   Bruno Blondé and Ilja Van Damme, 'The Shop, The Home and the Retail Revolution, Antwerp, Seventeenth-Eighteenth Centuries', *Città e Storia*, 2 (2007): 337.

40.   Clark, 'The Shop within?', 96.

41.   Riddy, '"Burgeis" Domesticity in Late-Medieval England', 25.

42.   Cox, *The Complete Tradesman: a Study of Retailing,* 15.

43.   Ibidem.

44.   Welch, *Shopping*, 163.

45.   Clark, 'The Shop Within?', 74.

46.   Welch, *Shopping*, 151.

47.   D. Garrioch, 'House names, Shop signs and Social Organization in Western European Cities, 1500–1900', *Urban History Review*, 21 (1994): 20–48.

48.   De Munck, 'Guilds, Product Quality and Intrinsic Value', 113; Bert De Munck, 'One counter and your own account. Redefining Illicit labour in Early Modern Antwerp', *Urban History* 37, no 1 (2010): 41; Welch, *Shopping in the Renaissance*, 143.

49.   Harding, 'Shops, Markets and Retailers', 158–159; Van Damme, *Verleiden en Verkopen*, 131.

50.   Stabel, 'From the Market to the Shop', 93.

51.   Deneweth, *Goede muren*, 46.

52.   Ibidem, 46.

53.   Blondé and Van Damme, 'The Shop, the Home', 342.

54.   Van de Velde, 'Het ambacht der stoeldraaiers, zeef-en waslichtmakers, te Brugge', 2.

55.   For a full list of these inventories and the occupations of the guildsmen see appendix 1.

56.   Jean C. Wilson, *Painting in Bruges at the Close of the Middle Ages* (Philadelphia: The Pennsylvania State University Press, 1998), 137.

57.   '[...] dies es te verstane, dat deghene vanden voorseiden ambochte (*guild of painters*), die wercken op cameren of achterwaert vande strate, ende gheenen tooch en hebben binnen haerlieder werchuuse, dat die zullen moghen houden eenen tooch daert hemlieden ghelieven zal [...]' Nieuwen Groenenbouck, fol° 206 and published in Van de Velde, *De ambachten van de Timmerlieden en de Schijnwerkers te Brugge*, 13.

58. Bert De Munck, 'From religious devotion to commercial ambition? Some marginal notes on the religious material culture of the Antwerp crafts in the 16ᵗʰ century', in *From Quinten Metsijs to Peter Paul Rubens. Masterpieces from the Royal Museum reunited in the Cathedral*, ed. Ria Fabri and Nico Van Hout (Antwerp: De Kathedraal vzw & Bai Publishers, 2009), 21–31.

59. De Geïntegreerde Taalbank, Historische Woordenboeken, *mersenier*.

60. De Munck, 'Guilds', 118; Mui, Hoh-Cheung and Lorna H. Mui, *Shops and Shopkeeping in Eighteenth-Century England* (London: Mcgill Queens University Press, 1989); Bruno Blondé et al., *Retailers and Consumer Changes in Early Modern Europe. England, France, Italy and the Low Countries*. (Tours: Presses Universitaires François-Rabelais, 2005).

61. CAB, Klerken van de Vierschaar, J. Dingne, 1563.

62. CAB, Klerken van de Vierschaar, Beernaerts, book 47, 1530.

63. SAB, Proosdij van Sint-Donaes, Wettelijke Passeringen, reg. 1294, 1480.

64. Baatsen, *A Bittersweet Symphony*, 107–110.

65. Welch, *Shopping*, 147.

66. Ibidem, 143.

67. Cox, *The Complete Tradesman*, 77–80.

68. Bert De Munck, 'Guilds, Product Quality and Intrinsic Value. Towards a History of Conventions?', *Historical Social Research*, Special Issue: *Conventions and Institutions from a Historical Perspective* 36, no 4 (2011): 105.

69. De Munck, 'One Counter on your own Account'.

70. Ibidem, 38.

71. SAB, Proosdij van Sint-Donaes, Wettelijke Passeringen, reg 1295, 1502.

72. CAB, Klerken van de Vierschaar, Bisschop, Book 3, 1584.

73. SAB, Proosdij van Sint-Donaes, Wettelijke Passeringen, reg 1292, 1469.

74. Marc Ryckaert, *Brugge*, (Brussels: Gemeentekrediet, 1991).

75. Walsh, 'Shop Design and the Display of Goods', 164.

76. Van Damme, *Verleiden en Verkopen*, 147; Harald Deceulaer, *Pluriforme Patronen en een Verschillende Snit. Sociaal-Economische, Institutionele en Culturele Transformaties in de Kledingsector in Antwerpen, Brussel en Gent*, 1585–1800 (Amsterdam: Aksant, 2001), 90.

77. CAB, Klerken van de Vierschaar, Dingne, 1562.

78. SAB, Proosdij van Sint-Donaes, Wettelijke Passeringen, reg 1292, 1464.

79. CAB, Staten van Goed, 1e reeks, n°48, 1564.

80. *Vriesche* or *Friesche lakens* were a cheaper variant of cloths. See Sturtewagen, *All Together*, 119.

81. R. De Peuter, *Brussel in de 18de eeuw: Sociaaleconomische Structuren en Ontwikkelingen in een Regionale Hoofdstad* (Brussels: 1999); R. De Peuter, 'Textielwinkels in Achttiende-eeuw Brussel', in *Mag het iets meer zijn? Detailhandel en Distributie van Consumptieartikelen in de*

Nederlanden, 1450–1850, ed. R. De Peuter and H. Soly (Brussels: VUB Press, 2006). See also; Van Damme, *Verleiden en Verkopen,* 145–146.

82. Walsh, 'Shop Design and the Display of Goods, 167.

83. Blondé and Van Damme, 'The Shop, the Home', 344–345.

84. Sturtewagen, *All Together Respectably Dressed,* 79–80.

85. The Dutch word *Reden* means processing a piece of fabric: see *Groot woordenboek der Nederlandse Taal – Geïntegreerde Taaldatabank,* 'reden', consulted 10th of March 2017, http://gtb.inl.nl/iWDB/search?actie=article&wdb=VMNW&id=ID39133&lemma=reden

86. CAB, Klerken van de Vierschaar, De Mommengy, 1541.

87. CAB, Klerken van de Vierschaar, De Mommengy, 1541.

88. Elizabeth Currie, 'Diversity and Design in the Florentine Tailoring Trade, 1550–1620', in *The Material Renaissance,* ed. Michelle O'Malley and Evelyn Welch (Manchester: Manchester University Press, 2007), 163–164.

89. CAB, Klerken van de Vierschaar, De Mommengy, 1541.

90. CAB, Klerken van de Vierschaar, Gheeraerts, 1571.

91. CAB, Klerken van de Vierschaar, Gheeraerts, 1583.

92. CAB, Klerken van de Vierschaar, Dingne, 1559.

93. CAB, Klerken van de Vierschaar, Gheeraerts, 1568.

94. CAB, Klerken van de Vierschaar, Dingne, 1559.

95. CAB, Klerken van de Vierschaar, Dingne, 1559.

96. Deneweth, *Goede muren,* 46–47.

97. CAB, Klerken van de Vierschaar, Gheeraerts, 1568.

98. CAB, Klerken van de Vierschaar, Gheeraerts, 1572.

99. CAB, Klerken van de Vierschaar, Dingne, 1561.

100. General State Archives Brussels, Rekeningen Raad van Beroerten, 246, f° 36r, 1567.

101. Ludo Vandamme, *De socio-professionele recrutering van de reformatie te Brugge, 1566–1567* (Master's Dissertation Leuven University, 1987).

102. A. Schouteet, *De zestiende-eeuwsche schilder en graveur Marcus Gerards,* Bruges (Bruges: Gidsenbond, 1941); E. Hodnett, *Marcus Gheeraerts the Elder of Bruges, London and Antwerp* (Utrecht: Haentjens Dekker & Gumbert, 1971). See also: Vandamme et al., 'Bruges in the Sixteenth Century', 445.

103. Wilson, *Painting in Bruges at the Close of the Middle Ages,* 169.

104. 'Those members of the guild of Saint Luke who worked in rooms at the back of the house (away from the street) and who did not have a counter in their house, were allowed to have it elsewhere.' *Nieuwen Groenenbouck,* fol° 206 and published in Van de Velde, *De ambachten van de Timmerlieden en de Schijnwerkers te Brugge,* 13.

105. Wilson, *Painting in Bruges*, 137; James W. H. Weale, 'Peintres Brugeois, Les Claeissens (1500–1656)', *Annales de la Société d'emulation de Bruges*, 61 (1911): 28.

106. CAB, Klerken van de Vierschaar, De Mommengy, 1541.

107. Peter Stabel, 'Guilds in Late Medieval Flanders: myths and realities of guild life in an export-oriented environment', *Journal of Medieval History*, 30 (2004): 187–212; Catharina Lis and Hugo Soly, *Werelden van Verschil* (Brussels: VUB Press, 1997); De Munck, 'Guilds, Product Quality and Intrinsic Value', 115; Bert De Munck, 'Construction and Reproduction. The Training and Skills of Antwerp Cabinetmakers in the Sixteenth and Seventeenth Centuries', in *Learning on the Shop Floor: historical perspectives on apprenticeship*, ed. Bert De Munck, Steven L. Kaplan and Hugo Soly (New York: Berghahn, 2007).

108. De Munck, 'One counter and your own account', 36.

109. Stefanie Gilté, 'Het Bakkersambacht te Brugge: Samenstelling en Werking', *Handelingen van het Genootschap voor Geschiedenis*, 137(2000): 128.

110. CAB, Klerken van de Vierschaar, Dingne, 1569.

111. CAB, Klerken van de Vierschaar, De Mommengy, 1542.

112. CAB, Staten van goed, 1ᵉ reeks, n°61, 1567.

113. Gilté, 'Het Bakkersambacht te Brugge', 131–133.

114. Blondé and Van Damme, 'The Shop, the Home', 346.

115. Andrew Brown and Jan Dumolyn (eds.), *Medieval Bruges, c. 850 – c. 1550* (Cambridge: Cambridge University Press, 2018).

116. For an overview and discussion of this shift from the traditional draperies to the new and light draperies see: Sturtewagen, *All Together*, 120–121; John Munro, 'Medieval Woolens: Textiles, Textile technology and Industrial Organization, c 800–1500', in *The Cambridge History of Western Textiles*, ed. D. Jenkins (Cambridge: Cambridge University Press, 2003), 181–227.

117. Sturtewagen, *All Together*, 120–121.

118. Peter Stabel, 'Working Alone? Single Women in the Urban Economy of Late Medieval Flanders (thirteenth-early fifteenth centuries', in *Single Life and the City, 1200–1900,* ed. Julie De Groot, Isabelle Devos and Ariadne Schmidt (Basingstoke: Palgrave MacMillan, 2015), 40.

119. Ibidem, 41; Peter Stabel, 'Working Women and Guildsmen in the Flemish Textile Industries (13th and 14th century). Gender, Labour and the European Marriage Pattern in an Era of Economic Change', *forthcoming*.

120. CAB, Klerken van de Vierschaar, Dingne, 1562.

121. Groot Woordenboek der Nederlandse Taal, Geïntegreerde Taaldatabank, http://gtb.inl.nl/iWDB/search?actie=article&wdb=WNT&id=M071540&lemma=twijnen, consulted on 16th March 2017.

122. In the craft of the silk twiners.

123. John H. Munro, 'Textile Technology in the Middle Ages', in Munro, John H., *Textiles, Towns and Trade: essays in the economic history of late medieval England and the Low Countries* (Aldershot: Variorum, 1994), 23–24.

124. CAB, Klerken van de Vierschaar, De Mommengy, 1540.

125. CAB, Klerken van de Vierschaar, Plocquoy, 1546.

126. Although here, again, the source has its limitations in considering rooms.

127. CAB, Klerken van de Vierschaar, Dingne, 1560.

128. CAB, Klerken van de Vierschaar, Bisschop, 1585.

129. CAB, Klerken van de Vierschaar, Gheeraerts, 1566.

130. CAB, Klerken van de Vierschaar, Gheeraerts, 1572.

131. Munro, 'Textile Technology', 23.

132. Ibidem, 23.

133. Berend Dubbe, *Thuis in de Late Middeleeuwen. Het Nederlandse Burgerinterieur 1400–1535* (Zwolle: Uitgeverij Waanders, 1980).

134. Blondé and de Laet, 'Owning paintings', 68–84; De Staelen, *Spulletjes*, 133.

135. CAB, Klerken van de Vierschaar, Dingne, 1562.

136. CAB, Klerken van de Vierschaar, Dingne, 1568.

137. CAB, Klerken van de Vierschaar, Dingne, 1568.

138. CAB, Klerken van de Vierschaar, De Quester, 1561.

139. CAB, Klerken van de Vierschaar, Coolman, 1542.

140. Erik Duverger, 'Tapijtwevers, tapijthandel en tapijtwerk in Brugge van de late middeleeuwen tot in het begin van de achttiende eeuw', in *Brugge en de Tapijtkunst*, ed. Guy Delmarcel and Erik, Duverger (Bruges/Moeskroen: Louis de Poortere, 1987), 50–52.

141. Ibidem, 62.

142. CAB, Klerken van de Vierschaar, Gheeraerts, 1569.

143. Hans Van Werveke, *De koopman-ondernemer en de ondernemer in de Vlaamsche lakennijverheid van de Middeleeuwen,* Mededelingen van Koninklijke Vlaamsche Academie voor Wetenschappen, Letteren en Schone Kunsten van België (Antwerpen/Utrecht: Standaard Uitgeverij/ De Haan nv, 1946), 5.

144. Stabel, 'Working Alone? Single Women in the Urban Economy of Late Medieval Flanders (thirteenth-early fifteenth centuries)'.

145. Peter Stabel and Jeroen Deploige, 'Textile entrepreneurs and textile workers in the medieval city', in *Golden times: wealth and status in the Middle Ages,* ed. Veronique Lambert et al. (Tielt: Lannoo Publishing, 2016), 241–280.

146. De Munck, 'One Counter', 28.

147. Van de Velde, *De ambachten van de Timmerlieden en de Schijnwerkers te Brugge: hun wetten, hun geschillen en hun gewrochten van de XVe tot de XIXe eeuw*, 124.

148. 'Not to deceive people'. Van de Velde, 'Het kuipersambacht te Brugge', 67.

149. De Munck, 'One Counter', 43.

150. De Munck, 'Guilds, Product Quality and Intrinsic Value', 107.

151. De Munck, 'One Counter', 41.

152. Walsh, 'Shop Design and the Display of Goods', 175.

153. De Munck, 'From religious devotion to commercial ambition?', 21–31.

154. Some shops were called as such in the inventories (*winckele*), but in other cases the floor could fulfill similar functions to a room labelled *winckele*.

155. Kate Giles, 'A Table of Alabaster with the Story of the Doom': The Religious Objects and Spaces of the Guild of Our Blessed Virgin, Boston (Lincs)', in *Everyday Objects*, ed. Richardson and Hamling, 267–285; Johan Dambruyne, *Corporatieve middengroepen: aspiraties, relaties en transformaties in de 16de-eeuwse Gentse ambachtswereld* (Ghent: Academia Press, 2002), 114–115.

156. Blondé and Van Damme, 'The Shop, the Home', 346.

157. Sarah Pearson, 'Houses, Shops, and Storage: Building Evidence from Two Kentish Ports', in *The Medieval Household in Christian Europe, c. 850 – c. 1550 Managing Power, Wealth, and the Body,* ed. Cordelia Beattie, Anna Maslakovic and Sarah Rees Jones (Turnhout: Brepols, 2003), 431. Or in the words of Arlette Farge: 'le logement et la rue se mêlent l'un à l'autre sans qu'on sache exactement où commence l'espace privé où finit l'espace public' Arlette Farge, *Vivre dans la Rue à Paris au XVIIIe siècle* (Paris: Editions Gallimard, 1979), 36.

158. Blondé and Van Damme, 'The Shop, the Home', 347.

159. Decuelaer, 'Prêt-a-porter, gender en gezondheid', 111.

160. Deneweth, *Goede muren*, 52.

161. E.S. Cohen, 'Honor and Gender in the Streets of Early Modern Rome', *Journal of Interdisciplinary History*, 22 (1992): 597–625; Heidi de Mare, 'The Domestic Boundary as Ritual Area in Seventeenth-Century Holland', in *Urban Rituals in Italy and the Netherlands*, ed. de Mare and Vos (Assen: Van Gorcum, 1993), 109–131.

162. Welch, *Shopping*, 134.

The Merchant in the *Contoor*

1. Franco Franceschi, 'Business Activities', in *At Home in Renaissance Italy*, ed. Ajmar-Wollheim and Dennis, 166.

2.   Ibidem, 166; Sarti, *Europe at Home*, 89–91.

3.   James M. Murray, 'Handels- en Financiële Technieken', in *Hanzekooplui en Medicibankiers. Brugge, Wisselmarkt van Europese Culturen*, ed. André Vandewalle (Ghent: Uitgeverij Ludion, 2002), 119.

4.   Franceschi, 'Business Activities', 168.

5.   Leah R. Clark, 'Collecting, Exchange, and Sociability in the Renaissance *Studiolo*', *Journal of the History of Collections* 25, no 2 (2013): 169–170 and 172; Peter Thornton, *The Italian Renaissance Interior: 1400–1600* (London and New York: Weidenfeld & Nicolson, 1991), 296.

6.   Currie, *Inside the Renaissance Casa*, 70–71.

7.   Ruvoldt, 'Sacred to Secular', 640.

8.   Clark, 'Collecting, Exchange, and Sociability', 171–172.

9.   It is only very recently, though, that attention has shifted from the studies of the rich and famous in renaissance Italy (such as the studiolo of Isabella d'Este (see S. Campbell, *The Cabinet of Eros. Renaissance Mythological Painting and the Studiolo of Isabella d'Este* (New Haven: Yale University Press, 2006) and the members of the De Medici family to similar rooms in more modest merchants' homes. See: Currie, *Inside the Renaissance House*, 70–71 and Luke Syson, 'The Medici Study', in *At Home in Renaissance Italy*, ed. Ajmar-Wollheim and Dennis, 288–293.

10.   Clark, 'Collecting', 172.

11.   Syson, 'The Medici Study', 288–293.

12.   Currie, *Inside the Renaissance House*, 70.

13.   Thorton, *The Scholar in his Study*, 77.

14.   Van Borm, *Hiëronymus in huis*, 23.

15.   Van Borm, *Hiëronymus in huis,* 18. One exception to this rule is the research on seven-teenth-and early eighteenth century studies in the houses of Dutch Calvinist preachers: Jaap van der Veen, 'Eenvoudig en Stil. Studeerkamers in zeventiende-eeuwse woningen, voor-namelijk te Amsterdam, Deventer en Leiden', in *Wooncultuur in de Nederlanden*, 137–171.

16.   Sven Dupré, 'Trading Luxury Glass, Picturing Collections, Consuming Objects of Knowledge in Early-Seventeenth Century Antwerp', in *Silent Messengers The Circulation of Material Objects of Knowledge in the Early Modern Low Countries*, ed. Sven Dupré and Christoph Lüthy (Münster: Lit Verlag, 2011), 267–282.

17.   Ibidem.

18.   Clark, 'Collecting', 171.

19.   Sven Dupré and Christoph Lüthy, 'Introduction: Silent Messengers. The World of Goods and the Circulation of Knowledge in the Early Modern Netherlands', in *Silent Messengers*, ed. Dupré and Lüthy, 1–2.

20.   For an overview of these inventories with contoren see appendix 2.

21. CAB, Klerken van de Vierschaar, Dingne (1568–1570), 1569.

22. CAB, Staten van Goed, 2ᵉ reeks, 15489, fᵒ 1r–26v, 1596.

23. Van der Veen, 'Eenvoudig en stil', 142–143.

24. CAB, Staten van Goed, 2ᵉ reeks, 15489, fᵒ 1r–26v, 1596.

25. Sarti, *Europe,* 131; Thornton, *The Scholar,* 27–28.

26. Currie, *Inside the Renaissance House,* 70.

27. The case of the English tradesman Thomas van Thottenay (1476) is treated as a specific case since his inventory was taken by reason of an economic debt. The contoor is the only room that was mentioned in the inventory, so it is difficult to connect it with the other rooms in the house. Most probably Thomas was a temporary resident in Bruges in an unidentified house on the Nieuwe Gentweg at the time the inventory was made. Judging from the goods that were inventoried, the room was indeed used as some sort of office.

28. CAB, Klerken van de Vierschaar, Dingne (1559–1560), fᵒ 175, 1559.

29. CAB, Klerken van de Vierschaar, Dingne (1564–1565), 1564.

30. Baatsen, Blondé, De Groot and Sturtewagen, 'Thuis in de Stad', 269.

31. CAB, Klerken van de Vierschaar, Dingne (1568–1570), 1569.

32. Thornton, *The Scholar in his Study,* 77.

33. Franceschi, 'Business Activities', 169.

34. Ibidem, 170.

35. CAB, Klerken van de Vierschaar, DeQueester (1561–1562), 1561.

36. CAB, Staten van Goed, 1e reeks, n° 65, fᵒ 1r–20r, 1568.

37. Inneke Baatsen, Bruno Blondé and Carolien de Staelen, 'Antwerp and the Material Renaissance. Exploring the social and economic significance of crystal glass and majolica in the Sixteenth-century', in *The Routledge Handbook of Material Culture in Early Modern Europe,* ed. David Gaimster, Tara Hamling and Catherine Richardson (Abingdon: Routledge, 2017), 12.

38. Baatsen, *A Bittersweet Symphony,* 194.

39. Ibidem, 194.

40. Deneweth, 'Brugge zoekt en vindt alternatieven', 90; Brulez, 'Brugge en Antwerpen in de 15de en 16de eeuw, 15–37; J. Maréchal, *Europese aanwezigheid te Brugge. De vreemde kolonies (XIVde-XIXde eeuw)* (Bruges: s.n., 1985), 82–89 and 90–173; William D. Jr. Phillips, 'Local Integration and Long-Distance Ties: The Castilian Community in Sixteenth-Century Bruges', *Sixteenth Century Journal* 17, no 1 (1986): 33.

41. Baatsen, Blondé and De Staelen, 'Antwerp and the Material Renaissance', 12.

42. Baatsen, *A Bittersweet Symphony,* 194.

43. Currie, *Inside the Renaissance House,* 83.

44. CAB, Klerken van de Vierschaar, Dingne (1564–1565), 1566.

45.   General Archives Brussels, Council of Troubles, 249, f° 1r–13r, 1567.

46.   Ibidem, 83; Jim Bennett, 'Scientific Knowledge', in *At Home in Renaissance Italy*, ed. Ajmar-Wollheim and Dennis, 172–173.

47.   Dupré, 'Trading Luxury Glass', 276. Pieter Hendrik Winkelmans (1595) had three maps as well, but it is unclear whether they hung in his hall or small contoor (situated in the hall). After calculating the ratio for maps, it seems that the hall and the floor yield the highest scores. It was therefore most likely that maps were located in halls and floors (or threshold spaces, spaces where people would end up after entering the house), rather than contoren (with the exception of Domenicus Vaerheil). Unfortunately, we do not know what was actually depicted. See also: Frederik Buylaert, Jelle De Rock and Anne-Laure Van Bruaene, 'City Portrait, Civic Body, and Commercial Printing in Sixteenth-Century Ghent', *Renaissance Quarterly* 68, no 3 (2015): 803–839.

48.   Paula Findlen, *Possessing Nature. Museums, Collecting, and Scientific Culture in Early Modern Italy* (Berkely: University of California Press, 1994), 293–294.

49.   Pamela H. Smith and Paula Findlen, 'Commerce and the Representation of Nature in Art and Science', in *Merchants & Marvels. Commerce, Science and Art in Early Modern Europe*, ed. Pamela H. Smith and Paula Findlen (New York: Routledge, 2002), 5.

50.   CAB, SVG, 1e reeks, n° 336, 1563.

51.   Pamela H. Smith, *The Business of Alchemy: Science and Culture in the Holy Roman Empire* (New Jersey: Princeton University Press, 2016).

52.   See for the word *alembijt* or *alembic*: Groot woordenboek der Nederlandse Taal, Geïntegreerde Taaldatabank, http://gtb.inl.nl/iWDB/search?actie=article&wdb=MNW&id=01199, consulted on 8th May 2017.

53.   Personal communication with the city archeologist of Bruges.

54.   Antonio Clericuzio, 'The Internal Laboratory. The Chemical Reinterpretation of Medical Spirits in England (1650–1680)', in *Alchemy and Chemistry in the 16th and 17th Centuries*, ed. Pivo Rattansi and Antonio Clericuzio (Dordrecht:, Kluwer Academic, 1994), 51–83.

55.   Lawrence Principe, 'Laboratory', in *Reading the Inventory: The Possessions of the Portuguese Merchant-Banker Emmanuel Ximenez (1564–1632) in Antwerp*, ed. Christine Göttler and Sarah Joan Moran, http://ximenez.unibe.ch/laboratory/, consulted on 26/10/2021.

56.   Tara E. Nummedal, 'Practical Alchemy and Commercial Exchange in the Holy Roman Empire', in *Merchants & Marvels*, ed. Smith and Findlen, 201; Vincent Van Roy, 'Tussen Overlevering en Empire? Vier zestiende-eeuwse receptenboekjes onder de loep genomen', in *De medische renaissance anders bekeken (1400–1600)*, ed. Ivo De Leeuw, Cornelis van Tilburg and Vincent Van Roy (Apeldoorn, Garant, 2006), 135.

57.   Nummedal, 'Practical Alchemy', 206–207.

58. CAB, Klerken van de Vierschaar, Plocquoy, f° 245, 1550.

59. Findlen, *Possessing Nature*, 298–299.

60. Ibidem, 302; Ruvoldt, 'Sacred to Secular', 648.

61. Cited in Thornton, *The Scholar in his Study*, 167.

62. Currie, *Inside the Renaissance House*, 76.

63. Thornton, *The Scholar in his Study*, 169.

64. Johan Veeckman and Claire Dumortier, 'La production de verres à Anvers', 70.

65. Ludo Vandamme, 'Inleiding', in *Een Stad vol Boeken. Bibliotheken en leescultuur in Brugge in de 16ᵈᵉ eeuw*, ed. Ludo Vandamme (Bruges: City of Bruges, 1998), 3. For an overview of extensive libraries in Antwerp see: Ria Fabri, 'Diversche boeken van verscheyden taele, soo groot als cleyn. Aspecten van het Antwerpse privé-boekenbezit in Rockox' tijd', in *Rockox' huis volgeboekt. De bibliotheek van de Antwerpse burgemeester en kunstverzamelaar Nicolaas Rockox (1560–1640),* exhibition catalogue (Antwerp: KBC, 2005), 9–27.

66. André Vandewalle, 'De Spaans-Brugse koopliedenfamilie Pardo en haar boekenbezit', in *Een Stad vol Boeken*, ed. Ludo Vandamme, 11.

67. A. Dewitte, 'De bibliotheek van een kanunnik. Alle de boucken van Jacob de Heere 1546–1602', in *Een Stad vol Boeken*, ed. Ludo Vandamme, 7; A. De Poorter, 'Le Manuel de Jacques de Heere', *Handelingen van het Genootschap voor Geschiedenis* (1901): 1–127.

68. Elly Cockx-Indestege, and Willem Heijting, 'De Doorbraak van de Drukkunst in Roerige Tijden. Het Nederlandse Boek in de Zestiende Eeuw', *Jaarboek voor Nederlandse Boekgeschiedenis*, 17 (2010): 117; Fabri, 'Diversche boeken', 17.

69. Ibidem, 102–103.

70. Vandamme, 'Inleiding', 3.

71. Ibidem, 3–4.

72. Jessica E. Buskirk, 'Salve Maria Gods Moeder Ghepresen'. The Salve Regina and the Vernacular in the Art of Hans Memling, Anthonis de Roovere and Jacob Obrecht', in *The Transformation of Vernacular Expression in Early Modern Arts*, ed. Joost Keizer and Todd M. Richardson (Leiden: Brill, 2012).

73. Cockx-Indestege and Heijting, 'De doorbraak van de drukkunst in roerige tijden', 95–96.

74. Thorton, *The Scholar in his Study*., 10. See also: Franceschi, 'Business Activities', 169–171.

75. Ruvoldt, 'Sacred to Secular', 644.

76. Ibidem, 640; Clark, 'Collecting, Exchange and Sociability', 171–184; Thornton, *The Scholar in his Study*, 77.

77. Ibidem, 643.

78. *The Literary Works of Machiavelli*, ed. John Hale, Oxford, Oxford University Press, 1961, 139. Cited in Ruvoldt, 'Sacred to Secular', 643.

79.   Sturtewagen, *All Toghether*, 173–174.

At the Heart of the Home: Rooms at the Heart of Domestic Culture

1.   Baatsen, Blondé and De Groot 'The Kitchen between Representation and Everyday Experience', 169; De Staelen, *Spulletjes*, 375; Sara Pennell, *The Birth of the English Kitchen, 1600–1850* (London: Bloomsbury, 2016).

2.   Baatsen et al., 'The Kitchen', 169.

3.   Ibidem, 169; Baatsen, Blondé, De Groot and Sturtewagen, 'Thuis in de Stad', 255–256; Alison A. Smith, 'Family and Domesticity', in *A Cultural History of Food in the Renaissance*, ed. Ken Albala (New York: Berg, 2012), 138.

4.   Currie, *Inside the Renaissance House*, 11–13; Marl Gardiner, 'Buttery and Pantry and their antecedents: idea and architecture in the English medieval house', in *Medieval Domesticity*, ed. Goldberg and Kowaleski, 37–65.

5.   Krohn, 'Picturing the Kitchen', 20–34; McIver, 'Let's Eat', 159–173; Françoise Piponnier, 'From Hearth to Table. Late Medieval Cooking Equipment', in *Food. A Culinary History from Antiquity to the Present*, ed. J.-L. Flandrin and M. Montanari (New York: Columbia University Press, 1999), 339–346.

6.   Buxton, *Domestic Culture*, 229.

7.   *De Re Aedificatoria* by Leon Battista Alberti (1450 – printed in 1485) see: Deborah Krohn, *Food and Knowledge in Renaissance Italy: Bartholomeo Scappi's paper on Kitchens* (New York: Routledge, 2015), 85–86; Baatsen, *A Bittersweet Symphony*, 216–217.

8.   Currie, *Inside the Renaissance House*, 39–40; Sarti, *Europe at Home*, 138–139; Buxton, *Domestic Culture*, 229–230.

9.   Margaret Sullivan, 'Aertsen's Kitchen and Market Scenes: Audience and Innovation in Northern Art', *The Art Bulletin* 81, no 2 (1999): 236–266.

10.   Nuechterlein, 'The Domesticity of Sacred Space in the Fifteenth-Century Netherlands', 49–80.

11.   John Loughman, 'Between Reality and Artful Fiction: The Representation of the Domestic Interior in Seventeenth-Century Dutch Art', in *Imagined Interiors. representing the domestic interior since the Renaissance*, ed. Jeremy Aynsley and Charlotte Grant (London: Victoria& Albert Museum, 2006), 72–97, De Laet, *Brussel Binnenskamers*, 114.

12.   Baatsen, Blondé and De Groot, 'The Kitchen', 165–166. See also: Simon Schama, *The Embarrassment of Riches. An Interpretation of Dutch Culture in the Golden Age,* (Berkeley and Los Angeles: University of California Press, 1988), 155–156; Baatsen, *A Bittersweet Symphony*, 236.

13. De Staelen, *Spulletjes*, 111; Toon Caers, *'Ende ierst in de coecken.' Kook- en eetgerei in zestiende-eeuws Antwerpen* (Bachelor's Dissertation, University of Antwerp, 2010), 8; Baatsen, Blondé and De Groot, 'The Kitchen', 170.

14. De Staelen, *Spulletjes*, 111.

15. Heley, *The material culture of the tradesmen,* 311–312.

16. Baatsen, Blondé and De Groot, 'The Kitchen', 170; Caers, *'Ende ierst in de coecken'*, 8.

17. Merwin Corbeau, 'Pronken en Koken. Beeld en Realiteit van Keukens in het Vroegmoderne Hollandse Binnenhuis', in *Mensen en Dingen. Betekenissen van Materiële Cultuur*, Special Issue of *Volkskundig Bulletin*, ed. Gerard Rooijakkers 19, 3 (1993), 354–375; Baatsen, Blondé and De Groot, 'The Kitchen', 170.

18. Baatsen, Blondé and De Groot, 'The Kitchen', 171; Hohti, 'Domestic Space and Identity', 375.

19. There is a difference between confiscation records and post mortem inventories since appraisers of post mortem inventories were often less accurate in naming separate rooms. The second sample period (1450–1500) yields much lower results regarding the presence of kitchens, but this is mainly due to the limited number of inventories with room indication.

20. See also: Baatsen, *A Bittersweet Symphony*, 248–249.

21. More information about food culture and dining habits can be found in the PhD thesis of Inneke Baatsen, *A Bittersweet Symphony*.

22. Loughman and Montias, *Public and Private Spaces*, 26.

23. *Peasants by the Hearth*, Pieter Aertsen, c 1560, Oil on Wood, Antwerp, Museum Mayer van den Bergh.

24. Paul Vandenbroeck, 'Genre Paintings as a Collective Process of Inversive Self-Definition, c. 1400 – c. 1800, II: Peasant Iconography and the Concept of Culture', *Jaarboek van het Koninklijk Museum voor Schone Kunsten* (2006): 94–161.

25. For a similar argument, see also: Claudia Goldstein, *Pieter Bruegel and the Culture of the Early Modern Dinner Party* (Aldershot: Ashgate, 2013).

26. Baatsen, Bondé and De Groot, 'The Kitchen', 176–177.

27. Baatsen, De Groot and Sturtewagen, 'Single Life in Fifteenth-Century Bruges', 191–192; Gardiner, 'Buttery and Pantry', 37–65.

28. CAB, SVG – 2e reeks – 17270, 1590, f° 1r–6v.

29. Jef Weyns, *Volkshuisraad in Vlaanderen: naam, vorm, geschiedenis, gebruik en volkskundig belang der huiselijke voorwerpen in het Vlaamse land van de middeleeuwen tot de eerste wereldoorlog* (Beerzel: Ter Speelbergen, 1974); Antoon Viaene, 'Kleine Verscheidenheden', *Biekorf*, 74 (1973): 313.

30. John Gloag, *The Englishman's Chair. Origins, design and social history of seat furniture in England* (London: Allen & Unwin, 1964), 48.

31. Baatsen, Blondé and De Groot, 'The Kitchen', 176.

32. Baatsen, Blondé and De Groot, 'The Kitchen', 177.

33. Ibidem, 177–178.

34. Corbeau, Merwin, 'Pronken en Koken', 354.

35. Claudia Goldstein, 'Artifacts of Domestic Life. Bruegel's Paintings in the Flemish Home', in *Wooncultuur in de Nederlanden*, ed. Jan de Jong, 177. Goldstein even claimed that for Antwerp 'household inventories show dining rooms and kitchens to have had similar amounts – if different types – of decoration'.

36. Only 32 inventories out of a total of 332 (inventories with rooms) mention a type of decoration (painting, statue, holy-water font, mirror) in the kitchen.

37. Sara Pennell, *The Birth of the English Kitchen, 1600–1850* (London: Bloomsbury, 2016).

38. Donal Cooper, 'Devotion', in *At Home in Renaissance Italy*, ed. Aymar-Wollheim and Dennis, 192.

39. Ibidem, 192.

40. CAB, Klerken van de Vierschaar, Ghyselin & Smout (1539–1542), 1540, f° 75r/v.

41. Smith, 'Family and Domesticity', 143.

42. De Staelen, Spulletjes, 117. For Antwerp Carolien De Staelen did find some 'eetcamere', or literally rooms where one could eat, but the number of entries was limited to only 7 and they seemed to have occurred only among the wealthiest households of her sample. Claudia Goldstein also came across only a limited number of references to dining rooms in the Antwerp sources, and those dining rooms she did encounter were situated only in the city palaces of the Antwerp city elite like Jan Noirot. See: Claudia Goldstein, *Pieter Bruegel and the Culture of the Early Modern Dinner Party* (Aldershot: Ashgate, 2013). For Amsterdam, see: Loughman and Montias, *Public and Private Spaces*, 26.

43. Antoon Viaene, 'Woning en Handwerk. Bouwstoffen voor een Archeologisch Glossarium', *Biekorf*, 62 (1961): 414–415. See also: Baatsen, *A Bittersweet Symphony*, 334.

44. Viaene, 'Woning en Handwerk', 415.

45. Patricia Fortini Brown, 'The Venetian Casa', in *At Home in Renaissance Italy*, ed. Ajmar-Wollheim and Dennis, 58.

46. SAB, PSD – TBO112 3e serie – 1482, 1596.

47. CAB, Klerken van de Vierschaar, Vandcvcldc (1585–1600), 1586, f° 17v–18r.

48. CAB, Klerken van de Vierschaar, Vandevelde (1585–1600), 1586, f° 21v–22r.

49. Overton, *Production and Consumption*, 131; Buxton, *Domestic Culture*, 225–226. See also: Mark Girouard, *Life in the English Country House: a Social and Architectural History* (New Haven: Yale University Press, 1978).

50. De Laet, *Brussel Binnenskamers*, 112.

51.   Overton, *Production and Consumption*, 133.

52.   Roger A. Ekirch, 'Sleep We Have Lost: Pre-Industrial Slumber in the British Isles', *American Historical Review* 106, no 2 (2001): 344; Roger A. Ekirch, *At Day's Close: Night in Times Past* (New York: W. W. Norton & Company, 2005).

53.   Ekirch, 'Sleep we have lost', 344.

54.   Sasha Handley has further elaborated on this topic of bed-sharing in her study on the emergence of a new set of 'sociable' sleeping habits among certain sections of English society in the years 1660 to 1760, a habit that reintroduced the culture of bed-sharing but only at certain moments in time. See: Sasha Handley, 'Sociable Sleeping in Early Modern England, 1660–1760', *History. The Journal of the Historical Association* (2013): 80.

55.   Ekirch, 'Sleep we have lost', 345; Gerrit Verhoeven, '(Pre)Modern sleep. New evidence from the Antwerp criminal
court (1715–1795)', *Journal of Sleep Research* (2020): 1–7.

56.   Ibidem, 364.

57.   Verhoeven, '(Pre-)modern sleep.', 6–7; Gerrit Verhoeven, 'Onder de Wol. Slapen en sluimeren in het achttiende-eeuwse Antwerpen', *Tijd-Schrift* 10, no 1 (2020): 7–19.

58.   Ibidem

59.   Karl Dannenfeldt, 'Sleep: Theory and Practice in the Late Renaissance', *Journal of the History of Medicine and Allied Sciences* 41, no 4 (1986): 415–441. See also: Hollie L. S. Morgan, *Beds and Chambers in Early Modern England, Readings, Representations and Reality* (York: York Medieval Press, 2017).

60.   Dannenfeldt, 'Sleep', 416.

61.   Ibidem, 420.

62.   Ibidem, 425; Morgan, *Beds and Chambers*, 13–16.

63.   John E. Crowley, *The Invention of Comfort. Sensibilities and Design in Early Modern Britain and Early America* (Baltimore: Johns Hopkins University Press, 2001), 8–10.

64.   Buxton, *Domestic Culture*, 176–184.

65.   Overton et al., *Production and Consumption*, 90–98.

66.   Overton et al. *Production and Consumption*, 90; McShane and Begiato, 'Making Beds, Making Households', 7.

67.   SAB, WP – Reg 1295, 1502.

68.   CAB, Klerken van de Vierschaar, Mommengy (1541–1543), 1541.

69.   CAB, Klerken van de Vierschaar, Telleboom (1559–1560), 1559, f° 10.

70.   Overton, *Production and Consumption*, 90–98.

71.   Handley, 'Sociable Sleeping'

72.   SAB, PSD – TBO112 3e serie – 1270, 1560, f° 1r–18r.

73.   CAB, Klerken van de Vierschaar, Mommengy (1541–1543), 1541.

74.   Currie, *Inside the Renaissance House*, 46.

75.   CAB, Klerken van de Vierschaar, Telleboom (1559–1560), 1559, f° 10.

76.   SAB, PSD – TBO112 3e serie – 1270, 1560, f° 1r–18r.

77.   CAB, Klerken van de Vierschaar, Vandevelde (1585–1600), 1585.

78.   Morgan, *Beds and Chambers*, 45.

79.   Currie, *Inside the Renaissance House*, 49.

80.   Baatsen, Blondé, De Groot and Sturtewagen, 'Thuis in de Stad', 275–276; Annie Carlano
      and Bobbie Sumberg, *Sleeping Around. the bed from Antiquity to Now* (Indiana University:
      Museum of International Folk Art, 2006); McShane and Begiato, 'Making Beds, Making
      Households', 10; De Groot, 'Zorgen voor later', 1–15.

81.   SAB, WP – Reg 1295, 1502.

82.   CAB, Klerken van de Vierschaar, Gheeraerts (1566–1569), 1567.

83.   CAB, Klerken van de Vierschaar, Telleboom (1559–1560), 1559, f° 10.

84.   CAB, Staten van Goed – 1e reeks – 336, 1563.

85.   Dannenfeldt, 'Sleep in the Late Renaissance', 425.

86.   Overton, *Production and Consumption*, 136.

87.   Ibidem, 136.

88.   Sara Pennell, 'Making the Bed in Later Stuart and Georgian England', in *Selling Textiles in
      the Long Eighteenth Century. Comparative Perspectives from Western Europe*, ed. Jon Stobart
      and Bruno Blondé (Basingstoke: Palgrave Macmillan, 2014), 31–32; Hollie L.S. Morgen,
      Beds and Chambers in Early Modern England, Readings, Representations and Reality (York:
      York Medieval Press, 2017); McShane and Begiato, 'Making Beds, making households: the
      domestic and emotional landscape of the bed in early modern England', Unpublished paper
      given at 'The Body in Bed' Seminar Series, Royal Holloway, (London, 2010), 19; Baatsen,
      Blondé, De Groot and Sturtewagen, 'Thuis in de Stad', 275–276.

Introduction: Domestic Objects in Context

1.   Soja, *Post-Modern Geographies,* 7; Jerram, 'Space', 400–419.

2.   Richardson and Hamling (eds), *Everyday Objects.*

3.   See also the discussion in Inneke Baatsen, Bruno Blondé, Julie De Groot and Isis Sturtewagen,
      'At home in the city: the dynamics of material culture', in *City and society in the Low Countries,
      1100–1600,* ed. Bruno Blondé, Marc Boone and Anne-Laure Van Bruaene (Cambridge:
      Cambridge University Press, 2018), 192–219.

4.   Giorgio Riello, 'The Material Culture of Walking: Spaces of Methodologies in the long
      Eighteenth Century', in *Everyday Objects*, ed. Richardson & Hamling, 42.

5.   Evans, 'Enlivening the Archive', 40.

6.   Buxton, *Domestic Culture*, 35–36.

Devotion on Display? Paintings in Domestic Interiors

1.   School for poor boys in Bruges.

2.   CAB, 1ᵉ reeks – 620, 1583.

3.   Klerken van de Vierschaar, Jan Digne, ?, n°210, f° 299. '*Petronella Heve, haar eerste man Loys
      de la Faulx, hun dochter Josyne. Haar tweede man Remeus Ommejaegher.*'

4.   See also: Paul Huvenne, *Pieter Pourbus, meester-schilder, 1524–1584* (s.l.: Gemeentekrediet,
      1984), 177.

5.   Huvenne, *Pieter Pourbus*, 177.

6.   Frank Trentmann, *Empire of Things. How We Became a World of Consumers, from the Fifteenth
      Century to the Twenty-First* (London: Allen Lane an imprint of Penguin Random House UK,
      2016), 4.

7.   Thomas E. Dale, 'Transcending the Major/Minor Divide: Romanesque Mural Painting,
      Color, and Spiritual Seeing', in *From Major to Minor. The Minor Arts in Medieval Art History*,
      ed. Colum Hourihane, 23–42.

8.   Michael North and David Ormrod, 'Introduction. Art and its Markets', in *Art Markets in
      Europe, 1400–1800,* ed. Michael North and David Ormrod (Aldershot: Ashgate, 1998), 1–6.

9.   Richardson, Hamling and Gaimster, 'Introduction', in *The Routledge Handbook of Material
      Culture in Early Modern Europe*, ed. Richardson, Hamling and Gaimster, 10.

10.   Kristina Joekalda, 'What has become of the New Art History?', *Journal of Art History* 9, no 9
      (2013).

11.   Among others: Maximiliaan Martens, *Artistic Patronage in Bruges Institutions, ca 1440–1482*
      (PhD Dissertation, University of California, 1992); Jean Wilson, Jean, *Painting in Bruges
      at the Close of the Middle Ages*; Maryan W. Ainsworth, 'The Business of Art: Patrons,
      Clients, and Art Markets', in *From Van Eyck to Bruegel. Early Netherlandish Painting in The
      Metropolitan Museum of Art,* ed. Maryan W. Ainsworth Keith Christiansen (New York:
      The Metropolitan Museum of Art, 1998), 23–37; Filip Vermeylen, *Painting for the Market:
      Commercialization of Art in Antwerp's Golden Age* (Turnhout; Brepols, 2003); Dan Ewing,
      'Marketing Art in Antwerp, 1460–1560: Our Lady's Pand', *The Art Bulletin* 72, no 4 (1990):
      558–584; Peter Stabel, 'Organisation corporative et production d'oeuvres d'art à Bruges à

la fin du Moyen Age et au début des Temps modernes', *Le Moyen Age,* 113 (2007): 91–134; Brecht Dewilde, *Portretten en de markt: het familiebedrijf Claeissens in zestiende-eeuws Brugge,* (Master's Dissertation, Catholic University of Leuven, 2007); Michelle O'Malley, *The Business of Art: Contracts and the Commissioning Process in Renaissance Italy* (New Haven: Yale University Press, 2005); De Neil Marchi,'Size and Taste. Taking the Measure of the History of the Art Markets', in *Economia e Arte Secc. XIII-XVIII*, ed. Simonetta Cavaciocchi, (Florence, Istituto Internazionale di Storia Economia "F.Datini" Prato, 2002), 79–81.

12. Van Oosterwijk, *Vergeten Meesters*, especially 19–30.

13. Dewilde, *Portretten en de Markt*

14. For example: Maryan Ainsworth (ed.), *Petrus Christus in Renaissance Bruges,* 1995; Dewilde, *Portretten en de Markt;* Stabel, 'Selling Paintings in Late Medieval Bruges'; Martens, *Artistic Patronage in Bruges Institutions, ca 1440–1482* and others.

15. Hamling and Richardson, *Everyday Objects*; Marta Ajmar-Wollheim, Flora Dennis and Ann Matchette (eds), *Approaching the Italian Renaissance Interior. Sources, Methodologies and Debates* (Oxford: Blackwell Publishing, 2007).

16. I actually prefer the term 'users' to 'consumers' because they actively put objects to use even when not displaying them.

17. Among Others: Nuechterlein, 'The domesticity of sacred space in the fifteenth-century Netherlands', 49–79; Diana Webb, 'Domestic Space and Devotion in the Middle Ages', in *Defining the Holy*, 31; Henk Van Os, *The art of devotion in the late middle ages in Europe, 1300–1500* (New Jersey: Princeton University Press, 1994); Nico Van Hout, *Vlaamse Primitieven. De Mooiste Tweeluiken (*Ghent: Ludion, 2007); Roger Wieck, *Painted Prayers. The Book of Hours in Medieval and Renaissance Art* (New York: George Braziller, inc, 1999); Caroline Walker Bynum, *Christian Materiality. An Essay on Religion in Late Medieval Europe* (New York: Zone Books, 2011).

18. Buskirk, 'Salve Maria Gods Moeder Ghepresen'.

19. Webb, 'Domestic Space and Devotion', 31.

20. Vermeylen, *Painting for the Market*; Bert Hendrickx, *Het schilderijenbezit van de Antwerpse burger in de tweede helft van de zestiende eeuw: een socio-economische analyse,* (Master's Dissertation, Catholic University of Leuven, 1997); Maximiliaan Martens and Natasja Peeters, 'Paintings in Antwerp Houses (1532–1567)', in *Mapping Markets for Paintings in Europe*, ed. De Marchi and Van Miegroet, 35–53; Dan Ewing, 'Marketing Art in Antwerp, 1460–1560: Our Lady's Pand', *The Art Bulletin* 72, no 4 (1990): 558–584.

21. Bert Timmermans, 'Networkers and Mediators in the 17th Century Antwerp Art World: The Impact of Collectors-Connoisseurs on Artistic Processes of Transmission and Selection', in

Luxury in the Low Countries: Miscellaneous Reflections on Netherlandish Material Culture,
1500 to the Present, ed. Rengenier Rittersma (Brussels: Faro, 2010), 109–134.

22.   Vermeylen, *Painting for the Market*; De Staelen, *Spulletjes*

23.   Vermeylen, *Painting for the Market.*

24.   Martens, 'Some Aspects of the Origins of the Art Market in Fifteenth-Century Bruges', 19–27.

25.   Stabel, 'Selling Paintings in Late Medieval Bruges'; Wilson, *Painting in Bruges at the Close of*
       the Middle Ages.

26.   Stabel, 'Organisation corporative et production d'oeuvres d'art à Bruges, 91–134

27.   Martens, 'Aspects of the Origins of the Art Market'.

28.   Nuechterlein, 'The domesticity of sacred space', 50.

29.   Brecht Dewilde, 'De productie en verkoop van schilderijen in het zestiende-eeuwse Brugge', in
       Vergeten Meesters, ed. Van Oosterwijk, 23.

30.   Ibidem, 23–24.

31.   Dewilde, 'De productie en verkoop', 26–27.

32.   De Staelen, *Spulletjes*, 24–56.

33.   City Archive Bruges, Staten van Goed, 1e reeks – n° 65, 1568.

34.   Jacob Verdam, *Middelnederlands Handwoordenboek* ('s-Gravenhage: Nijhoff, 1973): *tafele*;
       Martens and Peeters, 'Paintings in Antwerp Houses'

35.   Martens, 'Some Aspects of the Origins of the Art Market in Fifteenth-Century Bruges', 19–27.

36.   The term *drap peint*, used in fourteenth-century documents generally refers to paintings on
       linen. The Middle Dutch *beschreven cleedt* is more or less the same as the French *drap peint* and
       therefore refers to canvas painting as well. see: Diane Wolfthal, *The Beginnings of Netherlandish*
       Canvas Painting: 1400–1530 (Cambridge: Cambridge University Press, 1989), 3.

37.   De Staelen, *Spulletjes*, 184–198.

38.   http://www.atilf.fr/dmf/, Dictionnaire du Moyen Français (1330–1500), accessed on 20th of
       January 2016

39.   Nuechterlein, 'The domesticity of sacred space in the fifteenth-century Netherlands', 49–79;
       Hohti, *Artisans, Object, and Everyday Life in Renaissance Italy*, 267–268.

40.   John Michael Montias, 'How notaries and other scribes recorded works of art in seven-
       teenth-century sales and inventories', *Semiolus: Netherlandish Quarterly for the History of Art*
       30, no ¾ (2003): 217–235.

41.   CAB, Guillaume Bibau, Stokhouder, 1567–1568, n°9–304.

42.   André Vandewalle, 'De stokhouders te Brugge. Het geval Adriaenssens (1678–1694)', in
       Jaarboek van Vlaams Centrum voor Genealogie en Heraldiek (1982): 463–476.

43.   Pearson Chi Square=0,03<0,05 so there is a statistically significant correlation between the level of detail in the description of the painting and its resale price. Cramer's V is 0,9 so there is a strong correlation between the two variables.

44.   Blockmans, 'The Creative Environment', 15; Wim Blockmans, 'Bruges the European Commercial Centre', in Valentin Vermeersch (ed.), *Bruges and Europe* (Antwerp: Mercator, 1992), 40–55; Lorne Campbell, 'The Art Market in the Southern Netherlands in the Fifteenth Century', *The Burlington Magazine*, 118 (1976): 188–198.

45.   Deneweth, 'Brugge zoekt en vindt alternatieven'; Brulez, 'Brugge en Antwerpen in de 15de en 16de eeuw', 15–37; Dewilde, *Portretten en de markt.*

46.   Brown and Dumolyn (eds.), *Medieval Bruges, c. 850 – c. 1550.* Especially interesting is Chapter X. After the Middle Ages: the Withering Away of a Metropolis.

47.   State Archives Brussels (NAB), CC – 13773, f° 34v–35r, 1439.

48.   Wilson, *Painting in Bruges at the Close of the Middle Ages,* 41–84; Stabel, 'Selling Paintings in Late Medieval Bruges', 89–105; Dewilde, *Portretten en de markt*

49.   Blockmans, 'The Creative Environment', 14.

50.   J. P. Sosson., 'Une approche des structures économiques d'un métier d'art: la corporation des peintres et selliers de Bruges (XVe – XVIe siècles)', *Revue des archéologues et historiens d'art de Louvain*, 3 (1970): 91–100.

51.   Dewilde, 'De Productie en Verkoop', 19–20.

52.   Brown and Dumolyn (eds.), *Medieval Bruges, c. 850 – c. 1550* – Especially interesting: Chapter X. After the Middle Ages: the Withering Away of a Metropolis.

53.   Martens and Peeters, 'Paintings in Antwerp Houses', 35–53.

54.   Ibidem, 42.

55.   Philippe Benedict, 'Towards the Comparative Study of the Popular Market for Art: the Ownership of Paintings in Seventeenth-Century Metz', *Past and Present*, 109 (1985): 105.

56.   CAB, Staten van Goed – 1ᵉ reeks – 1595, f° 1r–44v.

57.   CAB, Staten van Goed – 1ᵉ reeks – 1586, f° 17v–18r.

58.   Blockmans, 'The Creative Environment', 20.

59.   Wolfthal, *The Beginnings*, 7.

60.   Rachel Billinge, Lorne Campbell et al., 'Methods and Materials of Northern European Painting in the National Gallery, 1400–1550', *Technical Bulletin Volume* 18 (1997): 10.

61.   Billinge, Campbell et al., 'Methods and Materials', 10.

62.   Ibidem, 24–25.

63.   Wolfthal, *The Beginnings*, 6.

64.   L., Gilliodts-Van Severen, *Mémoriaux de Bruges*, Bruges, Imprimerie de L. De Plancke, 1913, article 367 'Conflit entre la corporation des peintres et les décorateurs de tentures dits "cleerscrivers"', 406–407.

65.   Apprenticeship, entry into the guild, the quality of the products, the prices of goods and the salaries of the guildsmen were already regulated by the guild. See: Peter Stabel, 'Organisation corporative et production d'œuvres d'art à Bruges à la fin du Moyen Age et au début des Temps Modernes', *Le moyen âge: revue d'histoire et de philologie*, 113 (2007): 91–134, 98.

66.   Gilliodts-Van Severen, *Mémoriaux de Bruges*, Bruges, article 367, 406–407.

67.   Bloom, 'Why Painting?'.

68.   Gilliodts-Van Severen, *Mémoriaux de Bruges*, article 367 'Conflit entre la corporation des peintres et les décorateurs de tentures dits 'cleerscrivers', 406–407; Mander, 'Painted Cloths', 130–131.

69.   Karel Van Mander, *Het Schilder-Boeck waer in voor eerst de leerlustighe iueght den grondt der edel vry schilderconst in verscheyden deelen wort voorghedraghen, daer nae in dry deelen t'leven der vermaerde doorluchtighe schilders des ouden en nieywen tijds* (Haarlem, s.n., 1604), f° 203r and 203v. 'In these days artisans made large cloths with large images, used to cover walls like tapestries.'

70.   Diane Wolfthal, *The Beginnings of Netherlandish Canvas Painting: 1400–1530* (Cambridge: Cambridge University Press, 1989), 8.

71.   Ibidem, 12.

72.   Wolfthal, *The Beginnings*.

73.   J. Maréchal, *Europese aanwezigheid te Brugge. De vreemde kolonies (XIVde-XIXde eeuw)* (Bruges: s.n., 1985), 82–89 and 90–173; William D. Jr. Phillips, 'Local Integration and Long-Distance Ties: The Castilian Community in Sixteenth-Century Bruges', *Sixteenth Century Journal* 17, no 1 (1986): 33.

74.   Wim Blockmans, 'Fondans en melencolie de povreté. Leven en Werken in Brugge, 1482–1584', in *Bruges and the Renaissance: Memling to Pourbus*, ed. Maximiliaan Martens (Ghent: Stichting Kunstboek/Ludion 1998), 16–32.

75.   This theme was the subject of the international conference 'Netherlandish Art and Luxury Goods in Renaissance Spain. Trade, Patronage and Consumption' at the University of Leuven (4–6 February 2016) organised by Illuminare – Centre for the Study of Medieval Art | KU Leuven. See also: Dewilde, 'De Productie en Verkoop', 21; Didier Martens, 'De Familie Claeissens en Pieter Pourbus in de Iberische wereld: tussen Vlaams exotisme en inculturatie', in *Vergeten Meesters*, ed. Van Oosterwijk, 95–96.

76.   Hans Van Miegroet, 'New Data Visualisations on the Mechelen Export Industry and Artist Migration Patterns', *De Zeventiende Eeuw*, Special Issue *Art on the Move* 31, no 1 (2015): 179–190.

77. Personal communication with Prof. Dr. Maximiliaan Martens on 8 February 2016. This assumption is also corroborated by the research of Diane Wolfthal: see Wolfthal, *The Beginnings*, 22.

78. Alonso Hilario Casado 'Brugge, centrum van uitwisseling met Spanje', in *Hanzekooplui en Medicibankiers. Brugge, wisselmarkt van Europese culturen*, ed. André Vandewalle et al. (Oostkamp: Stichting Kunstboek, 2002), 56.

79. Didier Martens, *Peinture Flamande et Goût Ibérique aux XVème et XVIème Siècles* (Brussels: Le livre Timperman, 2010); Jan Karel Steppe, 'Spaans mecenaat en Vlaamse kunst in de zestiende eeuw', in *Luister van Spanje en de Belgische Steden, 1500–1700*, part 1, Europalia 85 España (Brussels: Gemeentekrediet, 1985); Dominique Marechal, 'De Diaspora van de Brugse Renaissance', in *Brugge en de Renaissance*, ed. Martens, 64.

80. Dewilde, 'De Productie', 25.

81. General Archives Brussels, Accounts of the Audit Office (*Rekenkamer*), 23482–23487, *Six Comptes rendus par Jacques Vanden Heede, de la perception du droit de deux pour cent à Bruges, Damme et l'Ecluse du 15 décembre 1551 au 12 août 1554*. See: Pinchart, A. *Inventaire des archives des Chambres des Comptes, précédé d'une notice historique sur ces anciennes institutions*, part IV.

82. Steppe, 'Spaans mecenaat', 248–249.

83. Casado Alonso, 'Brugge, centrum van uitwisseling met Spanje', 56.

84. CAB, Spanish Archive, Staten van Goed, Velasco de Béjar, 1555.

85. CAB, Protocollen van de klerken van de Vierschaar, Gheeraerts, 1586–1588, f° 95r.

86. Vermeylen, *Painting for the Market,* 148–149.

87. Martens and Peeters, 'Paintings in Antwerp Houses', 46.

88. Martens 'Tussen Artistieke Traditie en Vernieuwing', 57.

89. Blondé, 'Art and Economy', 388.

90. Martens (ed.) *Brugge en de Renaissance. Van Memling tot Pourbus, Notities*, 59, 87, 108 and 122.

91. Dewilde, *Portretten en de markt*; Martens, 'Tussen Artistieke Traditie en Vernieuwing'.

92. Blockmans, 'Fondans en melencolie de povreté', 31–32.

93. For this graph, all the religious themes we came across (saints, Jesus, Our Lady, New and Old Testament scenes) were put into the category 'Religion'.

94. Katelijne Van der Stighelen, *Hoofd en Bijzaak. Portretkunst in Vlaanderen van 1420 tot nu* (Leuven: Davidsfonds, 2008), 60–70.

95. Vermeylen, *Painting for the Market,* 149 and 161–162.

96. De Staelen, *Spulletjes*, 212. We have compared the variety of themes of the paintings in the Antwerp samples of Carolien De Staelen with the variety of themes registered in our own samples and calculated whether this difference between Antwerp and Bruges was based on

coincidence. The 0- hypothesis – the observation of a difference in taste between the two centres is based on coincidence – was rejected. Pearson Chi-Square = 0,000.

97. Webb, 'Domestic Space and Devotion in the Middle Ages', 45.

98. Greig et al. 'Introduction: Gender and Material Culture', 7.

99. Heley, *The material culture of the tradesmen of Newcastle upon Tyne,* 117–126; Salter, 'Some differences in the cultural production of household consumption', 405; Hamling and Richardson (eds), *Everyday Objects*, 14.

100. Nuechterlein, 'The domesticity of sacred space', 61; Noël Geirnaert, 'Bruges and the Northern Netherlands' in Vermeersch, Valentin (ed.), *Bruges and Europe*, Antwerp, Mercatorfonds, 1992, 82–83.

101. Nuechterlein, 'The domesticity of sacred space', 72.

102. Erwin Panofsky, 'Imago Pietatis: ein Beitrag zur Typengeschichte des "Schmerzensmanns" und der "Maria Mediatrix", in *Festschrift für Max Friedländer zum 60. Geburtstag* (Leipzig: E.A. Seemann, 1927), 261–308. For the development of the art historical concept, see Karl Schade, *Andachtsbild: Die Geschichte eines kunsthistorischen Begriffs* (Weimar: Verlag und Datenbank für Geisteswissenschaften, 1996). See also: Van Os, *The Art of Devotion in the Late Middle Ages in Europe, 1300–1500* (Amsterdam: Rijksmuseum, 1994).

103. Jacqueline Marie Musacchio, 'The Madonna and Child, a host of saints and domestic devotion in Renaissance Florence', in *Revaluing Renaissance Art*, ed. Gabriele Neher and Rupert Shepherd (Aldershot: Ashgate, 2010), 154.

104. Buskirk, 'Salve Maria Gods Moeder Ghepresen', 66.

105. Ibidem, 71.

106. Musacchio, 'The Madonna and Child', 155.

107. Guido Marnef, *Antwerp in the Age of Reformation. Underground Protestantism in a Commercial Metropolis, 1550–1577* (Baltimore/London: The John Hopkins University Press, 1996), 196.

108. Vandamme, *De socio-professionele rekrutering van de reformatie te Brugge.*

109. Ibidem.

110. Marnef, *Antwerp in the Age of Reformation,* 196–199.

111. Vandamme, *De socio-professionele rekrutering van de reformatie te Brugge,* 318–320. List of names.

112. Vermeylen, *Painting for the Market*; Martens and Peeters, 'Paintings in Antwerp Houses (1532–1567)', 35–53; Hendrickx, *Het schilderijenbezit van de Antwerpse burger in de tweede helft van de zestiende eeuw.*

113. Till-Holger Borchert, 'Some Thoughts about Form and Function of Early Flemish Portraits', in *Staging the Court of Burgundy: proceedings of the conference "The Splendour of Burgundy" in 2009* (Turnhout, Brepols, 2011), 201.

114. Van Hout et al. (eds.), *Vlaamse Primitieven. De Mooiste Tweeluiken.*

115. Silver, 'Arts and Minds: Scholarship on Early Modern Art History (Northern Europe)', 354–355.

116. Lorne Campbell, 'Diptychs with Portraits', in *Prayers and Portraits: Unfolding the the Netherlandish Diptych*, ed. John Oliver Hand and Ron Spronk (New Haven: Yale University Press, 2007), 33–45.; Lorne Campbell, *Renaissance Portraits: European Portrait-Painting in the Fourteenth-Fifteenth and Sixteenth Centuries* (New Haven: Yale University Press, 1990.; Van der Stighelen, *Hoofd en Bijzaak*, 33.

117. Van der Stighelen, *Hoofd en Bijzaak*, 60–70.

118. Borcher, 'Some Thoughts about Form and Function of Early Flemish Portraits', 201.

119. Erving Goffman, *The Presentation of Self in Everyday Life* (New York: Anchor Books, 1959).

120. Peter Burke, 'The Presentation of Self in the Renaissance Portrait', chapter 2, 150–151.

121. Goffman, 'Introduction', in Goffman, Erving, *The Presentation of Self.*

122. CAB, Klerken van de Vierschaar, Gheeraerts (1590–1602), 1591.

123. Among others: Loughman and Montias, *Public and Private Spaces*; Blondé and De Laet, 'Owning paintings; Martens and Peeters, 'Paintings in Antwerp Houses'.

124. Greig, Hannah, Hamlett, Jane and Leonie Hannan, 'Introduction: Gender and Material Culture', in Greig, Hannah, Hamlett, Jane and Leonie Hannan (eds.), *Gender and Material Culture in Britain since 1600,* London/New York, Palgrave Macmillan, 2016, 7.

125. only when there was no randomness noticeable in the inventory

126. Van de Velde, Arthur, *De Ambachten van de Timmerlieden en de Schrijnwerkers te Brugge. Hun Wetten, hun Geschillen en hun Gewrochten van de XIVe tot de XIXe eeuw*, Gent, A. Siffer/ Koninklijke Vlaamsche Academie, 1909, 139. 'But joiners were allowed to make cupboards 'in the style of an altar', in rooms or chambers, with or without canopy.'

127. Henk Van Os, *The Art of Devotion in the Late Middle Ages in Europe, 1300–1500* (London/ Amsterdam: Merrell Holberton, 1994), 131–132.

128. Oliver Kik, 'Rond den Heerd. Schoorsteenwangen en Haardstenen in de Gruuthuse Collectie', *Museumbulletin Musea Brugge* 36, no 3 (2016): 4–9.

129. Ibidem; Hans Lägers, *Hertsteen en Cronement. Haardstenen uit de zestiende en zeventiende eeuw* (Utrecht: Stichting Matrijs, 2006).

130. Vickery, *Behind closed doors,* 29.

131. Ibidem, 29.

132. Borcher, 'Some Thoughts about Form and Function of Early Flemish Portraits', 201.

133. Erik Duverger, *Brugge en de Tapijtkunst* (Brugge/Moeskroen: Louis de Poortere, 1987), 86; Brown and Dumolyn (eds.), *Medieval Bruges, c. 850 – c. 1550.*

For Public Elegance and Private Comfort

1. The words *Elegantiae publicae et commoditati privatatae* appeared over the entrance of the fifteenth-century Palazzo Castani in Milan. See: Sarti, *Europe at Home*, 129.
2. Jacob Burckhardt, *The Civilization of Renaissance Italy*, (transl.) L. Goldsheider (London, s.n., 1945), 227. Also in Bruno Blondé, 'Shoppen met Isabella d' Este. De Italiaanse renaissance als bakermat van de Consumptiesamenleving?', Stadsgeschiedenis 2, no 2 (2007): 139.
3. Trentmann, *Empire of Things*, 30.
4. John E. Crowley, 'The Sensibility of Comfort', *American Historical Review* 104, no 3 (1999): 750.
5. Ibidem, 751; Rybczynski, *Home. A Short History of an Idea*, 20–22.
6. Danièle Alexandre-Bidon, 'Le confort dans la maison médiéval. Une synthèse des données.', in *Cadre de vie et manières de'habiter (xiie-xvie siècle)*, ed. Danièle Alexandre-Bidon, Françoise Piponnier and Jean-Michel Poisson (Turnhout: brepols, 2006), 129–144, 129–130; Riddy, '"Burgeis" domesticity in late-medieval England', 14–17.
7. Alexandre-Bidon, 'Le confort dans la maison médiéval', 130–131.
8. Ibidem, 140–141; Penelope Eames, *Furniture in England, France and the Netherlands from the twelfth tot the fifteenth century*, part of: *Furniture History*, 13 (1977); Carlano and Sumberg, *Sleeping Around. The Bed from Antiquity to Now*, 35–36.
9. Trentmann, *Empire of Things*, 30.
10. Translated as 'Good manners'
11. J. Van Vloten, 'Levensmanieren naar een handleiding der 16e eeuw. Meegedeeld door Prof. J. van Vloten', *Dietsche Warande*, 6 (1864): 349. The booklet of Erasmus is titled: *Goede, manierlijcke zeden, hoe de jonghers gaen, staen, eten, drincken, spreeken, swijghen, ter tafelen dienen, ende de spijse ontghinnen sullen, met vele andere schoone Ghecolligeert vvt diuersche autheuren, ende meer andere gheleerde Boecken, door Vrage ende Antvvoorde ghestelt.* Published by Jan van Waesberghe, inde Cammenstrate, inden Schilt van Vlaenderen, 1587.
12. Trentmann, *Empire of Things*, 4.
13. Ibidem, 271.
14. Giorgio Riello, 'Fabricating the Domestic: The Material Culture of Textiles and the Social Life of the Home in Early Modern Europe', in *The Force of Fashion in Politics and Society. Global Perspectives from Early Modern to Contemporary Times*, ed. Beverly Lemire (Aldershot: Ashgate, 2010), 43.
15. Marc Boone and Walter Prevenier (eds), *Drapery Production in the Late Medieval Low Countries: Markets and Strategies for Survival (14th-16th Centuries)* (Leuven: Garant, 1993); Sturtewagen, *All Together Respectably Dressed*, 115–135.

16. Katherine Anne Wilson, 'Tapestry in the Burgundian Dominions. A complex and prob-lematic object', in *La cour de Bourgogne et l'Europe. Le rayonnement et les limites d'un modèle culturel*. Actes du colloque internationale tenu à Paris les 9, 10 et 11 octobre 200, ed. Werner Paravincini (Paris, 2011), 322.

17. Frances Pritchard, 'The Uses of Textiles, c. 1000–1500', in *The Cambridge History of Western Textiles*; ed. David Jenkins (Cambridge: Cambridge University Press, 2003), 355.

18. Alexandre-Bidon, 'Le confort dans la maison médiéval. Une synthèse des données.', 129–130; Riddy, '"Burgeis" domesticity in late-medieval England', 14–17.

19. Crowley, 'The Sensibility of Comfort', 750.

20. ...without aspiring to search for the cradle of the concept of comfort in the living rooms of fifteenth and sixteenth century Bruges.

21. Riello, 'Fabricating the Domestic', 49; Margaret Ponsonby, *Stories from Home: English Domestic Interiors, 1750–1850* (Aldershot: Ashgate, 2007), 111; Sarti, *Europe at Home*.

22. Baatsen et al. 'Thuis in de stad: dynamieken van de materiële cultuur'

23. Baatsen et al. 'Thuis in de stad', 275–276; Carlano and Sumberg, *Sleeping Around.*, 35–36.

24. Say is a twilled woolen fabric.

25. Borchert, 'De ontdekking van de Brugse schilderkunst'.

26. Wilson, 'Tapestry in the Burgundian Dominions.', 316–317.

27. Sturtewagen, *All Together*, 115–135

28. John Gloag, *A social history of furniture design from B.C. 1300 to A.D. 1960* (London: Crown, 1966).

29. Hester C. Dibbits, 'Between Society and Family Values: The Linen Cupboard un Early-Modern Households', in *Private Domain, Public Inquiry: Families and Life-Styles in the Netherlands and Europe, 1550 to the present*, ed. Anton Schuurman, and Pieter Spierenburg (Hilversum: Verloren, 1996), 125–145.

30. John Gloag, *The Englishman's Chair. Origins, design and social history of seat furniture in England* (London: Allen & Unwin, 1964), 1–2.

31. Goldberg, 'The Fashioning of Bourgeois Domesticity in Later Medieval England: a Material Culture Perspective', 125; Overton, *Production and Consumption*, 91.

32. We have to be aware, though, that in reality, this calculation may be an underestimate of the number of seats, because benches may have offered more seats than we now assume.

33. Trentmann, *Empire of Things*, 30.

34. Crowley, *The Invention of Comfort*, 7.

35. Trentmann, *Empire of Things*, 43.

36. Penelope Eames, 'Furniture in England, France and the Netherlands from the 12th to the 15th century', *Furniture History*, 13 (1977): 181.

37.   https://www.vam.ac.uk/collections, Victoria and Albert Museum, London, consulted on 27th August 2016.

38.   Gloag, *The Englishman 's Chair*, 41.

39.   Baatsen, De Groot and Sturtewagen, 'Single Life in Fifteenth-Century Bruges', 191–192; Gardiner, 'Buttery and Pantry and their antecedents', 37–65.

40.   Victor Chinnery, *Oak Furniture. The British Tradition. A History of Early Furniture in the British Isles and New England* (Woodbridge: Antique Collectors' Club, 1986).

41.   State Archives Brussels, CC – 13773, 1439, f° 36v–37r.

42.   Ibidem, CC – 13773, 1438, f° 23r/v; Ibidem, CC – 13774, 1439, f° 46v–47r and ibidem, CC – 13774, 1444, f° 46v–47r.

43.   Nuechterlein, 'The domesticity of sacred space', 72.

44.   Rogier van der Weyden, c. 1434, Oil on panel, 89 cm × 36.5 cm (35 in × 14.4 in), the Louvre, Paris, and Galleria Sabauda, Turin.

45.   Master FVB, c. 1480, engraving on paper, 204 mm (8.03 in) x 161 mm (6.34 in), Rijksmuseum Amsterdam (among others).

46.   Jean Gessler (ed.), *Le Livre des Mestiers: De Bouc vanden Ambachten, Het Brugsche Livre des Mestiers en zijn navolgingen* (Brugge, s.n., 1931), 8 or f° 3r.

47.   Alexandre Pinchart, *Archives des arts, sciences et lettres: documents inédits publiés et annotés par Alexandre Pinchart réimpression anastatique de l'édition de Gand, 1860* (Ghent: Hebbelynck, 1994), 42–49. See also: Baatsen, De Groot, Sturtewagen, 'Single Life in Fifteenth-Century Bruges', 192.

48.   'The Virgin had to be seated on a richly dressed bed, curtains opened'.

49.   Pinchart, *Archives des arts, sciences et lettres,* 42–49. 'And next to the bed a high chair should be placed, like it is done in Brabant and Flanders and many other places'.

50.   State Archives Brussels, CC – 13773, 1438, f° 23v-24r.

51.   Gloag, *The Englishman's Chair*, 3.

52.   State Archives Brussels, CC – 13773, 1438, f° 25r/v.

53.   Master of Flémalle, Merode Altarpiece, c. 1427–1434, oil on panel, Central panel: 25 1/4 x 24 7/8 in. (64.1 x 63.2 cm), The Cloisters, Metropolitan Museum of Art, New York.

54.   Master of Flémalle, Werl Alterpiece, C. 1438, oil on panel, Museo del Prado.

55.   Gloag, *The Englishman's Chair*, 5.

56.   SAB, WP – Reg 1293, 1476.

57.   Berend Dubbe, *Huusraet. Het stedelijke woonhuis in de Bourgondische tijd* (Hoorn: Uitgeverij Poldervondsten, 2012), 62.

58.   Van de Velde, 'Het kuipersambacht te Brugge'.

59.   Ibidem; De Staelen, *Spulletjes*, 278–279.

60. Holy Family at Work, Hours of Catherine of Cleves, in Latin, Illuminated by the Master of Catherine of Cleves, ca. 1440, Tempera on vellum, 7 1/2 x 5 1/8 in. (192 x 130 mm), Utrecht, The Netherlands.

61. Baatsen, Blondé and De Groot, 'The Kitchen between Representation and Everyday Experience.', 174. See also the chapter on the kitchen in this book.

62. CAB, Gheeraerts (1586–1588), 1584.

63. CAB, 2e reeks – 16059, 1569, f° 1r–32r.

64. Gloag, *The Englishman's Chair*, 48.

65. Baatsen, Blondé, De Groot, 'The Kitchen between Representation and Everyday Experience', 176.

66. Gloag, *The Englishman 's Chair*, 58; Katherine C. Grier, 'Bodily Comfort and Spring-Seat Upholstery', in *Culture and Comfort. People, Parlors and Upholstery, 1850–193,* ed. Katherine C. Grier (New York: Strong Museum, 1988), 106.

67. Ninya Mikhaila and Jane Malcolm-Davies, *The Tudor Tailor: Reconstructing Sixteenth-Century Dress* (s.l.: Costume & Fashion Press, 2006).

68. Personal communication with Isis Sturtewagen

69. De Staelen, *Spulletjes*, 273.

70. Ria Fabri, 'La Chaise d'Espagne dans les Pays-Bas des 17ième et 18ième siècles', *L'Estampille*, 115 (1979), 30; Ria Fabri, *De Spaanse Lerenstoel: Bijdrage tot de studie van het zitmeubel in de Zuidelijke Nederlanden (XVI-XVIIIe eeuw)* (PhD Dissertation, Catholic University of Leuven, 1977), 116–118.

71. Fabri, 'La Chaise d'Espagne', 36.

72. Ibidem, 30.

73. City Archive Antwerp, N, 1331, f° 37r–46r, 1588.

74. De Staelen, database Antwerp inventories; De Staelen, *Spulletjes*, 274–275.

75. CAB, SVG – 1e reeks – 65, 1568, f° 1r–20r and CAB, SVG – 2e reeks – 15415, 1597, f° 1r–37v.

76. De Staelen, *Spulletjes*.

77. Buxton, *Domestic Culture*, 176.

78. Dubbe, *Huusraet. Het Stedelijke Woonhuis in de Bourgondische Tijd*, 65; Sara Pennell, 'Making the Bed in Later Stuart and Georgian England', in *Selling Textiles in the Long Eighteenth Century. Comparative Perspectives from Western Europe*, ed. Jon Stobart and Bruno Blondé (Basingstoke: Palgrave Macmillan, 2014), 31–33.

79. Dubbe, *Huusraet*, 67. A *rabat* was an ornately decorated, mostly fringed or pleated strip of fabric, used as part of the bed curtains or canopy but also often used as a decorative detail on mantelpieces.

80.   A. P. E Ruempol, and A. G. A. van Dongen (eds.), *Huisraad van een Molenaarsweduwe: gebruiksvoorwerpen uit een 16de-eeuwse boedelinventaris* (Rotterdam: Museum Boymans-Van Beuningen, 1986).

81.   Baatsen et al. 'Thuis in de stad', 276.

82.   Ibidem, 276.

83.   CAB, Dingne (1568–1570), 1569.

84.   De Groot, 'Zorgen voor later?', 12; Sarti, *Europe at home,* 45–46.

85.   Thijs Lambrecht, 'Slave to the wage? Het dienstpersoneel op het platteland in Vlaanderen (16de-18de eeuw)', *Oost-Vlaamse Zanten* 76, no 1 (2001): 32–78; Sarti, *Europe at Home*, 42–45; Christiane Klapisch-Zuber, 'Women servants in Florence during the fourteenth and fifteenth centuries', in *Women and work in pre-industrial Europe*, ed. Barbara Hanawalt (Bloomington: Indiana University Press, 1986), 68.

86.   Vandamme, 'Huizenonderzoek en materiële cultuur in het zestiende-eeuwse Brugge', 88; Currie, *Inside the Renaissance House*, 49–50.

87.   Ileen Montijn, *Tussen Stro en Veren. Het Bed in het Nederlandse Interieur* (Wormer: Inmerc, 2006), 11.

88.   Buxton, *Domestic Culture*, 178.

89.   Currie, *Inside the Renaissance House*, 49.

90.   Sarti, *Europe at Home*, 130.

91.   Sturtewagen, *All Together*, 296.

92.   CAB, Staten van goed – 2e reeks – 1597, f° 1r–37v, 1597.

93.   Sturtewagen, *All Together*, 122.

94.   Herman Van der Wee, 'Consumptie van Textiel en Industriële Ontwikkeling in de Steden van de Nederlanden tijdens de late Middeleeuwen en de Nieuwe Tijd: aanzet tot een Werkhypothese, in *"Proeve 't al, 't is prysselyck": Verbruik in Europese Steden (13ᵈᵉ-18ᵈᵉ eeuw). Liber Amicorum Raymond van Uytven*, ed. Walter Prevenier et al. (Antwerp: UFSIA, 1998), 343; John Munro, 'Medieval Woollens: Textiles, Textile Technology and Industrial Organisation, c. 800–1500, in *The Cambridge History of Western Textiles*, ed. D. Jenkins (Cambridge: Cambridge University Press, 2003), 184.

95.   Sturtewagen, *All Together*, 122.

96.   Ibidem, 121.

97.   For an overview and discussion of this shift from the traditional draperies to the new and light draperies, see: Sturtewagen, Isis, *All Together Respectably Dressed.*, 120–121.

98.   Ibidem, 149

99.   Sarti, *Europa at Home*, 130.

100.   De Staelen, *Spulletjes*, 269.

101. See also Inneke Baatsen's findings considering sociability in the context of dinner: Baatsen, *A Bittersweet Symphony. The Social Recipe of Dining Culture in Late Medieval and Early Modern Bruges*, 321.

102. Phillips, 'Local Integration and Long-Distance Ties'; CAB, Spanish Archive, Registro de Pedro de Paredes.

103. CAB, Spanish Archive, Staten van Goed, Vélasco de Béjar, 1555.

104. Stabel, 'Le goût pour l'Orient', 118.

105. Belozerskaya, *Luxury Arts of the Renaissance,* 95.

106. Vanwelden, *Productie van Wandtapijten*, 24.

107. Wilson, 'Tapestry in the Burgundian Dominions', 316; J.C. Smith, 'Portable Propaganda: Tapestries as Princely Metaphors at the Courts of Philip the Good and Charles the Bold', *Art Journal* 48, no 2 (1989).

108. Guy Delmarcel, *Flemish Tapestry, 15th to 18th century* (Tielt: Lannoo, 1999).

109. Wilson, 'Tapestry in the Burgundian Dominions.', 316–317.

110. Vanwelden, *Productie van Wandtapijten*

111. Delmarcel and Duverger, *Brugge en de Tapijtkunst*, 37.

112. Wilson, 'Tapestry in the Burgundian Dominions', 324.

113. Ibidem, 317. See also: Katherine Anne Wilson, 'In the chamber, in the garde robe, in the chapel, in a chest: The possession and uses of luxury textiles. The case of Later Medieval Dijon', in *Europe's Rich Fabric. The Consumption, Commercialisation and Production of Luxury Textiles in Italy, the Low Countries and Neighbouring Territories (Fourteenth-Sixteenth Centuries)*, ed. Katherine Anne Wilson and Bert Lambert (Aldershot: Ashgate, 2016), 11–34, especially 11–12.

114. Delmarcel and Duverger, *Brugge en de Tapijtkunst*, 37.

115. Ibidem, 56.

116. Antoon Viaene, 'Carpite – carpette – karpet, 1300–1600', *Biekorf,* 70 (1969): 37–40.

117. Personal communication with Peter Stabel.

118. By 'cushion' we mean the cushions that were used to sit on or lean against, not the pillows used for sleeping on. Pillows were considered part of the bedding and not as decorative textiles.

119. Marco Spallanzani, *Oriental Rugs in Renaissance Florence* (Florence: Studio Per Edizioni Scelte, 2007), 52.

120. Ibidem, 51.

121. Sturtewagen, *All Together*, 129.

122. Jeroen Puttevils, 'Trading Silks and Tapestries in Sixteenth-Century Antwerp', in *Europe's Rich Fabric: The Consumption, Commercialization, and Production of Luxury Textiles*, 131-156. Also cited in Sturtewagen, *All Together*, 126.

123. Sturtewagen, *All Together*, 129.

124. Ibidem, 129.

125. Ibidem, 132.

126. Ibidem, 127.

127. Vanwelden, *Productie van Wandtapijten*; Delmarcel and Duverger, *Brugge en de Tapijtkunst*, 62–63.

128. Puttevils, 'Trading Silks and Tapestries in Sixteenth-Century Antwerp', 133; Vanwelden, *Productie van Wandtapijten*, 93; Filip Vermeylen, *Art and Economics. The Antwerp Art Market of the Sixteenth Century* (PhD Dissertation, Columbia University, 2000).

129. Delmarcel and Duverger, *Brugge en de Tapijtkunst,* 30.

130. Delmarcel, *Flemish Tapestry*, 181 and 184.

131. Ibidem, 184.

132. Delmarcel and Duverger, 'Brugse verdures en de schilderkunst', in *Brugge en de tapijtkunst*, ed. Delmarcel and Duverger, 107–112.

133. CAB, Plocquoy, 1545, f° 368.

134. CAB, Dingne (1561–1562), 1561.

135. CAB, Staten van Goed – 2ᵉ reeks – 15901, 1583.

136. CAB, Staten van Goed – 1e reeks – 126, 1574.

137. CAB, Spanish Archive, 1569, Jasper de Caestre.

138. CAB, Gheeraerts (1590–1602), 1591. The inventory was of Bruges nobleman Charles de Fonteynes; CAB, Staten van goed – 2e reeks – 1597, the inventory of Marie Pardo.

139. Wim Hüsken, Bart Stroobants and Els van der Jeugt, *Goudleer in Mechelen* (Mechelen: Stedelijk Museum Hof van Busleyden, 2004).

140. Johan Dambruyne, 'Het is al goud dat blinkt. Het succesverhaal van de vroegmoderne Mechelse goudleernijverheid', in *Werken aan de Stad. Stedelijke Actoren en Structuren in de Zuidelijke Nederlanden, 1500–1900*, ed. Margot De Koster et al. (Brussels: VUBpress, 2011), 69.

141. Puttevils, 'Trading Silks and Tapestries', 135; Delmarcel and Duverger, *Brugge en de tapijtkunst*, 73–82.

142. NAB, Accounts of the Audit Office (Rekenkamer), 23482–23487, Six Comptes rendus par Jacques Vanden Heede, de la perception du droit de deux pour cent à Bruges, Damme et l'Ecluse du 15 décembre 1551 au 12 août 1554. See: Pinchart, A. Inventaire des archives des Chambres des Comptes, précédé d'une notice historique sur ces anciennes institutions, part IV.

143. Belozerskaya, *Luxury Arts of the Renaissance,* 95.

144. James Bloom, 'Animated Bodies: The Performance of Images at the Burgundian Court', in *Staging the court of Burgundy: proceedings of the conference "The splendour of Burgundy"*, ed. Anne Van Oosterwijck et al. (London: Miller, 2013).

145. De Staelen, *Spulletjes*, 156–164. Although a thorough investigation of these murals and frescos would be interesting to consider as part of the interior decoration of many houses also in Bruges, it is beyond the scope of this research. Therefore, it is not included in this book.

146. Among others: John Munro, 'The Anti-Red Shift – To the Dark Side: Colour Changes in Flemish Luxury Woollens, 1300–1550', *Medieval Clothing and Textiles,* 3 (2007): 55–95.

147. Sturtewagen, *All Together*, 157.

148. Ibidem, 179.

149. Ibidem, 180.

150. Munro, 'The Anti-Red Shift – To the Dark Side'.

151. Raymond Van Uytven, 'Rood-Wit-Zwart: kleurensymboliek en kleursignalen in de Middeleeuwen', *Tijdschrift voor Geschiedenis*, 97 (1984): 464–467.

152. De Staelen, *Spulletjes*, 166–167.

153. Sturtewagen, *All Together*, 179–180.

154. Van Uytven, 'Rood-Wit-Zwart', 449.

155. Ibidem, 449–450.

156. Personal communication with dr. Jeanne Nuechterlein.

157. Sturtewagen, *All Together*, 163.

158. Ibidem, 158.

159. Unfortunately, no variations in shade were specified in the inventories for the flat textiles.

160. Judith Hofenck de Graeff, *The Colourful Past The Origins, Chemistry and Identification of Natural Dyestuffs* (London: Archetype Publications Ltd, 2004), 215.

161. Jill Goodwin, *A Dyer's Manual* (London: Pelham Books Ltd., 1982), 60.

162. Katherine Anne Wilson, 'Commerce and Consumers: The Ubiquitous Chest of the Late Middle Ages', *The Journal of Interdisciplinary History* (2021): 1–28.

163. De Staelen, *Spulletjes*, 286.

164. State Archives Brussels, CC – 13773, f° 25v–26r, 1438.

165. SAB, WP – Reg 1292, 1460.

166. Dibbits, 'Between Society and Family Values'

167. Wilson, 'The household inventory as urban 'theatre' in late medieval Burgundy', 341–342.

168. CAB, SVG – 2e reeks – 16059, f° 1r–32r, 1569.

169. Wilson, 'Commerce and Consumers: The Ubiquitous Chest of the Late Middle Ages', 1–28.

170. SAB, WP – Reg 1295, 1502.

171. Riello, 'Fabricating the Domestic', 47.

172. Wim De Clercq, Jan Dumolyn and Jelle Haemers, 'Vivre Noblement: Material Culture and Elite Identity in Late Medieval Flanders', *Journal of Interdisciplinary History* 38, no 1 (2007): 1-31.

173. Blondé, Stabel et al., 'Retail Circuits in Medieval and Early Modern Europe: an Introduction', 9.

General Conclusions

1. Evans, 'Enlivening the Archive'.
2. Ibidem.
3. Anne-Laure Van Bruaene, Bruno Blondé and Marc Boone, 'Verstedelijking en Stadshistoriografie', in *Gouden Eeuwen. Stad en Samenleving in de Lage Landen 1100–1600,* ed. Anne-Laure Van Bruaene, Bruno Blondé and Marc Boone (Ghent: Academia Press, 2016), 25.
4. Riddy, '"Burgeis" Domesticity in Late Medieval England', 2008, 14–36. See also the work of Daniel Jütte on the value of gates, locks and walls in the pre-modern city: Daniel Jütte, *The Strait Gate. Thresholds and Power in Western History* (New Haven: Yale University Press, 2015).
5. King, Chris, 'Domestic Buildings', 115.
6. See also: Denis, 'In search of material practices', 1–16.

BIBLIOGRAPHY

Archival Sources

Post-mortem inventories

City Archive Bruges, Staten van Goed, 1st and 2nd series.
General State Archive, Chambre des Comptes, n° 13773 and 13774.

Confiscation inventories

City Archive Bruges, Ledgers of Beernaerts (1530–1532), Berlot (1560–1563), Bisschops
(1569–1595), Coolman (1541–1545), De Queester (1561–1562), De Rouf (1589–1603),
Dingne (1550–1584), Gheeraerts (1566–1602), Ghiselin & Smout (1528–1549), Mommengy
(1541–1561), Pancoucke (1560–1562), Philippet (1583–1585), Plocquoy (1543–1560), Smet
(1531–1539), Telleboom (1559–1560) and Vandevelde (1585–1600).
State Archive Bruges, Old Archive, Legal Proceedings, series 1292, 1293, 1294, 1295 and 1233.
General State Archive, Old Archive, Raad van Beroerten, Series 249.

Other

City Archive Bruges, Old Archive, Series 203, account book by G. Bibau, 1576–1568.
General Archives Brussels, Accounts of the Audit Office (Rekenkamer), 23482–23487, Six Comptes
rendus par Jacques Vanden Heede, de la perception du droit de deux pour cent à Bruges,
Damme et l'Ecluse du 15 décembre 1551 au 12 août 1554.
City Archive Bruges, Spanish Archive, Staten van Goed.

Literature

Ainsworth, Maryan W. 'The Business of Art: Patrons, Clients, and Art Markets.' In *From Van Eyck to Bruegel: Early Netherlandish Painting in The Metropolitan Museum of Art*, edited by Maryan W. Ainsworth and Keith Christiansen, 23–37. New York: The Metropolitan Museum of Art, 1998.

Ajmar-Wollheim, Marta, and Flora Dennis. *At Home in Renaissance Italy*. London: Victoria and Albert Museum, 2006.

Ajmar-Wollheim, Marta, Dennis, Flora, and Ann Matchette (eds.) *Approaching the Italian Renaissance Interior: Sources, Methodologies and Debates*. Oxford: Blackwell Publishing, 2007.

Ajmar-Wollheim, Marta, Dennis, Flora, and Ann Matchette. 'Introduction. Approaching the Italian Renaissance Interior: Sources, Methodologies, Debates.' *Renaissance Studies* 20, no. 5 (2006): 623–628.

Alexandre-Bidon, Danièle. 'Le Confort dans la Maison Médiéval. Une Synthèse des Données.' In *Cadre de Vie et Manières de'Habiter (xiie-xvie siècle)*, edited by Danièle Alexandre-Bidon, Françoise Piponnier, and Jean-Michel Poisson. Caen: Publications du CRAHM, 2006.

Allerston, Patricia. 'Consuming Problems: Worldly Goods in Renaissance Venice.' In *The Material Renaissance*, edited by Michelle O'Malley and Evelyn S. Welch, 11–46. Manchester: Manchester University Press, 2010.

Anseeuw, Jan et al. *Achter Brugse Muren: op zoek naar Materiële cultuur in Brugge, 1500–1800*. Bruges: Levend Archief, 2014.

Appadurai, Arjun (ed.). *The Social Life of Things: Commodities in Cultural Perspective*. Cambridge: Cambridge University Press, 1988.

Ariès, Philippe. *Centuries of Childhood: A Social History of Private Life*. London: Pimlico; New Ed edition, 1996.

Arnade, Peter, Howell, Martha, and Walter Simons. 'Fertile Spaces: The Productivity of Urban Space in Northern Europe.' Special volume, *Journal of Interdisciplinary History* 32, no. 4 (2002): 515–548.

Aynsley, J., and C. Grant *Imagined Interiors: Representing the Domestic Interior since the Renaissance*. London: Victoria and Albert Museum, 2006.

Ayres, J. *Domestic Interiors: The British Tradition 1500–1850*. New Haven: Yale University Press, 2001.

Baatsen, Inneke, Blondé, Bruno, and Carolien De Staelen. 'Antwerp and the "Material Renaissance": Exploring the Social and Economic Significance of Crystal Glass and Majolica in the Sixteenth Century.' In *The Ashgate Research Companion to Early Modern Material Culture*, edited by David Gaimster, Tara Hamling, and Catherine Richardson, 436–451. Aldershot: Ashgate 2017.

Baatsen, Inneke, Blondé, Bruno, and Julie De Groot. 'The Kitchen between Representation and Everyday Experience. The Case of Sixteenth-Century Antwerp.' In *Trading Values in Early Modern Antwerp*, edited by Christine Götler et al, 162–184. Leiden: Brill, 2014.

Baatsen, Inneke, De Groot, Julie, and Isis Sturtewagen. 'Single Life in Fifteenth-Century Bruges. Living Arrangements and Material Culture at the Fringes of Urban Society.' In *Single Life and the City, 1200–1900*, edited by Julie De Groot, Isabelle Devos, and Ariadne Schmidt, 179–202. Basingstoke: Palgrave Macmillan, 2015.

Baatsen, Inneke. 'A Bittersweet Symphony: The Social Recipe of Dining Culture in Late Medieval and Early Modern Bruges (1438–1600).' PhD diss., University of Antwerp, 2016.

Baatsen, Inneke et al. 'Thuis in de Stad. Dynamieken van de Materiële Cultuur.' In *Gouden Eeuwen: stad en samenleving in de Lage Landen, 1100–1600*, edited by Anne-Laure van Bruaene et al, 251–285. Ghent: Academia Press, 2016.

Baetens, Roland, and Bruno Blondé. 'Wonen in de Stad: Aspecten van de Stedelijke Wooncultuur.' In *Stad in Vlaanderen. Cultuur en Maatschappij, 1477–1787*, edited by Jan van der Stock, 63–64. Brussels: Gemeentekrediet, 1991.

Benedict, Philippe. 'Towards the Comparative Study of the Popular Market for Art: The Ownership of Paintings in Seventeenth-Century Metz.' *Past and Present* 109 (1985): 105.

Bennett, Jim. 'Scientific Knowledge.' In *At Home in Renaissance Italy*, edited by Marta Aymar-Wollheim and Flora Dennis, 172 – 174. London: Victoria and Albert Museum, 2006.

Benson, John, and Laura Ugolini. 'Introduction. Historians and the Nation of Shopkeepers.' In *A Nation of Shopkeepers: Five Centuries of British Retailing*, edited by John Benson and Laura Ugolini. London: Tauris, 2003.

Billinge, Rachel et al. 'Methods and Materials of Northern European Painting in the National Gallery, 1400–1550.' *Technical Bulletin* 18 (1997): 6–55.

Blockmans, Wim. 'Bruges the European Commercial Centre.' In *Bruges and Europe*, edited by Valentin Vermeersch, 40–55. Antwerp: Mercator, 1992.

Blockmans, Wim. 'Fondans en melencolie de povreté. Leven en Werken in Brugge, 1482–1584.' In *Bruges and the Renaissance: Memling to Pourbus*, edited by Maximiliaan P. J. Martens, 16–32. Ghent: Stichting Kunstboek, 1998.

Blockmans, Wim. 'The Creative Environment: Incentives to and Functions of Bruges Art Production.' In *Petrus Christus in Renaissance Bruges: An Interdisciplinary Approach*, edited by Maryan Ainsworth, 11–20. New York: Metropolitan Museum of Art, 1995.

Blondé, Bruno, and Veerle De Laet. 'Owning Paintings and Changes in Consumer Preferences in the Low Countries, Seventeenth–Eighteenth Centuries.' In *Mapping Markets for Paintings in Europe, 1450–1750*, edited by Neil De Marchi and Hans J. Van Miegroet, 68–84. Brepols: Turnhout, 2006.

Blondé, Bruno et al. (eds.) *Buyers and Sellers: Retail Circuits and Practices in Medieval and Early Modern Europe*. Turnhout: Brepols, 2006.

Blondé, Bruno, and Ilja Van Damme. 'The Shop, The Home and the Retail Revolution, Antwerp, Seventeenth-Eighteenth Centuries.' *Città e Storia* 2 (2007): 335–350.

Blondé, Bruno, and Wouter Ryckbosch. 'In "Splendid Isolation". A Comparative Perspective on the Historiographies of the "Material Renaissance" and the "Consumer Revolution".' *History of Retailing and Consumption* 1, no. 2 (2015):105–124.

Blondé, Bruno et al. *Retailers and Consumer Changes in Early Modern Europe: England, France, Italy and the Low Countries*. Tours: Presses Universitaires François-Rabelais, 2005.

Blondé, Bruno et al. *Trend en Toeval. Inleiding tot de Kwantitatieve Methoden voor Historici*. Leuven: Leuven University Press, 2015.

Bloom, James. 'Animated Bodies: The Performance of Images at the Burgundian Court.' In *Staging the Court of Burgundy: Proceedings of the Conference 'The Splendour of Burgundy'*, edited by Anne van Oosterwijck et al. London: Miller, 2013.

Bloom, James. 'Why Painting?' In *Mapping Markets for Paintings in Europe, 1450–1750*, edited by Neil De Marchi and Hans J. Van Miegroet, 17–31. Brepols: Turnhout, 2006.

Boone, Marc, and Walter Prevenier (eds). *Drapery Production in the Late Medieval Low Countries: Markets and Strategies for Survival (14th-16th Centuries)*. Leuven: Garant, 1993.

Borchert, Till-Holger. 'De ontdekking van de Brugse schilderkunst.' In *Brugge en de Renaissance. Van Memling tot Pourbus*, edited by Maximiliaan Martens. Ghent: Ludion, 1998.

Borchert, Till-Holger. 'Some Thoughts about Form and Function of Early Flemish Portraits.' In *Staging the Court of Burgundy: Proceedings of the Conference 'The Splendour of Burgundy'*, edited by Wim Blockmans and Anne van Oosterwijk. London: Miller, 2013.

Brown, Andrew, and Jan Dumolyn (eds.). *Bruges. A Medieval Metropolis, c. 850 – c. 1550*. Cambridge: Cambridge University Press, 2018.

Brulez, Wilfried. 'Brugge en Antwerpen in de 15de en 16de eeuw: een tegenstelling?' *Tijdschrift voor Geschiedenis* 83 (1970): 15–37.

Burckhardt, Jacob. *The Civilization of Renaissance Italy*. Translated by L. Goldsheider. Oxford: Oxford University Press, 1945.

Burke, Peter. 'The Presentation of Self in the Renaissance Portrait.' In *The Historical Anthropology of Early Modern Italy*. Cambridge: Cambridge University Press, 2005.

Buskirk, Jessica E. '"Salve Maria Gods Moeder Ghepresen." The Salve Regina and the Vernacular in the Art of Hans Memling, Anthonis de Roovere and Jacob Obrecht.' In *The Transformation of Vernacular Expression in Early Modern Arts*, edited by Joost Keizer and Todd M. Richardson, 59–97. Leiden: Brill, 2012.

Buxton, Antony. *Domestic Culture in Early Modern England*. Woodbridge: Boydell Press, 2015.

Caers, Toon. '"Ende ierst in de coecken." Kook- en eetgerei in zestiende-eeuws.' Bachelor's thesis, University of Antwerp, 2010.

Campbell Lorne. 'Diptychs with Portraits.' In *Prayers and Portraits: Unfolding the Netherlandish Diptych*, edited by John Oliver Hand and Ron Spronk, 33–45. New Haven: Yale University Press, 2007.

Campbell, Lorne. 'The Art Market in the Southern Netherlands in the Fifteenth Century.' *The Burlington Magazine* 118 (1976): 188–198.

Campbell, Lorne. *Renaissance Portraits: European Portrait-Painting in the Fourteenth-Fifteenth and Sixteenth Centuries*. New Haven: Yale University Press, 1990.

Campbell, Erin, Miller, Stephanie, and Elizabeth Carroll Consavari. 'Introduction.' In *The Early Modern Italian Domestic Interior, 1400–1700*, edited by Erin Campbell, Stephanie Miller, and Elizabeth Carroll Consavari. Aldershot: Ashgate, 2013.

Carlano, Annie, and Bobbie Sumberg. *Sleeping Around: The Bed from Antiquity to Now*. Santa Fe: Museum of International Folk Art, 2006.

Carlson, Elisabeth. 'Dazzling and Deceiving: Reflections in the Nineteenth-Century Department Store.' *Visual Resources* 28, no. 2 (2012): 117–137.

Cavallo, Sandra, and Silvia Evangelisti. *Domestic Institutional Interiors in Early Modern Europe*. Aldershot: Ashgate, 2009.

Chinnery, Victor. *Oak Furniture. The British Tradition. A History of Early Furniture in the British Isles and New England*. s.l.: Antique Collectors' Club, 1986.

Cieraad, Irene. 'Introduction: Anthropology at Home.' In *At Home: An Anthropology of Domestic Space*, edited by Irene Cieraad, 1–12. Syracuse: Syracuse University Press, 1999.

Clark, David. 'The Shop within?: An Analysis of the Architectural Evidence for Medieval Shops.' *Architectural History* 43 (2000): 58–87.

Clark, Leah R. 'Collecting, Exchange, and Sociability in the Renaissance *Studiolo*.' *Journal of the History of Collections* 25, no. 2 (2013): 171–184.

Clericuzio, Antonio. 'The Internal Laboratory: The Chemical Reinterpretation of Medical Spirits in England (1650–1680).' In *Alchemy and Chemistry in the 16th and 17th Centuries*, edited by Piyo Rattansi and Antontio Clericuzio, 51–83. Dordrecht: Kluwer Academic, 1994.

Cockx-Indestege, Elly, and Willem Heijting. 'De Doorbraak van de Drukkunst in Roerige Tijden. Het Nederlandse Boek in de Zestiende Eeuw.' *Jaarboek voor Nederlandse Boekgeschiedenis* 17 (2010): 93– 139.

Cohen, E. S. 'Honor and Gender in the Streets of Early Modern Rome.' *Journal of Interdisciplinary History* 22 (1992): 597–625.

Cohen, Elisabeth, and Thomas Cohen. 'Open and Shut: The Social Meanings of the Cinquecento Roman House.' *Studies in the Decorative Arts* 9, no. 1 (2002): 61– 84

Cohn, Samuel. 'Renaissance Attachment to Things: Material Culture in Last Wills and Testaments.' *The Economic History Review* 65, no. 3 (2012): 984–1004.

Colish, Marcia. *The Mirror of Language: A Study of the Medieval Theory of Knowledge.*, Lincoln: University of Nebraska Press, 1983.

Cooper, Donal. 'Devotion.' In *At Home in Renaissance Italy*, edited by Marta Aymar-Wollheim and Flora Dennis, 190–203. London: Victoria and Albert Museum, 2006

Corbeau, Merwin. 'Pronken en Koken. Beeld en Realiteit van Keukens in het Vroegmoderne Hollandse Binnenhuis.' Special issue, *Mensen en Dingen. Betekenissen van Materiële Cultuur: Volkskundig Bulletin*, edited by Gerard Rooijakkers 19, no. 3 (1993): 354–375.

Cox, Nancy. *The Complete Tradesman: A Study of Retailing, 1550–1820*. Aldershot: Ashgate, 2000.

Crowley, John E. 'The Sensibility of Comfort.' *American Historical Review* 104, no. 3 (1999): 749–782.

Currie, Elizabeth. *Inside the Renaissance House*. London: Victoria and Albert Museum, 2006.

Currie, Elizabeth. 'Diversity and Design in the Florentine Tailoring Trade, 1550–1620.' In *The Material Renaissance*, edited by Michelle O'Malley and Evelyn S. Welch. Manchester: Manchester University Press, 2014.

D'Hondt, Jan et al. (eds.). *Huizenonderzoek & stadsgeschiedenis: handelingen van het colloquium op 28 november 2008 in Brugge*. Bruges: Levend Archief, 2009.

D'Hooghe, Catharina. *De huizen van het Zuidproosse te Brugge van ca. 1400 tot 1920*. Brussels: Algemeen Rijksarchief, 1997.

Dale, Thomas E. 'Transcending the Major/Minor Divide: Romanesque Mural Painting, Color, and Spiritual Seeing.' In *From Major to Minor: The Minor Arts in Medieval Art History*, edited by Colum Hourihane, 23–42. Princeton: Princeton University Press, 2012.

Dambruyne, Johan. 'Het is al goud dat blinkt. Het succesverhaal van de vroegmoderne Mechelse goudleernijverheid.' In *Werken aan de Stad. Stedelijke Actoren en Structuren in de Zuidelijke Nederlanden, 1500–1900*, edited by Margot de Koster et al. Brussels: Vrije Universiteit Brussel Press, 2011.

Dambruyne, Johan. *Corporatieve middengroepen: aspiraties, relaties en transformaties in de 16de-eeuwse Gentse ambachtswereld*. Ghent: Academia Press, 2002.

Dannenfeldt, Karl. 'Sleep: Theory and Practice in the Late Renaissance.' *Journal of the History of Medicine and Allied Sciences* 41, no. 4 (1986): 415–441.

Davidoff, Leonore, and Catherine Hall. *Family Fortunes: Men and Women of the English Middle Class 1780–1850*. London: Routledge, 1987.

Davis, D. *Fairs, Shops and Supermarkets: A History of Shopping*. Toronto: University of Toronto Press, 1966.

De Clercq, Wim, Dumolyn, Jan, and Jelle Haemers. 'Vivre Noblement: Material Culture and Elite Identity in Late Medieval Flanders.' *Journal of Interdisciplinary History* 38, no. 1 (2007): 1–31.

De Groot, Julie. 'Zorgen voor later? De betekenis van de dienstperiode voor jonge vrouwen in het laatmiddeleeuwse Gent herbekeken.' *Stadsgeschiedenis* 6, no. 1 (2011): 1–15.

De Laet, Veerle. *Brussel Binnenskamers. Kunst- en Luxebezit in het Spanningsveld tussen Hof en Stad, 1600–1735*. Amsterdam: Amsterdam University Press, 2011.

De Marchi, Neil. 'Size and Taste. Taking the Measure of the History of the Art Markets.' In *Economia e Arte Secc. XIII-XVIII*, part 2, edited by Simonetta Cavaciocchi, 79–81. Florence: Istituto Internazionale di Storia Economia "F.Datini" Prato, 2002.

De Mare, Heidi, and Anna Vos. 'Urban Rituals in Italy and the Netherlands.' In *Urban Rituals in Italy and the Netherlands: Historical Contrasts in the Use of Public Space, Architecture and the Urban Environment*, edited by Heidi de Mara and Anna Vos, 5–25. Assen: Van Gorcum, 1993.

De Mare, Heidi. 'The Domestic Boundary as Ritual Area in Seventeenth-Century Holland.' In *Urban Rituals in Italy and the Netherlands: Historical Contrasts in the Use of Public Space, Architecture and the Urban Environment*, edited by Heidi de Mara and Anna Vos, 109–131. Assen: Van Gorcum

De Meyer, Ingrid. 'De Sociale Structuren te Brugge in de 14e eeuw', *Studiën betreffende de sociale strukturen te Gent, Brugge en Kortrijk in de 14de en 15de eeuw,* Heule, 1971, 7–78.

De Munck, Bert. 'Guilds, Product Quality and Intrinsic Value. Towards a History of Conventions?' Special issue, *Historical Social Research: Conventions and Institutions from a Historical Perspective* 36, no. 4 (2011): 103–214.

De Munck, Bert. 'Construction and Reproduction. The Training and Skills of Antwerp Cabinetmakers in the Sixteenth and Seventeenth Centuries.' In *Learning on the Shop Floor: Historical Perspectives on Apprenticeship*, edited by Bert de Munck, Steven L. Kaplan, and Hugo Soly. New York: Berghahn, 2007.

De Munck, Bert. 'From Religious Devotion to Commercial Ambition? Some Marginal Notes on the Religious Material Culture of the Antwerp Crafts in the 16th Century.' In *From Quinten Metsijs to Peter Paul Rubens: Masterpieces from the Royal Museum Reunited in the Cathedral*, edited by Ria Fabri and Nico van Hout, 21–31. Antwerp: De Kathedraal, 2009.

De Munck, Bert. 'One Counter and Your Own Account: Redefining Illicit Labour in Early Modern Antwerp.' *Urban History* 37, no. 1 (2010): 26–44.

De Peuter, R. 'Textielwinkels in Achttiende-eeuw Brussel.' In *Mag het iets meer zijn? Detailhandel en Distributie van Consumptieartikelen in de Nederlanden, 1450–1850*, edited by R. de Peuter and E. Steegen. Brussels, 2006.

De Staelen, Carolien. 'Spulletjes en hun betekenis in een commerciële metropool. Antwerpenaren en hun materiële cultuur in de zestiende eeuw.' PhD diss., University of Antwerp, 2007.

Decavele, J. 'Protestantse invloeden in Brugge in het midden van de 16de eeuw: een internationaal netwerk.' *Tijdschrift voor Nederlandse Kerkgeschiedenis* 16 (2013): 6–23.

Deceulaer, Harald. 'Pret-à-porter, gender en gezondheid. De veelvuldige betekenissen van huiszoekingen bij kleermakers en oudekleerkopers in het laat-16de-eeuwse Antwerpen.' In *Werelden van Verschil: Ambachtsgilden in de Lage Landen*, edited by Catharina Lis and Hugo Soly. Brussels: Vrije Universiteit Brussel Press, 1997.

Deceulaer, Harald. *Pluriforme Patronen en een Verschillende Snit. Sociaal-Economische, Institutionele en Culturele Transformaties in de Kledingsector in Antwerpen, Brussel en Gent, 1585–1800.* Amsterdam: Aksant, 2001.

Delmarcel Guy. *Flemish Tapestry, 15th to 18th century.* Tielt: Lannoo, 1999.

Delmarcel, Guy, and Erik Duverger. *Brugge en de Tapijtkunst.* Bruges: City of Bruges, 1987.

Deneweth, Heidi. 'Moving Up or Down the Housing market. Real Estate and Social Change in Bruges, 1550–1670.' Paper presented at the Tenth European Social Science History Conference, Vienna, 2014.

Deneweth, Heidi. 'Brugge Zoekt en Vindt Alternatieven.' In *Brugge*, edited by V. Vermeersch. Antwerp: Mercatorfonds, 2002.

Deneweth, Heidi. 'Een Demografische Knoop Ontward? Brugse Bevolkingscijfers voor de Vroegmoderne Tijd.' *Handelingen van het Genootschap voor Geschiedenis te Brugge* 147, no. 1 (2010): 3–48.

Deneweth, Heidi. 'Licht zonder Zicht. Burenovereenkomsten rond Lichtinval en Privacy in Vroegmodern Brugge.' *Tijd-Schrift* 5, no. 2 (2015): 7–20.

Deneweth, Heidi, d'Hondt, Jan, and Kathleen Leenders. *Een huis in Brugge. Vademecum voor de historische studie van woningen, eigenaars en bewoners.* Bruges: Levend Archief, 2001.

Deneweth, Heidi. *Huizen en Mensen. Wonen, verbouwen, investeren en lenen in drie Brugse wijken van de late middeleeuwen tot de negentiende eeuw*, part 1. PhD diss., Vrije Universiteit Brussel, 2008.

Deneweth, Heidi. *Goede Muren maken Goede Buren. Verbouwingen en buurtleven in Brugge, 1500–1800.* Bruges: Van de Wiele, 2020.

Denis, Britt. 'Home, Sweet Home?! Publiek en Privaat onder de Loep in Negentiende-eeuws Antwerpen (1880).' *Volkskunde* 116, no. 2 (2015): 129–150.

Denis, Britt. 'In Search of Material Practices: the Nineteenth-Century European Domestic Interior Rehabilitated.' *History of Retailing and Consumption* (2016): 97–112.

Dewilde, Brecht. 'Portretten en de Markt: het Familiebedrijf Claeissens in Zestiende-eeuws Brugge.' Master's thesis, Catholic University of Leuven, 2007.

Dewitte, A. 'Chronologie van de Reformatie te Brugge en in het Brugse Vrije (1485–1593).' In *Brugge in de Geuzentijd. Bijdragen tot de Geschiedenis van de Hervorming te Brugge en in het Brugse Vrije tijdens de 16de eeuw*, edited by Dirk van der Bauwhede, 34–44. Bruges: Westvlaamse Gidsenkring, 1982.

Dibbits, Hester C. 'Between Society and Family Values: The Linen Cupboard un Early-Modern Households.' In *Private Domain, Public Inquiry: Families and Life-Styles in the Netherlands and Europe, 1550 to the Present*, edited by Anton Schuurman and Pieter Spierenburg, 125–145. Hilversum: Verloren, 1996.

Douglas, Mary. 'The Idea of a Home: a Kind of Space.' *Social Research* 58, no. 1 (1991): 287–307.

Dubbe, Berend. *Thuis in de Late Middeleeuwen. Het Nederlandse Burgerinterieur 1400–1535*. Zwolle: Waanders, 1980.

Dubbe, Berend. *Huusraet. Het stedelijke woonhuis in de Bourgondische tijd*. Hoorn: Poldervondsten, 2012.

Dupré, Sven, and Christoph Lüthy. 'Introduction: Silent Messengers. The World of Goods and the Circulation of Knowledge in the Early Modern Netherlands.' In *Silent Messengers: The Circulation of Material Objects of Knowledge in the Early Modern Low Countries*, edited by Sven Dupré and Christoph Lüthy. Münster: Lit Verlag, 2011.

Dupré, Sven. 'The Value of Glass and the Translation of Artisanal Knowledge in Early Modern Antwerp.' In *Trading Values in Early Modern Antwerp*, edited by Christine Götler et al. Leiden: Brill, 2014.

Dupré, Sven. 'Trading Luxury Glass, Picturing Collections, Consuming Objects of Knowledge in Early-Seventeenth Century Antwerp.' In *Silent Messengers: The Circulation of Material Objects of Knowledge in the Early Modern Low Countries*, edited by Sven Dupré and Christoph Lüthy, 267–282. Münster: Lit Verlag, 2011.

Duverger, Erik. 'Tapijtwevers, tapijthandel en tapijtwerk in Brugge van de late middeleeuwen tot in het begin van de achtiende eeuw.' In *Brugge en de Tapijtkunst*, edited by Guy Delmarcel and Erik Duverger, 50–52. Bruges: Louis de Poortere, 1987.

Eames, Penelope. *Furniture in England, France and the Netherlands from the Twelfth to the Fifteenth Century*. London: Furnitures History Society, 1977.

Ekirch, Roger A. 'Sleep We Have Lost: Pre-Industrial Slumber in the British Isles.' *American Historical Review* 106, no. 2 (2001): 343–386.

Ekirch, Roger A. *At Day's Close: Night in Times Past*. New York: W. W. Norton, 2005.

Evans, Adrian B. 'Enlivening the Archive: Glimpsing Embodied Consumption Practices in Probate Inventories of Household Possessions.' *Historical Geography Volume* 36 (2008): 40–72.

Ewing, Dan. 'Marketing Art in Antwerp, 1460–1560: Our Lady's Pand.' *The Art Bulletin* 72, no. 4 (1990): 558–584.

Fabri, Ria. '"Van een gestocken tresoirken tot een rare schrijffcabinet" of Antwerpse kasten van de laat-16de tot de vroeg-18de eeuw: typologie en gebruik.' In *Opgeruimd staat netjes. Bergmeubelen van eind 16de tot begin 20ste eeuw*. Leuven: Museum Leuven, 1997. Exhibition catalogue.

Fabri, Ria. 'De "inwendighe wooninghe" of de binnenhuisinrichting.' In *Stad in Vlaanderen. Cultuur en Maatschappij, 1477 1787*, edited by Jan van der Stock, 127–140. Brussels: Gemeentekrediet, 1991.

Fabri, Ria. 'La Chaise d'Espagne dans les Pays-Bas des 17ième et 18ième siècles.' *L'Estampille* 115 (1979): 30.

Fabri, Ria. 'De Spaanse Lerenstoel: Bijdrage tot de studie van het zitmeubel in de Zuidelijke Nederlanden (XVI-XVIIIe eeuw).' PhD diss., Catholic University of Leuven, 1977.

Farge, Arlette. *Vivre dans la Rue à Paris au XVIIIe siècle*. Paris: Editions Gallimard, 1979.

Findlen, Paula. *Possessing Nature: Museums, Collecting, and Scientific Culture in Early Modern Italy*. Berkeley: University of California Press, 1994.

Fortini-Brown, Patricia, 'The Venetian Casa.' In *At Home in Renaissance Italy*, edited by Marta Aymar-Wollheim and Flora Dennis, 50–66. London: Victoria and Albert Museum, 2006.

Franceschi, Franco. 'Business Activities.' In *At Home in Renaissance Italy*, edited by Marta Aymar-Wollheim and Flora Dennis, 166–172. London: Victoria and Albert Museum, 2006

Frelick, Nancy (ed.). *Specular Reflections: The Mirror in Medieval and Early Modern Culture*. Turnhout: Brepols, 2016.

Gardiner, Mark. 'Buttery and Pantry and Their Antecedents: Idea and Architecture in the English Medieval House.' In *Medieval Domesticity: Home, Housing and Household in Medieval England*, edited by P. J. P. Goldberg and Maryanne Kowaleski, 37–65. Cambridge: Cambridge University Press, 2008

Garrard, Rachel P. 'English Probate Inventories and Their Use in Studying the Significance of the Domestic Interior, 1570–1700.' *A. A. G. Bijdragen* 23 (1980): 55–81.

Garrioch, D. 'House Names, Shop Signs and Social Organization in Western European Cities, 1500–1900.' *Urban History Review* 21 (1994): 20–48.

Geirnaert, Noël. 'Bruges and the Northern Netherlands.' In *Bruges and Europe*, edited by Valentin Vermeersch. Antwerp: Mercatorfonds, 1992.

Giles, Kate. "'A Table of Alabaster with the Story of the Doom": The Religious Objects and Spaces of the Guild of Our Blessed Virgin, Boston (Lincs).' In *Everyday Objects: Medieval and Early Modern Material Culture and Its Meanings*, edited by Catherine Richardson and Tara Hamling, 267–285. Aldershot: Ashgate, 2010.

Giles, Kate. 'Seeing and Believing: Visuality and Space in Pre-Modern England.' *World Archaeology* 39, no. 1 (2007): 105–121.

Gilliodts-Van Severen, Louis. *Coutumes des Pays et Comté de Flandre: quartier de Bruges*, 2 vols. Brussels: Gobbaerts, 1874–1874.

Giltè, Stefanie. 'Het Bakkersambacht te Brugge: Samenstelling en Werking.' *Handelingen van het Genootschap voor Geschiedenis* 137 (2000): 126–151.

Girouard, Mark. *Life in the English Country House: A Social and Architectural History*. New Haven: Yale University Press, 1978.

Gloag, John. *A Social History of Furniture Design from B.C. 1300 to A.D. 1960*. London: Cassell, 1966.

Goffman, Erving. *The Presentation of Self in Everyday Life*. New York: Anchor Books, 1959.

Goldberg, Jeremy, and Maryanne Kowaleski. 'Introduction. Medieval Domesticity: Home, Housing and Household.' In *Medieval Domesticity: Home, Housing and Household in Medieval England*, edited by Jeremy Goldberg and Maryanne Kowaleski. Cambridge: Cambridge University Press, 2008.

Goldberg, Jeremy. 'The Fashioning of Bourgeois Domesticity in Later Medieval England: a Material Culture Perspective.' In *Medieval Domesticity: Home, Housing, and Household in Medieval England*, edited by Jeremy Goldberg and Maryanne Kowaleski. Cambridge: Cambridge University Press, 2009.

Goldstein, Claudia. 'Artifacts of Domestic Life. Bruegel's Paintings in the Flemish Home.' *Wooncultuur in de Nederlanden, Nederlands Kunsthistorisch Jaarboek*, edited by Jan de Jong, 51 (2001): 177.

Goldstein, Claudia. *Pieter Bruegel and the Culture of the Early Modern Dinner Party*. Aldershot: Ashgate, 2013.

Goldthwaite, Richard. 'The Empire of Things: Consumer Demand in Renaissance Italy.' In *Patronage, Art and Society in Renaissance Italy*, edited by F. W. Kent and P. Simons, 153–175. Oxford: Oxford University Press, 1987.

Goldthwaite, Richard. *Wealth and the Demand for Art in Italy, 1300–1600*. Baltimore: John Hopkins University Press, 1993.

Goodwin, Jill. *A Dyer's Manual*. London: Pelham Books Ltd., 1982.

Gottdiener, Mark. *The Social Production of Urban Space*. Austin: University of Texas Press, 2010.

Greig, Hannah, Hamlett, Jane, and Leonie Hannan. 'Introduction: Gender and Material Culture.' In *Gender and Material Culture in Britain since 1600*, edited by Hannah Greig, Jane Hamlett, and Leonie Hannan. London: Palgrave Macmillan, 2016.

Grier, Katherine C. 'Bodily Comfort and Spring-Seat Upholstery.' In *Culture and Comfort: People, Parlors and Upholstery, 1850–1930*, edited by Katherine Grier. New York: Strong Museum, 1988.

Griffith Winton, Alexa. 'Inhabited Space: Critical Theories and the Domestic Interior.' In *The Handbook of Interior Architecture and Design*, edited by Lois Weinthal and Graeme Brooker. London: Bloomsbury Press, 2013.

Guerzoni, Guido. 'Liberalitas, Magnificencia, Splendor: the Classic Origins of Italian Renaissance Lifestyles.' In *Economic Engagements with Art*, edited by Neil De Marchi and Craufurd D. W. Goodwin, 332–378. Durham, NC: Duke University Press, 1999.

Guerzoni, Guido. 'Servicing the Casa.' In *At Home in Renaissance Italy*, edited by Marta Aymar-Wollheim and Flora Dennis, 146–152. London: Victoria and Albert Museum, 2006.

Hamling, Tara, and Catherine Richardson. 'Introduction.' In *Everyday Objects: Medieval and Early Modern Material Culture and its Meanings*, edited by Tara Hamling and Catherine Richardson, 1–23. Aldershot: Ashgate, 2010.

Handley, Sasha. 'Sociable Sleeping in Early Modern England, 1660–1760.' *History. The Journal of the Historical Association* 98, no. 1 (2013): 79–104.

Heley, Gwendolynn. *The Material Culture of the Tradesmen of Newcastle upon Tyne 1545–1642: The Durham Probate Record Evidence*. Durham: Durham University, 2007.

Hendrickx, Bert. 'Het schilderijenbezit van de Antwerpse burger in de tweede helft van de zestiende eeuw: een socio-economische analyse.' Master's thesis, Catholic University of Leuven, 1997.

Heynen, Hilde, 'Modernity and Domesticity: Tensions and Contradictions.' In *Negotiating Domesticity: Spatial Productions of Gender in Modern Architecture*, edited by Hilde Heynen and Baydar Gülsüm, 1–29. London: Routledge, 2005.

Hilario Casado Alonso. 'Brugge, centrum van uitwisseling met Spanje.' In *Hanzekooplui en Medicibankiers. Brugge, wisselmarkt van Europese culturen*, edited by André Vandewalle et al. Oostkamp: Stichting Kunstboek, 2002.

Hofenck de Graeff, Judith. *The Colourful Past The Origins, Chemistry and Identification of Natural Dyestuffs*. London: Archetype Publications Ltd., 2004.

Hohti, Paula. 'Domestic Space and Identity: Artisans, Shopkeepers and Traders in Sixteenth-Century Siena.' *Urban History* 37, no. 3 (2010): 372–385.

Hohti, Paula. '"Conspicuous" Consumption and Popular Consumers: Material Culture and Social Status in Sixteenth-Century Siena.' *Journal of the Society for Renaissance Studies* 24, no. 5 (2010): 654–670.

Hohti, Paula. *Artisans, Objects, and Everyday Life in Renaissance Italy: The Material Culture of the Middling Class*. Amsterdam: Amsterdam University Press, 2021.

Howell, Martha C. 'Fixing Movables: Gifts by Testament in Late Medieval Douai.' *Past and Present* 150, no. 1 (1996): 3–45.

Howell, Martha C. *Commerce before Capitalism in Europe, 1300–1600*. Cambridge: Cambridge University Press, 2010.

Hüsken, Wim, Stroobants, Bart, and Els van der Jeugt. *Goudleer in Mechelen*. Mechelen: Stedelijk Museum Hof van Busleyden, 2004.

Huvenne, Paul. *Pieter Pourbus, Meester-Schilder 1524–1584*. Bruges: Gemeentekrediet and City of Bruges, 1984.

Jardine, Lisa. *Worldly Goods: A New History of the Renaissance*. London: W. W. Norton, 1998.

Jerram, Leif. 'Space: A Useless Category for Historical Analysis?' *History and Theory* 52 (2013): 400–419.

Joekalda, Kristina. 'What Has Become of the New Art History?' *Journal of Art History* 9, no. 9 (2013): 1–7.

Johnson, Matthew. *English Houses 1300–1800: Vernacular Architecture, Social Life*. London: Pearson, 2010.

Jordanova, Ludmilla. *The Look of the Past: Visual and Material Evidence in Historical Practice*. Cambridge: Cambridge University Press, 2012.

Kik, Oliver. 'Rond den Heerd. Schoorsteenwangen en Haardstenen in de Gruuthuse Collectie.' *Museumbulletin Musea Brugge* 36, no. 3 (2016): 4–9.

King, Chris. 'Domestic Buildings: Understanding Houses and Society.' In *The Routledge Handbook of Material Culture in Early Modern Europe*, edited by Catherine Richardson, Tara Hamling, and David Gaimster, 116. London: Routledge, 2017.

King, Chris. 'The Interpretation of Urban Buildings: Power, Memory and Appropriation in Norwich Merchants' Houses, c. 1400–1660.' *World Archaeology* 41, no. 3 (2009): 471–488.

Krohn, Deborah. 'Picturing the Kitchen: Renaissance Treatise and Period Room.' *Studies in Decorative Arts* 16, no. 1 (2008/2009): 20–34.

Krohn, Deborah. *Food and Knowledge in Renaissance Italy: Bartholomeo Scappi's Paper on Kitchens.* New York: Routledge, 2015.

Lägers, Hans. *Hertsteen en Cronement. Haardstenen uit de zestiende en zeventiende eeuw*. Utrecht: Stichting Matrijs, 2006.

Lambrecht, Thijs. 'Slave to the wage? Het dienstpersoneel op het platteland in Vlaanderen (16de-18de eeuw).' *Oost-Vlaamse Zanten* 76, no. 1 (2001): 32–78.

Lefebvre, Henri. *La Production de l'espace*. Paris: Éditions Anthropos, 1974.

Lesger, Clé. *Het Winkellandschap van Amsterdam. Stedelijke structuur en winkelbedrijf in de vroegmoderne en moderne tijd, 1550–2000*. Hilversum: Verloren, 2013.

Lindow, James. *The Renaissance Palace in Florence: Magnificence and Splendour in Fifteenth-Century Italy*. Aldershot: Ashgate, 2007.

Lis, Catharina, and Hugo Soly. *Werelden van Verschil*. Brussels: Vrije Universiteit Brussel Press, 1997.

Loughman, John, and J. M. Montias. *Public and Private Spaces: Works of Art in Seventeenth-Century Dutch Houses*. Zwolle: Waanders, 2000.

Loughman, John. 'Between Reality and Artful Fiction: The Representation of the Domestic Interior in Seventeenth-Century Dutch Art.' In *Imagined Interiors: Representing the Domestic Interior since the Renaissance,* edited by Jeremy Aynsley and Charlotte Grant, 72–97. London: Victoria and Albert Museum, 2006.

Marechal, Dominique. 'De Diaspora van de Brugse Renaissance.' In *Brugge en de Renaissance. Van Memling tot Pourbus*, 2 volumes, edited by Maximiliaan Martens. Bruges: Stichting Kunstboek, 1998.

Maréchal, J. *Europese aanwezigheid te Brugge. De vreemde kolonies (XIVde-XIXde eeuw)*. Bruges: Genootschap voor Geschiedenis, 1985.

Marnef, Guido, and Hugo de Schepper. 'Raad van Berocrten (1567–1576).' In *De Centrale Overheidsinstellingen van de Habsburgse Nederlanden (1482–1795)*, edited by Erik Aerts et al., 469–477. Brussels: Algemeen Rijksarchief, 1994.

Marnef, Guido. *Antwerp in the Age of Reformation: Underground Protestantism in a Commercial Metropolis, 1550–1577*. Baltimore: The John Hopkins University Press, 1996.

Martens, Didier. *Peinture Flamande et Goût Ibérique aux XVème et XVIème Siècles*. Brussels: Le livre
Timperman, 2010.

Martens, Maximiliaan. 'Some Aspects of the Origins of the Art Market in Fifteenth-Century Bruges.'
In *Art Markets in Europe, 1400–1800*, edited by M. North and D. Ormrod, 19–27. Aldershot:
Ashgate, 1998.

Martens, Maximiliaan, and Natasja Peeters. 'Paintings in Antwerp Houses (1532–1567).' in
Mapping Markets for Paintings in Europe, 1450–1750, edited by Neil De Marchi and Hans J.
Van Miegroet, 35–53. Brepols: Turnhout, 2006.

Martens, Maximiliaan. *Artistic Patronage in Bruges Institutions, ca. 1440–1482*. PhD diss., University
of California, 1992.

Matchette, Ann. 'To Have or to Have Not: The Disposal of Household Furnishings in Florence.'
Renaissance Studies 20, no. 5 (2006): 704.

McIver, Katherine A. 'Let's Eat: Kitchens and Dining in the Renaissance Pallazo and Country Estate.'
In *The Early Modern Italian Domestic Interior, 1400–1700: Objects, Spaces, Domesticities*, edited
by E. J. Campbell et al., 159–173. Farnham: Ashgate, 2013.

McShane, Angela, and Joanne Begiato. 'Making Beds, Making Households: The Domestic and
Emotional Landscape of the Bed in Early Modern England.' Unpublished paper, forthcoming
2017.

Melchior-Bonnet, Sabine. *The Mirror: A History*. New York: Routledge, 2002.

Michelant, Henri (ed.). *Le Livre des Mestiers; dialogues français-flamands composes au XIVe siècle par
un maître d'école de la ville de Bruges*. Paris: Librairie Tross, 1875.

Mileson, Stephen. 'Openness and Closure in the Later Medieval Village.' *Past and Present* 234
(2017): 3–37.

Montias, John Michael. 'How Notaries and Other Scribes Recorded Works of Art in Seventeenth-
Century Sales and Inventories.' *Semiolus: Netherlandish Quarterly for the History of Art* 30,
no. 3/4 (2003): 217–235.

Montijn, Ileen. *Tussen Stro en Veren. Het Bed in het Nederlandse Interieur*. Wormer: Inmerc, 2006.

Morgan, Hollie L. S. *Beds and Chambers in Late Medieval England – Readings, Representations and
Realities*. York: York Medieval Press, 2017.

Mui, Hoh-Cheung, and Lorna H. Mui. *Shops and Shopkeeping in Eighteenth-Century England*.
London: McGill Queens University Press, 1989.

Munro, John H. 'Textile Technology in the Middle Ages.' In *Textiles, Towns and Trade: Essays in the
Economic History of Late Medieval England and the Low Countries*, edited by John H. Munro.
Aldershot: Variorum, 1994.

Munro, John H. 'Medieval Woolens: Textiles, Textile Technology and Industrial Organization, c. 800–1500.' In *The Cambridge History of Western Textiles*, edited by D. Jenkins, 181–227. Cambridge: Cambridge University Press, 2003.

Munro, John H. 'The Anti-Red Shift – To the Dark Side: Colour Changes in Flemish Luxury Woollens, 1300–1550.' *Medieval Clothing and Textiles* 3 (2007): 55–95.

Murray, James M. 'Handels- en Financiële Technieken.' In *Hanzekooplui en Medicibankiers. Brugge, Wisselmarkt van Europese Culturen*, edited by André Vandewalle. Ghent: Uitgeverij Ludion, 2002.

Musacchio, Jacqueline Marie. 'The Madonna and Child, A Host of Saints and Domestic Devotion in Renaissance Florence.' In *Revaluing Renaissance Art*, edited by Gabriele Neher and Rupert Shepherd. Aldershot: Ashgate, 2010.

North, Michael, and David Ormrod. 'Introduction: Art and Its Markets.' In *Art Markets in Europe, 1400–1800*, edited by Michael North and David Ormrod. Aldershot: Ashgate, 1998, 1–6.

Nuechterlein, Jeanne. 'The Domesticity of Sacred Space in the Fifteenth-Century Netherlands.' In *Defining the Holy. Sacred Space in Medieval and Early Modern Europe*, edited by Andrew Spicer and Sarah Hamilton, 49–79. Aldershot: Ashgate, 2005.

O'Malley, Michelle. *The Business of Art: Contracts and the Commissioning Process in Renaissance Italy*. New Haven: Yale University Press, 2005.

Olsen, Roberta et al. *The Biography of the Object in Late Medieval and Renaissance Italy*. Oxford: Oxford University Press, 2006.

Orlin, Lena Cowen. 'Fictions of the Early Modern English Probate Inventory.' In *The Culture of Capital: Property, Cities and Knowledge in Early Modern England*, edited by Henry S. Turner. Basingstoke: Routledge, 2002.

Orlin, Lena Cowen. *Locating Privacy in Tudor London*. Oxford: Oxford University Press, 2007.

Overlaet, Kim, and Inneke Baatsen. 'Zilveren lepels in het zestiende-eeuwse Mechelen: luxueus eetgerei of betekenisvolle gedinckenisse?' *Tijd-Schrift. Heemkunde en lokaal-erfgoedpraktijk in Vlaanderen* 11 (2015): 16–29.

Overton, Mark, Whittle, Jane, Dean, Darron, and Andrew Hahn. *Production and Consumption in English Households, 1600–1750*. London: Routledge, 2004.

Overton, Mark. 'A Computer Management System for Probate Inventories.' *History and Computing* 7, no. 3 (1995): 135–142.

Panofsky Erwin, 'Imago Pietatis: ein Beitrag zur Typengeschichte des "Schmerzensmanns" und der "Maria Mediatrix."' In *Festschrift für Max Friedländer zum sixty. Geburtstag*, 261–308. Leipzig: E.A. Seemann, 1927.

Pardailhé-Galabrun, Annik. *La Naissance de l'Intime. 3000 Foyers Parisiens XVIIe-XVIIIe siècles*. Paris: Presses Universitaires de France, 1988.

Pearson, Sarah. 'Houses, Shops, and Storage: Building Evidence from Two Kentish Ports.' In *The Medieval Household in Christian Europe, c. 850 – c. 1550. Managing Power, Wealth, and the Body*, edited by Cordelia Beattie, Anna Maslakovic, and Sarah Rees Jones. Turnhout: Brepols, 2003.

Pendergrast, Mark. *Mirror Mirror: A History of the Human Love Affair with Reflection*. New York: Basic Books, 2009.

Pennell, Sara. 'Making the Bed in Later Stuart and Georgian England.' In *Selling Textiles in the Long Eighteenth Century: Comparative Perspectives from Western Europe*, edited by Jon Stobart and Bruno Blondé. Basingstoke: Palgrave Macmillan, 2014.

Pennell, Sara. 'Pots and Pans History: The Material Culture of the Kitchen in Early Modern England.' *Journal of Design History* 11, no. 3 (1998): 201–216.

Pennell, Sara. *The Birth of the English Kitchen, 1600–1850*. London: Bloomsbury, 2016.

Phillips, William D. Jr. 'Local Integration and Long-Distance Ties: The Castilian Community in Sixteenth-Century Bruges.' *Sixteenth Century Journal* 17, no. 1 (1986): 33–49.

Piponnier, Françoise. 'From Hearth to Table. Late Medieval Cooking Equipment.' In *Food: A Culinary History from Antiquity to the Present*, edited by J.-L. Flandrin and M. Montanari, 339–346. New York: Columbia University Press, 1999.

Ponsonby, Margaret. *Stories from Home: English Domestic Interiors, 1750–1850*. Aldershot: Ashgate, 2007.

Priestley, Ursula, and P. J. Corfield. 'Rooms and Room Use in Norwich Housing, 1580–1730.' *Post-Medieval Archaeology* 16 (1982): 93–123.

Pritschard, Frances. 'The Uses of Textiles, c. 1000–1500.' In *The Cambridge History of Western Textiles*, part 1, edited by David Jenkins. Cambridge: Cambridge University Press, 2003.

Puttevils, Jeroen. 'Trading Silks and Tapestries in Sixteenth-Century Antwerp.' In *Europe's Rich Fabric: The Consumption, Commercialization, and Production of Luxury Textiles in Italy, the Low Countries and Neighboring Territories (Fourteenth-Sixteenth Centuries)*, edited by Bart Lambert and Katherine A. Wilson. Aldershot: Ashgate, 2016.

Richardson, Catherine, and Tara Hamling. 'Introduction.' In *Everyday Objects: Medieval and Early Modern Material Culture and Its Meanings*, edited by Catherine Richardson and Tara Hamling. Aldershot: Ashgate, 2010.

Richardson, Catherine, Hamling, Tara, and David Gaimster. 'Introduction.' In *The Routledge Handbook of Material Culture in Early Modern Europe*, edited by Catherine Richardson, Tara Hamling, and David Gaimster, 10. London: Routledge, 2017.

Richardson, Catherine, and Tara Hamling. *A Day at Home in Early Modern England. Material Culture and Domestic Life, 1500–1700*. New Haven: Yale University Press, 2017.

Riddy, Felicity et al. 'The Concept of the Household in Later Medieval England.' In 'The Later Medieval English Urban Household,' edited by Sarah Rees Jones et al. *History Compass* 4 (2006): 5–10.

Riddy, Felicity. '"Burgeis" Domesticity in Late Medieval England.' In *Medieval Domesticity: Home, Housing and Household in Medieval England*, edited by Jeremy Goldberg and Maryanne Kowaleski, 14–36. Oxford: Oxford University Press, 2008.

Riello, Giorgio. 'Fabricating the Domestic: The Material Culture of Textiles and the Social Life of the Home in Early Modern Europe.' In *The Force of Fashion in Politics and Society: Global Perspectives from Early Modern to Contemporary Times*, edited by Beverly Lemire. Aldershot: Ashgate, 2010.

Riello, Giorgio. 'Things Seen and Unseen. The Material Culture of Early Modern Inventories and Their Representation of Domestic Interiors.' In *Early Modern Things. Objects and their Histories, 1500–1800*, edited by Paula Findlen, 125–150. London: Routledge, 2015.

Rublack, Ulinka, 'Matter in the Material Renaissance.' *Past &Present* 219, no. 1 (2013): 41–85.

Ruempol, A. P. E., and A. G. A. van Dongen (eds.). *Huisraad van een Molenaarsweduwe: gebruiksvoorwerpen uit een 16de-eeuwse boedelinventaris*. Rotterdam: Museum Boymans-Van Beuningen, 1986.

Ruvoldt, Maria. 'Sacred to Secular, East to West: The Renaissance Study and Strategies of Display.' *Renaissance Studies* 20, no. 5 (2006): 640.

Rybczynski, Witold. *Home: A Short History of an Idea*. New York: Pocket Books, 1987.

Ryckaert, Marc et al. (eds.). *Brugge, de Geschiedenis van een Europese Stad*. Tielt: Lannoo, 1999.

Ryckaert, Marc. 'Van grafelijke residentiestad tot middeleeuwse handelsmetropool.' In *Brugge*, edited by Valentin Vermeersch, 62–86. Antwerp: Mercatorfonds, 2002.

Ryckaert, Marc (ed.). *Historische Stedenatlas van België: Brugge*. Brussels: Gemeentekrediet, 1991.

Salter, Elisabeth. 'Some Differences in the Cultural Production of Household Consumption.' In *The Medieval Household in Christian Europe, c. 850 – c. 1550. Managing Power, Wealth, and the Body*, edited by Cordelia Beattie et al., 391–407. Turnhout: Brepols, 2003.

Sarti, Rafaela. *Europe at Home. Family and Material Culture 1500–1800*. New Haven: Yale University Press, 2002.

Schama, Simon. *The Embarrassment of Riches: An Interpretation of Dutch Culture in the Golden Age*. Berkeley: University of California Press, 1988.

Schuurman, Anton. 'Is huiselijkheid typisch Nederlands? Over huiselijkheid en modernisering.' *Low Countries Historical Review* 107, no. 4 (1992): 745–759.

Schuurman, Anton. 'Probate Inventories: Research Issues, Problems and Results.' In *Probate Inventories: a New Source for the Historical Study of Wealth, Material Culture, and Agricultural Development*, edited by van Ad der Woude and Anton Schuurman. Wageningen: Wageningen Landbouwhogeschool, 1980.

Shuger, Debora. 'The "I" of the Beholder: Renaissance Mirrors and the Reflexive Mind.' In *Renaissance Culture and the Everyday*, edited by Patricia Fumerton and Simon Hunt. Philadelphia: University of Pennsylvania Press, 1999.

Silver, Larry. 'Art and Minds: Scholarship on Early Modern Art History (Northern Europe).' *Renaissance Quarterly* 59, no. 2 (2006): 351–373.

Smail, Daniel Lord. *Legal Plunder: Households and Debt Collection in Late Medieval Europe.* Cambridge, MA: Harvard University Press, 2016.

Smith, Pamela H. *The Business of Alchemy: Science and Culture in the Holy Roman Empire.* Princeton: Princeton University Press, 2016.

Smith, Alison A. 'Family and Domesticity.' In A *Cultural History of Food in the Renaissance*, edited by Ken Albala. New York: Berg, 2012.

Smith, Pamela H., and Paula Findlen. 'Commerce and the Representation of Nature in Art and Science.' In *Merchants & Marvels: Commerce, Science and Art in Early Modern Europe*, edited by Pamela H. Smith and Paula Findlen. New York: Routledge, 2002.

Smith, Pamela H., and Tonny Beentjes. 'Nature and Art, Making and Knowing: Reconstructing Sixteenth-Century Life-Casting Techniques.' *Renaissance Quarterly* lxiii (2010): 128 – 179.

Smith, J. C. 'Portable Propaganda: Tapestries as Princely Metaphors at the Courts of Philip the Good and Charles the Bold.' *Art Journal* 48, no. 2 (1989): 123–129.

Sosson, J. P. 'Une approche des structures économiques d'un métier d'art: la corporation des peintres et selliers de Bruges (XVe – XVIe siècles).' *Revue des archéologues et historiens d'art de Louvain* 3 (1970): 91–100.

Spallanzani, Marco. *Oriental Rugs in Renaissance Florence*. Florence: Studio Per Edizioni Scelte, 2007.

Stabel, Peter. 'Working Alone? Single Women in the Urban Economy of Late Medieval Flanders (thirteenth-early fifteenth centuries).' In *Single Life and the City, 1200–1900*, edited by Julie de Groot, Isabelle Devos, and Ariadne Schmidt. Basingstoke: Palgrave MacMillan, 2015.

Stabel, Peter. 'Organisation corporative et production d'oeuvres d'art à Bruges à la fin du Moyen Age et au début des Temps modernes.' *Le Moyen Age* 113 (2007): 91–134.

Stabel, Peter, and Jeroen Deploige. 'Textile Entrepreneurs and Textile Workers in the Medieval City.' In *Golden Times: Wealth and Status in the Middle Ages in the Southern Low Countries*, edited by Veronique Lambert et al., 241–280. Tielt: Lannoo, 2016.

Stabel, Peter, and Michiel, Wagenaar. 'Stadsgeschiedenis. Uitgangspunten van een nieuw tijdschrift.' *Stadsgeschiedenis* 1, no. 1 (2006): 1–6.

Stabel, Peter. 'From the Market to the Shop. Retail and Urban Space in Late Medieval Bruges.' In *Buyers and Sellers. Retail Circuits and Practices in Medieval and Early Modern Europe*, edited by Bruno Blondé et al. Turnhout: Brepols, 2006.

Stabel, Peter. 'Guilds in Late Medieval Flanders: myths and realities of guild life in an export-oriented environment.' *Journal of Medieval History* 30 (2004): 187–212.

Stabel, Peter. 'Le Goût pour l'Orient. Demande cosmopolite et objets de luxe à Bruges à la fin du Moyen Âge.' *Histoire Urbaine* 30 (2011): 21–40.

Stabel, Peter. 'Le Rouge et le Noir en Flandre. Vêtements et Couleurs en Milieu Bourgeois au Bas Moyen Age (Bruges première moite du XVe siècle).' forthcoming.

Stabel, Peter. 'Markets and Retail Circuits of the Late Medieval Countries. Economic Networks and Socio-Cultural Display.' In *Fiere e Mercatie. Nella Integrazione delle Economie Europee Secc. XIII-XVIII*, edited by Simonetta Cavaciocchi, 797–817. Florence: Le Monnier, 2001.

Stabel, Peter. 'Selling Paintings in Late Medieval Bruges: Marketing Customs and Guild Regulations Compared.' In *Mapping Markets for Paintings in Europe, 1450–1750*, edited by Neil De Marchi and Hans J. van Miegroet, 89–105. Brepols: Turnhout, 2006.

Stobart, Jon. 'Shopping Streets as Social Space: Leisure, Consumerism and Improvement in an Eighteenth Century Town, 16060–1840.' *Economic History Review* 55 (2002): 31–50.

Sturtewagen, Isis. *All Together Respectably Dressed. Fashion and Clothing in Bruges During the Fifteenth and Sixteenth Centuries*. PhD diss., University of Antwerp, 2016.

Sullivan, Margaret. 'Aertsen's Kitchen and Market Scenes: Audience and Innovation in Northern Art.' *The Art Bulletin* 81, no. 2 (1999): 236–266.

Tafur, Pero. *Andanças é viajes de pero tafur por diversas partes del mundo avidos 1435–1439*. Madrid, 1874. English Translation: Tafur, Pero, *Travels and Adventures, 1435–1439*, translated by M. Letts. London, 2005 – 1ste ed. 1926.

Thornton, Peter. *The Italian Renaissance Interior: 1400–1600*. London: Weidenfeld & Nicolson, 1991.

Timmermans, Bert. 'Networkers and Mediators in the 17th Century Antwerp Art World: The Impact of Collectors-Connoisseurs on Artistic Processes of Transmission and Selection.' In *Luxury in the Low Countries: Miscellaneous Reflections on Netherlandish Material Culture, 1500 to the Present*, edited by Rengenier Rittersma, 109–134. Brussels: Faro, 2010.

Torti, Anna. *The Glass of Form: Mirroring Structures from Chaucer to Skelton*. Cambridge: D. S. Brewer, 1991.

Tosh, John. *Manliness and Masculinities in Nineteenth-Century Britain: Essays on Gender, Family and Empire*. Harlow: Pearson, 2005.

Trentmann, Frank. *Empire of Things: How We Became a World of Consumers, from the Fifteenth Century to the Twenty-First*. London: Penguin Random House, 2016.

Unwin, Tim. 'A Waste of Space? Towards a Critique of the Social Production of Social Space.' *Transactions of the Institute of British Geographers* 25, no. 1 (2000): 14–17.

Van Borm, Sarah. *Hiëronymus in huis. Geleerdencultuur in de Zuidelijke Nederlanden: het Sint-Romboutkapittel van Mechelen, 1495–1554*. Master's thesis, University of Antwerp, 2015.

Van Damme, Ilja. *Verleiden en Verkopen. Antwerpse Kleinhandelaars en hun klanten in tijden van crisis (ca. 1648–ca. 1748)*. Amsterdam: Aksant, 2007.

Van Damme, Ilja. 'Pendelen tussen revoluties en tradities Recent historisch onderzoek naar de
    kleinhandel in de late middeleeuwen en de nieuwe tijd (ca. 1450–ca. 1850).' *Stadsgeschiedenis* 2,
    no. 1 (2007): 54–65.

Van der Stighelen, Katlijne. *Hoofd en Bijzaak. Portretkunst in Vlaanderen van 1420 tot nu.* Zwolle:
    Waanders, 2008.

Van der Wee, Herman. 'Consumptie van Textiel en Industriële Ontwikkeling in de Steden van de
    Nederlanden tijdens de late Middeleeuwen en de Nieuwe Tijd: aanzet tot een Werkhypothese.'
    In *"Proeve 't al, 't is prysselyck": verbruik in Europese steden (13de–18de eeuw)*, edited by Raymond
    VanUyten and Walter Prevenier. Antwerp: Liber Amicorum Raymond van Uytven, 1998.

Van Hout, Nico. *Vlaamse Primitieven. De Mooiste Tweeluiken.* Ghent: Ludion, 2007.

Van Male, Zegher. *Lamentatie van Zegher van Male behelsende wat datter aenmerckensweerdich
    geschiet is ten tyde van de geuserie ende de beeltstormerie binnen ende omtrent de stadt van
    Brugghe*, edited by C. Carton Ghent: L. Maatschappij der Vlaemsche Bibliophilen, 1859.

Van Miegroet, Hans. 'New Data Visualisations on the Mechelen Export Industry and Artist Migration
    Patterns.' *De Zeventiende Eeuw, Special Issue Art on the Move* 31, no. 1 (2015): 179–190.

Van Os, Henk. *The Art of Devotion in the Late Middle Ages in Europe, 1300–1500.* Princeton:
    Princeton University Press, 1994.

Van Oosterwijk, Anne (ed.). *Vergeten Meesters. Pieter Pourbus en de Brugse schilderkunst van 1525 tot
    1625.* Bruges: Snoeck, 2017.

Van Roy, Vincent. 'Tussen Overlevering en Empire? Vier zestiende-eeuwse receptenboekjes onder de
    loep genomen.' In *De medische renaissance anders bekeken (1400–1600)*, edited by Ivo de Leeuw,
    Cornelis van Tilburg, and Vincent Van Roy. Antwerp: Garant, 2006.

Van Uytven, Raymond. 'Rood-Wit-Zwart: kleurensymboliek en kleursignalen in de Middeleeuwen.'
    Tijdschrift voor Geschiedenis 97 (1984): 464–467.

Van Uytven, Raymond. 'Stages of Economic Decline: Late Medieval Bruges.' In *Peasants and Townsmen
    in Medieval Europe: studia in honorem Adriaan Verhulst*, edited by Jean-Marie Duvosquel and Erik
    Thoen, 259–269. Ghent: Belgisch Centrum voor Landelijke Geschiedenis, 1995.

Van Uytven, Raymond. *De Zinnelijke Middeleeuwen.* Leuven: Davidsfonds, 1998.

Van Werveke, Hans. *De koopman-ondernemer en de ondernemer in de Vlaamsche lakennijverheid van
    de Middeleeuwen.* Antwerp: Antwerpen Standaard-Boekhandel, 1946.

Vandamme, Ludo. 'Het Calvinisme te Brugge in beweging (1560–1566).' In *Brugge in de
    Geuzentijd. Bijdragen tot de Geschiedenis van de Hervorming te Brugge en in het Brugse Vrije
    tijdens de 16de eeuw*, edited by Dirk van der Bauwhede and Marc Goetinck, 102–122. Brugge:
    WerkgroepHerdenkingsbundel en Uitgaven Westvlaamse Gidsenkring, 1982.

Vandamme, Ludo. 'Huizenonderzoek en materiële cultuur in het zestiende-eeuwse Brugge.' In *Huizenonderzoek en stadsgeschiedenis*, edited by Brigitte Beernaert et al. Bruges: Brugge Levend Archief, 2009.

Vandamme, Ludo. 'Inleiding.' In *Een Stad vol Boeken. Bibliotheken en leescultuur in Brugge in de 16de eeuw*, 3. Bruges: City of Bruges, 1998.

Vandamme, Ludo. 'Sluis en Brugge (1587–1604): de handelsvaart op het Zwin herleeft.' In *Niemandsland in Staats verband: West-Zeeuws-Vlaanderen ten tijde van de Republiek en daarna*, edited by A. R. Bauwens, 17–32. Aardenburg: Heemkundige Kring West-Zeeuws-Vlaanderen, 2004.

Vandamme, Ludo. *De socio-professionele recrutering van de reformatie te Brugge, 1566–1567*. Master's thesis., Rijksuniversiteit Gent, 1987.

Vandewalle, André, and K. Van Damme (eds.). *Hanzekooplui en Medicibankiers: Brugge, wisselmarkt van Europese culturen*. Oostkamp; Stichting Kunstboek, 2002.

Vandewalle, André. 'De Spaans-Brugse koopliedenfamilie Pardo en haar boekenbezit.' In *Een stad vol boeken: Bibliotheken een leescultuur in Brugge in de 16e eeuw*, edited by Ludo Vandamme et al., 11. Bruges: City of Bruges, 1998.

Vandewalle, André. 'De stokhouders te Brugge. Het geval Adriaenssens (1678–1694).' *Jaarboek van Vlaams Centrum voor Genealogie en Heraldiek* (1982): 463–476.

Veeckman, Johan, and Claire Dumortier. 'La production de verres à Anvers: les données historiques.' In *Majolica and Glass from Italy to Antwerp and Beyond. The Transfer of Technology in the 16th and 17th Century*, edited by Johan Veeckman et al. Antwerp: City of Antwerp, 2002.

Veldman, Ilja M. 'From Indulgence to Collector's Item: Functions of Printmaking in the Netherlands.' In *Images for the Eye and Soul: Functions and Meaning in Netherlandish Prints (1450–1650)*, 9–17. Leiden: Primavera Press, 2006.

Vermeylen, Filip. 'Art and Economics. The Antwerp Art Market of the Sixteenth Century.' PhD diss., Columbia University, 2000.

Vermeylen, Filip. *Painting for the Market: Commercialization of Art in Antwerp's Golden Age*. Turnhout: Brepols, 2003.

Viaene, Antoon. 'Kleine Verscheidenheden.' *Biekorf* 74 (1973): 313.

Viaene, Antoon. 'Woning en Handwerk. Bouwstoffen voor een Archeologisch Glossarium.' *Biekorf* 62 (1961): 414–415.

Vickery, Amanda. 'Golden Age to Separate Spheres? A Review of the Categories and Chronologies of English Women's History.' *The Historical Journal* 36, no. 2 (1993): 383–414.

Vickery, Amanda. *Behind Closed Doors. At Home in Georgian England*. New Haven: Yale University Press, 2010.

Walker Bynum, Caroline. *Christian Materiality: An Essay on Religion in Late Medieval Europe*. New York: Zone Books, 2011.

Walker, Lynne. 'Home Making: An Architectural Perspective.' *Signs* 27, no. 3 (2002): 823–835.

Walsh, Claire. 'Shop Design and the Display of Goods in Eighteenth-Century London.' *Journal of Design History* 8, no. 3 (1995): 157–176.

Warwick, Genevieve. 'Looking in the Mirror of Renaissance Art.' *Art History: Journal of the Association of Art Historians* 39, no. 2 (2016): 251–281.

Weale, W. H. James. 'Peintres Brugeois, Les Claeissens (1500–1656).' *Annales de la Société d'emulation de Bruges* 61 (1911): 49–71.

Weatherill, Lorna. *Consumer Behavior and Material Culture in Britain 1660–1760*. London: Routledge, 1988.

Webb, Diana. 'Domestic Space and Devotion in the Middle Ages.' In *Defining the Holy. Sacred Space in Medieval and Early Modern Europe*, edited by Andrew Spicer and Sarah Hamilton. Aldershot: Ashgate, 2005.

Welch, Evelyn S. 'Public Magnificence and Private Display. Giovanni Pontano's *De splendore* (1498) and the Domestic Arts.' *Journal of Design History* 15, no. 4 (2002): 211–221.

Welch, Evelyn S. 'Scented Gloves and Perfumed Buttons: Smelling Things in Renaissance Italy.' In (ed.), *Ornamentalism: Accessories in Renaissance Europe*, edited by M. Bella Mirabelle. Ann Arbor: University of Michigan Press, 2012.

Welch, Evelyn S. *Shopping in the Renaissance. Consumer Cultures in Italy, 1400–1600*. New Haven: Yale University Press, 2005.

Weyns, Jef. *Volkshuisraad in Vlaanderen: naam, vorm, geschiedenis, gebruik en volkskundig belang der huiselijke voorwerpen in het Vlaamse land van de middeleeuwen tot de eerste wereldoorlog*. Beerzel: Ter Speelbergen, 1974.

Wieck, Roger. *Painted Prayers. The Book of Hours in Medieval and Renaissance Art*. New York: George Braziller, Inc., 1999.

Wilson, Jean C. *Painting in Bruges at the Close of the Middle Ages. Studies in Society and Visual Culture*. University Park: Pennsylvania State University Press, 1998.

Wilson, Katherine Anne. 'Tapestry in the Burgundian Dominions. A Complex and Problematic Object.' In *La cour de Bourgogne et l'Europe. Le rayonnement et les limites d'un modèle culturel*, edited by Werner Paravincini. Ostfildern: Jan Thorbecke Verlag, 2013: 317–331.

Wilson, Katherine Anne. 'The Household Inventory as Urban "Theatre" in Late Medieval Burgundy.' *Social History* 40, no. 3 (2015): 342.

Wilson, Katherine Anne. 'Commerce and Consumers: The Ubiquitous Chest of the Late Middle Ages.' *The Journal of Interdisciplinary History* 51 (2021): 337–404.

Winstanley, Michael J. *The Shopkeeper's World, 1830–1914*. Manchester: Manchester University Press, 1983.

Withers, Charles W. J. 'Place and the "Spatial Turn" in Geography and in History.' *Journal of the History of Ideas* 70, no. 4 (2009): 637–658.

Wolfthal, Diane. *The Beginnings of Netherlandish Canvas Painting: 1400–1530*. Cambridge: Cambridge University Press, 1989.

Wolfthal, Diane. *In and Out of the Marital Bed: Seeing Sex in Late Medieval and Early Modern Art*. New Haven: Yale University Press, 2011.

Woodall, Joanna. 'De Wisselaer. Quentin Matsys's Man Weighting Gold Coins and his Wife, 1514.' In *Trading Values*, edited by Christine Götler et al., 58. Leiden: Brill, 2014.

Woolgar, C. M. *The Senses in Late Medieval England*. New Haven: Yale University Press, 2007.

Yiu, Yvonne. 'Der Spiegel: Werkzeug des Künstlers oder Metapher der Malerei? Zur Deutung des Spiegels in: Produktionsszenarien in der nordischen Malerei des 15. und frühen 16. Jahrhunderts.' *Zeitschrift für Kunstgeschichte* 68, no. 4 (2005): 475–488.

Fig. 1. Portraits of Jan van Eyewerve (left) and his wife Jacquemyne Buuck (right),
Pieter Pourbus, 1551, Oil on Panel, © Groeningemuseum, Bruges, www.artinflanders.be

Fig. 2. Detail of the shop in The Rooster and the counter in front of the shop,
detail in the portrait of Jacquemyne Buuck, Pieter Pourbus, 1551, Oil on Panel,
© Groeningemuseum, Bruges, www.artinflanders.be

Fig. 3. Closer detail of the shop in *The Rooster* and the counter in front of the shop, detail in the portrait of Jacquemyne Buuck, Pieter Pourbus, 1551, Oil on Panel, © Groeningemuseum, Bruges, www.artinflanders.be

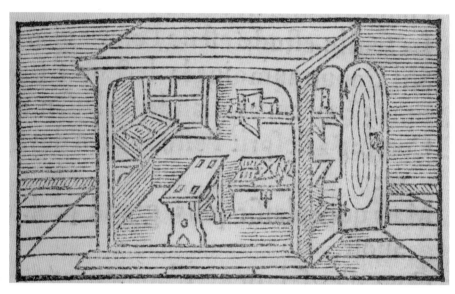

Fig. 4. Detail of a woodcut 'le blason de l'estude', Gilles Corrozet, Les Blasons Domestiques contenantz la décoration d'une maison honneste, et du mesnage estant en icelle, invention joyeuse et moderne, Paris, 1559, © Bibliothèque nationale de France, Rés. Ye-1380, 33

Fig. 5. Erasmus working in a room with wooden shuttering, Portrait of Erasmus of Rotterdam, Quentin Metsijs, 1517, Oil on panel, transferred to canvas, © Gallerie Nazionali di Arte Antica, Roma (MIBACT) - Bibliotheca Hertziana, Istituto Max Planck per la storia dell'arte/Enrico Fontolan

Fig. 6. A Hanseatic merchant portrayed in his office, Portrait of the Merchant Georg Gisze,
Hans Holbein the Younger, 1532, Oil on wood, © Staatliche Museen, Berlin,
bpk / Kupferstichkabinett, SMB / Dietmar Katz

Fig. 7. Spanish-Moorish plate, 15ᵗʰ century, anonymous, Bruges, © Musea Brugge / OCMW Brugge, O.OTP0008.XXI, www.artinflanders.be

Fig. 8. Saint Hieronymus in his Study, Albrecht Dürer, 1514, Kupferstichkabinett,
© Staatliche Museen, Berlin, bpk / Gemäldegalerie, SMB / Jörg P. Anders

Fig. 9. Kitchen scene of staff preparing food. The Four Elements: Fire, Joachim Beuckelaer, 1570, Oil on canvas, London, © The National Gallery

Fig. 10. Kitchen interior with hearth, furniture and utensils. The Miracle of the Broken Sieve, Jan II van Conincxloo, 1552, left panel of diptych, Oil on panel, Brussels, © Royal Museum of Fine Arts, www.artinflanders.be

Fig. 11. Prayer bench, 15th century, Bruges, © Musea Brugge / OCMW Brugge, O.OTP0035.
VII, www.artinflanders.be

Fig. 12. 'The Great Bed of Ware', carved oak bed, probably from Ware, Hertfordshire, UK, about 1590. © Victoria and Albert Museum, London

Fig. 13. In the bed of the abbot a small diptych is hanging as a charm
to ward off all evil. Portrait of Abbot Christiaan de Hondt,
Master of 1499, c. 1500, Panel, 30 x 14 cm, Antwerp,
© Royal Museum of Fine Arts, www.artinflanders.be

Fig. 14. Left and right panels of the altarpiece of Remi Ommejaeghere and Petronella Herve, Pieter Pourbus, 16th Century, oil on panel, © Bruges Church of Our Lady, www.artinflanders.be

Fig. 15. Painting of Madonna and Child in the study of the Cardinal. Cardinal Albrecht of Brandenburg as St. Jerome, 1526, Lucas Cranach the Elder, German, 1472-1553, Oil on wood panel, 45 1/4 x 35 1/16 inches, SN308, Bequest of John Ringling, 1936, Collection of The John and Mable Ringling, Museum of Art, © the State Art Museum of Florida, a division of Florida State University

Fig. 16. Left and right panels of altarpiece of Juan Pardo and his wives Anna Ingenieulandt
en Maria Anchemant, Bruges, © Musea Brugge, www.artinflanders.be

Fig. 17. Pendant portraits of Christoffel Ghuyse and Elisabeth Van Male, Pieter Pourbus, 16th Century, Bruges, © Musea Brugge, www.artinflanders.be

Fig. 18. Religious painting displayed on a cupboard. Next to the bed a colored print is
nailed to the wall. The Annunciation, Joos Van Cleve, c. 1525, Oil on Wood, New York,
© The Metropolitan Museum of Art, CC0

Fig. 19. Ornament of a Mantelpiece, head of a man, 15th Century, Bruges, © Musea Brugge,
www.artinflanders.be

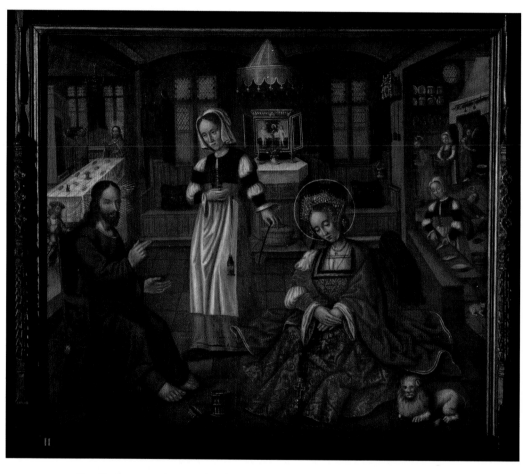

Fig. 20. A woman is preparing food using a driestael or a three-legged stool.
Detail from Christ in Bethany, in the house of Martha and Mary, Anonymus, 16th Century,
Oil on Canvas, Bruges, © Musea Brugge, www.artinflanders.be

Fig. 21. Armchair, made in France, c. 1580, Walnut, © Victoria and Albert Museum, London

Fig. 22. A throne-like chair is standing next to the canopied bed. The Annunciation,
Master of FVB, c.1480, Copper plate Engraving, Amsterdam, © Rijksmuseum

Fig. 23. Saint Barbara sitting on a bench before the
hearth. The bench is decorated with a red coloured
banker and some red cushions on the seat. Werl
Altarpiece, right panel of St. Barbara, Robert Campin,
1438, Tempera on Panel, Madrid, © Museo del Prado

Fig. 24. Joseph sits on a barrel-shape chair. Holy Family at Supper, Hours of Catherine of Cleves, c. 1440. MS M.917, pp. 150–151. © The Morgan Library & Museum, New York

Fig. 25. Backstool fitted with leather, 1660-1700, © Victoria and Albert Museum, London.

Fig. 26. Bed with red curtains. The Birth of John the Baptist (miniature from the Très Belles Heures de Notre-Dame), Jan van Eyck, c.1422. Body colour on parchment.
© Museo Civico d'Arte Antica, Turin, Italy

Fig. 27. Bed, 17th century (with 19th century details and textiles), Bruges, © OCMW Brugge, www.artinflanders.be

Fig. 28. Bruges-styled verdure of wool and silk, fragment, Bruges, © Musea Brugge, www.artinflanders.be

Fig. 29. Bruges-styled tapestry hanging of wool and silk, Bruges, © Musea Brugge,
www.artinflanders.be

Fig. 30. Cushion cover with the arms of Sacheverell, Silk and wool, with silver and silver-gilt thread, Sheldon Tapestry Workshops (maker), Warwickshire (possibly, made), 1600-1620 (made), © Victoria and Albert Museum, London

Fig. 31. Cabinet, 16th Century, Bruges, © Musea Brugge, www.artinflanders.be